Running
with the Moon

Jonny Bealby was born in Lincolnshire in 1963.
Educated in England, Scotland and Canada, he
developed a passion for travel and on leaving
college journeyed extensively in Australasia and
the Far East. Returning to the UK he became a
sound engineer before forming his own rock band,
Tin Gods, in 1984. The group recorded four
singles and one album before splitting up in 1989.
He has had many jobs including stunt horse rider,
circus roustabout and motorcycle courier. He was
elected a Fellow of the Royal Geographical
Society in 1992 and lives in London.

JONNY BEALBY

Running
with the Moon

A BOY'S OWN ADVENTURE

Mandarin

The author is grateful for permission to
quote seventeen words from *The Great Railway Bazaar*
by Paul Theroux (Hamish Hamilton, 1975)
copyright © Paul Theroux, 1975.
Reproduced by permission of Hamish Hamilton Ltd.
He also expresses his thanks to HarperCollins
Publishers Ltd for permission to quote from
The Last Battle by C. S. Lewis.

A Mandarin Paperback

First published in Great Britain 1995
by William Heinemann Ltd
This edition published 1996
by Mandarin Paperbacks
an imprint of Reed International Books Ltd
Michelin House, 81 Fulham Road, London SW3 6RB
and Auckland, Melbourne, Singapore and Toronto

Reprinted 1996

Copyright © Jonny Bealby 1995
The author has asserted his moral rights

A CIP catalogue record for this title
is available from the British Library
ISBN 0 7493 2098 2

Printed and bound in Great Britain
by Cox & Wyman Ltd, Reading, Berkshire

This book is for Melanie

'Wherever your travels take you,
the moon is always there,
and I am the moon . . .'

Contents

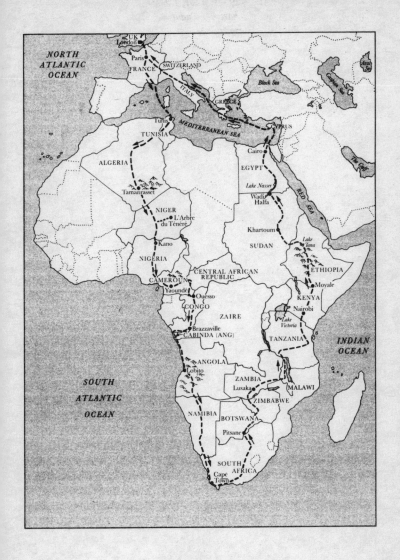

Prologue
Srinagar, Kashmir

Something was wrong, I knew instantly, almost before I woke up. Melanie lay on her back, her breathing shallow and uncertain. It seemed to be getting weaker. I leant over and touched her face. She was burning up, soaked in sweat, clammy, as though she had a high fever.

I jumped out of bed, a tight feeling of panic gripping my chest.

'What the hell's wrong with you?' I shook her. 'Come on babe, wake up.' . . . Nothing. I shook her again, still nothing. I slapped her gingerly and even found myself throwing water in her face, thinking, 'Well it works in the movies,' but this was no film, this was horribly real. There was nothing, save her rasping, ever-decreasing, breath.

Help, Jonny. Get help!

I ran to the door and looked out on a crisp, bright October morning. Mist rose effortlessly from the lake which stretched away to the edge of the valley and the white peaks of the Himalayas beyond. Javed, the youngest of the Nadro family, was passing by, preparing breakfast for the houseboat guests.

'Javed, something's wrong with Mel. Quick, get that German who arrived last night . . . I need help.'

He hurried away, reading the urgency on my face.

I ran back into the room. She lay in the same position, pale and inert. Her eyes were now slits, only the whites showing. Panic seized me completely, an iron fist holding me. I was paralysed with fear and confusion.

Kneeling by the side of the bed, I slipped my arm under her neck and held her.

Then it happened; she exhaled a small breath and with it she was gone. Just like that. There was no struggle, no pain or last-second realisation of what was happening to her, she just went, as vividly as if she had got up and walked out of the door. I stared in frozen horror as my wife, my future, my hopes and my dreams disappeared before my eyes.

'What is wrong?' asked Marcus, the German policeman who now stood behind me, 'Can I help?'

'Do something,' I yelled hysterically. 'I think she's . . .'

'We must get her on the floor,' he said, the training of his profession taking over. We carried her across the rosewood room and laid her down. The silk blouse she was wearing clung to her body and her hair stuck to her face.

'You blow in her mouth,' he instructed, 'and I will massage her heart.' I did as I was told. I blew and he pumped but there was nothing.

'Wake up,' a voice inside me was screaming. 'What the hell are you doing, you can't go like this . . . WAKE UP!' But deep down I knew she'd gone, I'd seen her go. I knew but I couldn't believe.

Marcus sat up, shocked. His eyes would not meet mine. He said simply, '. . . she's dead.'

PART ONE

Moonshadow
London – Yaoundé

1 African Dreams

The Mediterranean. Two years later.

With the ship lurching and staggering in the storm I felt drunk long before I was. Soon people were throwing up. Nobody cleared the vomit away, it was simply sprinkled with sawdust much in the way Italian waiters cover pasta with parmesan cheese. Neil and I sat in the bar with Pierre, a fellow traveller from France. North African men squeezed in beside us smoking and drinking coffee and alcohol. The latter surprised me, their smoking did not. The smell was suffocating.

As I began to feel sick, annoyed with myself for getting carried away and drinking too much, I started to feel blue. On the World Service evening news the announcer had given us the depressing information that Zaire, a country almost unavoidably on our route, had just broken out in civil unrest, all the foreign nationals were being evacuated and the borders closed. Neil and Pierre were locked in an unbelievably boring conversation about bikes – Do Yamaha wheels take seven-inch or eight-inch spokes? Which nut takes a nineteen-millimetre spanner? – so when the man next to me plonked his turbaned head on my shoulder and started to snore, I decided to get some air. Vicious forks of lightning split the sky like cracks in the firmament. The waves pounded the hull and spray lashed my face. A fierce wind took my Manchester United cap clean off my head and planted it somewhere between Corsica and Ibiza. It seemed apt, considering they'd just lost their first match of the season, but it only helped to bring me down a little further.

I had been thinking a lot about Mel recently, especially on the journey down through France, and now I missed her more than ever. She was, after all, my travelling partner, not Neil. She should have been there. Her beautiful little face would have been so excited at the prospect of another journey. Normally, large expanses of water act as a calming influence on me, but not then. The ferocity and anger of the sea seemed to reflect my own feelings. Buffeted and damp, I

5

fought my way back inside, sank onto an empty bench, and slept.

By morning the storm had passed, and with it my dejected spirits – it looked like being a fine day. Standing on the bow, we seemed to be heading straight into the sun, away from Europe and its troubled past and on towards a new, exciting beginning. Zaire may have been in turmoil, as, no doubt, were countless other African states, but so what? I had never assumed the journey was going to be easy, I wouldn't have wanted it so. Africa. This was what I had been waiting for.

At noon I had my first experience of African bureaucracy. We had all been lined up to have our passports stamped at the purser's office. After a wait of one and a half hours I finally reached the front, only to be told:

'Non, monsieur, nous sommes fermés pour le déjeuner. Retournez à deux heures.'

I bit my tongue. *Now, now, Jonny, remember, this is Africa, learn patience.* 'Bon, d'accord. Merci.'

At two there was no queue and our passports were stamped 'toute de suite'.

The closer we got to Africa, the thinner the clouds became. A plane passing overhead, leaving behind a fluffy white vapour trail, achieved in a few minutes what had taken us more than thirty hours. As I pulled up a chair and waited impatiently for my first glimpse of Africa, fishing boats and cargo ships sailed by along the horizon. Gulls appeared overhead and the sun sank towards the west, sending a glistening silver pathway to the edge of the world. And then, creeping out of the evening haze, came the black, jagged profile of the dark continent.

Down in the ship's hold my bike had fallen against the side of a truck and the brake lever was bent. Loaded up, we moved down the ramp and into the African night. There was surprisingly little hassle at customs. *If all the border crossings are as easy, the trip will be a breeze.* What an absurd thought. Within minutes we were through the gates and on our way to the city centre with Pierre, who had tagged along, assuming the lead. 'I know the way,' he announced. Quite how, I couldn't imagine, considering he hadn't been here before, but I chose not to question him and to follow instead. Pierre was as ungainly a sight on his bike as John Wayne in ballet shoes. His long, gangly body looked enormous and his knees stuck out like those of a bad horseman, while his elbows jutted out at right-angles as if somehow to give him more balance. Within minutes of leaving the port my misgivings were confirmed. We came to a small roundabout with one route clearly signposted to Tunis. Pierre disregarded the information, opting instead for an unlit dirt track which led us between a row of derelict houses to a dead end by the sea. *I don't like following people*, I grouched to myself.

Eventually we drove into Tunis, ten kilometres in the dark across the salt flats, and looked for a beer. But this was now the Arab world and there were few bars. We parked on the pavement outside a hotel; Neil's bike was top-heavy and fell over into the gutter. The hotel bar was closed.

An avenue of trees in the middle of the large street led from a broken clock tower, past the hotels, airline offices and restaurants, to the Great Mosque at the other end. It seemed surprisingly quiet for a capital city and there was a conspiratorial feeling, as if the men, huddled together in the cafés, drinking coffee, smoking and playing backgammon, were talking about us. There were no women. Round a fountain in the centre of the boulevard flower sellers and traders closed their stalls, another day's work done.

Luckily we found a pizzeria open and, having had our beer and something to eat, left the town to find a beach on which to sleep. It had already gone eleven. We headed for a place I'd heard of, or, more accurately, thought I'd heard of, on the sea about twenty kilometres to the east of Tunis, called Hammon Lif. When we got there I was not so sure. Most of the buildings looked derelict, or worse, as if they'd been through a war. It was how I imagined Beirut to look: twisted pieces of metal poked out of the rooftops and piles of rubble blocked the pot-holed streets. The roads were deserted.

Boarded up breeze-block huts with low surrounding walls lined the beach. One of these would have made an excellent place to camp for the night – sheltered from the wind and offering at least a little security, like a castle wall, for we were all nervous. The only problem was that they were littered with human excrement. Indeed, all the shelter nearby, including a short pier, had been soiled.

We parked behind one of the huts, got out our sleeping bags and lay down under the moon and stars for our first

African night. Not that this was exactly the African night I'd dreamed of: the wild animals, the cicadas, camp fires and *ju-ju* huts . . . no, all that would come later. I was simply caught up in the excitement of having finally arrived and the thought of what lay ahead. I was the pebble in a catapult, pulled back to breaking point, about to be sent hurtling towards whatever destiny had in store. Total freedom. At that moment I wouldn't have changed places with anyone.

What's that? I opened my eyes and realised that the stars and moon were no longer visible. *There it is again.* Another drop of water hit my face. On my right-hand side, Neil's mind was obviously going through a similar cycle. He reached the same conclusion and sat up.

'It's raining,' he said, but Pierre slept on. We were up in a flash, feverishly packing things away and covering them with our waterproof tarpaulins. Neil gave Pierre a prod in the back and he too prepared himself for the storm.

'What do we do now?' asked Neil. The rain was already getting heavier.

'I don't know. I guess we should go and find some shelter.'

'Preferably without the shit,' cut in Pierre, rubbing his eyes.

'What? And leave the bikes here?' asked Neil.

A good point: the whole reason we had left Tunis was so that we could stay close to the bikes. But it was four o'clock in the morning and still pitch-black; also they were quite well hidden and I couldn't really believe that anyone would be out in this weather, never mind stealing motor bikes.

'I think they'll be safe,' I said. 'We can't stand here all night, it might go on for ages.'

'I'm not sure,' ventured Neil. 'I think one of us should stay.' By now we were all starting to get wet.

'All right,' I said, thinking of a compromise, 'I'll hang around here, you go and find some shelter, then come back and we'll chain them up and take the tank bags with us.' The tank bags housed all of our most crucial possessions. Reluctantly Neil agreed and set off with Pierre, while I crouched under a plastic sheet.

My ecstasy of a few hours ago had evaporated. The flimsy cover was of little use against the mounting squall; the violent wind tore it from my grasp and rain ran down my neck. Suddenly the thought of changing places with someone else was highly appealing.

Finally, they returned to collect me. Carrying our tank bags, we walked back across a sodden dirt football pitch to the partially lit street on the other side. Most of the lights were broken but the few still burning emitted a soft yellow glow over this baneful spot. The storm was now fiercer than ever, the rain lashing our faces and the wind howling around our ears. Out to sea, on the far horizon, lightning flashed, illuminating the whole sky like a nuclear explosion.

For all my careful planning, I had neglected to bring any waterproofs. 'No, we won't need them in North Africa,' I'd told Neil, authoritatively. 'The Sahara virtualiy meets the Mediterranean, and it doesn't rain in the desert, everyone knows that. By the time we get south to the forests we should have missed the rains.' Now, huddled under a six-foot by three-foot corrugated iron awning in jeans and a leather jacket, trying to stave off the inevitable, I felt pretty stupid. Neil looked smugly on from the warmth of his Drizabone. My sole consolation was Pierre's denim jacket: his only line of defence against this unexpected storm. We were both soaked, for this 'shelter' as Neil had called it, was quite obviously built to shade a milk stall from the sun. Still, it was marginally better than nothing.

The rain continued unabated. Neil went walkabout and eventually returned, like Noah's dove, with good news. He had found a small shop, open, where we could shelter. The old shopkeeper was so relieved to find we only wanted to share his roof that he showered us with hospitality: coffee, buns and cigarettes as well as introductions to his entire family. He had clearly been scared half to death by this soaking wet, leather-clad white man in a green military cap sauntering out of the darkness.

'I thought the Germans had returned,' he joked with us later.

The muezzin called the faithful to prayer, the dawn broke and the rain continued. After a while it was the turn of the schoolchildren to brave the elements. They seemed to get a lot more enjoyment out of it than we did. Splashing through the puddles on the yellow sand roads they stopped and stared, a little bemused by the sight of the three strangers in their local shop.

After an age of waiting and a hundred cups of coffee, we realised that this rain just wasn't going to stop. At about

9

eleven we packed the bikes up properly, said goodbye to Fiarzi and his family and departed, resigned to the fact that today we were going to be wet.

We had one job to do back in town before we could leave Tunis for sunnier climes – we needed our Nigerian visas from the British Embassy. For some reason this visa can be very hard to get from the Nigerian Embassy in London, but in Tunis the British Embassy acts on behalf of the Nigerians, which makes life much easier.

We made a tentative plan with Pierre to find a hotel together but when I saw his ridiculous figure disappear the wrong way up a one-way street I decided I'd followed him far enough.

'Thank God for that,' said Neil, evidently feeling the same, 'at least we won't have to worry about him any more.' It wasn't that Pierre was such a bad bloke, it was just that we wanted to experience these first few hours on our own, without distractions from outsiders.

It was great to have Neil along – a joy to be sharing the adventure with such an old friend. Here was someone I knew and trusted so well: totally dependable, with a heart as big as a wheel, and, given half a chance, as wild as any man I knew. Any reservations I might have had in England about asking him to come had gone. I felt sure we'd make a good team.

Even though the weather showed no signs of improving, having been issued with our visas, we decided to leave Tunis and head for the holy city of Kairouan, 110 miles away.

The sky was leaden and oppressive. I had imagined all African rain thundering down thick and fast and then stopping to give the sun a chance, but this could have been English drizzle: continuous and unspectacular. The narrow roads were clogged with traffic: cars, tractors, lorries and horse-drawn carts, most of which also seemed to be heading south.

A Mercedes swung out of a side street very nearly taking Neil with it. He skidded onto the verge but just managed to hold the bike up while swearing obscenities at the driver. Grimy trucks barged their way past us and buses stopped abruptly in our path.

Fighting our way down those pot-holed streets, it occurred to me that this whole journey would be like a real life video game. How many lives we would have, how many levels and phases there would be and whether a beautiful princess would be waiting at the end to be saved from the jaws of a fire-breathing dragon, only time could tell. But, as the rain thrashed our faces and mad Tunisian drivers did their best to use up some of those precious lives, I knew this was just the beginning, the first stage, and an easy one for starters.

Fifty miles from Tunis, near a small farming town called El Fad, the rain stopped. The African sun broke through the clouds and showed itself for the first time. There were olive groves on the hillsides, small crumbling whitewashed houses and avenues of eucalyptus trees. The air was clean and fresh, washed by the rain, which I hoped would be the last we would see. Neil offered me his jacket, which I ruefully accepted as by now my clothes were soaked and I was very cold.

We drove on into bibleland. What a buzz! Our bikes had become time-machines zooming down a warp straight into the Old Testament. Goatherds and shepherds grazed their flocks, farmers tilled the land with oxen, mules pulling loads of hay worked their way down the tracks and beautiful bright-eyed children came rushing from their homes. They smiled and waved, their innocent faces full of excitement. I felt sure that no matter how many children I waved at on this trip, they would always bring a smile to my face. We drove on, happy to be alive. I started to sing.

As we turned off the main road onto a dirt track which led into the back streets of Kairouan the picture changed. Mud brick walls were falling apart, goats and donkeys rummaged through the rubbish and children fought and threw stones. The rural scene which had seemed so magical only a few minutes ago, now, reflected in the town, seemed dirty, desperate and far more real.

We came to a roundabout where, obviously looking a little confused, we were offered help by a man on a moped. His name was Abdul.

'We need to get to the hotel El Marhala,' I said. 'Can you show us the way?'

'Yes, of course. I take you very nice hotel. Yes, you get beer. Of course you bikes will be safe. Yes, there is hot water, and no, it is very cheap for you,' he said, answering our questions. 'It is bestest hotel in town. My brother owns it. You like it. Follow me.'

The Hotel Les Aghlabites was run-down but elegant, a pale green three-storeyed building on the corner of the main square. It looked rather like a mosque. A group of men wearing red fezzes sat round a table outside the entrance, talking and drinking coffee. Donkeys pulling carts carried vegetables across the square and through the main gate of the old city wall to the market beyond.

Unfortunately this was not the whole picture. For Muslims, Kairouan is the fourth most holy city; it is very beautiful and very old and therefore well-marked on the tourist map. Out of our bedroom window six or seven empty coaches could be seen, their floppy-hatted cargo exploring the narrow alleyways and mosques of the old town, or they were being persuaded to buy carpets over cups of mint tea. They would be rounded up at the allotted hour and herded back to a more familiar world of Club Med hotels, banana daiquiris and holiday reps, memories of their day in the Sahara already beginning to fade. It was the world from which we were escaping.

Having sorted us out with a perfectly adequate room, Abdul departed, promising to return later to take us to the only bar in town. There was no beer at the hotel and no running water, let alone hot, but our bikes were safe. We relaxed and waited for Abdul. Two hours later, as good as his word, he came to collect us.

'I take you to bar tonight and tomorrow you will come see my carpets.' Of course there had to be something behind his generosity, but confident that neither of us would buy a rug, we duly agreed.

After we had dined off roast goat's head, eye-balls and all, Abdul led us down a labyrinth of dark streets, hopping over open sewers and avoiding piles of rubbish. Mangy cats scurried out of our way and disappeared through cracks in walls, while veiled women stared silently from the security of their homes. Their expressions made me feel uneasy. The bar was crowded and noisy, thick smoke partially obscured the pale strip lighting. There was only canned beer and we ordered three each in case it ran out as Abdul had warned us it might.

Abdul was a likeable man, about our age and very good-looking. He had strong Arab features: a sharp nose, angled chin and thick black hair cut short but, unusually, no moustache. From his neat Western clothes it was clear that he took pride in his appearance. He could speak six languages and had girlfriends in most European countries, he said, and with his obvious charm and good looks, who was I to disbelieve him? People were eager to meet us and buy us beer which, far from running out, seemed to flow ever more freely. The more beers we had, the more settled in we felt.

Out of the corner of my eye I noticed an unkempt, bearded man propping up the bar on the far side of the room. Obviously drunk, he was gesticulating angrily in our direction. After a few more minutes he staggered over.

'What d'you come from?' He slurred, but without waiting for an answer continued. 'You British . . . you Margaret Thatcher cow . . .' He was dribbling and unable to focus but he had something to say and was determined to express it. 'You stupid America, what d'you know about? . . . ugh . . . nothing . . . aargh . . . Bush, you, he know nothing.' As he went on it became perfectly obvious what was coming. 'Saddam, Saddam Hussein he knows, Allah praise his name. He, Saddam, but you . . . you, your John Major, he know nothing.'

By this stage most of the occupants of the bar had quietened and were watching the spectacle. I felt embarrassed as did Neil. We both did the British thing and tried to pretend it was not happening. Like a drunk on the underground we ignored him and hoped he'd go away. No such luck. He swung round and spilled some beer over Neil. Abdul was up first and tried to grab the drunk but he staggered backwards into Neil who by now was pretty annoyed. *Please stay calm, Neil, the last thing we need is a fight.* The drunk lashed out again, this time towards Neil's face. It was a feeble, unconvincing strike which Neil easily parried with his left arm. But there was anger in Neil's eyes now, his famous temper was about to blow. *Oh, Christ, here we go.*

Then something happened that quite surprised me. Five other men pushed Abdul aside and unceremoniously dragged the drunk, still ranting about 'the cow Thatcher . . .' and 'you pig shit America . . .', to the door and threw him outside.

It was only a few months after the Gulf War and although many of the Arab governments had sided with the West, most of the Muslim men in the street, I believed, supported Saddam. This show of help for us was therefore quite unexpected, and very welcome. It made me realise, however, that in this part of Africa, especially in bars, we would have to take care.

The next morning, as promised, we went to see Abdul's government carpet co-op, secure in the knowledge that we really were only going to look. Riding already overladen motor bikes around Africa we needed carpets like we needed a sun-bed. But Abdul, naturally, had other ideas.

The shop itself had been the music room of a pasha and was still quite exquisite. Rich wooden galleries, stained dark with age, clung to the walls at unnatural angles and a spectacular mosaic floor took us through two small rooms into a large chamber at the back. Here the carpets were on display. We sat and waited for tea. Once the refreshments had arrived and we were comfortably seated, Abdul went into his well-rehearsed sales pitch.

'These are the holy carpets of Kairouan. Kairouan fourth most holy city so these carpets very nice. They made from lambs' wool and woven by the women. One carpet, it take four month to make and has many knots.' I'd seen better. The woven ones were not of particularly good quality and were too gaudy for my taste, but the deep red and blue embroidered ones were very desirable.

'This is the sign of Fatima's hand, the daughter of Allah,' Abdul went on, 'and here you see the steps to the holy mosque, here in Kairouan. These carpets very holy, make you much luck. You buy, you no regret. You not buy, you regret.'

After ten minutes of spiel both Abdul and I could tell that Neil's defences were weakening. He had made the potentially disastrous mistake of expressing an interest – like a boxer sensing victory, Abdul ploughed on, pushing home his advantage.

'Aarrh! You have a good eye my friend, these two are very special and favourites of mine. You see . . .'

It's not that I was in any way above all this, on the contrary, I'm about as gullible as they come. I've twice been talked into buying carpets I didn't really want, but I had no intention of making it a hat trick. I was simply surprised at Neil, who is usually so careful. Then again, I expect this man could sell ice to the Eskimos. Forty minutes later, a price had been agreed and Neil walked out with, not one, but two small, embroidered Tunisian carpets.

We drove through the afternoon. The olive groves, chilli fields and fruit farms gave way to arid scrub and sand. Though the sky was partially obscured by haze, the air felt surprisingly cool. Leaving Kairouan well after one o'clock had killed any hope of reaching Tozeur by nightfall. A hundred and thirty miles on we came to the small oasis town of Gafsa where, with darkness at our heels, we found a place and camped down for the night.

I woke with the dawn. The early morning sun cast long shadows across the sand and the deep blue sky, scratched with wispy pink clouds, made a dramatic backdrop for the rocky hills behind. The tent was perched on the brow of a smaller hill which overlooked a blaze of green date palms. Below us they stood out like a cricket pitch in an urban sprawl. The reason for my eagerness to rise at a time normally reserved for fishermen and the faithful was simply that I was frozen half to death. The light-weight sleeping-bag I'd brought was no match for the bitter temperatures of the cloudless desert sky and rather than lie there shivering in the tent I got up to enjoy this most beautiful time of day. For me it is always the best time – the whole day stretching before you like a blank page to be filled with what beauty, what experiences and what hardship?

Eventually Neil stirred and crawled out. He smashed his head on the lamp, trod on his cooker and tripped headlong over a guy rope; it was not a good start to the day. He picked himself up and, grumbling under his breath, set about making a cup of tea. We packed up and moved out with me in the lead. Neil is not bothered who goes first whereas I like to see the open road ahead of me. We had only fifty-odd miles to drive to Tozeur which is the last town before the Algerian frontier, where the Sahara starts in earnest. There we could service the bikes and prepare them and ourselves for the desert. It would be our last chance. We reached the main road and turned south. Yes, I thought, the Sahara, at last.

* * *

My Africa dream was conceived several months earlier at the tail-end of a roller-coaster depression that took me to rock bottom. Returning home from India I felt nothing. A large part of me hadn't come back at all and was still in Kashmir watching myself cremating Mel not seventy-two hours since we had kissed each other good-night. I felt quarantined by my oldest friends, as if I suffered a nameless disease leaving my emotions too vulnerable and brittle to risk shattering with the wrong word or expression. The people closest to us found it hard to look me in the eye, let alone bring up Mel's name in conversation. They seemed nervous, almost guilty that it hadn't happened to them. Everyone tried their best to help but they didn't know how to deal with or share in my grief, and I couldn't handle their embarrassed sympathy. I tried to work but that was impossible. And everywhere I went I saw Mel's face. All I could think of was to put as much distance as possible between myself and anything familiar.

I found a job as a ski-instructor in Pennsylvania, sharing cold, dirty accommodation the size of a dolls' house with six teenage acid heads, whose idea of meaningful dialogue was ordering a take-away pizza. The change was as dramatic as the effect on my spirits: I started a new downward spiral of exhaustive introspection. After work I'd often find myself down at the local supermarket staring vacantly into a freezer full of frozen peas, trying to puzzle it all out. Sometimes I'd reach an illuminating conclusion and, for a while, feel some sense of relief, only for another wave of emptiness to knock me back down, making me realise that my answers were no answers at all. A few minutes later, over the fruit and veg, the cycle would begin again.

I knew that the storm had to break sometime soon. Breakdown or miracle cure – I couldn't see a middle ground. Of course the solution was far simpler and less melodramatic. Her name was Natalie. An extremely pretty, healthy-looking Swiss girl with wavy, auburn hair and cute little freckles. We became friends on the slopes and when the season finished, she invited me to stay in Washington where she worked as an au pair. One evening at a nightclub, I had worked out, for some reason, that it was 150 days since Mel had died and I went into a massive slump. After asking what the problem was Natalie picked me up, kissed me on the lips and, like a therapist sensing that drastic measures are called for, said, 'I think it is tam that we med luv.'

The strangest part of the experience was how completely natural it seemed. I hadn't so much as kissed another girl since meeting Mel over five years before, and the isolation I had felt since her death had left me too numb and frozen to spark any interest in sex. Now, under the covers with a new lover, it somehow felt entirely right. There was no guilt or regret, in fact it seemed as though Mel, fed up with seeing me so lost and lonely, had taken a hand in turning the tide. Any man lucky enough will know that there's nothing quite like being seduced by a warm-hearted and desirable woman to bolster your ego, restore your confidence and make you walk tall. Natalie hadn't answered any of the tortured questions I was still asking myself but she had, at least, delivered me back into the real world.

Back home in England however, the roller-coaster ride was far from over. Now that I had emerged from my cocoon of grief, being back in the land of the living suddenly seemed the greater evil. I was living alone in our London flat: our home, filled with our possessions and plans. My band had split up, the business I was setting up with Mel had disintegrated and I was wasting my days as a motor-cycle courier enjoying nothing, except perhaps whisky. I may have been the latest in a long line of grieving souls to seek solace in a bottle, but it was still a pretty good place to hide and, in the short-term, soak up a lot of pain. The one person who could truly understand my sorrow was not around when I needed her most. And that was the cause of the pain.

But Mel was there. Or at least there were times when I was so sure, I swear I could almost feel her hands caressing my hair. I felt in my bones that she was watching and willing me to get the hell out of the ruined remains of what might have been, and get on with whatever was next. Then, out of the blue, came two much needed pieces of good luck.

Eighteen months previously I had damaged my left knee in a motor-cycle accident. As it was in no way my fault I was advised to sue but told that I could expect little over £1,000 in compensation. When my solicitor called, one cold February morning, with the news that he'd managed to get £6,500, you can imagine my surprise and delight. After I had paid his fees and various other debts, I was left with a very healthy five grand. Money may not buy happiness but it undoubtedly makes things possible. Two days later Mel's mum Ann rang up: she and her partner Robert had been asked to look after a house in Kenya for six months, they didn't want to but wondered if I did. Naturally I jumped at the opportunity.

By all accounts Matropi is a beautiful house, set in the middle of a coffee plantation, up in the hills just outside Nairobi. It has a spectacular terraced garden, with brightly coloured bougainvillaea, jacaranda and acacia trees, spilling down to a waterfall and river where, in the evenings, buck come to drink. It has five double bedrooms, a large, cool living room and a veranda on three sides. All in all, a very special Kenyan house. Just having something to look forward to and plan for improved my spirits enormously. I took Swahili lessons in London and made preparations to ship a motor bike out to meet me. Quite what I'd do when I got there I didn't know. Perhaps I'd learn to fly, or maybe get work on one of the many safaris. I didn't care. I would be out of England into a Karen Blixen world of wild game, natives and freedom.

About a month before I was due to leave, I was told I couldn't have Matropi after all. The owner rang me to say that because of his ill-health he had been forced to sell the property. Well, they say the way to make God laugh is to tell him your plans, but I was getting a little fed up with His constant chuckling at my expense.

Back to the Glenmorangie and depressions? I'd finally kicked myself out of those shadowlands and was determined not to slide back in. The Africa bug was now in my system; I'd read and dreamed too much about it simply to discard my plans like a cancelled weekend. A friend suggested that I should drive a motor bike there. The more I thought about the idea the more I liked it.

When I was a child of ten my parents, with an uncle and aunt, had bought two Landrovers and driven them from England to Kenya. The excellent cinefilm they made had been my first insight into exotic foreign travel – it had captivated my interest. I would play on the lawn with bows and arrows they had brought home, bash away on the bongos and could often be seen scrambling through thickets in the garden in my new safari suit, looking, I imagined, like a mini Roger Moore, pretending to stalk a gorilla – usually one of my brothers – in deepest Zaire. Images of strange people and vast scenery intrigued me and I hoped even then that one day I would be lucky enough to go there. I had travelled a good deal in other parts of the world but Africa had always struck me as the continent of challenge and adventure – and perhaps that was what I needed more than anything. In the old days I could have joined the Foreign Legion or fought on some distant outpost for Queen and country. But nowadays there is no empire to build and no relevant wars to fight: if you want adventure you've got to go out and find it.

I'd tried to settle down like my friends but for me things had worked out differently. Here was an opportunity that I could take which was denied them. I could journey to places they could only dream of, meet people and experience cultures that haven't changed since time immemorial. Why, I could be like Burton or Livingstone. I would sleep in mud huts given to me by hospitable Chiefs. I would cross wastes and ford rivers. I'd grow thirsty in the heat of the desert and struggle through mud in the rainforest. I'd be free, free to go where I liked, when I liked, self-sufficient on my iron horse, travelling on a wing and prayer. *Romantic fool!*

In my mind's eye I could see the bike, exactly how I wanted it to look. I lay awake at night, lost in fantasy: *I'll spray the bike desert-sand colour and get some trans-Africa transfers made. I'll build a jerry can rack for the front and make aluminium panniers for the back. They'd have to be strong. They would be strong. A Yamaha XT 600 Ténéré will be the bike. Yes, they're reliable and fairly cheap second-hand. And, more important, they look right. After all, if I'm going to do this journey I might as well look the part! Besides, isn't Ténéré the name of a Saharan desert? Perhaps I could drive the bike 'home'.*

It didn't take long for me to realise that losing Matropi wasn't such bad news after all. As the planning stage gathered momentum and the reverie turned to reality, I discovered that this obsession was taking over from the grief. If I started to feel down, I took out a brochure on tents and cookers and wondered which one I should take. I've never seen the point in pessimism, which I suppose makes me, by nature, an optimist, but during the last couple of years this had been a near-impossible quality to retain; slowly it was returning. And Melanie? Well, wherever she was, however near or far, I strongly believed that she was sharing in my excitement and overjoyed that I had taken my life and destiny back into my own hands. I even started running in order to get fit, but luckily pulled a muscle in my hip on the fourth day and was forced to stop. I'd get fit soon enough holding 250 kilograms of machinery upright, I thought. Yes, Africa on a motor bike, what a perfect idea!

* * *

Looking back in my rear-view mirror, I was surprised not to see Neil. Surprised? I don't know why. It was not unusual for him to be lagging behind. Already, in the first few days of the journey, I had become accustomed to this. I would be packed up and ready to go a full ten minutes before Neil would decide to re-pack. That's just how we were. Neil slow, irresolute but thoughtful, while I'm fast, impatient and forgetful. For although I'd be sitting there, with my engine running, urging him to hurry up, he would inevitably hand me something I'd left behind. Sometimes hanging on to it until later for greater effect. *Slow down and let him catch up. He's probably taking a leak.*

After a couple of minutes I noticed a square breeze-block building up ahead on the right-hand side of the road. As I got closer I saw it was a derelict restaurant; there was still no sign of Neil so I decided to wait in its shade.

Where the hell was he, I wondered? Could he have had a crash? No, this was Neil, it was bound to be something trivial. Maybe he was having a cigarette, oblivious to my worry? After a couple of minutes I heard the rumbling of an engine, not of a bike but of an old truck rolling over the hill and down the road towards me. As it got closer I saw a turbaned Arab signalling to me, pointing back up the road.

So something had happened. It wasn't just a toilet or fag stop. I climed onto my bike and drove back fast, my mind in something of a turmoil. *Maybe he's had a puncture. Unlikely – brand-new tyres on a perfect asphalt road . . . Could be the chain's come off. Maybe the bike's just broken down or maybe . . . Oh hell, let's not jump to any conclusions, he's bound to be fine.*

I came over a rise in the road and my heart lurched. Far off in the distance was the sight I hadn't even dared to consider. A large white coach which had nearly hit me a little earlier had stopped in the middle of the road. There was a crowd gathering around something on the other side – evidently Neil. 'Oh no!' I thought. 'Please, God, not again.'

* * *

Neil's African dream had started more as an English nightmare. In the summer of '89 he was married, at one of the most romantic weddings I've ever witnessed, to a lovely, vivacious girl called Kate. They lived a stone's throw from me in London and upon my return from America they were much-appreciated friends. But when the dark clouds of recession started to gather, their work in the glamorous but fickle world of film production dried up, the already crippling mortgage grew bigger and things started to go downhill. Around this time I was offered Matropi and asked if they would like to share it with me. Travel can be a cure for many things. As one writer put it:

'Oh, I've got a headache . . .'

'Would you like an aspirin?'

'No, I think I'll go to India.'

If India can cure a sore head, I thought, surely Kenya could put a spark back into a troubled relationship. But, as you know, Matropi fell through, and so, sadly, did their marriage. It hit Neil hard.

Neil is not only a very old friend and a fellow biker, but also a compassionate and courageous man, sometimes hot-headed but always looking to do the right thing. One Christmas Eve, attending the midnight service at his local church, some drunken louts started jeering outside. Neil's broad-set chin jutted out in annoyance. Rather than ignore it like everyone else he went outside and saw them all off single-handedly. He is also the most popular person I know, with a bulging address book and the ability to get on with anyone – if you were looking for an ambassador to a hostile alien nation, you might well pick Neil. Through his work in the film industry he'd done plenty of travelling already and, like myself, was desperate to get away from painful memories. It seemed fairly natural that I should ask him along and, after some hesitation on both sides, we decided to make the journey together.

Although heartbroken and confused, the idea of Africa got to Neil. He was preoccupied to be sure, but did his best to cope with the preparations, which I'm sure helped him as they did me. He bought an identical bike to mine and we drove them up to my father's farm to set about equipping them for the dream. They were both second-hand, mine had done 15,000 miles and needed some work doing on it, whereas Neil's had done only 6,500 and just needed a good service.

We sanded them down and sprayed them desert army colours (because of the Gulf War there was plenty of this paint around). We built the frames and panniers and fixed them onto the bikes. Two ten-litre jerry cans on the front, added to the twenty-five-litre tank, would provide us with thirty-five litres of petrol and ten of water. I estimated that with these we had a range of over 350 miles in good conditions, but not much over 250 in bad. The front rack was designed in such a way that it would also act as protection for our legs in the event of crashes and falls.

In the lockable aluminium boxes at the rear we would carry most of our possessions. The real problem of what to take, and what not to, became clear. There is no literature on the subject, you simply have to guess. I took far too much. First came the absolute essentials: tool kit, bike manual, foot pump and puncture repair kit, three oil filters, a set of brake pads, cables, inner tubes and a few other odds and sods. Then there was the camping equipment: petrol cooker, pots and pans – designed like a Russian doll to save space, a Swiss Army knife, a fork and spoon, enamel mug, compass . . . and so on. Then the medical box with hypodermics, bandages, plasters, scalpel and even a needle and thread. (With the all-purpose travel health guide I was quite confident I could whip out Neil's appendix and stitch him back up – whether he'd survive was another matter.) The most interesting addition to the medical supplies were some oral morphine tablets a doctor friend gave us. I insisted on taking – or should that be looking after? – these as I was sure that once Neil got his hands on them they would never have reached the African continent. (None returned.)

So what else? Well the list went on and on. Every time I looked in *Field and Trek* there was something else I was sure I couldn't do without. An oil lamp, for instance. (The lid came off the specialised oil and it spilt over everything before I'd even used it.) A water purifier. (When I did finally need it, after 6,500 miles, it filtered one and a half litres of water before breaking irreparably.) There were salt'n'pepper dispensers, mosquito coils and their holders, J-cloths, Wet Ones, egg holders and many other such vital accessories. In our semi-confused state they all seemed indispensable – even, quite literally, a collapsible kitchen sink. In the event only a few were used, at least by us. Were they of any use to the Africans with whom they ended up? I hope so. I suppose my theory was 'If I've got it and don't need it I can give it away, but if I haven't got it and need it . . .' So I packed those panniers to bursting point and drove around Africa like Santa Claus.

One most unlikely optional extra that proved an undeniable success was a canvas fishing chair, with arms. It collapsed in such a way that, placed over the back frame of the bike, it made a rack upon which my clothes bag, sleeping-bag and my share of the oversized tent could sit. Not only was it a welcome luxury after a long ride in the desert, it was also very practical.

Clotheswise I started out with very little and returned with even less. A few T-shirts, a pair of jeans and shorts, a jumper and my trusty old leather jacket. Toiletries: what you would imagine. I also took a couple of good, thick books (*Lonesome Dove* and *The Quincunx*) and a sheet sleeping-bag. Then, up front, came the tank bag, the heart of our possessions. It was an extremely natty holdall that attached to a plastic base, which in turn attached to the petrol tank. You simply unclipped it, pulled out some straps and it turned into a neat little rucksack. In it we housed all our valuables and documents: passport, driving licence, vaccination certificate and carnet de passage. Mine also carried my camera equipment and film, short-wave radio, diary and pens. In brief they contained everything we could not afford to have stolen. Wherever we went the tank bags would go as well, at least in theory.

Eventually the day came to leave. The bikes stood, as my fantasy said they would, with friends and well-wishers gathered round. As I walked across the garage to greet them, dressed in my black leather jacket, knee-pads, boots and gloves, my helmet in one hand and tank bag in the other, I felt like a test pilot about to try out a new jet, Chuck Yeager about to push the outside of that envelope. I have to say, I felt very proud.

We drove out of the London fog and into the dream. Later, the white cliffs of Dover slowly receded from view as these two self-exiling Englishmen were, at last, on their way.

'Take a good look,' Neil said nostalgically, putting a comforting hand on my shoulder, 'It'll be a long time before we see them again.'

* * *

I hurried through the parting crowd, my heart thumping like the clappers of hell. I saw Neil's face contorted in agony and began to laugh. The sheer joy of seeing him alive! Though he was obviously in considerable pain, this was just fantastic. On realising what this probably meant for Neil, I stopped.

'Oh mate,' he winced through clenched teeth, 'I've blown it. I think I've fucking blown it.'

'What happened? Are you all right? Can you feel everything?'

'It's my leg. I should have put her down. I'm sorry, I'm . . . oh shit!' He rolled back his head, his eyes filling with tears.

'Don't worry, Neilo, everything'll be fine. Now, which leg is it?'

'The left one . . . near the bottom.' Before I could stop him, a fat, broken-nosed Arab with rotting teeth had picked the leg up and given it a good squeeze. Maybe his camels or goats are used to such heavy-handed treatment but poor Neil was not. He let out a sharp yelp, cursing the man and his mother.

I pushed the Arab away and tried to give Neil more room. Fortunately the coachload of tourists decided the show was over and made their way back to the bus, gossiping quietly. I placed my jacket under Neil's head and lit him a cigarette.

'What happened?' I asked again.

'I don't know, I just wasn't looking . . . I came off the road, somersaulted and, damn . . . how's my bike? And my tank bag? Where's my bag, Jonny . . . get it, my bag?' He started to shake.

'It's here. Don't worry, it's all fine. It's as well you were wearing this.' I showed him his helmet. There was a deep gash three or four inches long just above the temple. I vowed then never to drive without wearing mine.

'Has an ambulance been called?' I asked the fat Arab, not in the least sure that there were such things out there.

'La police arrive bientôt,' he replied.

'Okay, just relax. Let's have a look at that leg.'

'It's bloody sore but maybe it's only sprained.' I looked again, and although there was only a slight abrasion I doubted it, the shape seemed decidedly squiffy.

'How's the bike?' He asked again, drawing deeply on the cigarette. It lay in a heap just off the road. The front end was badly bent and the fairing smashed, but he didn't need to know.

'It's fine,' I lied. 'What about your leg? Can you move your toes?' He could not.

A blue van pulled in next to the damaged machine. The driver, wearing a djellaba and turban, with teeth as bad as our fat friend's, got out.

'Qu'est que c'est le problème?' he asked. With a motor bike

mangled in the dirt and a man lying in agony it seemed like a remarkably stupid question. *My wife here has just had her jewellery stolen?*

'Mon ami, il a eu un accident.'

'Arh . . .' he grunted, as if he really had needed the explanation.

'Would you like that we take him to the hospital in Tozeur?' Up until this point I hadn't even been sure that there was a hospital within a hundred miles. It was quite a relief.

'What do you think?' I asked Neil. 'I think the most important thing is to get you to the hospital. Let the police find us, I'm sure they will soon enough.'

He agreed.

After re-packing a mountain of pumpkins, we got the bike in the back of the van and Neil in the front. This time our over-enthusiastic, fat friend tried to throw Neil over his shoulder as though he were a bag of corn. Again he hollered with pain and I felt it too. All loaded up, we left.

Fifteen minutes after our arrival at the hospital I held the hand of a thoroughly defeated man. His leg was indeed broken, as were two ribs. Neil's African dream was at an end . . . Game over player one.

2 Blue Veils, Brown Eyes

Tozeur, Tunisia

'Damn it J.B.,' Neil said through his pain, 'I'm going to go on.' It took three days for the reality of the situation to sink in.

The fibula had snapped in the middle – not bad as leg breaks go but bad enough. We'd been told it would take a month to heal; but how strong would it be? Falls are guaranteed in the desert. If the bike fell the wrong way and the leg broke again a hundred miles from anywhere, what then? And the bike? After completing the inevitable formalities with the police, I set about trying to mend it, but I'm no mechanic and could only bodge it up. Had we been in Malawi or Zambia, the bike could have hobbled to Cape Town, but the fact was we still had to cross the Sahara. With bent forks it was simply impossible. Just to complicate matters further, if we weren't in Algeria within three weeks our visas would no longer be valid.

So all that was on the one hand. On the other was Neil's dream. Not only had he put his heart and soul into it, he had also invested over £3,000. To see it destroyed barely 200 miles into Africa was a catastrophe. Not to mention the fact that he was my partner and the thought of setting out for Cape Town alone was, well, daunting to say the least. I promised to help him all I could but the situation was taken out of my hands. Neil's leg got more and more painful as each day passed and it soon became obvious that there was really no choice.

'A limb is more important than a trip,' Neil said resignedly. 'I must go home.' Four days later he was in hospital in France and although it was another three months before I found out the full story, it was just as well he was.

We had always imagined danger would come from external sources such as bullets or knives, wild animals or deadly diseases, but I was now painfully aware that the most dangerous aspect of the journey would probably be holding a heavy, two-wheeled machine upright all the way to the Cape. I had selfishly thought of the trip as my show, in which Neil was merely playing a supporting role, but to him it was every bit as important. This time, it seemed, God was laughing at him.

To say that I felt blue, as I sped along the road towards the Algerian border, would make me a master of understatement. I felt terrible: guilty for having persuaded Neil to come, mean for leaving him and utterly sorry for what had happened. Added to this, in Niger the Tuareg were taking vehicles from Westerners at gunpoint, in Nigeria there were maniacs on the loose, armed with machetes, intent on chopping people up, and I was fast approaching one of the most notorious border crossings in Africa. I had expected to feel better once I got going, but I didn't. Cape Town was over 10,000 miles away; it might as well have been on Pluto.

'Arrh, you musician?' asked the cheerful-looking customs man as he studied my immigration card. The room was dark and airless. A huge map of Africa sprawled across to the wall, dwarfing me and my confidence.

'Yes . . .' I replied a little nervously, never quite sure if it's a good or a bad thing to be. In Europe it often means being pulled aside and given the once over. In Africa it proved to be different.

'This good,' he smiled. 'I think you play rock'n'roll, yes?' Humming some indistinguishable tune, he started to play an imaginary guitar. 'Me, I like Beatles.' To eat or to listen to I wondered?

This friendly fellow in no way resembled the bastard, 'I'll give you a six hour search', baksheesh-demanding customs officer I'd been warned about. On the contrary, both he and his colleagues were nothing short of charming. The Algerian border turned out to be a classic example of why you shouldn't believe everything you've been told until you've seen it for yourself. In Africa, as I would soon discover, travellers love to tell a melodramatic story. I suppose it makes them feel braver and more intrepid if they have coped with a difficult situation themselves, or serves as a useful excuse if they do not wish to.

Within twenty minutes I had shaken hands and said my goodbyes and was crossing the frontier to enter the Sahara proper.*

For the first time in a week my spirits were high. The whole Sahara stretched before me, 2,000 miles wide, like an ocean of mystery. I headed west along the northern edge of the Grand Erg Oriental towards the trans-Saharan highway. Wave upon wave of scrubless yellow dunes unrolled. There were few villages, just sand. I remembered reading somewhere that when carried to their extremes things take on the characteristics of their opposites. Landscapes are no exception. My surroundings reminded me of the top of an Alpine range: the power lines looked like ski-lifts and the sand like snow, only the people were missing. At times the whole road vanished under drifts of sand. I had to go steady as hitting one at fifty would have been disastrous.

A seed of optimism had burst in my chest, now I was really on my way. Neil was gone and that seemed unbelievably cruel, but I couldn't help feeling that perhaps, for me, this was always the way it was supposed to be. This journey wasn't simply about having fun, thrashing a motor bike thousands of miles across Africa. There was a much bigger – more important – reason than that. It was easy to over-romanticise the link between the journey and my grief – like Sir Lancelot, carrying my pain with my primus – but there were obvious connections between the two. I needed answers and I wanted peace. With every mile I wouldn't automatically be granted these – sitting at border posts and avoiding pot-holes would not be enough. I would have to be pushed to new lengths, perhaps to the edge. Travelling with Neil would have been too easy – a problem shared – making this impossible. I had to be alone and, as I motored along under the bright desert sky, it seemed as though fate had made it so.

At a small village I bought some tomatoes and chillies from a market trader. Dark strangers in djellabas and turbans milled about the colourless streets; curious about me, they stopped and talked in undertones. As I left, a mangy dog gave chase, as if telling me what the men hadn't the nerve to say. It gave up when I reached the edge of the village but schoolchildren, dressed in white coats, followed its lead and threw stones. Apparently this is something of a national sport, and happens to everyone; I took two direct hits but was too excited to be put out. A few miles on I

*Three days later, in a raid by FIS, the Islamic fundamentalists, the border was attacked and four of these men were killed.

parked amongst some dunes to lunch in peace on a sardine and tomato sandwich.

Towards evening the wind picked up and danced a million grains of sand down the road before me. As the sun blurred into a crimson wash I pulled off the main road into Touggourt and, happy with my first day's solo progress, splashed out on the best hotel in town. It cost just five pounds.

The following day I got away in good time and soon had the wind at my back. The scenery changed as I drove west. Gone were the rolling *Beau Geste* dunes. Here the land was flatter, with thousands of tiny bushes like whiskers on an old man's face. I could see for miles in every direction. Never had I witnessed such space and openness. Wild camels roamed the desert plains while carcasses fed the scavenging birds.

I was driving on, happy but cold, when up ahead I saw a road-block. I wasn't sure what to expect but I'd been told to be cautious and to prepare for the worst.

'So . . . you is Inglis, I think?' said the policeman. He was about fifty-five, rather plump, grey-haired and with eyes that never stopped smiling. He didn't really speak but chortled, as if everything to be said was humorous. It was hard to imagine him carrying out any pernicious activity. I knew I had nothing to fear.

'Yes.' I tried to match his grin.

'You know where you are?'

I pointed at the map. 'About here I think.'

His face became grave and he shook his head. 'No, no, no, my friend. You is here.' He pointed to Morocco. Then his face split again in two. 'I joke . . . I joke . . . I like you Inglis. You funny, crazy men I think. Look, this is road to Ghardara but is very bad.' He pointed down a sand track. 'This also road to Ghardara and is very nice. I think you take this one. Ha! But you is Inglis, so maybe you take bad one.'

'No. No. I'll take the good one.'

'Aarr . . . ha! ha!' he chuckled. 'Maybe you not so crazy, where you going?'

'South Africa.'

'South Africa?' He was amazed and again burst out laughing; his wonderful beaming face made me laugh too.

'You more than crazy. I know it – you Inglis, all crazy. If you go to South Africa I think you need many luck.'

For a moment I thought he was going to take some out of his pocket and hand it to me. Instead, he slapped me on the back and went away talking and laughing to himself. So much for bastard Algerian policemen. I came to three more road-blocks that day, none of the others even bothered to stop me.

In the late afternoon I crested a ridge and found Ghardara below me. As the sun lost height and sank towards the west, its golden light lengthened the shadows across the pastel buildings. On the top of the biggest hill an imposing minaret stood proudly, like a holy man, with the sprawling town below kneeling in veneration. From here it was south all the way to Nigeria and, for all I knew, to the end of the continent.

As I was parking on the main street I heard a voice over my shoulder.

'I wouldn't leave your bike there if I was you.' I turned round to see a lanky, dark-haired Welshman. 'That's where we left our Landrover and all our passports and documents have been lifted. Bastard Arabs! They'll take anything. Damn them I say.'

Before I had a chance to answer he was gone, obviously very angry. I bumped into him and his friend a little later on but rather wished I hadn't as they were both still surly and resentful. It seemed that they had been trying to deliver their Landrover to someone in Malawi but had been turned back at the closed Zairean border. Okay, it was bad news, but things could be worse. Surely that's what travelling is all about? Highs and lows. Good luck and bad. Even poor Neil with a broken leg and a dream in tatters had eventually been able to find the absurd, funny side to it. They had at least seen a large part of Africa, still had their vehicle and were in good health. I tried to put this point of view to them but with little success.

'It's all right for you, with all the time in the world. We only had a month to do it in. Now we've got to wait here for a week to get new papers. I don't know what work'll say . . . we work you know.'

A Danish motor cyclist I met that evening was also turning round and going back.

'I have heard that the situation in the desert is very bad.' It turned out to be no more than I already knew, which wasn't very much. The Tuareg were said to be robbing overlanders in the desert south of Tamanrasset, on a couple of occasions taking their trucks. But there were hundreds of vehicles going across each week and less than a handful had been hit. I found it hard to understand his defeatism. I don't mean to sound fearlessly heroic, I am not, but you don't plan a trip like this without anticipating some danger. Perhaps my motives for risk-taking were stronger than his, but to turn and flee at the first whiff of trouble seemed ludicrous – why not save yourself the bother and just tour France instead?

The next morning there was one thing I had to do before I could leave for El Golea – get insurance. These days in London it's hard enough to get motor-cycle cover for the UK – ask about Africa they laugh you out of the office. It had to be done here, country by country. So far I had been lucky that no one had demanded to see it. I asked the hotel receptionist for directions.

'Oh non – c'est fermé, m'sieur. Aujourd'hui est vendredi, demain c'est ouvert.' I'd forgotten again. Friday is the Islamic holy day and all businesses are shut. I'd either have to risk it and hope that I wouldn't be stopped, or wait in Ghardara an extra day.

I think as a consequence of losing Neil I was keen to get some distance under my belt. The thought of what I was doing seemed so daunting that I wanted to get well into the Sahara before I had a chance to stop and think. On the other hand, the blue Chinagraph line tracking my progress on the map had already made something of an impression, and Ghardara seemed a nice enough place. Besides which, it is asking for trouble driving round a country like Algeria without your papers in order. Although I'd been fortunate to meet only friendly officials the rumours had to come from somewhere. I'd stay and look around.

Most of the day I spent wandering the narrow streets, exploring the mosques and watching the animated cast of the colourful market. There were buyers, sellers, browsers and beggars, talking, smoking and drinking tea. The fragrance of spices and freshly cut flowers did it best to mask the earthier smells left behind by goats and donkeys. Given the arid countryside I'd just driven through, I found the selection of perfect vegetables on sale nothing short of amazing. There were also carpets and clothes,

31

sandals and slippers, chickens, books and all manner of cheap electrical appliances.

At the far end of the market square, between the carpet sellers and a donkey cart, there was a hullabaloo. Many people gathered excitedly, watching something and laughing. When I got close enough to peer over their heads, I saw a dark brown snake wriggle up the sleeve of a walnut-faced Arab and then emerge from the bottom of his djellaba to the shrieks of joy of all who watched. The sun was low as I made my way back towards the hotel.

'You want change money?' said a voice from behind me. I turned and saw a young face, faintly lit, at the entrance to a dark alleyway.

'You want change money I give you good price.' I was a little surprised that he was talking to me in English since few people here could. I had some dollars I'd smuggled in just for this purpose and now seemed like as good a time as any.

'What price will you give me?'

'You come this way, I give you good price.'

I followed him down the alleyway, dodging some fleeces which hung on strings from the balcony above, round a corner and through an ill-fitting wooden door. I found myself in a musty, unpainted room.

'You sit here,' he said, pointing to a flimsy wooden chair up against the wall. He sat on a stool facing me. A young girl perched on the window-ledge in the corner, studying a thick book, evidently doing her homework. A dim electric light bulb did its best to brighten the gloom.

Many countries in Africa have very strict currency import and export controls, and in my experience, none are so rigorously enforced as in Algeria. Upon entry, a currency declaration form must be filled in, stating exactly how much money you have. Every time you change money, you must get an official stamp on the form to show that it was legally changed. If this form is not kept in perfect order you can have big problems on leaving the country. Hence the booming black market in hard currency. If you do manage to get some undeclared money into the country, you can get nearly twice as much for it as at the official rate of exchange. It is however, like all good scams, not without risk. If you are unlucky enough to get caught, either at the border or while changing it, you can expect at least a few days, possibly months, in jail. And I wouldn't wish an Algerian jail on anyone.

'How much you want change?' asked Yousef.

'Well . . . er . . . only fifteen dollars actually. It's all I have.' It wasn't, but it was all I needed. From what I could see of his expression in the gloom, he was crestfallen at the puny sum.

'I give you thirty dinar for one dollar,' he said. Since the bank was giving twenty-seven I knew I could get better, even for my meagre deal.

'You said you give me good deal, I can get fifty for one dollar.'

'No, this is too much. I give you thirty-five.' And so it continued until we both settled for forty-two.

'Tell me, Yousef, how come you speak English?'

'I learn it so I can make business with the tourist.' This seemed as good a reason as any.

'And is this your sister?' I asked, tipping the chair on its back legs. Before Yousef had a chance to answer my question the back legs gave way and I crashed to the floor. Teachers always said this bad habit would one day do neither myself nor a chair any good. Now they were proved right. That sort of thing is always embarrassing even if the audience is only two Algerian children. The little girl started to giggle as I tried unsuccessfully to mend the damage. Yousef said it didn't matter but I could see that it did. It was the only chair in the room, possibly in the house. Of course I would have to pay for it. I gave him 200 dinar and left muttering words of apology, my short career in currency smuggling a total waste of time.

From Ghardara the trans-Saharan highway carves its way directly south across the heart of the desert, which does its best to reclaim it. For the first 1,000 miles the road is asphalt and in good condition, but from Tamanrasset there is no road at all, over 500 miles of sand and rocks as far as Arlit in Niger. It was on this stretch of piste that the Tuareg were said to be causing the trouble. Still, I had to get there first and I knew there would be a lot more information in Tam. All the overlanders gather there to form convoys before making the big push south.

Having got my insurance and filled up with petrol, I was away by ten. The further south I drove, the pinker the sand became – almost orange. The plains expanded and the road got straighter. As far as the eye could see was flat, arid

33

nothingness. Then vertical flat-topped rocks appeared. At first there were just a few, then more and more until I was driving down a canyon. Jutting straight out of the earth to about 500 feet, they were as menacing as those in Monument Valley, seen in countless cowboy films. The strange thing about them was that they all levelled out at exactly the same height, as though God had sliced their tops off with one swish of a sickle.

There were dunes later on, huge and forbidding, marching towards the road. To get a better look, I stopped on a ridge where the edges of the road dropped sharply away on either side. While I was sitting absorbing this strange sight, another motor bike pulled up behind mine and a man and a woman dismounted.

'Eh gov, d'you know where we can get a beer round 'ere? Ah'm that bloody parched me liver's swearing at me. Ah'm like as not gonna pass out unless I get one . . . Oh, an' by the way, I'm Steve an' this es Sue, ma missus.'

It was hard to know what to say. One minute I was musing on the amazing creations of nature and the next I was being accosted by a Yorkshireman looking for a beer.

'El Golea I should think, it can't be very far now.'

'Aye, that's about what we thought,' said Steve. 'D'you fancy one ye'sen?'

As a matter of fact I did. Driving all day in the desert is thirsty business. Excluding the grumpy Welshmen, these were the first Brits I'd seen, and bikers to boot. It seemed likely that they would be decent company so I agreed and we drove the last fifty miles in convoy.

It didn't take long for Steve to find a hotel with a bar and we were soon sitting round our beers. Steve was indeed amusing. A loquacious man, no taller than five foot five, his lively face wearing a bandit-style moustache, he sat eagerly on the edge of his chair, the quicker to express the next thing to come into his head. Sue, on the other hand, was quiet and thoughtful. She didn't say much and when she did it was usually to reprimand Steve for exaggerating one of his countless stories. 'Oh, Steeeve . . .' she'd say, 'he never ded.' But Steve wouldn't mind, he'd just turn to me and giggle like a naughty schoolboy.

I have always been a bit wary of men who talk about drink or women in the first five minutes of meeting. It usually means they can't get by without the former and aren't getting any of the latter, but Steve was a pure delight. I'm sure, as his wife insisted, his tales should be taken with the proverbial pinch of salt, but he was a natural story-teller and his tales were all amusing or interesting. One of them, about an Indian in Dubai, where Steve had been working with Sue, was particularly bizarre.

The story concerned a man from Punjab who had been accused of a rape which he almost certainly did not commit. He was duly taken before the court, found guilty and given a five-year jail sentence.

Some 'kindly' fellow prisoners told him that in one year's time he would be able to appeal against his conviction. 'Learn the Koran inside out,' they said, 'learn to speak Arabic, change your name, become a Muslim and the judge will assuredly give you back your freedom.'

The Indian took the advice.

One year later he stood in the dock and the judge said to him, 'I hear you have changed your name and become a Muslim.'

'Yes, sir.'

'You have learnt the Koran?'

'Yes, sir.'

'You can speak and write Arabic?'

'Yes, sir.'

'And you are a good Muslim?'

'Yes, sir, I am.'

'Well, this is most unfortunate for you. Under the Holy Law of Islam, to which this court adheres, the penalty for rape as a Muslim is life. Take him away.'

The next day I drove on across a barren gravel plain which ran almost all the way to In Salah. The wind was strong and chill but carried no sand. Just outside the town there was a cutting where the road broke through and dipped away out of sight. As I rounded the corner, for the first of many times on this journey, I couldn't believe my eyes. I had reached the edge of an escarpment and before me, hundreds of feet below, lay an extraordinarily beautiful arid valley. The surface, covered by bright yellow desert flora, was pierced by jet-black granite buttes and inselbergs. It was as though I had been beamed down to another planet.

In the camp site that night there were fifteen of us sitting around eating couscous and talking. Most of the campers were engaged in a scam which was new to me but which I would soon see being executed by many others. Hugo, an affable Dutchman with whom I later crossed the roadless desert, explained that because Niger is a landlocked country there is a chronic shortage of decent cars. As there are no import restrictions on vehicles you can just drive them in, overland through Algeria, and get three or four times what you paid for them in Europe. It's just about as simple as that, except of course for the little problem of crossing the Sahara. At Arlit, the first town across the Niger border, plenty of dealers are ready to take vehicles off your hands. Hugo had a Peugeot estate, the preferred choice, though some had Mercs, and Maurice, a Frenchman on his twelfth trip, had a minibus. He reckoned that after two more trips, which were definitely getting more dangerous, he would have made enough money to live with his girlfriend in South America for two years. A fat Belgian had figured it out the best. He didn't have just one vehicle, he had a truck and low-loader with five cars on its back. On reaching Niamey, Niger's capital, he would sell the lot and fly back ten grand richer. It sounded quite tempting.

What a long-haired German called Marcus was doing did not sound tempting at all.

'I am volking across the Sahara,' he told us. The collective gasp of amazement was quickly followed by a barrage of questions as to the likelihood of his succeeding in such a venture. He answered with confidence that bordered on arrogance. 'Oh, ya, I am very determined.' We were all suitably impressed.

Still, I guessed that if someone could push a wheelbarrow across (Geoffrey Howard, in 1975), it must be possible, but I, for one, was pleased to have a motor bike. At seven the next morning, when I passed him a few kilometres out of town, I gave him a wave and wished him luck. You can, therefore, imagine my surprise when I saw him two days later in the hotel bar in Tamanrasset, drinking a beer.

'You're a quick walker,' I said. 'Five hundred miles in two days is pretty good. Why don't you walk to Cape Town, you'd be there next Monday.'

'Ah, my feet ver sore, ya. A truck gave me lift. It is of no matter.'

All was fine until I got to within fifty miles of the Arak gorge. The wind whipped up and hit me so fast it was hard to know where it came from or what had caused it. It didn't matter, it was there sure enough – a notorious Saharan sandstorm. The sand cut and slashed like a cat-o'-nine-tails. It wiped the contented smile from my face, replacing it with a squinting grimace. For the first few miles I battled on, sometimes leaning the bike as much as thirty degrees to stop myself being blown over. I knew I had only a few miles to go till the gorge would lend me sanctuary but each one felt like ten. The sand got in everywhere. It penetrated my goggles and blocked my eyes. I turned my head away, closing one eye, but it was no good, I knew I must stop. There was so much sand in the air that the sun was barely visible – a thick, painful blizzard of dirt. Through the murk I saw a black shape up ahead. When I got closer I saw it was Steve and Sue huddled behind their bike. I pulled up beside them and we sat in contemplative silence while the earth did its best to erase us from its surface. When I did open my eyes I could barely see ten yards ahead in a place where previously I had been able to see for miles. We waited for nearly two hours while the sand slowly buried us. It did not let up or show any likelihood of doing so.

'We might as well make a dash for the gorge,' I shouted to Steve. 'We could be waiting here all night.'

'Aye, keep your lights on and we'll follow close behind.'

The road was invisible a lot of the time and twice I drove off it into deep sand. Mile by mile we plodded on, no faster than twenty miles an hour, fighting the forces of nature. But at last, standing like a citadel of peace and security, out of the gloom came the faint and welcome outline of the Arak gorge.

Despite all the hardship and discomfort one inevitably suffers on a bike, it is, I'm sure, the most satisfying means of transport, at least on a trip like this. In a Landrover or truck you can simply wind up the windows and pour yourself a coffee, cocooned in Western comfort. Not so on a bike. Whether it be sandstorm, torrential rain, fierce wind or even a swarm of locusts, indeed anything God, nature or the devil can throw at you, you must take it. There is nowhere to hide. But when the challenge is over and you have succeeded, the feeling of satisfaction is unbeatable.

At about seven, the wind dropped as quickly as it had risen and the evening was still. We camped about forty miles into the gorge, making sure we were above any wadis as flash flooding can be lethal. Indeed, they say more people die from drowning in this part of the Sahara than they do from thirst. A storm up in the Hoggar mountains, which we were now entering, can quickly result in torrents of water down below.

We were joined by Frank and Iliana, a German couple who had been with us in In Salah. They were travelling south in a four-wheel-drive camper van. Not only did they have coffee but they also had cold beer, some of which they shared with us along with a meal of spaghetti bolognaise.

We retired at about nine thirty but sleep did not come easily. Lying on the sand, without the protection of the tent which I had had to dispense with since leaving Neil, I was soon very cold. The icy chill of the starlit desert sky penetrated my body and settled on my bones as though I were dead. The desert at night can be unimaginably tranquil and serene, but that night I could not take comfort in it. I had been too busy and excited by what I was doing to dwell for long on the loss of Neil but now I felt lonely for the first time since his departure. Steve and Sue were huddled in their tents and Frank and Iliana were together in their van. Looking up at the stars I saw Mel's face and missed her terribly. Surely that's what it's all about, having someone with whom to share moments like this. What the hell was I doing belting across Africa? Trying to escape from the shackles of a broken heart? Trying to impress friends who wouldn't really understand? Or was I trying to prove something to myself? I didn't know, but whatever the reason, as I lay there under the distant heavens, it all seemed just a little pointless without love.

I was so dirty and tired by the time I reached Tamanrasset I decided to stay in a hotel and sod the camp site. I don't mind sleeping rough and consider myself just about as hardy as the next man, but if there's a hotel to be had at not much greater expense, I'll take it.

First I tried the Hotel Dassine, which I found boarded-up and then the Tinhinane, which had no rooms available. This only left the more up-market Hotel Tahat.

There wasn't much to be said for the Tahat as I soon discovered. There was no hot water – I'd just about given up hoping that there ever would be – and the light didn't work in the room which I shared with a thousand flies. The one thing it did have going for it was its receptionist. She looked absolutely delicious. On arrival I walked up the steps of the capacious lobby and accidentally caught her eye. She left her place behind the desk and came over.

'Bonjour, m'sieur, comment puis-je vous aidez?' For a moment all my French deserted me. Confronted by this vision of loveliness, I could say nothing. *Come on, Jonny, pull yourself together, you've talked to pretty girls before.*

'Err . . . pardon, mademoiselle . . .' She was smiling at me, either conscious of the effect she was having or simply being polite. '. . . Mais, avez vous une chambre pour la nuit?'

'Oui, m'sieur, c'est quatre cent vingt dinar.' After an embarrassing pause during which I first translated the French to 420 dinar and then converted that to sterling, I realised it was over twelve pounds. This was far more than I could afford for one night, but I couldn't let her know that. Besides, I was tired and in need of a treat. *Okay, just this once.*

'Oui, d'accord. C'est bien, merci.'

With the same enchanting smile she took my passport so she could fill in the ledger later. As she leant down to get my key I couldn't help but notice the most perfectly shaped breasts hidden behind a pale silk shirt. I looked away quickly, embarrassed that she might have seen. Apparently she had not. She just gave me the key and watched with some amusement as I struggled with my luggage out of the back door towards my room.

It's funny how a fully grown man can react to a beautiful woman. She had probably treated me like any other guest, smiled and been polite. But had I seen something more than that, or was it just my vanity hoping so? I must have looked a sight: filthy, scruffy and I probably smelt as well. But . . . if I was not very much mistaken . . . there had been a certain something . . . a kind of sparkle in her eyes that seemed to be for me. I went to sleep with that in mind.

I was awoken by a swarm of flies so thick I couldn't tell if the ceiling was black or white. The room was small and airless; I opened the shutters but it made no difference. I packed a bag with what I thought I might need for a night at Assekrem, the hermitage at the top of the Hoggar mountains fifty miles to the east, and went to reception to check out.

The bright, morning light reflecting off the marble floor filled the room. Giant yucca plants stood by the doorless doorways like sentries guarding the tomb of a Pharaoh. Other guests made their way to and from the dining room, lingering for a while to take in the notices on the information board.

She was there again, even more beautiful than the vision I'd slept with. Her long black hair fell easily across her shoulders, tumbling a short way down her back. She wore no make-up; there was no need as her golden skin was perfect. Her face was almost childlike with a little nose, delicate chin and the softest cheeks. As I approached the desk, her almond eyes, as dark and bright as polished onyx, lit up. Her infectious smile was as radiant as the stars.

'Bonjour, Jonatan,' she said, pushing back some hair that had fallen across her cheek. 'Bien dormi?'

I'm not usually too keen on people calling me by my Christian name. I associate it with being accused of something, told off, but from her it sounded delightful. And, more importantly, it meant she'd taken the trouble to remember it from my passport which she now handed back. *Surely she doesn't do that for all the guests.*

'Oui, merci,' I replied, grinning stupidly.

There were three other people working behind the desk and all seemed to take an interest in me. They asked questions, in a mixture of English and French, such as where was I going, what was I doing and where had I been, to which I replied as best I could. Then she asked, I thought for the hotel register, 'What is your occupation?'

'Oh, je suis musicien.'

'Vraiment?' she asked excitedly. 'What do you play?'

'Ugh ... la guitar et je suis chanteur.' A fatal mistake and one I regretted immediately.

'Oh! C'est très bon. Please sing something for me.' Instantly, all the others were joining in, asking me to sing. Why can't I ever learn to keep my big mouth shut? I hate singing alone to people at the best of times but without a guitar, and to a girl I was seriously contemplating carrying off into the sunset, it was a disaster; but I knew I had no choice. So what should I sing? 'Only the lonely' by Roy Orbison was all that came to mind. Of all things. What a jerk. I sang some of it, felt utterly stupid, and blushed. She seemed to enjoy it, or at least pretended to, and clapped.

We talked some more but eventually my business was completed and, after leaving my luggage with them for safe-keeping, I turned to go.

'Au revoir.'

'Au revoir, Jonatan. If you return after two o'clock for your things I will be here working.'

'Bon. D'accord.' I left feeling as high as the place I was about to visit. I didn't even know her name.

Assekrem, meaning End of the World, stands at an altitude of 9,000 feet, in an area of the Hoggar mountains known as Atakor and getting there proved to be my first real challenge. I left Tamanrasset on a dusty road which passed the police check-point and led on into a labyrinth of wadis. The air was dry and hot and the sun slammed down relentlessly upon my back. The sand was thick and deep ruts made progress hard. They seemed to make the front and back wheels go in different directions and twice I nearly fell. After an hour, I clambered out of the riverbed and onto a flat gravel plain where the going was easier. At a Tuareg encampment I took a wrong turn and wasted ten miles in a loop back towards Tam. Again a shabby dog, much like a greyhound, appeared from nowhere and gave chase. It got close, for a moment snapping at my heels. On this terrain it possessed much the same speed as the bike, though thankfully less stamina. It soon gave up and limped away, barking at the dust.

The bike heaved and spluttered as I drove high up into the range. Black mountains, like the rotting teeth of a giant, jutted vertically out of the gums of the earth. It was a landscape of tortured sculptures forming distant peaks, oppressive, almost evil . . . the devil's backyard. Narrow tracks, composed of sharp rock and lava flow, hammered the bike's suspension and rattled every bone in my body. At times the going was so steep the bike slid backwards on the shale, losing power because of the altitude. I expected spokes to break, oil seals to leak or tyres to burst. I passed Ilamen, a mighty piece of rock which towered 3,000 feet above me. How wonderful it felt to be driving under the Finger of God, bound for the End of the World.

The front wheel hit an unseen gully and I was knocked off balance. I fell hard, my first fall in Africa, leaving me with a slightly strained right shoulder. Brushing myself off, I continued up the track and eventually rounded a corner to enter the refuge below the hermitage itself. It had taken four hours to cover fifty miles.

There was a chill wind whistling through the malign peaks

41

as I parked outside. I was relieved to get into the main room of the refuge and gratefully accepted a thick, black coffee. I sat down in a comfortable chair, much to the relief of my back, and let Dawn, a friendly Canadian girl who was up there with two friends, tell me about the man who was mad enough to want to live in this lonely place.

It seems that Charles du Foucauld was something of a wealthy rogue before 1905 when he caught religion big time in Morocco. He took his vows as a Trappist monk, gave away most of his money and came out to Tamanrasset to help the Imazighen, or Tuareg. After a while even Tam proved too busy for this mystic so he came to the Atakor and built the hermitage as a place of contemplation. The isolation of the place and the hardness of the life nearly killed him, as a result he didn't stay long before returning to Tam, which did. (In 1916 the Tuareg of Tassili joined forces with the Libyan Sennousi and, bribed by the Germans to make trouble for the French, went on a raiding party to Tam. By mistake, for it was well-known that he was a holy man, du Foucauld was shot by an overexcited boy of fifteen.) Still, as I looked out of the window onto the evil landscape of black volcanic rock, rock which had at some point ripped through the surface of the earth in a most violent manner, it was hard to imagine how du Foucauld could have worshipped anything other than Satan. If hell could be imagined, surely this was it.

The dormitory was warm. I had fully expected to sleep outside so was relieved to find a sponge mattress and some shelter. Sitting cross-legged facing each other in the corner of the room were two Tuareg men. Their traditional veils hung loosely from their heads and the swords they always carried lay at their sides. The veil – or chech – is what makes the Tuareg distinctive. It consists of a piece of cotton between three and five metres long, traditionally dyed indigo, wrapped around the face and head with only a slit left for the eyes. To explorers of old, the Tuareg were known as the blue men because the dye from the veils stained their faces. The dim light from a solitary oil lamp sent their sinister shadows sliding across the wall. Their Tamachek voices continued uninterrupted, an expressionless flow of sound. We settled ourselves for the night.

There was a time when the Tuareg were the unrivalled warriors of the Sahara. The sight of their blue veils could

42

strike fear into the heart of the hardest man. As mercenaries, protecting the desert convoys and the isolated people of the oases, they gained substantial rewards. They also bred highly valued camels and traded salt from their mines at Bilma, but a combination of drought, hostile governments and a fall in demand for salt led to the slow but definite demise of this once great tribe. Most Tuareg have left the desert to live in hardship in towns where they look for work as security guards, handicraft sellers or, if they're lucky, guides.

Mohammed and Maktar were of Berber descent. Both having lost their livestock in the droughts of the eighties, they had been forced to travel north from their homes in Niger. They now drove Landrovers for the tourists wishing to see the area. Between them, on a pile of hot coals, sat a small, enamel teapot, its contents simmering gently. Maktar poured the mint tea into three small glasses and passed them round. No one from a culture such as theirs would ever indulge themselves before making sure that everyone else had been invited to partake. Indeed, I was soon to realise that the less people have the more generous they are. There is no question of 'giving', it is as natural as breathing. They rolled some spliffs of hashish, passed them round too, and, warming to their audience, told us tales of their past.

After a while the dope took over, my body fell asleep and my brain gave up the battle of translating from French. I sank back and let it all wash over me, thoroughly contented. I was 9,000 feet up, in a house at the End of the World, listening to warriors talk. It didn't matter that I couldn't understand – I knew what they were saying. I closed my eyes and drifted to sleep.

By the time I woke, the sky was already a psychedelic mass of colour. Hurriedly I pulled on my jeans and staggered outside. It was cold, by God. My breath turned white as I clambered from the dormitory up the zigzag path towards the hermitage, stopping every few yards to catch my breath. I reached the little house at the top, looked east and was awestruck. A *mélange* of colours filled the sky while stars were still in evidence above. As the sun slipped up from behind the Martian landscape it seemed as though it were doing so for the first time, like the birth of a new planet.

The effect was marred slightly by a truckload of Australian overlanders who had arrived late the night before.

'Lizzy, have you finished the Vegemite!' shrieked a girl. And though Lizzy swore she had not, the ensuing argument was hardly conducive to my daydream interplanetary exploration. They sat in a row on the edge of the cliff, with enough camera equipment to open a shop. Knowing they had just as much right to be there as I did not lessen my resentment. Was this what Africa would be like all the way south? Would there always be truckloads of backpackers? I don't mean to sound like a travel snob but, after all, this was the End of the World. I began to realise that if unspoilt Africa was what I desired, if I really wanted to go to places which few people see, where that tribal chief would lend me his hut, I would have to get off this well-trodden route. I walked a little way down from the peak and sat watching in solitude, wishing I'd been born a hundred years earlier.

Six hours later, without any wild dogs, Bedouin camps or falls, I was back in Tam – the town with the beautiful girl. I found the camp site and secured myself a dusty but comfortable zeriba, or grass hut. Nervously, I made my way back to the hotel to collect my belongings. Half of me hoped she wouldn't be there. I could get my things with the minimum of fuss and be gone, into the desert, the whole thing remembered as a fleeting fancy. The other half, the less cowardly side, prayed she'd be there, although I really wasn't sure why.

I arrived at the hotel, made my way up the steps past the yuccas, and approached the desk. Her head was buried in a ledger, concluding some business. I stood in front of her, smiled and waited. At first I had wanted to turn and run but I hadn't, and now I was pleased, even calm. She looked up and smiled.

'Ah, bonjour Jonatan,' she said excitedly. 'Est-ce que Assekrem était bien?'

'Oui, c'était magnifique, merci; mais la route était un peu mal. Mais . . . comment tu t'appelles?'

'Amel.' It was a beautiful name, pronounced a-mel, and struck me as an astonishing coincidence. She had got up and was now standing in front of me with only the desk between us. I asked her to spell her name for me. She wrote it down in large swirly writing and told me that in Arabic it means 'hope'.

I crossed off the 'A' and told her about Mel. I don't know why, for I very seldom tell anyone, especially strangers, but somehow it seemed right. Her face became grave as she offered her condolences. I changed the subject – and some money – really as an excuse to stay longer. I hung around as long as I could, at a loss as to know what to do. I couldn't just ask her out for a drink – it's not like that there. I wanted to tell her she was the most beautiful girl I'd ever seen, that I'd give anything to hold her, to kiss her, hell, just to sit and look at her. But how could I? I was leaving for the border the following morning, the whole situation was hopeless. I sat outside the hotel for ten minutes, wishing I had said something, wondering what to do. It seemed too ridiculous, too bizarre. Could I really be feeling crazy about this girl I'd only just met? And if so, was I not mad to be turning my back on her? How could I ignore what my heart seemed to be telling me? Was it the same feeling I'd had for Mel that first time? It really felt like it was . . .

The Meeting

8.35 p.m. January 15th

'Bringgg . . .' The piercing sound of the door bell echoed through the house. 'Damn,' I muttered as I burned my hand on the casserole. 'Okay, just coming. Emma, can you do something with the stew. It's all dried out.' I'd never had anyone to dinner before and was as nervous as a rabbit trapped by headlights.

A week earlier, at a party in the country given by mutual friends, I had become re-acquainted with Tania. She had grown up a lot since I had last seen her some three years back and now, at nineteen, was a beauty to behold. She had the sultry looks of a Romanian gypsy with high cheek-bones and large brown eyes. In her black velvet dress she had had little difficulty in holding my attention for most of the night.

She was beautiful, yes, and good fun, but was she right for me? I wasn't sure. But I also knew that if I didn't make an effort, I'd probably never find the right girl. 'It's no use waiting for that thunderbolt,' I told myself. So I asked her to dinner and she accepted.

The closer the big day got the more nervous I became. What was I going to cook? A fry-up was about all I was good for, and who else should I invite? Was I being stupid getting so worked up? Could I really imagine Tania as my girlfriend? I'd had relationships before, of course,

*but they had never lasted long; somehow we'd just never clicked. What I
wanted was the big one – Love – a soulmate. Would Tania be different,
would she be the one? It was hard to see what we actually had in common.
Worrying that she might be feeling just the same way, I decided to check
that she still wanted to come.*

*'Yes, of course, I'm really looking forward to it,' she said when I
called her at work. 'It'll be fun, but . . . er . . . would you mind if
I brought a friend?' Evidently she too was unsure.*

'No, no, not at all.' I tried to hide my disappointment.

*'You'll really like her,' she went on, rubbing in her uncertainty. 'You
know, she's into music, bands and all that.' So I figured I'd just wait
and see.*

*I reached the front door and took a deep breath. It had been raining
all day and had only recently stopped. A strong breeze rippled the puddles.
It blew Tania's hair across her face, she pushed it away with her hand. I
bent down to kiss her on the cheek.*

'Hi,' she said brightly, handing me a bottle of wine. 'This is Mel.'

*A ripple of electricity ran down my back – so thunderbolts happen
after all. She was perhaps not as classically beautiful as her friend but
in her pale blue eyes she seemed to carry a secret, a certain spirit I had
never seen before. It wasn't so much the way she looked as the spark that
came from within.*

*I knew in an instant that she was the one. She was the girl I'd been
waiting for. The girl I spent countless nights with alone in my bed. The
girl who would make me whole. I knew it as certainly as I knew my own
name.*

*Surprising myself, I bent forward and kissed her. 'Come on in,
I'm afraid I've burnt the stew.'*

I returned to the camp site with my mind in something of a
muddle. I could just drive off into the desert the following day
and in a week or two I would probably have forgotten all about
Amel. But on the other hand . . .

Then an idea came to me. I would write her a letter in French,
telling her how I felt, and give her my Kenyan bangle. It was the
only thing I had worth giving, besides perhaps a torque-wrench
which I doubted she would have much use for. Yes, she'd like
that.

I reckoned she would not be on duty that evening as she'd
worked the day shift, so I thought I'd give it to one of the other

receptionists to pass on to her in the morning. I realised that this would give her no chance to respond as I'd be gone, but the futility of the situation didn't seem to bother me – at least she'd know how I felt.

With my mind made up, I was much happier. I sat back on the dusty mattress in my zeriba and wrote the letter. That completed, all I had to do was to persuade Steve to come with me for a beer, and that was never going to be a problem. At eight o'clock we set off, Steve ignorant of my scam.

As we walked up the steps of the hotel the plan fell apart, for there, standing facing the other way, at the far end of the lobby, was Amel. *Oh no, what can I do now? I can't give it to one of the receptionists. They'll just call her over and . . . well . . . that's far too intense.* I raced for the sanctuary of the bar, hoping she wouldn't turn round, and that Steve wouldn't notice her, for he knew I liked her. I was nervous, very nervous, and in need of a drink.

After a couple of beers I felt much better, as did the whole situation. *She's probably gone by now, it'll be fine. Go and change some money and if everything's cool you can hand the present over and get out.* My mind made up, I acted. But as soon as I showed my face in the entrance hall I realised that this plan was doomed to failure as well.

'Ah, Jonatan. M'sieur Jonatan,' the receptionists called excitedly.

'Bonsoir.' I was a little confused, not really knowing why I had suddenly become so famous. One of the other girls disappeared and within a minute she was back with Amel. She was out of her smart work clothes, wearing jeans and a T-shirt, with her hair tied up at the back – the look suited her. We were now on the same side of the counter and I was filled with Dutch courage.

At once the whole world seemed to implode, with Amel and I at its centre. It didn't matter that we spoke different languages or came from cultures a million miles apart, it was obvious that our feelings for each other were the same. I felt things I hadn't done in ages. All those precious emotions I had been forced to keep a lid on for more than two years resurfaced. Amel had woken me up.

'You'll find someone else, of course you will,' friends used to say reassuringly, but I had been far from convinced that I would. 'To have what I've had once is more than many people get,' I would think. 'Why should I be so lucky as to have it all again?' They had often set me up at dinner parties with single girls, I'd even had affairs with one or two, but nothing whatsoever had stirred inside, it had been as though my emotions were dead. Yet here I was, quite literally in the middle of the Sahara desert, with a girl I had known for only a matter of minutes, deliriously excited as that treasured feeling of total, uninhibited joy consumed me again. In some ways she even reminded me of Mel: the enthusiasm and speed with which she talked, the way she pushed a loose strand of hair behind her ear, her figure, and there was even some resemblance in the features of her face. But what grabbed me the most, sending my heart all aflutter, was her captivating, ever-present smile. From it radiated an excitement and passion for life that had me hooked. And when I caught the sweet, fresh fragrance of her body as I whispered something in her ear I could have cried with delight. Instead I laughed. We sat close to each other talking, smiling and holding hands. I felt no guilt – it all seemed so absurdly right.

Amel was witty and enthusiastic. She didn't giggle for the sake of it when my French was wrong, but she did take the micky. She told me she came from Algiers from a large family but, fed up with the harsh rules Islam imposes on women in the north, she had applied for the relative freedom of a job in Tam. When her father had finally consented to her taking it, a decision most Algerian parents would not have contemplated, she had jumped at the chance.

'The best thing I ever did,' she said happily, 'and now I meet you.' Her colleagues cackled from behind the desk. They seemed delighted that Amel should be so happy. Neither of us was quite sure what was going on.

It was honestly about the last thing I expected to happen, and must be considered highly unusual. In a country where unveiled girls over twelve, let alone beautiful women of twenty-three, are seldom seen, I was falling head over heels in love and it seemed the feeling was reciprocated. It didn't matter that the whole situation was hopeless, I was enchanted – I could have sat there all night.

I gave her the letter with which she was very pleased and excited. 'Pre-arranged . . .' she kept saying, waving it above her head. 'He must like me.'

'I do. I do.' *I think you're bloody gorgeous*. She kept it unopened, saying she would read it later, when she was alone in her room.

Again the time came for me to leave her. For the last time? I kissed her good-night and, unable to find Steve, left, walking on a cloud.

Hugo was sitting at the entrance to the camp site wearing a smart new chech of deep blue. From a distance he looked great, just like one of the Tuareg he was talking to. I had to tell someone about my strange evening, so I poured it out to him. Then a friend of Hugo's came over, carrying a bottle of whisky. Franz was a tall, strikingly good-looking Dutchman. He was dark, wore a battered dusty hat and with his long thick hair straggling out at the sides, looked something like a Red Indian. It turned out that he was the driver of a Dutch overland group of fifteen who, unbeknown to me, was supposed to be coming with our convoy in the morning. For one reason or another they had decided to leave twenty-four hours later and, if I wanted to, I could go with them. An extra day in Tam! I could hardly believe it. Maybe I could get Amel out of the hotel and away from prying eyes. Yes, an extra day – what a buzz! We sat around a tiny, crackling fire, beneath a quarter-moon and drank the whisky. I couldn't stop talking. I hadn't felt so happy in years.

In the morning I made my arrangements for crossing the desert. It was ridiculous, here I was about to drive 500 miles across nothing but sand and all I could think about was this girl. I hadn't considered how much petrol might be needed, or food, or even water. I took Hugo's advice and hastily got an extra fifteen litres of petrol to see me through to Alit. He told me there would be no petrol at In Guezzam, on the border, and kindly offered to carry it for me. His advice turned out to be good.

I had a shower and went to see Amel. It was after eleven by the time I turned up and as she had been expecting me early to say goodbye she thought I was not coming. Relieved, she gave me a smile. We arranged to meet in town at five.

The desert comes right up the main street in Tamanrasset. It blocks the doorways and piles up in drifts like snow on a New York sidewalk. The road was wide, shaded by flat-topped acacia trees and lined with single-storeyed mud-brick houses. Tall Tuareg, dressed in blue and white robes, sauntered along, some on foot, some on camels; they have the same indolent stride. I sat on a bench under a tree and waited. It was hot even though the sun was low in the sky. The air was still, there was no breeze.

'Ah, Jonny le Targui,' Amel said, referring to the chech I was now wearing. We walked slowly down the muggy street to the courtyard where my bike was parked. She'd never been on a motor bike before and loved it. The feel of her hugging me tight, her front pressed into my back and her chin resting on my shoulder, was wonderful. The sun was setting as we drove out of town into the desert. We stopped and sat under a date palm to watch it.

'Jonatan, why did we meet?'

'I'm not sure.' I put my arm round her and held her close. Again I could smell the glorious perfume of her skin. I breathed it in deep, forcing it into my memory in the hope of being able to recall it later. 'Maybe one day we'll know.'

After a moment she smiled. 'Our paths have crossed once, they may do so again.'

'I hope so,' I said, as much to myself as to her. I leant forward and kissed her cheek.

'Insh' Allah,' she said, her soft, dark eyes resting on me. 'It is all in the hands of God.'

3 Taking the Ténéré Home

Tamanrasset, Algeria

As our convoy moved out of the camp-site gates it was as much as I could do to concentrate on what was to come. All I could think about was what I was leaving behind. *You're crossing the Sahara, Jonny, forget her for the moment and get on with the job in hand.*

Most of the convoy had left on schedule the day before. I wasn't sure if our depleted numbers made us more or less of a target. Our group consisted of the truck, Hugo's car and myself, just enough to fulfil the requirements for travel in the area. We checked out with the police on the edge of town and trundled off into the unknown.

The road soon deteriorated into a pot-holed track which finally petered out completely. At first the ground was firm and the going easy. The land was flat and lifeless, devoid of any vegetation. Except for us, the only movement was a shimmering heat haze on every horizon; we moved on like ants in a sand-pit.

I spotted what looked like a good route through a canyon of bare rocks but was almost immediately swallowed up by a patch of soft sand. The front wheel went down instead of forward and buried itself. Had I been on my own it would have taken a day to dig it out, with help it took half an hour.

In the afternoon, with the heat increasing, corrugations started to appear. Formed by wheels and erosion they were small undulations on the surface of the track, about a foot apart and six inches high. Going slowly was a nightmare as they rattled me around like a fair-ground ride. If I went faster, in order to skim over their tops, the risk of crashing and injuring myself was far greater.

As the day progressed the scenery became more spectacular. There were large orange dunes away to the west with jagged black rocks peeking out in contrast to the bright sand. The horizon was as far away in front as it was from side to side, but after more than 200 miles I was beginning to tire and was pleased

51

when Franz started looking for a place to camp. We found one almost immediately, behind a cluster of boulders, a mile or so off the main route. After listening on the World Service to the last fifteen minutes of United–City live from Maine Road – to lots of sad looks from the overlanders, who thought our environment was more interesting! – I noticed Hugo beckoning to me with one hand while holding up a bottle of whisky with the other. He looked quite surreal, silhouetted as he was by the sun. In his baggy trousers and shirt, with his head and neck wrapped in a five-metre chech, he could almost have been an ancient warrior holding up the severed head of a vanquished foe. I pulled out my enamel mug, picked up my chair and wandered over to join him.

Hugo loved the desert. This was his third trip to Niger. To him it represented the freedom of the world. All this space and so few people, was, he said, like suddenly finding yourself on your own little planet. All the hassles of big city living were rendered meaningless next to the sheer vastness of these surroundings. There was nowhere he'd rather be. On the surface he was a happy man, always joking and playing the fool, but underneath the bravado he carried a heavy heart. Three of the six members of his family, his mother and two sisters, had died by suicide in the last five years. He didn't dwell on this shocking revelation to seek sympathy but just told me as if it were something I should know. After a while we were joined by Franz, who was pleased with the first day's progress. We sat calmly in the twilight, drinking and talking.

The moon, like a distant pearl, rose high, lighting up the desert as though it were under celestial street lamps. The whisky mellowed me and restored my strength, which had been sapped by the strenuous day. Feeling warm and satisfied, I climbed to the top of one of the rocks and stared out across the silvery night. Moonshadows flickered across the barren ground. Orange sparks from a fire crackling beneath me flew up high past my head. REM played on the car stereo and I started to dance. It must have been a strange sight: a tall man in a chech dancing in the eerie light, but then again, who was there to see? Out here, there was no one, not even a lizard, just us.

I lay awake on the sand that night, under the peaceful moon and stars, thinking of two girls. I felt sad to have left Amel but happy to have known her. *Did I do the right thing in leaving her? Well, what else could you have done? You couldn't stay in Tam for ever and it would have been impossible to have whisked her off to Cape Town. Yes, you did the right thing, you did the only thing. The journey is what you're here for. At least you've proved you can love again.* I'd write, and, as she would say, 'Insh' Allah'. And then I thought of Mel. 'We'll think of each other as the moon,' she'd once said before going away for a while. 'When we look at it, it'll bring us closer together.' *I wouldn't even be here in this wonderful place if it weren't for you, and I certainly wouldn't be the person I am. I can't have you back, I know, but often I wish . . . I sometimes wonder if you died for me? I know that's self-centred, considering how many other lives you've touched, but to me it seems that way. And now I can feel you watching over me, just like this friendly moon, helping me, guiding me. Perhaps you are travelling with me after all; another of our journeys.* I felt closer to her then than I had done in a long while. *Yes, maybe that's it. Some special souls like you are sent here to earth to help us lesser spirits, but are then taken away to guide us from afar.* At least, then, in the ubiquitous serenity of the desert, it seemed so. And had she now led me to love?

'If I died I'd want you to love again.' I hadn't given it much thought at the time – I'd told her not to be so silly – but I did now. It seemed unlikely that new love could be with Amel; even though I was sure that our feelings for each other had been real, the odds were too heavily stacked against us. But sooner or later Mel would lead me to lasting love, of that I now felt sure. I snuggled deep inside my sleeping-bag, an inner warmth repelling the cold night air.

The next morning was hell. There was no early run of hard track to get warmed up on, it was straight into the soft stuff and by seven thirty I'd had two hard falls. The first happened when I was trying to keep up my speed to clear an area of soft sand, rutted with tracks. At about forty-five miles per hour the front wheel hit a rut running adjacent to my line. The wheel went left while the rest of us went straight on, condemning me to a breakfast of sand. The hardest part was having to pick myself up to carry on quickly for fear of losing the truck. Within ten minutes it had happened again. This time I left the track completely and went somersaulting over the handle-bars. The fall wrenched my shoulder again so, dejected and in some pain, I gave my bags to Franz. With the lighter load, the going

53

was easier and I had no more bad falls that day.

At noon, with the temperature soaring, we came across Steve's convoy in a large gully of soft sand, 200 yards wide. Because of their numbers, they had been forced to go much slower than us. It was a vehicle graveyard: burnt-out cars and overturned vans, on their sides or upside down, stripped of dignity and anything of value, lying dead where they'd stopped – casualties of the Sahara. The gully proved to be a major problem for most of the four-wheeled vehicles. Hugo got badly grounded, as did Frank and Iliana. I got through quickly and for the first time that day was glad to be on a motor bike. Ben, a German biker, had not fared so well. Earlier he'd had a bad fall in which the front of his bike had been smashed up; it was now being carried by a truck. Steve, too, looked a little shaken.

In the early afternoon the plains opened up. With the soft sand behind us, I flew along, leaving nothing but a trail of dust in my wake. Desert riding, far from being a drag, now became a joy. We reached In Guezzam at about four. It was a one-horse town to be sure, though I expect the horse had had the sense to bolt. As Hugo had predicted, there was no petrol. In fact, there was not very much at all, save for a few ramshackle buildings that looked as if a half-decent shower would wash them away. We pushed on to the border, twelve miles south, exactly 3,000 miles from London.

If you thought that a customs post in the middle of the Sahara would be a quiet little place, peopled by a few intrepid travellers carefully filling out the various exit papers, you'd be wrong. There was a mêlée of all sorts. There were overlanders, bikers, car drivers and backpackers, Algerians heading south and Nigeans coming north. It seemed strange, on a frontier which consists of over 500 miles of nothing but sand and rocks, that everyone should funnel down to one point no larger than a football field, go through a gate and out the other side into the same nothingness as before.

By the time I got through into no man's land it was dark. After a good supper, cooked by one of the Dutch girls, I wandered off and lay down behind some rocks. I fell asleep quickly.

I woke with a start. Panic gripped my chest and I felt a clammy sweat leak from my pores. *There's a fucking snake in the sleeping-bag. Keep calm. Don't move.* The night was still, as silent as the moon, save for the drumming of blood in my ears. I had heard that snakes sometimes keep warm by snuggling up to people, but sharing my bloody sleeping-bag! I lay there, without a muscle moving, for what seemed like eternity, slowly mustering up the courage to do something. It came and I acted. With all the speed I could muster I brought my hands round to the front, grasped the little bastard and leapt to my feet all in the same movement. I pulled hard, the bag closed tight round my neck and I fell in a heap to the floor.

Only then did I realise that this life-threatening snake was the harmless cord from the hood of the sleeping-bag. I sat up feeling rather stupid, hoping no one had noticed, but there was no one around and the night remained still. How much of it had been a dream I didn't know but the quicker I got myself a tent the better, I thought. I lay down again, shaken but relieved.

Later that night I froze. Out there in the heart of the desert the days are so hot they can poach your brain but at night the clear skies freeze your bones to Edinburgh rock. I was relieved to see the faint red glow in the east get brighter.

From here to Arlit was the danger zone. I was fairly confident that I would be all right. I couldn't really imagine a Targui wanting a motor bike, but Franz was pensive. Two days earlier we'd had word from a convoy coming north that a German truck had been hit. At first the driver had refused to part with the passengers' money. He soon changed his mind when one of the marauders put a hole through his trousers with a pistol. They lost 50,000 Deutschmark, but did at least keep their vehicle. The Tuareg were always the ones to get blamed for such happenings, but in a lot of cases, I believe, the robbers were simply bandits, desperadoes or opportunists using Tuareg dress as cover.

Others were less fortunate than the Germans. In the previous two weeks at least three vehicles had been stopped, the occupants given ten litres of water and told to walk the ten to fifteen kilometres to the border. They lost everything but the clothes on their backs. Because of this, there were rumours that the border was soon to be closed. We had got through one, we now had to get past the other and cover the 200 miles to Arlit.

We were lucky. Having reached the Niger customs post soon after seven, we were away by midday, which gave us just enough time to reach Arlit before dark. We saw no Tuareg, no bandits or anyone else for that matter. The sun sank lower as the moon rose over Arlit from the east. As we approached town on a narrow sand track the wind picked up, filling the air with a dense, grey dust. Through the murk I saw a sign welcoming the visitor. Some wit had crossed out Arlit and substituted:

WELCOME TO THUNDERDOME.

Shacks and stalls covered in animal skins lined the dirty, tumbledown streets. Goat, chicken and camel carcasses hung from poles, while throngs of poorly clad people haggled and jostled one another. The smoke from innumerable fires lay thick and, added to the dust, made breathing hard and visibility almost nil.

There were hawkers and traders, hookers and pimps, dealers and beggars. The town reeked of deprivation and depravity. It was as if the bike had once again become a time-machine, taking me back a few thousand years, depositing me in Sodom or Gomorrah. The transition from Arab- to black-Africa was as vivid as the people themselves. Semi-naked negro children ran after the truck shrieking, 'Cadeau! M'sieur, cadeau!' Some clambered aboard, their vibrant, happy faces bursting with energy. A border town for sure, reacting to the strict rules of Islam enforced by its northern neighbours; in Arlit, it seems, anything goes.

Having made use of the limited facilities of the hotel, we ventured out onto the street. Hugo and I were as excited as two schoolboys playing truant.

'Oh, mister,' leered a none too attractive good-time girl, 'I think we make love all night, yes?'

'But I have no money,' I responded weakly. Not that I intended spending any on her, but I was enjoying myself. For me, this was a new experience. Surrounded by five or six girls, leching and giggling at us, we walked on.

'I no want your money, baby. I want your love.' She put her arm through mine and pushed her face against my cheek. 'You big handsome man. I need you fuck me all night.'

'You do? Well, that's fine,' I said, pulling away, repelled by her looks and whisky-stained breath. 'But first I think I'll just go and get a drink with my friend.'

'Come on, Jonny, in here,' commanded Hugo, grabbing me by the other arm. I ducked from her grasp and shot through a doorway.

'Okay. But I see you later. Me – Chrissy.' Her voice faded into the noisy hubbub of the bar.

Inside, some men were playing dice, while others gambled with cards. Most of the European men had girls on their laps, and everyone had drinks in their hands. Algerians, Nigerians and Nigeans all enjoyed the liquor, while dead-pan Tuareg handicraft sellers glided between tables, exploiting anyone they could. The air was alive and buzzing with talk and laughter; it had the iniquitous atmosphere of a wild west brothel. We settled ourselves down in a courtyard at the back.

I have to admit to being totally amazed by this place. Nobody had so much as mentioned the town to me. I wish they had. So be warned, if you are male, and ever have the bizarre pleasure of finding yourself in Arlit, leave all but a little money in your hotel room and try not to get drunk. I'd just crossed the Sahara and was in a fine mood. I knew there would be more desert riding, but I was pleased with myself, proud even, and thought I'd earned a good time. I certainly had one.

At first we were stoical in our refusal to entertain any of the girls who presented themselves.

'Fuck off,' Hugo told them in no uncertain terms. 'We're not interested.' But I have to confess to finding the whole scene, especially the girls, quite enthralling. Most of them were from Nigeria and therefore could speak English, but talking to them was the first step on a slippery slope that led to the inevitable. The whisky flowed and the girls persisted. The ones we ignored quickly turned their attention to others and continued undeterred. The drunker I got, the more beautiful they became. I was tiring, my defences were weakening and the little devil's voice at the back of my head was getting louder. I knew that if I didn't get out of there fast, only one thing would happen.

At this point I could quite easily tell you that Hugo and I returned to our hotel and woke in the morning with nothing more than sore heads. However, the truth is we didn't leave. We stayed put and accepted our fate. I was a man, perhaps a stupid one, but a man nevertheless, who'd been starved of physical affection for a long time. Yes, I know I'd just fallen in love but perhaps that stirred the longing for feminine contact or, perhaps more accurately, it was just simple lust. Whatever the reason, good sense lost out and, to quote Oscar Wilde, 'I couldn't help it. I can resist everything except temptation.'

A pretty young whore came over and straddled herself across my crotch. She leant forward, giving me plenty of opportunity to appreciate her ample bosom and whispered in my ear, 'My name is Tina. Tonight we fuck.'

'Yep, Tina,' I replied, 'we probably will.'

Some time later we staggered out onto the street. It was long past midnight but there was still a crowd loitering mischievously in the semi-darkness. I walked at Tina's side, a lamb to the slaughter. She led me off the main street and into a maze of alleyways, well lit by the light of the moon. A soft breeze came out of the night, disturbing the rubbish which lay around our feet. Small mud hovels encroached on us like a crowd of lepers. Two drunken Arabs fell out of a doorway; one crashed against me and cursed. A cat screamed and ran across our path. A good omen? At the far side of a small yard we reached a low wooden door which she opened and I followed her inside.

The room was spacious and clean, if a little stuffy. It was divided in the middle by a tasselled bead drape. One side contained the bed, the other a chair and desk, both halves, you might say, dedicated to business. The walls were papered with tacky posters depicting Hollywood heroes and pop stars: Rambo, Bruce Lee and Michael Jackson. The floor was covered with a thick red carpet. Madonna played on the tape recorder. She led me to the bed, turned on a fan in the corner, and took off her clothes.

Was it fun? I suppose it was. To be honest I was a little too drunk to know. She took me back to the hotel, where she cleaned me out of practically all my toiletries, and ten dollars, and left with Joy, Hugo's girl. Anaesthetised by the booze, I was asleep in seconds.

I had intended staying two days in Arlit but by ten the next morning I was on my way south with my tail very much between my legs. The moment I'd woken up, a nervous shiver had run down the length of my spine. I tried to stay asleep in the vain hope that the memory of the night before would simply go away, that it would all turn out to be a weird dream. Unfortunately it did not. I couldn't believe I'd been so stupid. Sleeping with an African prostitute is like playing Russian roulette, more fun

58

perhaps and with slightly better odds but a death that is surely far worse. I tried to console myself with the fact that the sex had been 'safe' but it didn't help much. There was nothing I could do about it, however, except push it from my mind and pray, and in future take a good deal more care. I covered the 120 miles to Agadez quickly and set about losing my anguish by organising a little detour.

Back in London, studying the maps, I had discovered that the Ténéré desert – the place which lends its name to my bike – was not only a part of the Sahara but that it was only 200 miles off the main route south. How many Honda Hurricanes have been in a hurricane I wondered? How many Kawasaki Ninjas have been driven by one? And, come to that, how many Yamaha Ténérés have been there? Wouldn't it be nice to make mine one of the few?

This, however, is not as simple as one might think, for although the Erg du Ténéré, meaning 'Land of Fear', is reputedly the most beautiful of all the Saharan sand seas, it is also a killer. More people die in the Ténéré than in any other part of the desert. Because of this, the rules about going there are strictly enforced: groups must consist of at least two four-wheeled vehicles and be accompanied by a guide. Which left me, as a solo motorcyclist, at a distinct disadvantage.

I sat in the Tourist office looking at a man who, even by Tuareg standards, was a giant. He was talking on the phone. I suspected he was an Inaden, of mixed blood, probably descended from slaves of the Hausa or Fulani tribes from the south. He wore a light green chech and thick brown gandoura or robe. Every feature on his face was huge, like a caricature, and, running vertically above and below his left eye, there was a deep, red scar. He looked unnaturally mean.

With the shutters tightly closed, the room was dark and cool. Stray electric wires poked pointlessly out of a paintless wall. A fly buzzed; a chair creaked. I picked up a small globe which sat on the desk and fiddled with it nervously. He rang off.

'So, you want to go to the Ténéré?' His accent was clean, easy to understand.

'Yes,' I replied, 'I've heard it's very beautiful.'

'Beautiful, of course,' he said, 'but also very hard. Especially on a motor bike.'

'So I'm told. But I think I can manage it . . . it's important that I try.'

'And it is important to me that you do not die.' He smiled and a row of sparkling white teeth added light to the dingy room. 'I wouldn't mind, but I have my job and future to consider. My wife would be very mad if I lost it because of a crazy Englishman.'

I had felt very daunted by this ogre of a man, but now that he'd smiled I could see he was nothing more than a big teddy bear.

'I'll do my best to come back alive,' I said, putting the globe back on the table, adding with a grin, 'I would not want you to get in trouble with your wife, m'sieur.'

'Aarh . . . You are a thoughtful man,' he laughed, 'and I shall do my best to find you a group to go with, but at the moment there are no trips planned.' He stood up. 'Leave me the name of your hotel and I shall get word to you as soon as I know. At this time of year it should not be a problem.'

I wrote out the information on a pad, shook his enormous hand and left. All I could do now was wait.

A prosperous little town compared to the others I had seen in the Sahara, Agadez was a nice place to rest. It sits on the edge of the Air plateau with the Ténéré beyond. It has a mosque, complete with leaning minaret, a couple of relatively smart hotels, a very chic restaurant and even a small supermarket. Sandy pathways link gingerbread houses, and dusty streets carry languid camels whose intimidating cargoes watch through the slits in their veils. As in all desert places, the days are hot and the nights cold. After one night spent shivering in a zeriba at the camp site a few miles out of town, I moved to a hotel since the price was the same and the facilities far better. That's to say there was a bed. I did some maintenance on my bike, read, wrote and waited.

Steve and Sue passed through, as did most of the people I'd met along the way. Hugo turned up and sold his car for less than he had wanted. He moved on south and we arranged to meet in Kano. Then, late one afternoon while checking out the camel market, situated on a large dust bowl behind the mosque, I bumped into Dawn, the Canadian I'd met at Assekrem. She was with her friends, Martin and Jim.

'Ha, ha, have we got a surprise for you!' she cried smugly.

'Guess what it is?' She rummaged excitedly through her bag and pulled out a a white envelope. 'It's from your girl in Tam.'

'What? Amel?' I was incredulous. They were all smiling at me and I felt myself blush.

'Yeah,' said Martin, 'she's a real babe.'

'She was lovely,' continued Dawn sweetly. 'We went for dinner there a couple of nights ago. We all got talking to her and she asked if we knew you. When we said we did, and that we hoped to see you here, she asked if we'd bring you this letter.'

'It's amazing,' I said, staring at the handwriting.

'If we didn't catch you I was to send it to Poste Restante at Kano, but we did, so there you are.' It's always nice to be the bearer of good news and I could tell Dawn had thoroughly enjoyed her job as a messenger of love.

'Thank you,' I said, still a little stunned, but inside terribly excited that Amel had already got in touch. I looked at the writing again and then, without thinking, brought it to my nose. Of course it smelt of nothing but paper. I casually put it in my pocket, conscious that the others were still watching me. 'Shall we go and have a beer?'

The sun had gone and the light was growing discernibly dimmer. The breeders and buyers were packing up, leading their animals away, the heat of the day evaporating fast. We walked back into town as the muezzin cried. I read the letter quickly in the bar at the Hotel de l'Air. It was only a short note really, just telling me her address, wishing me luck and sending me her love; I vowed to write from Kano. I put the letter away and turned my attention to the others, feeling warm and content. Before too long we were all chatting away and I discovered it wasn't to be the only surprise they had for me.

'So what do you do back home, Jonny?' Martin asked. He was a slim, dark-haired New Yorker, with a large nose that rather dominated the rest of his face.

'Nothing now,' I said, 'but I used to be in a band.'

'Yeah? So was I. What was it called?'

'Oh, you wouldn't have heard of us,' I said. 'We were only small, based in London.' Dawn interjected with information I'd given her earlier. 'They were called the Tin Gods.'

'No!' Martin looked amazed. 'Bullshit! You weren't with them?' I thought at first that he wasn't being serious – how

61

could he possibly have heard of us? But as he went on, it became obvious that he had.

'I've got your tape back home, man. My pal at CBS, he gave it to me. It's great, I love it. What did you play?'

'I can't believe it, you've really got our album?' I shook my head. Now I was amazed. 'I was the singer.'

The Gig

10.35 p.m. January 21st

The lights flickered and the speakers strained as the last chord of the song fed back into a crescendo of noise. I hit hard at the strings of my guitar as the sound rose to a deafening pitch. To my right, Andy was doing the same and on my left Guy smiled. I lifted the guitar up to my head and looked back at Tom. With a final leap in the air I brought it down in time with his crashing cymbals, bringing our first gig to an end.

The stage was suddenly immersed in darkness. For a moment there was silence, as though no one were present. Then the cheer rang out, loud and strong from every corner of the club, from the balcony above and the dance floor in front. Guy was still smiling as he unplugged his bass guitar. He looked across and clenched his fist. Yes mate, I thought, *we've done it. From the first moment that we'd decided to put a band together, I'd been secretly dreading the day that I'd have to sing on stage. Now I'd done it and it was the best feeling I'd ever known. Evidently the others felt the same.*

The lights started to come up. I looked out across the sea of faces and spotted Mel not far away to my right. She was cheering. I took off my guitar and left the stage.

'I don't care what anyone else says,' I cried to her above the din, 'but you have to tell me if it was brilliant.'

She looked straight into my eyes, a huge grin on her face: 'It was absolutely brilliant.' I smiled back and gave her a hug.

'Yeah, it was bloody excellent,' slurred John, a great friend, as he thrust a pint of beer into my hand.

It wasn't, of course. I don't suppose first gigs often are. Andy's guitar strap had broken which meant he had had to play the last three songs sitting on his amp. Tom had split a drum skin. Guy broke a string and I had managed to sing an entire song in the wrong key. None of it had mattered though. At last we were out there being a real band, making our statement, playing songs we'd written. For months we'd been rehearsing, pretending to be musicians, but now we were – we would even get paid. The feeling was total – like scoring a goal at Old Trafford. It was the most satisfying thing I had ever done in my life.

We packed the gear away and loaded up my van. It was long past midnight by the time we got back to John's flat; Mel and I were the first to arrive. We sat close together waiting in the van under the cold light of the street lamps, talking and giggling about the events of the night. She'd brought me a present; a bottle of champagne. We opened it and drank. She laughed helplessly when the liquid exploded and shot up my nose making me splutter. The same thing happened to her.

Should I kiss her? *I kept on thinking*. Would she mind if I did? *I liked her so much I didn't want to blow it*. Surely she likes me, *I thought*. She's given me a red rose before the gig and a bottle of champagne after. How much more obvious could a girl be? *Twice, I nearly summoned up the courage but both times failed at the last. Towards the bottom of the bottle, I suddenly knew I could do it*. It will be easy Jonny, just lean across and do it. *She was looking out of the front windscreen, her sweet profile so animated as she talked. I moved towards her with no way of stopping . . .*

There was a knock at the window. John's tall, thin figure stood smiling in. 'Come on, you two,' he said, 'you'll freeze to death out here.'

More than a week after my arrival at Agadez, and on the verge of giving up on my journey to the Land of Fear, I was sent word in the form of Suliman, an old Targui in indigo garb.

'We have journey for you with French group,' he said. 'I am the guide. We leave tomorrow, first light.' He turned and, with a flail of his gandoura, was gone, like the genie back to his lamp.

The dirt track led out of Agadez, past the mud-brick houses and up onto the Air plateau. I thought this would be the easy part but I was wrong. The bull dust was so soft and deep that it completely obscured my vision. It got up my nose, into my eyes and, mixing with my sweat, caked hard on my face. In the sweltering heat and heavy air breathing was difficult, but the Landrovers pushed on at a punishing pace, mindless of my struggle. This was the Sahel, a small area of semi-desert savannah, sandwiched by sand. The barely discernible track wove its way through the low hills, passing small encampments. It's hard to believe that people actually live out here but they do. In hide tents and reed huts they eke out an existence from the parsimonious earth.

A strange sight appeared crawling towards us across a large bowl in the landscape. It looked like a long black caterpillar. As we got closer I could see it was a chain of camels; one of the famous salt caravans on its way back from Bilma, on the other side of the Grand Erg. There were three or four hundred camels in two long columns stretching back into the distance. We stopped to watch their slow passage.

In olden times, Suliman explained to me, you could have seen as many as 20,000 camels and 4,000 men. They would pick up the salt from the mines in Bilma and take it south to the Hausa markets of Nigeria to trade for cloth and livestock; but no longer.

'It is a bizarre sight, non?' said the Colonel reflectively, offering me some dates from a plastic bag, 'but I really don't know what will happen to them now.'

I was travelling with eight people from an organisation called 'Le Camion d'Espère'. They had three Landrovers and had been delivering medical equipment to hospitals in Niger. Colonel Guy Faveaux was their leader.

'Sorry, Colonel?'

'To the Tuareg, I mean. I think things are going to get a lot worse.'

'Why?'

'Yesterday,' he explained, 'I went to see the Sultan in Agadez. He told me that unless the Tuareg get what they want they will intensify the fighting. They have given the government until a week on Saturday to comply.'

'And what exactly do they want?'

'Azawad: it is their name for a homeland in the north. Like so many people in the world, the Kurds, the Palestinians, they have no country. When this area was carved up they were discarded. Now they want a piece for themselves, to live their own lives.'

'It doesn't sound like so much,' I said, chewing reflectively on another date, 'not when you consider the land they want.' Earlier in the year two Tuareg groups in Mali had achieved this, though I believe there were still troubles. The Colonel looked grave.

'You are right, of course, but they will not get it, and

therefore they will fight. You are lucky to be through my friend, and we must hurry north, because soon the border will have to be closed.'

I spat the last stone onto the dirt, kicking it away with my boot. The Colonel returned to the Landrover and started the engine.*

Towards midday the terrain changed again and we were forced to follow a wadi. The sand was soft and deep and a strange kind of straggly cacti lashed out, catching my body. The dust from the vehicles in front was intolerable. I got stuck three times and needed help to get free. By two p.m., the plateau was behind us and we were back out in the open on harder ground. Regs – great plains of gravel – stretched out into the distance, broken only by leafless thorn trees, but I was tired and starting to feel uncomfortable. My shoulders ached, my eyes stung and my throat was as dry as the land.

Again the track took a turn for the worse and the next twenty-five miles were atrocious. I fell six or seven times. Each time it was harder to push the bike up again and the last time I didn't bother. I sank to my knees, head down, and refused to go on without a rest. I barely had the energy to drink the water I so thirsted for. The French all gathered round.

'It is hard, yes?' they said with pitying laughter. How I wished they'd all just go away, sitting there in the comfort of their Landrovers, safe in their cocoons. I knew it was my choice but oh, how I resented their laughter when I hadn't even the energy to cry. I really didn't know if I could go on. Another forty miles, two hours at best, and soon the desert would start in earnest – the hardest part, surely – but I didn't want to leave my bike there and go on in the Landrover. Calling on every scrap of energy I had left, I stumbled to my feet.

'On y va,' I said, and climbed back on the bike.

My worries were ill-founded and soon I discovered that the worst really was behind us. We came to the end of the dirty brown earth and paused on the shore from which the orange dunes of the Ténéré stretched out endlessly. There were no

*Everything he said came to pass. Within days the fighting did get far worse, with attacks on government troops, border posts and, on occasion, tourists. Six weeks later the border was closed, and at the time of writing, over a year on, it remains so. The trouble with the Tuareg continues.

tracks here, no life at all, just perfect orange sand and clear blue sky. There was no shading or variation in colour, no shadows and no distraction in view. Total unreality. Scale became hard to judge, as did speed. Was I moving at all or was I stationary with the ground moving under me? It was hard to tell.

Suddenly I am back on Brighton Pier in my video game – the earth below and the heavens above. *What's that coming at me fast on the right? A camel carcass? Swerve, Jonny, swerve.* I do, just in time, and miss it, but there's another on the left. The stripped white rib cage laughing at me like a joker's mouth. There's another, and another. *Stay awake, open your eyes.*

The mesmeric landscape was drugging me. *Concentrate. Where are the others?* I looked up and saw a speck on the horizon. *Shit, lose them and you're dead, speed up.* I pulled back on the accelerator and started to fly. I was trapped in two dimensions, caught between the sand and sky. I hit a small dune I hadn't seen and took off into the air. I came down with a bump but just managed to hold the bike upright. The speck got bigger and turned back into a vehicle. For the next hour I threaded my way through the crescent dunes, lost on a tranquil sea of dreams.

The sun was low in the sky when we finally reached L'Arbre du Ténéré, the most isolated tree in the world. At least it had been until a Libyan truck driver crashed into it a few years ago. Now it's a strange monument, a metal totem pole. It's the halfway mark between Agadez and Bilma, and, since a camel fell into it, the site of a bad water hole. More importantly to me, it meant that I had made it.

I climbed to the top of the highest dune and sat in contemplation, staring out across the peaceful view. Crests of petrified waves, frozen where they broke, continued to eternity. They say that near Bilma shells can be found, proving that the sea itself was once here, and that this really was an ocean bed.

The sun balanced on a dune. It tilted and was gone, leaving the wispy clouds crimson; angry marks on the belly of the sky. All the sweat and pain had been worth it. *This is you, Jonny, not Livingstone or Burton or even Lawrence of Arabia – it's you!*

As if on cue, a full moon rose, bathing me in its silvery light, and stars twinkled high above. The night was as calm as the day had been harsh. The first stage of my journey was complete. I'd taken my Ténéré home.

4 (Another) Lonesome Traveller

Magaria, Niger

A fat, unshaven soldier wearing pyjama bottoms and a combat shirt sat behind a desk, eating fried grasshoppers and drinking beer. A pile of empties lay discarded on the floor. It was ten in the morning. In the corner of the dingy room an automatic rifle was propped against a camp-bed, the tip of its barrel resting on the wall. I put my carnet on the desk beside him and waited.

Without looking at me or saying a word he picked it up, belched, and put it on the far side of the desk, his greasy fingers marking the cover; he carried on munching. So, was this a case for a bribe? Everyone told me that it's the only way to get on in Africa. He had to sign it and let me out of Niger, of that I was sure, but how long would he take? I didn't want to spend three or four hours waiting but on the other hand I certainly didn't want to spend three or four days in jail. It was a risk and my pulse began to beat a little faster. Outside it was quiet and sultry. I felt beads of sweat on my forehead and wiped them away. I looked at the man again. Surely if anyone would accept a bribe he would, a more slovenly soldier was hard to imagine. Though he'd given up on the grasshoppers, he still showed no interest in the carnet. He nonchalantly leant back on his chair and took another slug of beer. I decided to risk it.

I walked round the desk, retrieved the carnet, placed 1,000 Central African Francs – about two pounds – in the section to be stamped and, holding my breath, handed it back. The soldier took it again, the expression on his face unchanged. A lizard crept silently along the wall behind him, froze for an instant, then disappeared through the unglazed window. He opened it up and his face split in two. Looking at me as if to say 'There you are, that wasn't so hard was it?', he stamped the carnet, handed it back and offered me a grasshopper. I was so relieved that I accepted before realising what I was doing. Dunked in a black sugary goo it was surprisingly good, rather like a spring roll.

Having cleared Nigerian customs, I was on the road to Kano, the country's Muslim capital. During the first ten miles there were no fewer than seven police checks. At each one a shabby soldier sat in a corrugated lean-to, either picking his teeth, snoozing or drinking beer. Some bothered me, some did not. Brick-makers cut themselves a living from the African earth, their work now evident in the villages that sprung up everywhere. Hausa herdsmen grazed their stock and children waved. Occasionally a small swarm of locusts would emerge from the sky, their large hard bodies hitting me like bullets. Groups of baboons ran across the road and humpbacked oxen ploughed the soil, encouraged by dark, solitary figures. Passing through a landscape of older and slower cultures, mine was the only vehicle on the crumbling road. It was quiet and still; though this did not last long.

The road widened as Kano greeted me. Battered trucks and cars spewed black smoke from their tired engines, their horns a discordant symphony of noise. A mass of miniature motor bikes hurried in and out of the traffic like soldier ants. Large dirty billboards proclaimed 'Guinness is good for you' and 'You're happy when smoking Salem'. At traffic lights an army of ragged children selling anything from screwdrivers and breath-fresheners to live chickens and rat poison hawked their wares through car windows. People everywhere. Elegant women in brightly coloured kampalas strutted the streets like jazzy birds, mangoes on their heads and children on their backs. The heat was intense and the contrast to the desert calm of the last six weeks overwhelming. I hurried through the bustling streets and, much to my relief, quickly found the tourist camp.

To my great delight my Dutch friend, Hugo, was still there, as well as two English Landrovers and a Swiss couple. All, except Hugo, who was flying home from Kano, were heading for Kenya. We realised that the decision, so far postponed, regarding in which direction to continue, would have to be made very soon.

During the past month we had received precious little information about Zaire but it seemed that the situation had improved somewhat, resulting in the borders being reopened. Two or three trucks had crossed the country and the news was that things were okay so long as you stuck to the north and took care in Kisangani, the only large town on the route. All were agreed that the risks seemed minimal and worth taking.

It had been Neil's and my plan all along to drive across Zaire to Kenya and then down to Cape Town if we so desired, but I now asked myself what were the alternatives? All of the 4,000 miles I had covered had been done in the company of other overlanders. I'd driven most days on my own but so far my vision of travelling like Burton was a long way from being realised. I was now aware that it would be dangerously easy to drive all the way to the Cape without so much as a whiff of adventure. I would meet the same Europeans, almost every night, on a route so well trodden that my journey would be considered quite usual.

From Kano most people head east into northern Cameroun, then cut across to Bangui in the Central African Republic where they all meet up to drive across the north of Zaire. From here it's plain sailing through Uganda and on into Kenya where hassle-free East Africa begins. There was a very good reason for this route being so well used. So far as anyone knew, it was the only one possible.

There were two other routes which, on the map at least, looked feasible. The first was simple: I could drive south through Nigeria to Douala in the Cameroun, catch a boat to Namibia or Cape Town and then drive back up the other side of the continent, possibly all the way home. For obvious reasons, I felt it would be cheating to catch a boat, but I did like the idea of driving all the way back to England; which left the second option. To drive through Gabon or the Congo, through Angola into Namibia and on to the Cape, which would mean I could still come up the other side – if my bike and body allowed. However, most of these countries were volatile, to say the least, and the guide books said very little about any of them, except that visas were practically impossible to obtain. What the hell, I thought. I'd drive to Yaoundé, the capital of Cameroun, and keep my options open. I would be bound to find more information there.

The journey down from Kano was relatively uneventful. No machete-wielding maniacs crossed me, the Muslims and Christians seemed to be in an unusual state of peace, and the road was good. The only battle in Nigeria was against the crushing heat. The pores of my body opened like floodgates. I was soaked whenever I was still.

The yellow earth turned to red as savannah gave way to forest – Nigeria to Cameroun. I crossed the border at Ekok, where a huge planked suspension bridge spans the Ejagham river, said goodbye to the asphalt road and hello to a dirt track that would now take me most of the way south. A thin, black snake slithered ominously across my path, reminding me that I was still without a tent.

The following day, on the road from Mamfé to Dchang, the going was more problematic. On the Michelin map the route was a nice yellow line, indicating a surfaced minor road. In reality it was virtually impassable. At a fork in the track I asked a soldier the way.

'You go here.' He pointed up a much narrower path which ran at a right angle to the main track. 'La route est bonne,' he said. 'On this machine it is easy. C'est bonne, c'est bonne.'

The dirt turned to rocks almost immediately and the gradient got steeper and steeper. There was precious little zigzagging, it just seemed to go straight on up for ever. Twice I fell off and had enormous difficulty raising the bike without letting it slide back down the slope. At the top I was given a thorough search by two inquisitive policemen which soon became a spectacle for half the village.

'What is this?' One of them said, holding up a tin of spaghetti.

'A tin of spaghetti,' I replied, trying not to let my eyes betray how idiotic I thought them.

'Open it,' he said. As this went on it became clear that both of them were illiterate as well as curious and only trying to alleviate a boring Sunday afternoon. Eventually the thinner of the two pulled out a plastic bag of white washing powder.

'Aah ha!' his face exploded into a grin that said: 'Now we've got you.'

They looked at it and sniffed it but were unable to make up their minds. Thinny licked his finger, stuck it into the powder and then into his mouth. I got the impression that he did this not because of any training he had been given, after all, you are unlikely to find cocaine in the Cameroun highlands, but rather because he'd seen an American actor do it in a cop video. Whatever the reason, the result was just what I hoped for. His face contorted in disgust as he spat out what had not already dissolved in his mouth. After that they left me in peace to pack up and move on.

I passed through Dchang that afternoon and arrived at Bafoussam in the early evening. The streets were alive with the dancing African rhythms of people, animals and vehicles. Just down the way from the Catholic mission, in which I had secured a bed, was a street market. Women sat in groups gossiping and selling a most astonishing selection of fruit and vegetables: yams, potatoes, onions, cassava, peppers, avocados, bananas, plantain, garlic, oranges, lettuces and others I didn't even recognise. Sweetcorn was roasting on converted oil drums and mobile wheelbarrow barbecues, loaded with fish and meat kebabs, moved up and down the street, filling the air with their scented smoke. I bought a kebab and a beer and sat on the pavement watching Africa. A thin, fingernail moon rose over the rooftops and with it my spirits, for the indecision about my route was hanging heavily on my mind. Looking down, Mel's golden Russian wedding ring, which I've worn since her death, caught my eye. I gave it a kiss – I had the feeling things would be okay.

The Kiss
8.45 p.m. January 23rd

It was a cold night in London. The wind had changed direction and now blew hard from the north, bringing with it the snow. It piled up high on the buildings and the parked car, sparkling orange under the streetlamps. I stamped my feet and blew warm air into my hands. There was a thud of feet descending the stairs and Tania came to the door.

'Hi! Mel is just doing the cooking. Come on in.'

They lived on the second floor of a converted Victorian town house. The living room was spacious and pleasantly decorated for a rented flat. At the far end of the room a table was laid for six and beyond it Mel appeared at the kitchen doorway. We greeted each other in our now customary anticipative kiss. The other guests arrived and we were soon all seated and enjoying a delicious chicken Florentine.

Mel was a fantastic cook. In fact it was her profession. She had studied at Leith's cookery school in Kensington and now worked for their catering department. Conversation between us never died and, as our nerves dissolved into glasses of wine, we became more and more animated. We seemed so in

71

tune. *'Exactly!' she'd exclaim excitedly. 'I know, I know . . . I love it too.'* Her liveliness and enthusiasm captivated me in a way I'd never experienced before. We laughed and chattered nineteen to the dozen, oblivious of the rest of the party.

At about eleven, with the meal well finished and our spirits high, Mel suggested we go for a drive.

'What – now?' I cried. *'But it's probably snowing.'*

'All the better, we can put the roof down. Come on.'

We made our apologies to the others, grabbed our coats and ran out onto the street. It had indeed started to snow again and large glistening flakes were falling, like feathers, refreshing the tired afternoon fall. We reached the car and pulled back the hood.

My MGB was my joy. It was bright red, with a black canvas roof and chrome spoke wheels. My sister Emma had picked it up for a song a few years before but, wanting something more practical, she had sold it on to me.

We drove out of the side street, the fresh snow creaking under the wheels, and turned down the New Kings Road. As we reached the Embankment we were greeted by the towers of Albert Bridge looking like a magic wintry castle lit up by the sprawling lights.

'It's called the wedding cake bridge,' Mel said, clearly enjoying its appearance. Looking at the pink marzipan paintwork and white icing-sugar frame, I could see why.

'Let's park and walk over it,' she suggested.

I pulled up against the kerb. There were few cars around and even fewer people. We walked in the snow which settled on our shoulders and hair to the centre of the bridge. It was beautifully quiet and still for London, the sounds dampened by the heavy snowfall. We stood in the middle holding hands, looking down the Thames, postponing the inevitable.

'Christ, Jonny,' said Mel, turning to me after a minute, *'if you're not going to do it, I guess I'll have to.'* She put her hands around my neck and pulled my lips to hers.

'Hello.' I turned at the sound of the English voice to see a thick-set man of about my age with mousy hair and a boyish face. 'Have you driven that from England?' He pointed at the bike but did not look hugely impressed.

'Yes, but I'm a bit lost now,' I replied. My map of Yaoundé was woefully inaccurate and I hadn't a clue where I was. 'Do you know where the Catholic mission is? I'm damned if I can find it.'

'You have done,' he laughed. 'It's just up this track here. Come on, I'll show you. My name's Tony, I'm saying there too.'

Tony was a lovely bloke who instantly became a good friend. He was bicycling round the world and had done an incredible 37,000 miles from Auckland to Yaoundé. In three years he had travelled through twenty-five countries on three continents and the fact that his home base in the UK was Oakham, less than ten miles from my own, gave us a instant affinity.

For the most part I found him an enigma. On the one hand he liked nothing more than travelling on his own. At one stage on his journey he had gone for three months without seeing another white man; indeed, he did his best to avoid them. Yet he was the life and soul of any social situation. Each night at dusk, as the bats emerged from the sanctuary of the mission roof to blacken the darkening sky, four or five of us would sit eating delicious grilled fish bought from one of the street vendors while listening to his stories.

To get as far as he had (with 145 punctures, fourteen buckled wheels, five broken chains and one cracked frame) showed not only an impressive presence of mind but amazing determination. He had waited six weeks on the coast of Indonesia for a lift to the Malaysian peninsula, only for the ship's captain to change his mind and refuse him passage. Undeterred, he had bribed one of the deckhands to smuggle him aboard and keep him hidden for the two-day journey. When the Burmese authorities had refused to give him a visa, as determined as ever, he had cycled through Thailand to the border, in the hope that a miracle might allow him in. None had come, but desperate not to be totally beaten he had followed the frontier river to a point where he could swim across, just so that he could say that he had set foot in the country. Halfway across the hundred-yard stretch he had heard some Thais shouting from behind. How nice to receive their encouragement, he had thought and waved at them. Having reached the other side and kissed the ground – or whatever one does in that situation – he had waved again and started to swim back. It was only when he was halfway across and saw the fervour on the bank grow to fever pitch that he had realised all was not well. They were pointing behind him, appearing quite crazed. Tony had turned but from water level could see nothing. Increasing his speed, a minute later he had crawled up the muddy bank and turned around. There, swinging their tails vigorously in the water, were three crocodiles. Why they hadn't attacked him he really couldn't say.

From Bangkok he'd flown to Bangladesh and cycled to Delhi, where he'd spent three weeks in the toilet with amoebic dysentery. In Cape Town the yacht he was working on had been caught in a storm off Cape Point and wrecked against the rocks and at the time Neil and I had arrived in North Africa, Tony had been aboard a Belgian military helicopter, bike and all, being air-lifted out of Zaire. He told these incredible stories not in order to impress, for he was naturally a modest man, but simply because we were interested.

From Brazzaville, where the paratroopers had dropped him off, he had come up through the Congo; he thought I could go that way if I wanted. 'It'll be hard,' he said, 'but what you'll see will be worth it.' There was a brief lull in the rains so if I was quick I could get through before they started again. While he showed me the route on the map, he also pointed out another track to the Congo, through southern Cameroun, which he'd heard had been taken by someone. He wasn't sure how long ago or even if they had succeeded but as it cut nearly 300 miles off the journey it seemed sensible to try it. Tony's passion excited me tremendously. His natural enthusiasm and encouragement for my trip made me believe that if I really wanted to, I could go anywhere.

So here it was, my chance at last to break away from the well-trodden route and try something new. Tony was the catalyst I needed and now I felt I had no choice. There were no boats available at Douala to take me down the west coast and I knew that if I went through Zaire with everyone else I would be fooling myself. This was what I had been waiting for: I would travel due south through Cameroun and the Congo to Angola.

Tony knew nothing about Angola though and suspected it would be extremely difficult to get into but, as so often seemed to be happening now, there was another lucky encounter in store for me. That night an American called Michael arrived at the mission.

'Yeah, you can get in. I did, but I think I was about the first. Huh, they put me on TV.' He was a dark, long-haired Californian. He'd only been to Luanda for a week but said it was 'real'.

'What you gotta do, man, is make out you're an investor. They're desperate for businessmen.' If he could pass as an investor, I saw no reason why I could not.

'Just make up a company, get yourself some letter-headed paper, print a letter and there's no problem. That's all I did. It's great, man.'

Julius, a local man to whom Tony had introduced me, secured the paper for me. It was made up by changing the title slightly but otherwise copying a genuine letter-heading from a document Tony had. Now I was a director and chief salesman of UK Agricultural Systems Ltd. Julius also got me a spare set of second-hand tyres (new ones not being available in this part of Africa) and some dodgy insurance. On paper it covered me for every country in Africa. I just prayed I would never need to make a claim. Hens, a wonderful Dutchman also staying at the mission, very generously gave me a tent he said he had no need of and piece of sponge to sleep on – the baked African soil was starting to give me back-ache.

My finances were the next thing to sort out as I would soon be out of money. Not wanting to travel with too much cash, and expecting Africa to be cheaper than it was proving to be, I had left England with only £1,000. It was a mistake and I should have carried far more. I had over £2,000 at home but the problem now, I thought, would be getting it. Telexing money to Africa is not advisable; it tends to get lost.

I need not have worried. At the British Embassy a delightful girl sorted it out for me. She faxed the Foreign Office in London and asked them to telephone my parents. The FO asked them to deposit £600 with a local bank for me. The bank then told the FO the money was there, the FO faxed the embassy and within twenty-four hours I was issued with the £600. And all for the charge of a tenner.

Within a week I was packed up and ready to go, my route now certain; at least in my head. Tony gave me a local map of Cameroun to help me through the south and his antimalarial tablets as he thought he would not be needing them any more (three days after leaving Yaoundé he came down with malaria and spent a week in hospital in Douala). Our visas came through on the same day and the following morning, when the time came for us to say goodbye, I really felt quite moved. Two lonesome travellers, at the crossroads of Africa, heading in opposite directions; he, north, to the trails of the desert, not knowing that a closed border would be blocking his path, while I would be continuing south, into the forests. We embraced like brothers.

'Right. Bye then.'

'Yeah, take care, drop me a line to Cape Town.'

'I'll give you a call,' he said with a smile, picking up the handset of the old desk telephone he had ludicrously strapped to his bicycle frame.

'Okay, reverse the charges if you like.' And pushing his laden bike before him he walked out of my journey.

PART TWO

Into the Trees
Yaoundé – Cape Town

5 Road to Nowhere

Sangmelima, Cameroun

South of Sangmelima the road took a distinct turn for the worse. The edges had been crumbling for some time, the pot-holes getting bigger and the bridges more precarious, as if the further from the capital it reached the less important the route became. The problem was that this road, like so many in Africa, did not have proper foundations. Molten tarmac had simply been poured onto the red earth in the hope that it would last for years. The weight of heavy vehicles had broken up the surface like ice on a puddle. Soon even the tarmac petered out.

The route Tony and I had pondered over cut from Sangmelima into deep forest, crossing the border at a place called Souanké. I was a bit dubious about the terrain depicted on the Michelin map, which showed a number of small rivers and marshes, but the track looked official enough. Indeed it was one of only two ways marked from Cameroun into northern Congo. The worry was that all my questions about the feasibility of this route were met with incomprehension.

'Why you want to go to the Congo?' people answered. 'This is no good. If it Cape Town you want, you must fly.' But I felt that if a track was marked, I would be able to make it. Besides, if, as Tony thought, someone had got through before, why couldn't I?

For fifty miles the track was wide and in good order. In fact it was often better than the tarmac for it was at least consistent. The forest was not so thick and stood back from the road, giving the long grass room to grow. The trees were tall with creepers crawling up their sides and hanging from their branches like snakes.

Every few miles the vista would widen to reveal a small village. A row of mud huts, thatched with grass, would appear on either side of the track, semi-naked children running mischievously over the dusty ground while their hopeful mothers sat by bamboo tables on the verges selling bananas, yams, aubergines and black-market petrol. Some waved, while others appeared bemused. A luckless chicken bolted across the road, just at the wrong moment, decapitating itself in my front wheel. It was becoming obvious that now I was well off any route tourists trod. My feelings of excitement grew.

At Djoum I filled up with petrol, passed the inevitable football game and found the police station. Although nearly a hundred miles from the border it was the last town of any significance and therefore housed the customs. The police station, painted pale green and with a black iron roof, was situated just off the main drag in one of the few brick buildings the town had to offer. I parked and walked towards the doorless entrance, trying not to squash the enormous stag beetles which lay *en masse* on the grassy floor. There was no glass in the windows, just dirty wooden shutters hanging from the walls at various angles. A dark face appeared at one of them and beckoned me inside. In a shabby, paintless office at the end of a corridor the Chief of Police reluctantly stamped me out of the country. It was obvious from his expression that he thought me mad.

The road soon narrowed and the forest grew more dense. Deep gullies, formed by the torrents of water which amass at the height of the rains, ran like scars down the centre of the track before slanting away into the foliage. I had to be careful not to slide into them – they would almost certainly have made me fall and would pose a struggle to get out of. The track dipped and rose, steeply in places. Sharp rocks threw me off balance and muddy pot-holes slowed me down. I could hear the barking of primates and the screeching of birds above the steady rumble of the engine but as yet, to my relief, there was no water.

At Mintom I stopped for the night. The rain was getting heavier and the light was almost gone. Bright pairs of eyes appeared in darkened doorways, the braver ones slowly showing the rest of themselves. Chickens stopped their pecking, a goat bleated and a naked child ran for the sanctuary of his hut. Smoke from charcoal fires lingered in the air. I parked on a corner of flat dirt just away from the huts, took off my helmet and face-mask and walked towards a young Jack-the-lad. A smiling girl stood hiding in his wake.

'Puis-je dormir ici ce soir, m'sieur?' My words did not have the desired effect though, and they, and three others who had now appeared, were simply reduced to giggles. One, however, showed me the upright palms of his hands in a gesture of 'wait' and disappeared. A minute later he returned with a man of about forty. I repeated my question, in response to which I got a smile and a 'Mais, bien sûr'.

Francis, as was his name, started to take charge of the situation, treating me as if I were the chief of a neighbouring tribe. Soon most of the village had summoned up the courage to come and view their visitor, so he proudly translated their questions and my answers. He was desperate to help. Each time I put something on the ground he would pick it up and hand it back to me with a big smile, only for me to nod and put it down again. Soon they were all at it, convinced that they were making my life easier. I was feeling damp and irritable so the whole situation soon became terribly annoying.

It was then that I experienced, for the first of many times, the dilemma Tony had discussed with me: whether it was better to camp in the wilds of the jungle, and risk attacks from animals or brigands, or to become a source of amusement, a freak show, in the relative security of a village. Not a hard choice, I hear you say, but believe me, having fifty or more people huddled round watching your every move, fiddling with your possessions and slowly encroaching on your space after a long, hard ride, is one of the most claustrophobic feelings I have ever experienced. After an hour of this I felt a fight with a twenty-foot python would have been preferable.

Of course their curiosity was understandable. They had seldom, if ever, seen anything like my equipment. I found the best way to handle the situation was to play up to them. The tent I had been given by Hens made the greatest stir. I rolled it out on the floor and secured the corners with pegs and a hammer, holding each item up in the air for all to see, like a magician with his props. The plastic poles, held together by a cord of elastic, pinged easily into two long bendy sticks. By feeding these through the loops and attaching them to opposite corners a perfect dome tent was created in a matter of seconds. There were gasps of amazement followed by a low-pitched murmur.

One of the onlookers, a soldier from some nearby barracks, told me, after a brief study of my papers, that the last foreigner had come through here nearly a year ago.

'He is your brother, no?'

He looked quite upset when I explained that both my

81

brothers were, to the best of my knowledge, happily wrapped up with their wives in England.

'No,' he said after a minute of thought, his face now in a big grin, 'this brother, he from Denmark.'

'Oh. That brother.'

I asked him more about the Dane, obviously the person Tony had heard of, and the possibilities of making it through to the Congo. He knew little. Twice a year the army patrolled as far south as Mbalam, which he thought I could reach, but he wasn't sure after that. My informant presumed the Dane had made it. He had passed through and had not been seen coming back.

If he had made it, could I? I crawled inside my home, away from the stares of those penetrating eyes, to contemplate that worrying question. *Would it not be more sensible to turn round and find another way? It wouldn't really be giving up, I could still be on this new, unexplored western route.* But something inside me said that it would. 'If I can go on, I must go on' had, from somewhere, become the new motto of the journey. An uncontrollable force was pushing me forward and I knew, no matter what I told myself or however many reasons I could think of for turning round, come dawn the next day there was only one direction in which I would be heading. After making a cup of coffee, laced with a large splosh of whisky, things seemed a little brighter. I made some soup on my astonishingly user-unfriendly petrol stove, vowing to change it for a gas one at the first opportunity, listened to the news from London and fell asleep.

It wasn't long before the water appeared. Small puddles at first which got longer, deeper and more frequent the nearer to the Congo I got. Until Alakdi the forest held back from the track and gave me room to see the obstacles to be confronted, but afterwards it closed in around me like a witch's cloak. Creepers and plants flicked my mask, the firmer branches bruising my arms and legs. The bike slithered, the back wheel spinning on the mud as the tyre struggled to grip. I fought a losing battle to hold it upright. Twice the front wheel went from under me, throwing me hard against the damp foliage and undergrowth that comprised the jungle floor. High above, the sun was bright and the occasional beam of light which managed to penetrate the dense cavern refracted tiny rainbows through the moisture in the air. I sweated like a horse and fought for every mile.

I pushed on to the border in the hope of making Souanké by nightfall but, soon after midday, a few miles north of Mbalam and less than twenty miles from the Congo, I found myself in a little glade, looking at a river and bridge. The bridge was nothing more than three large tree trunks and would have presented a precarious crossing at the best of times, but now it was broken, smashed in the middle and submerged in fast-flowing water.

I took out a damp cigarette and pulled on it deeply as tears welled in my eyes. I desperately missed everyone and everything. A pint with John, a spliff with Guy, a chat with Tania. Oh, to eat a roast, watch a film, sleep in a bed. The worst part was not being forced to give up, but the utter frustration of having to go back through all the crap I'd just fought. *Back to Yaoundé and then what? Is there another route round? Yes, there's bound to be. Keep your chin up, it's not the end of the world. Try to make it back to Mintom tonight and Yaoundé tomorrow. It'll all seem better then.* Tony had made me believe I could do anything – evidently I was wrong. I took one last look at the piece of nature that had beaten me, flicked my cigarette in it, and left.

Each mile going back seemed twice as long as the ones going out, when I had still had hope – that vital ingredient – that everything would work out okay, that I'd make it through and that the struggle would be worth it. Now, retracing my steps, the battle seemed totally pointless. I didn't make it back to Mintom that night. Two hours after turning round I had the first mechanical problem of the journey. The strain on the aluminium boxes had caused them to bend inwards and each time the suspension pushed down, which was practically every second, the box on the left smashed onto the wheel nut, thus halving my area of bounce. As I struggled down the track, no faster than fifteen miles per hour, it was as much as I could do to stop myself crying. Quite a problem considering my visibility was horrendous anyway.

I mended the box temporarily in Alakdi where I stayed the night. The next day I passed through customs at Djoum where the Chief, with a 'told you so' expression, stamped my passport in ten seconds flat. It was lucky I had a multiple-entry visa. The day after that I was back at the mission in Yaoundé, studying the map once more.

6 Things That Go Bump in the Night

Yaoundé, Cameroun

Mercia, a jovial, English-speaking Camerounian, stood next to me beside a trestle table in the compound of the mission. She was as large around the middle as she was tall, in her late thirties, with a deep, rich voice as soft as treacle. It was mid-afternoon and the air was wet with humidity. The washing she had done for me that morning still hung damply on the line; I had given up any hope of it drying.

'Ya can go here,' she said in her pidgin tongue, her short, blunt finger stabbing the map of the Central African Republic at a place called Solo. 'Fram here ya get d'boat. It take ya dan stream ta Ouesso, an fram dere it easy. Ya get nadda boat aaaall d'way ta Brazzaville, but after dat . . .' she looked up to the heavens and shook her enormous breasts, 'God help ya boy.'

'He will,' I said reassuringly. 'He will.'

I liked Mercia. Wrapped in her bright, orange kampala, printed with segments of green and red water melons, she was a fantastic sight. She helped out at the mission doing the washing and cleaning and lived on the grounds with her two children in a hut behind a large mafumeira tree. Her husband, she said, worked in town; I had seen him only once.

Whichever way I looked at the map, the rivers of the Congo basin crossed my route like a diagram of arteries in a biology textbook. It seemed inevitable that at some point I would be forced to travel down one of them. Not that this bothered me; on the contrary, after my recent experience, the thought of putting my bike on a boat for a few hundred miles was rather appealing. It looked feasible, so long as there was a boat. It would entail driving east out of Yaoundé, back on the main route to Berberati in the Central African Republic and then south to Solo where, 200 miles north of Ouesso, the Sangha river widens considerably. It was at Ouesso that I could either join the route Tony had taken through the rainforests of the Congo or, as Mercia suggested, take the boat all the way to the capital. I knew which option I preferred.

I felt the heat radiate from her motherly body as she stood fidgeting slightly. Her five-year-old son, Nonye, walked towards us. Embarrassed by my attention, he hid his face against his mother's leg.

'I t'ink you go lak everyone else.' She glared at me as fiercely as she was able before reaching down to pick up her son. He moulded to her bosom and hip as though they were one. 'Thes way ain't no good. Ya don know wat mite b'like in Angola – it's a crezy ples ya no. But I s'pose it up to ya.' She turned and walked away, tut-tutting to herself.

The mission's seedy labrador, which had been watching us keenly, scratched a flea from behind its left ear. It stood up, shook itself and wandered off in the direction of the kitchen, leaving me to dwell on these matters alone. I looked at the map again. A journey down the Sangha and Congo rivers, wasn't that Joseph Conrad country? Into the heart of darkness? The romantic chord was struck. Besides, I had no choice. It would take at least three weeks to obtain a visa for Gabon, by which time the rains would have started again. No, this was the only way left unless I was to abandon my dream and follow the others into Zaire. All Mercia's worrying about Angola was surely a little dramatic; no one else had been so concerned. The infant peace accord seemed to be holding and if it really was as dangerous as she thought they wouldn't let me in anyway.

I sat back in my chair and picked up a copy of the daily newspaper. For the first time in a long while I became aware of the date. A familiar feeling swelled inside, a bittersweet ache of magic and loss. I took a deep breath and turned my eyes to the sky. It was 20 December, Mel's birthday.

The Dinner
8.15 p.m. December 20th

'How do I look?' she asked, standing up and throwing me a beaming smile.

'Gorgeous, sweetheart, bloody gorgeous.' I walked over and nuzzled her cheek. 'The taxi's here. Come on. Let's go.'

It was no lie. She did look great. Melanie was one of those people who make the best of what they have. She was only five foot three, but her body was perfectly proportioned. Imaginatively, her friends had once called her Melons but the teenage puppy fat had slowly fallen off to reveal a body of beauty. Her lively face was a joy to watch. Sweet, rather than beautiful, it was shaped like a heart with a full-lipped mouth, neat little chin and the clearest skin I'd ever seen. Her nose, according to her, was a mite too long, but far from detracting from her looks it seemed to me to enhance them. She had grown her dark hair and it now rested gently on her shoulders. As it was her birthday, we were going out to dinner. We left the apartment and climbed into the minicab.

We'd lived in several places since we'd met – she in one flat and I at another – but as we seemed to spend every night together we decided to move in with each other. Through a friend of a friend we found a flat just over the river in East Putney. It was large and convenient and not too expensive.

Living together was great and our relationship blossomed because of it. Mel was just so easy. She was seldom angry or sullen – in all the time we'd been together I couldn't remember our having an argument – and she was never given to temper tantrums. But Mel certainly wasn't dull – she could, and often did, hold her own with anyone I knew – she just seemed to understand things better than most. She had changed jobs and now worked, by day only, at a restaurant in Knightsbridge, while I was still pushing my band. When the group was first formed I had fully believed that we'd write a few songs, get a deal and be megastars by Christmas. After nearly two years of hard work I realised it would take a little longer but my belief in our ultimate fame never wavered – I knew I was destined to be a rock star.

Mel didn't seem to mind this. She enjoyed the gigs and the music and, knowing how much it meant to me, she supported me all the way. We'd become much more than lovers. We were also best friends. I turned sideways to look at her. One by one the orange street lamps lit up her face as we passed beneath them . . . yes she was all I wanted.

Le Quai St Pierre is a quiet little seafood restaurant in Kensington. It was our favourite, although actually we'd only been there twice because of the expense. John and Tania were already there, sitting at a table next to the lobster tank. There was a bottle of champagne in an ice-bucket.

'Happy birthday,' said Tania cheerfully. She handed Mel a small parcel wrapped in red and blue paper. When the two of them had been at school together, Mel and Tania had often fantasised about having two best friends as their boyfriends and amazingly it had happened. John and Tania met at the band's second gig and after an inauspicious start – John

*had spilled his pint over her – they had merged into a concrete relationship.
Excitedly, Mel tore off the paper and opened the box it contained. Her
face creased with delight when she pulled out its contents. The present
was a beautiful Indian necklace made of an array of delicately carved
silver mangoes. She took off her old chain and put the necklace round her
neck.*

*'I love it,' she said, studying her reflection in the window. 'One day
I should like to go to India.'*

It was impossible to get away very early in the morning
as the moisture from the trees and vegetation left everything
covered in a deep layer of dew. Waiting for the tent to dry out
completely would mean the loss of half a day, so there had to
be a compromise. I would leave about ten. This gave me time
to go down to a messy workshop at the bottom of the hill and
get my frame fixed.

Because of their poverty, and the lack of spare parts, Africans
have a great talent for fixing things. They patch things up time
after time to eke a few more precious years' work from a trusty
and often ancient friend. Trucks, cars and bikes, which in the
West would have been discarded decades before, still trundle
gamely down the streets of most African cities, emitting a mite
too much carbon monoxide but, out here, who's measuring?

In no time at all the mechanic had cut through the offending
piece of frame and welded it on higher up so it could no longer
hit the wheel nut. I then bolted the box back on, using washers
as spacers to move it out an inch. This provided enough width
for the suspension to move freely again. I gave my petrol cooker
to Mercia and, for a couple of quid, bought a second-hand gas
one from a German. On my way out of town I bought two spare
cylinders of gas and posted a letter to Amel.

At Obala the road split in two, west to Nigeria and east
to the Central African Republic. Five miles further on the
tarmac fell away beneath my wheels and the red earth tracks
began again. Up here, running along the northern edge of the
rainforest, the roads were in good condition and a joy to ride:
wide and smooth and for the most part free of corrugations. On
either side green laurel-like bushes were reddened with the soil
thrown up by passing vehicles.

Some way ahead a large cloud of dust blocked the road like a wall of London brick: a truck trailing a thick plume. It was either a matter of hanging back and travelling at its speed, about thirty miles per hour, or running the risk of overtaking it. Of course there was really no choice. Even with a bandana covering my mouth and nose, and the goggles and mask protecting my face, sitting in his wake was impossible. I could barely breathe and could see nothing. However, with my broken horn and the huge spray of earth being thrown into the air, he wouldn't see or hear me and I would be blinded for a few seconds. I pulled out beside the rear wheels, which maliciously spat stones and gravel, knowing that if anything was coming the other way it would be curtains. I flashed my lights and pulled back on the throttle. Then I was past, out of the dirt and through to the open road again. It was a logging truck with a huge tree trunk cut in three lying on its back. I passed many more that day.

With the sun sinking behind the trees and the heat of the day dissolving into a calm, still evening I pulled off the road into a clearing. There was a mango tree in the centre of an area about the size of a tennis court behind which, some five yards back, stood a derelict hut with a broken roof. If I moved close to the hut, I realised, I would be practically invisible from the road, hidden by a cluster of coarse grass on one side and the tree on the other. It seemed as good a place as any to camp for the night.

I unpacked the bike, put up the tent with the tarpaulin in front of the entrance, placed my chair on that, hung my light on the guy rope and put the cooker in front of the chair. Inside, I unrolled my sleeping-bag over a small piece of sponge, the length of my back, and lay my sheet sleeping-bag on top. The tank bag was on one side and the clothes bag on the other, with my machete (bought in Nigeria, made in Sheffield) close at hand. After arranging all this, I washed the dust from my face and hands in a saucepan of water, and I sat quietly in the luxury of my folding chair to smoke a cigarette of peace and take in the last half-hour of the day.

This became my routine. After a few days I had it down to a fine art and it would be little more than ten minutes before I would be sitting enjoying what had now become the best part of the day, the only time really to relax.

My evening meal also became something of a ritual and

almost all the way down the west side of Africa, if I was cooking for myself, I would perform the following:

Open a can of sardines in oil. (It was annoying when I hadn't read the label properly and found myself with sardines in tomato paste.) Pour the oil into the medium-sized pan. Chop up an onion or two and a clove of garlic and fry in the oil. After a few minutes, add some water and tomato purée, tomatoes if you're lucky enough to have any, and seasoning. Bring to the boil and simmer. Add the sardines and cook for a further two minutes.

Then cook the spaghetti (or rice) in the large pan. While draining the pasta, reheat the sardines, put them on the pasta and voilà! A delicious meal, full of protein, created with the minimum of fuss in fifteen minutes.

That day I had done well and covered over 200 miles. The bike was fine and I was in good spirits, so again I treated myself to a splash of whisky in my coffee. As it was too dark to read, I listened to a play on the radio and went to sleep with the huge orange moon low in the sky.

Suddenly I'm awake and for a second or two am totally unaware of where I am. It's pitch-black and silent, save for the quickening beat of my heart. I lie still, listening intently. There it is again, a twig snaps and the ground is scuffed. Something is moving slowly round the tent. Is it human, or animal, and if the latter, what kind? It stops. Silence reigns. The clammy sweat covering my body suddenly cools and I shiver, all senses acutely aware. As quietly as I can, for I do not want to shock the predator into action, I reach over and fumble in the darkness for the machete. I find it and grip its wooden handle tightly. *Why didn't I stay in a bloody village? I would have been safe there, but here, oh shit!*

I'm frightened by my position. The tent, at first a sanctuary, has now become a prison. I'm trapped inside my nylon cage at the mercy of whatever is lurking outside in the darkness. For a while the night is still and nothing moves, I can hear the tick-tock of my tiny alarm clock.

Again there's movement, louder and closer. Suddenly it prods the tent on the far side away from my head. I sit, bolt upright, clutching my weapon, the knuckles of my hand white with tension, my heart pounding like that of a captured bird. Should I shout to scare it away or stay quiet? For by now I'm convinced it's an animal. I can hear it breathing and sniffing as it tries to decipher the olfactory message. There could be leopards, jackals, various types of primates, even lions out there for all I know. What can it be? Again it prods, this time harder, pushing the fly-sheet in towards me. I shout and lash out at what I take to be its nose. It lets out a howl, a sound without mystery, and scampers away.

The terrifying creature that was going to tear me to pieces for a midnight snack was an inquisitive dog. It now stood, ten feet back, barking incessantly. Deeply relieved and breathing normally for the first time in what seemed like ages, I clambered out of the tent. By the wan light of the moon I could see it cowering back in the shadows. After a shout and a wave of my arms it disappeared into the night. I took a pull on the whisky bottle and lay down again but it took a while for sleep to return.

7 Black Mamba and the Commissar

No man's land, Cameroun and the Central African Republic

The only thing which lay in the no man's land separating Cameroun from the Central African Republic was a football pitch hewn roughly from the tall, thick bush. At the far end was the only goal and that had a broken cross-bar but this did not seem to detract from the enjoyment of the five or six youths who were trying desperately to kick a deflated ball through it. There had been no trouble getting out of Cameroun, and I hoped the same would be true of getting into the Central African Republic.

A gaunt soldier with sunken cheeks and a toothbrush moustache took my passport and started to digest its contents. The hut, which was only large enough for his desk, was rotten and frail, eaten by termites; more like a shed at the end of a forgotten garden than a border post. I stood waiting patiently at the doorway while his younger comrade examined my bike with a dubious look. It was Sunday lunchtime and the air was sticky and still. Flies buzzed and people milled about.

Watching the soldier's face contorted with concentration, it dawned on me that he was probably barely literate. He pondered over each visa and stamp, at one stage checking that he had the passport the right way up. Confident that he had, he returned to the front page with the photo on it and started to copy the information into a large book. My name was entered as Mr B. J. Guy, I was born in Facial Mole and had a Grantham for a distinguishing feature. I wondered whether I should try to correct him but thought better of it. It might have taken a week and besides I rather liked the sound of Facial Mole. It conjured up an enchanting little village from an Enid Blyton novel.

After a brief search I was told to report to a larger hut at the crossroads a mile further on. There my passport would be stamped. It had already taken half an hour.

The immigration office was a long, thin, wooden building, crowded inside and out. The heat, which was fierce in the street, was insufferable within. Waving their documents in the air, people jostled and pushed for position in the hope that one of the three officials would take notice. They seldom did. Luckily I was taller than most of them and the fact that I was white made me conspicuous. A portly official I took to be the boss came over. He was dressed in a traditional shirt with a large gold bracelet round his wrist and rings on his stumpy fingers.

'If you want stamp,' he said in English, 'you give me 3,000 CFA [Central African Francs]. Or you wait till morning.' This straightforward request explained the amount of gold he wore. The sum was not much, about six pounds, and not for the first time I was extremely thankful for corrupt officials. He made no attempt to hide the bribe but stamped my passport and, with a wave of his fat right hand, as though trying to freshen the stagnant air, passed me into my sixth African country.

Unfortunately though, in Africa, nothing is quite that simple. Although I was officially in the country, the bike was not and I now had to find the customs office. I found it a little further on and sat down to wait in the shade of a dalbergia tree. I waited three hours in the crushing heat before the boss, smiling and content, finally returned from his lunch, happy to stamp my carnet. By three thirty I was away again. It had taken nearly five hours. Still, better than waiting till morning.

The vista opened up. Some way below in the valley a large river wove its way, spanned by an iron grid bridge. I hadn't washed properly for three days and the thought of a swim was too much to resist. Besides, it looked like an ideal place to camp. When I looked at the map I realised that this was the Sangha river, my ticket to the Congo.

I was soon surrounded by people of all ages from the nearby village of Bania as I quickly went through my making-camp routine. I handed out some sweets to the younger ones and asked the oldest and most responsible-looking to keep an eye on my things. Then, attended by some of the children, I went to find a place to swim.

We crossed the road and walked through the long grass, which here was taller than me, down a sloping path to a little beach. In the middle of the river fishermen stood in tiny dugout canoes casting their nets towards the setting sun.

The children quickly divested themselves of their scanty

clothing and splashed happily in the water. I took off mine and joined them. The muddy riverbed squirmed up between my toes as the cool water engulfed me, taking away the strain from my shoulders and the heat from my body. After five minutes of a tiring game with the children, I pushed out towards the centre of the river. Their shrieks and laughter receded like echoes in a dream. How peaceful and still it was after the hard day's drive, the gentle waters lapping slowly by and the silent sky above.

It was a beautiful, misty morning. A thick fog, the colour of milk, lay on the river, obscuring it from view, just the metal girders at the top of the bridge giving away its presence. Women with large clay pots balanced on their heads walked past, looking at me inquisitively as I packed up camp. After my usual breakfast of oats, condensed milk and banana, I set off on another day's drive.

The sun was soon out, the road good and I was enjoying myself – until I rounded a corner where the forest closed in on the track. Obscured as it was by a shadow, I noticed the obstacle a moment too late. A broken green bottle lay in my path. I just managed to get the front wheel round it but not the rear. It made a large BANG followed by a depressing hiss. The bike sank to its knees like a wounded animal.

A puncture had to happen sooner or later – I'd been lucky to cover more than 6,000 miles without one. As I looked at the mess I was glad I'd bought the spare tyre from Julius. The jagged base of the bottle had cut a four-inch gash in the old tyre and in the inner tube, rendering both of them useless.

The problem with mending a puncture on this particular bike is that it has no centre stand on which to prop it up. I had to pull it over onto the side stand until the back wheel was well off the ground and then put a jerry can on the other side, under the engine, to hold it in place. This meant taking the wheel off and putting it on at an angle, which is quite a strain. Also the bike can fall over. Still, on that glorious morning, with the birds singing high up in the trees and the sun shining in patches on the rust-coloured road, it did not. With the help of some soap, the tyre came off easily. I put the new one over the rim, placed the tube inside that and, with a little more force than I had wanted to exert at eight thirty in the morning, finished the job. Feeling very pleased with myself – it had taken less than an hour – I

93

was back on the track to Solo, where Mercia's boat would be waiting.

A row of wooden huts, a thatched bar and a small army barracks stood back from the road, which had, just for the village, turned to asphalt. On the other side was the river, about as wide as the Thames at Westminster. What looked to be a small ferry was halfway across on its way to the mass of dense vegetation on the other side.

It is the law in the Central African Republic that you report to the police in every town. For the most part this is no great hassle as they are the best informed, know the most about the various routes and are therefore worth contacting anyway. At Solo the barracks were the same as usual; a breeze-block hut with steps leading up to a veranda with a door in the middle and a couple of small offices off either side. Set in the centre of a dusty compound, it had a rusting corrugated-iron roof, a puny flag pole and an acacia tree with a circle of white stones at its base. A dog and an unkempt soldier completed the picture. I climbed the steps and, following the direction of the soldier's pointing finger, entered one of the rooms.

'Boat, what boat?' the officer puzzled. 'There has been no boat from here for three years. You must go to Bangui.' He leant back and waved his hand at a fly.

'But, m'sieur,' I pleaded, 'I must get to Ouesso. I wish to go to the Congo, not Zaire. Is there really no boat at all . . . or any other way?'

'From Bangui you can get a boat. It take you direct to Brazzaville or Kinshasa, this is much better for you.' He looked pleased and self-important – confident he was right.

But Bangui was over 300 miles away in the wrong direction, a two-day drive at best, and the barge to which he was referring was notoriously foul. Packed with more than 600 people, violence and disease were commonplace. In fact, in the last couple of weeks, I had heard of an Englishman who had died of cerebral malaria while on board. The only food was said to be monkey and the journey lasted at least three weeks. But worse than all of this was the fact that Bangui was on the tourist route. I'd seen enough European travellers for the time being. I wanted to forge myself a new path south. I'd been forced back once and was determined not to let it happen again. As if reading my mind, the officer spoke.

'You could go to Lidjombo. There may be boat there that can take you to Ouesso . . . I don't know.'

I looked at my map. Lidjombo was another seventy miles south on the Sangha, but there was a problem. Normally every road and track was shown on the Michelin map. No route was marked that connected Solo to Lidjombo other than the river. I pointed this out.

'Oh yes, there is a track, a good track, from here to Bayanga and then to Lidjombo. You try it . . . you will see. Go back up this road and at the top of the hill, next to shop, turn right. Then straight on all the way.'

I found the shop, the shelves of which were piled high with miniature packets of biscuits, cans of sardines and gas cylinders. Unfortunately that was all. I asked the man behind the counter if Lidjombo was indeed this way. He assured me it was.

All of a sudden I was aware of smoke. Great clouds of it, thick and grey, billowing about on my left-hand side. There was a bank four feet high with huts set back on it. They were blazing and people were running. I was confused and couldn't see what was going on. Then I was in it. Flames leapt and danced all around me. The crackling was deafening, the heat painful and the smoke was blocking my lungs. I had been taken totally by surprise. I tried to suppress the desire to panic. *How long will it go on for? Should I try to turn round?* I could see the flames climbing high above me, the transparent vapour mutating the shapes and the fierce draught carrying the cinders away. To burn to death in the rainforest would be truly ironic. I had to keep going. *Stopping in this heat could be lethal. The tank might explode. I might get stuck, be trapped in a funeral pyre.* Then I was through, with the fire behind me; it was almost as if nothing had happened.

Strange – one second I'm fearing for my life and the next I'm perfectly safe. That was what was making this trip so exciting: the unknown. Round each corner anything could happen. The further I got, the more thrilling things were becoming; the harder the challenges, the greater the satisfaction after a success. It was only midday and I felt as though things were going my way.

This feeling did not last long. The track soon dipped off the plateau by the river and plunged headlong into the jungle once more. The going was firm, but the enormous gullies I encountered made progress painfully slow. Once my front wheel slid into one, diverting me straight into the slimy foliage. I had to unpack the bike before I could pull it clear. The forest squeezed me from both sides and gave precious little room for error.

By two o'clock I was at Bayanga, sitting in another police hut and was, to my utter frustration, again being told the same disappointing news.

'No, there will be no boat to Ouesso at Lidjombo.' The young guard couldn't have been much older than twenty and wore a benign expression on his thoughtful face. The worries of the world rested on his narrow shoulders. He seemed genuinely concerned about me, but couldn't understand what I was doing there in the first place.

'They should have told you in Solo,' he said. 'This very bad, you must go back.' He had a high-pitched voice and spoke with a strange accent. His French was far from good and he often fell back into his tribal tongue. As he went on, I found it harder and harder to understand him.

Sometimes, when I'm tired and things aren't going so well, my brain simply refuses to work properly. The longer I had spent in French-speaking countries, the easier I had found translation, but it could still be a struggle and when, like now, it was spoken in an incomprehensible accent and with at least half the words coming from an entirely different language my brain would plunge into a state of anarchy. 'NO, Jonny,' it would say. 'Piss off, I'm not going translate any more. I'm tired and fed up. If you want to know what's going on find someone who speaks my language.' It would then switch off and go into a sulk.

The man was still talking. I looked at him, then sunk my head in my hands in a gesture of defeat. Was I really going to be sent back again? I could hardly bear to think of it. I caught the words 'Commissar . . . be here soon . . . you wait.' I nodded and leant back against the wall.

The room was small but airy with the door open at my side. Through the window, behind the desk at which the soldier sat, there was a clear view down to the river. It seemed so easy, one boat that's all. How difficult could it be? I didn't want a luxury paddle-steamer, just a boat big enough to take my bike and me.

At least it was now quiet. The soldier, with a pained expression, read from the ledger in front of him. Even the lizard, which had been scurrying to and fro across the wooden floor, was now perfectly still, stuck horizontally to the wall. I could feel the muscles around my forehead begin to relax. I stretched my back and rubbed my temples slowly in circular motions and then looked down at my dirty hands. I saw Mel's ring and again gave it a kiss. *Come on babe, give me a break*.

'So, m'sieur,' said a voice at the door, 'You have come from England. My sister, she live in Manchester.'

I could hardly believe my ears. He spoke English. I felt like leaping to my feet and kissing the man but quickly suppressed the urge when I saw what he carried. He read my concern.

'You need no worry. It will no hurt you. At least no so long as I have hold of it.' Thoroughly enjoying himself at the sight of this near-petrified Englishman, he smiled hugely. He was short and portly, I guessed about five foot six, which made the thin black snake he held by the neck – if a snake can be said to have such a thing – about six feet long. He held it raised at arm's length above him. Its end dangled to the floor.

'Isn't it dead?' I saw the snake's limp body flicker a little.

'Oh, I do hope no, only stunned I think.' He crossed the room to the desk and issued an order in his own tongue. The junior quickly stepped aside with a flamboyant salute and went to a shelf from which he lifted down a large jar. In a former life it might have contained Branston Pickle but was now half-full of urine-coloured liquid which I took to be embalming fluid. 'For some reason,' he continued, 'and please no ask me why, the hospital say it better if the snake is no dead when it come in the jar. So I must be very careful. This one a Black Mamba, if he bite me I think it goodbye world.' He chuckled and coiled the snake into the jar. He would, of course, be rewarded for such a catch and by the look on his friendly face, I imagined the pastime paid quite well.

Having placed his bizarre trophy back on the shelf, he fitted his girth behind the desk and sat down. 'And so, what can we do you for?'

I explained my determination to get through to Ouesso and from there south to Brazzaville, that I had already been forced back once and had no wish to turn round again. And, if there was no boat at Lidjombo, did he know of any other way.

He sat back in his chair, chewing thoughtfully on a pencil. 'It is true my friend, there be no boat at Lidjombo so big as to take you to Ouesso. There no need for these boat – from there the timber go now by truck.' He turned and looked out of the window. The three tribal scars across his left cheek were deepened by his grave expression. Touched by his concern, I joined his gaze towards the river. Some children dived off a dugout canoe that was tethered to the bank while others splashed happily in the shallows. *So that's it. I'll have to go back to Bangui and get the bloody barge* . . .

'Umm . . .' something stirred in the officer's mind. 'You know, I am thinking, there may be way.' He leant forward and rested his elbows on the desk, the scars stretching as his face began to smile. 'If you can get machine in pirogue,' he said, pointing to where the children were playing, 'you can get to Ouesso.' He put the pencil down, looking very pleased with himself. As well he might be, I thought. Was he going to save the day?

'How?' I asked excitedly, taking out my map.

'You must continue to Lidjombo where you cross river back to Cameroun – here, at Bila.' The place was not on the map. I wrote down the name. 'From here there be new road, for the logging. It take you to main track to Moulondou. Then after er . . .' he stared at the ceiling as though seeking guidance, 'maybe five kilometres, you come to village. I no remember name. You take track to left. It take you to Kika. Boats go every time from Kika to Ouesso.' He stood up, smiling proudly. His junior giggled in the corner, pleased by our contentment.

'What about the pirogues. Are they big enough to take me?' The canoes I'd seen the fishermen using at Bania looked barely big enough for a man, never mind a 250-kilogram motor cycle. The one here didn't appear much larger.

'It may be possible, some are very big.' We stepped outside. 'Though maybe you must take machine to pieces.'

'Yes, maybe.' One thing was for sure, he had given me a lifeline and it was certainly worth a try.

The sun had already started its descent and I estimated I had another three hours of daylight left. If I was to cross the Sangha that night I had to get going. I shook the Commissar's hand, offering my profound thanks.

'It is no matter,' he said with a smile. 'If you are in Manchester please say hello to my sister. Her name is Keso . . . Mrs Keso Jones.'

8 Nothing is Impossible

Lidjombo, Central African Republic

The road to Lidjombo was magnificent. There were no gullies or pot-holes, no mud or water, just a perfect, dead-straight track. The trees were taller than before: giant hardwood, the colour of saffron, surrounded at their base by thick, deep green vegetation. A bush completely covered in cobwebs was beautiful with the sun shining through it, like a giant stick of candy floss. A mass of brilliant yellow butterflies burst into life and followed me on my way. The sunlight was dancing with the shadows, playing games with my vision. I was driving through an ethereal tunnel.

Silhouetted by the sun I saw something move across the track, way off in the distance. A trick of the light? I couldn't tell. Again I noticed movement ahead. It seemed to be a short figure, there one second but gone the next. I slowed my speed hoping to see it again. I did. Not just one but four men, forest dwellers – Baka pigmies, I assumed. They wore only loin cloths and beads, with leather thongs around their wrists and ankles and crude metal bracelets circling their biceps. They carried bows and spears and were painted with strange designs on their chests and faces. As I passed they sank back into the forest, making themselves invisible. Terribly excited, I pulled on my brakes, grabbed my camera, and ran back. They were nowhere to be found. The forest was silent.

An hour later I was at Lidjombo describing my plan to two more policemen.

'It is impossible, m'sieur.' He too had tribal scars, but bigger ones, slanted across his face like cat's whiskers. He was more interested in the news coming through on his large two-way radio than he was in me. How he could decipher the voice amongst the static I could not tell. It fell silent.

'I think I can do it, m'sieur,' I said. 'I wish to try.'

He shrugged, as if to say, 'It's your life.' He took my carnet and passport and stamped them out, effectively sealing my fate as I had no re-entry visa. I hoped I wasn't being foolhardy again.

'Okay, you can go,' the second one said, 'but I think we shall see you again. It *is* impossible.'

I stood up and shook their hands and, feeling more confident, replied, 'Nothing is impossible, m'sieur.' I grinned and walked out. I had proved that once before . . .

The Tower
5.57 p.m. January 23rd

'We can't,' said Mel, when I told her of my plan, 'it's impossible, they're bound to catch us.'

'They won't,' I assured her. 'We'll be fine as long as we get there just before one set of security guards goes off duty and leave just after the new ones arrive. They're so slack, honestly. I stayed for an hour today checking it out. They didn't even make me sign in.' We did one more trial run to watch the shifts change – feeling like a couple of bank-robbers – and then she agreed. After all, it was our second anniversary and we thought we might as well enjoy it in style.

'Leaf It to Us' was a small business owned and run by Paul and Vanessa, two great friends who lived just down the road from us. As the name suggests, its purpose was to supply and maintain office plants. They held various accounts around the metropolis, one of which happened to be the show flat in the yet to be completed Chelsea Tower. Generally speaking, it was Paul's job to make sure the plants were in good order by doing a once weekly circuit. When they took a holiday I was called in to do it. This time they were away for three weeks which had given me plenty of time to work things out.

We left the small florist's van in a quiet side road, collecting the watering can and bucket from the back and made our way towards the newly constructed building. I had kept Mel in the dark about the finer points of the plan as I wanted at least some of it to be a surprise – she was still unaware of the goodies I had hidden in the bucket and can. Automatic glass doors admitted us to the lobby where we nodded a half-greeting to one of the security guards – he was already clearing his desk, making ready to depart – and headed for the lift. The doors closed silently behind us and we glided effortlessly towards the fifth floor. We found the right corridor and reached the front door. It was quiet, for few of the flats had been sold. The key moved smoothly in the lock, and with a little look of triumph, I pushed the door open.

'Your room for the night, mademoiselle.'

*It was a beautiful flat. A parquet-floored hallway led into a
spacious open-plan living room and dining area. Large french windows
gave a spectacular view of the Thames and some of its sparkling bridges.
There were three bedrooms, the largest of which had a en suite marble
bathroom with an enormous jacuzzi bath. Mel grinned when she saw it.*

'Do you think the water's hot?' she asked.

I tried the tap and it was.

*The kitchen was neat and compact and after we'd done the plants we
set about laying out the picnic. I'd bought pâtés, cheese, salamis, and cold
meats, bread, olives and pickles, but what really made Mel's eyes dance
with glee was the sight of the two bottles of Château Margaux. We'd tried
it only once before but had both decided it was the most delicious drink in
creation. I was feeling a wonderful sensation of freedom and control, as
if it were us who made the rules and decided what could and could not be
done.*

*We ate our meal and drank our wine by candlelight. We had a
steaming hot bath and made love on the floor. When we left just after
nine the next morning, carrying our refuse and sore heads with us, no one
batted an eyelid.*

No track, just a steep grass bank, led down to a small beach
where five or six black pirogues bobbed up and down in the
water. The river here was vast, 500 metres wide, and the colour
of vegetable soup. Some children splashed noisily in the shallows
and a crowd quickly assembled. The sun was sinking fast, at best
there was an hour of daylight left. A young man of about my age
approached. His flared trousers were far too short and his shirt
was badly torn. The boots he wore were split at the toe.

'You want cross the river?' he asked in pidgin French.

'Yes, can you take me? I must get across tonight.'

'Of course. This is my pirogue.' He pointed at a long,
thin, dark wooden canoe, 'I make it myself.'

'Will it take the bike as well?' I enquired.

'Yes, yes . . . there is no problem.' His confidence implied
an everyday occurrence.

The dugout was quite wide, maybe three feet, and at least
fifteen feet long. The problem was its depth, which was no more
than two and a half feet. But although the centre of gravity would
be high, which might pull it over, if I partially dismantled the
bike, I thought it could be done. If the boat were to capsize and

condemn my machine to a watery end on the bed of the Sangha, so be it. I couldn't turn round again. I'd just have to risk it and put myself in the hands of the gods.

'Okay, how much?'

'No much,' he said looking serious. He glanced at the bike then at his pirogue, gauging the amount of effort that would be required on his part. After a moment he said, 'You pay 10,000 CFA.'

'Ten thousand!' I blurted out, unable to contain my shock. This was over twenty pounds. 'You're crazy. I wouldn't give you 10,000 if you took me all the way to Ouesso. I'll get someone else.' I turned quickly to walk away.

'Okay, m'sieur, how much you pay?' he asked eagerly, snapping at my heels, worried he might lose the deal.

'Five thousand and no more.' It still seemed like highway robbery, but I was getting more and more conscious of the weakening light. It would take a while to dismantle the bike and anyone else would probably charge as much.

'Okay,' he said, '7,000. It is a long way.'

I took out a 5,000-CFA note and the remains of my bottle of whisky.

'Here's 5,000, and if you get me to the other side in one piece you can have the whisky.' A particularly generous offer, I thought, and one he readily accepted. I realised, afterwards, that I could have got a considerably cheaper deal as whisky in those parts was about as rare as the travellers who brought it.

I went to work on my bike in front of a large crowd of curiosity-seekers. I unpacked the back end, emptied the boxes and started to take them off. But the bolts were caked in mud and had begun to rust, making progress difficult. As I turned the nut the bolt inside the box turned too. I had to kneel at an awkward angle to hold the bolt with a screwdriver while unthreading the nut. It was still extremely hot; the sweat dribbled from my forehead into my eyes and my head throbbed.

Faces surrounded me, watching my every move. I was tired and apprehensive. The claustrophobic feeling started to return and the more I tried to ignore it, the deeper it seemed to get. I retreated into myself, cutting off any acknowledgment of my surroundings. I was thankful for a village idiot who started shouting, for at least he distracted some of the attention. Eventually, though, the last bolt dropped off. I pulled the boxes clear and stood up.

I took the seat off, then the petrol tank, and pulled the jerry cans out of the rack, leaving a thin, skeleton bike. It looked embarrassed by its nakedness. I thought if anything went wrong, I'd rather blame myself, so, under my direction, we loaded up the bows with my luggage and then, with the help of a small army, wheeled the bike up a plank and into the pirogue. It wobbled a bit, causing my heart to flutter, but the two people I had positioned on either side held it steady while I wedged it as best I could with the boxes and jerry cans. One piece of luck was that the front frame was exactly the same width as the inside of the boat, which gave it natural stability. I handed out the last of my sweets and with my head pounding had a last look to the heavens. I whispered 'please' and climbed nervously aboard.

The orange sun, resting on the treetops of the far bank, sent a shimmering path to meet us. A mighty heron rose with a screech from the shore and set off downstream. Another bird cried and then, save for the gentle lapping of water against the side of the pirogue, there was silence. The boat was remarkably stable.

Satisfaction overwhelmed me. The headache from the village disappeared, my bodily aches dissolved into the peaceful waters and, comfortably blissful, I sat and let my brain unwind. This was utter contentment, like the night in the Sahara or the swim in the Sangha. A feeling so wonderful that should the pirogue have capsized and the bike sunk I'm really not sure I would have cared. Indeed, had death suddenly come I would have had no regrets or any problem in accepting it. Everything had been worth it for these few short minutes.

The first stars of the night appeared and behind us darkness was falling. Kamau and his brother were kneeling happily at the front paddling lazily while the current did most of the work. Small tufts of vegetation, dislodged from the thick mangrove on the banks, drifted with us. The occasional splosh of a surfacing fish was all that cut the tranquil silence. At last I had found it, the real Africa, the Africa of my dreams. I took a slug on the whisky, lit a cigarette and dangled my feet in the warm waters. I wanted the journey to last for ever.

9 Illegal Entry

Bila, Cameroun

In the gathering gloom, just before darkness, Kamau jumped from the pirogue and pulled the bows safely up the shingle. I was back in Cameroun. An area of the bank had been cleared, leading to a slope which rose gently from the river to an impressive compound above. In front of us there were huge lawns of rough grass which joined the forest 500 yards away. To the left, electric lights from workshops and offices flickered in the twilight and the lugubrious boom and clank of a generator resounded deep and continuous like the rhythm of a distant drum. A tall, white water tower stood in the centre and to the right were two Western bungalows.

'What is this?' I asked Kamau, as we reached the top, dragging various possessions with us. I had been expecting more dense forest and another night in the tent with sardine pasta but it was now quite obvious that I had stumbled across a major project, a logging station, I presumed.

'It is for the forest,' Kamau confirmed. 'There are some Frenchmen here. They live there I think.' He pointed to the nearest of the two bungalows.

So much for my unbastardised Africa I thought ruefully.

From the direction of the work area, out of the mist which was already falling over the river, came the headlights of a small, red car. It pulled off the road onto the grass and drove towards us. A young European got out, extending his hand to be shaken. He had tightly curled dark hair and eyes that popped from a podgy face.

'Bonsoir. Where have you come from?' he asked in English.

'London,' I replied. 'These guys have just got me across the river. I hoped it would be all right to camp here for the night and go on to Kika in the morning . . . if there is a route to Kika?'

He immediately put my mind to rest: 'Yes, the new track to Kika is very good. You will have no problems but you need not camp. Come.' He picked up two of my bags. 'We have a spare room in this house, you can have a shower.' He grinned. 'I think you need one, yes? And then you must have dinner with us. My name is Jean-Baptiste, I am Belgian.'

I gave Kamau the remains of the whisky, for which he showed great appreciation, thanked them both, and said goodbye. Their journey back would be a lot harder – against the current and in darkness – but they seemed unconcerned.

I followed Jean-Baptiste in the direction of the second bungalow.

There was a clatter from the roof of an open-sided garage, propped against the building. Two smallish monkeys held us in their huge green-eyed gaze for a second, screeched and jumped down, one chasing the other into the night.

'You must not worry about them,' Jean-Baptiste instructed me, 'they are harmless enough. Just make sure you close your doors. If you are lucky you may see the gorillas in the morning. We have two, they usually come out of the forest just after dawn.'

'Are they dangerous?'

'Oh no, they're almost tame. Lowland gorillas seldom attack humans.' That was encouraging news.

He led me through a cluttered room, a ping-pong table in one corner and a parrot in another, to a small but comfortable bedroom.

'Have a shower and come over when you are ready. We eat at seven thirty.'

Exhausted, I lay flat out on the bed for a while, congratulating myself. Travelling this way really was the best. Less than three hours before I was being told it was impossible and I would have to go back; now I was through, with a real possibility of reaching Ouesso, and it almost seemed by way of reward, was wallowing in relative luxury.

I made my way back across the dew-soaked lawn to the other bungalow. The river was now invisible, lost in a blanket of mist that had crawled up the banks and would soon smother the whole camp. A fluorescent security lamp perched on the water tower shimmered through the mist like a moon behind clouds. The rhythmical clicking of the insects below my feet was all that could be heard.

The living room was spacious and smart. Maroon-patterned rugs lay on the white-tiled floor and, at the far end, wicker sofas and armchairs were arranged round a coffee table. Oil paintings of rural European scenes hung from the whitewashed walls and a large green plant graced each corner; it had the feel of a modern French villa. At the end of the room nearest to the kitchen there was a dining table which I noticed had been laid for four. It was covered with a luxurious spread of imported French pâtés and cheeses.

Olivier, about fifty and from Nantes, introduced himself and offered me whisky and a cigarette.

'So you are trying to get to Cape Town, yes?' He handed me my drink. 'Well, tomorrow you can get to Kika and from there take a boat to Ouesso. This is not a problem.' His reassurance was comforting. 'Then you can take the boat from Ouesso to Brazzaville, but after this . . .' He lifted his shoulders, to which his eyebrows seemed attached, and took a sip of his drink. He paused in contemplation. 'Maybe you could join up with the rally. They might help you round Angola. That is not a place I should want to go to . . . I hear it is still very dangerous.'

'The rally?' I asked, a little confused.

'Bien, oui, m'sieur. Paris–Le Cap.' He said it with pride, as if by simply being French he was partly responsible for its success. 'I show you. It is in the *Paris Match*, I think.' He got up from the sofa and sorted through some magazines on a desk against the wall. I had heard that this year's rally, which normally goes from Paris to Dakar in Senegal, was going all the way to Cape Town, but while I'd been travelling I'd heard nothing about when it would be happening or what its route would be.

'Ah,' grunted Olivier with a satisfied smile. 'Voilà. Here is the route, and the dates they arrive in each place.' He handed me the magazine. 'It might be of use to you.'

The rally was to start on Christmas Day in Paris; it was now the evening of the twenty-third. Late on Boxing Day they would arrive in Tripoli and start the fast desert section. One hundred and fifty cars, 130 bikes and a hundred trucks, reaching speeds in excess of a hundred miles an hour, would cut a swathe through the deserts of Libya, Niger and Tchad and arrive in Yaoundé on 2 January. They would then race through the Gabon and on the seventh would arrive at Pointe Noire on the coast of the Congo.

From my point of view, this is where it got interesting. For security reasons they were not going to drive through Angola, but were to take a ship round it. If I could get to Pointe Noire by 7 January, perhaps I could hitch a ride. That gave me two weeks to get there with a 6,000-mile head start. It sounded easy, but I was in the middle of the rainforest and fully aware that anything could happen. Still, it was certainly worth bearing in mind. The rally was then to continue through Namibia and was expected to reach the Cape on 16 January, a staggeringly short twenty-four days from Paris.

A large white-faced monkey scrambled down from the heights of a thick hardwood tree, crossed the road in front of me and, using its tail as an extra hand, bolted up another tree on the other side. This gave me some satisfaction as I had been disappointed that the gorillas had been shy and not shown themselves. I had been looking forward to seeing them and had sat for an hour, waiting hopefully. 'Don't be too disappointed,' Jean-Baptiste had told me when I left, 'there are plenty more in the jungle.'

The road was in fantastic condition, smooth and easily wide enough for two trucks. The forest it passed through showed the effects of Jean-Baptiste's and the others' work. Although they claimed to be involved in environmentally friendly selective logging, the effect was still shocking. It was as if the forest were being thinned – like the hair on an old man's scalp. To get one tree out many more were destroyed, either crushed by falling trees and heavy machinery or cleared to make way for roads . . . roads which were now my only link with the south.

I sped along, leaving a long band of dust in my wake and soon reached the village of Mulondou. At the crossroads with the main track south, three languid soldiers sat in the shade of a lean-to, twenty yards back from the junction. On hearing my engine one climbed slowly to his feet.

The nearest point of immigration, Jean-Baptiste had informed me the previous evening, was at a place called Yokadouma, over 200 miles to the north. As he was sure there were no army checkpoints on this stretch of track, I had decided to drive to Kika without an entrance stamp in my passport in the hope that I could get out of Cameroun before any official knew I'd entered. It seemed Jean-Baptiste was wrong.

The soldier was watching me but had made no advance towards the road. Arms crossed, he stood next to his comrades who were still deep in conversation. If I stopped he would check my papers, giving him little option but to send

108

me back, or, worse still, arrest me for entering the country illegally. It was imperative to leave Kika without showing my passport to anyone. When I was ten yards from the junction he put up his hand. The others had stopped talking and were also looking in my direction. He still made no move towards the road. I turned onto the main track, 'waved' in a similar gesture to his, and sped south without looking back.

Kika, though not on my map, was obviously a place of some importance. Two miles out of the village I passed a grass airstrip and a large timber complex where millions of dollars worth of wood – some still trunks, some already cut – lay waiting for transportation.

It was a clear, balmy day. The sun was high and the heat strong, but for once not suffocating. Usually the air stuck to my body like a damp cloth but now, encouraged by a slight breeze, it gave light but welcome relief.

The long red track took me down past a row of rickety bamboo stalls all the way to the water's edge. It was mid-afternoon, a time when little happens, and there were few people about.

I parked on a mound where the hard, baked earth descended steeply to the river. There were some pirogues, larger than the one which had taken me across the Sangha, and a couple of big wooden boats which I assumed were used for transporting the timber. As I turned, I noticed a black Landcruiser parked up a side street where the stalls continued. Then, to my horror, I saw two large men in customs uniforms emerge from a bar. Unsurprisingly, they noticed me and drove over.

'Bonjour,' I said once they had alighted, extending my hand forcefully in the hope it might hide my nerves.

'I am sorry,' said the taller and obviously more important of the two, 'but my French is not so good.' He took my hand in a firm grip, his face split with an enormous smile. 'You see, I come from the other side of the country, from a small town called Mamfé, where we speak English. My name is Mojaninga, Captain Mojaninga. I think this is better for you too, no?' He finally dropped my hand.

'Really!' I tried cautiously to suppress the seed of hope which had just sprouted. 'Yes, yes. Much better for me, my French is very bad. I stayed in Mamfé . . . at the Hotel Lodge. The people there were very nice . . . there was one problem though

. . . I saw my first snake there, big and brown.' I wriggled with disgust.

'Oh, yes, my friend, you have seen the viper. They are very bad, very bad indeed.' He chuckled and looked over at my bike. 'You have big machine, it goes anywhere I think.'

'Well, almost. It's come all the way from London.' The Captain was clearly impressed, as I'd hoped he might be. 'I am now trying to get a boat from here to Ouesso and from there to Brazzaville. Do you think this is possible?' If I kept him talking, I figured he might just forget to look at my passport. He seemed a benign and charming fellow but if he remembered, save for a miracle, he would be forced to do his duty.

'Yes, of course it is possible,' he said, crouching down to inspect the engine of the bike. 'A boat goes most days to Ouesso, early in the morning I think, so you have missed today's.' He stood up, everything evidently in order. 'I am in charge of customs at Molondou, I only come here once a week . . .' *Just my luck.* '. . . so I am not exactly sure, but you will get there, there is no problem . . . tomorrow maybe.' His forehead was blistered with hundreds of tiny beads of sweat. He took off his beret and wiped them away. They returned instantly

My presence had again caused some excitement and five or six people hung around, listening inquisitively to our conversation which I doubt they understood. The other officer had wandered off, back in the direction of the bar. The whole situation sat on a knife-edge.

'Ah, you have a map,' said the Captain.

'Yes, would you like to see it?' I took it out of the tank bag and put it on the bonnet of his jeep. I had just swapped from the map of North Africa to the one covering Central and Southern Africa. It was large and impressive with no marks save a thin blue line in the top right-hand corner. I took out my Chinagraph and filled it in from Bila to Kika, roughly estimating their locations.

He was enthralled by it and was delighted when he found Mamfé. He gasped with astonished awe as I showed him the route I hoped to take to Cape Town, so, playing to my appreciative audience, I showed him my Sahara crossing on the map of the north. This staggered him. That anyone could cross the desert was hard for him to believe, but an Englishman on a motor bike – it was too much. I was not showing off, merely trying to get him on my side. Then I had an idea. I got another map, the one Tony had given to me in Yaoundé, from one of the boxes on the bike. It wasn't a Michelin map but it was a perfectly decent map of Cameroun.

'I'm sorry I can't give you these maps as I need them, but you might like this one, it's of Cameroun.'

He was most grateful and shook my hand again, honouring me once more with his friendly smile.

'Come,' he said, having tucked it in his pocket. 'I will take you to the logging company. You will be able to stay the night there and leave in the morning.' He paused for a moment. 'Tomorrow is Noël though, so maybe nothing goes.' He looked down at his feet, rubbing his chin. 'You wait here for a minute. I will find out for you.' He walked off up the dusty street.

Okay babe, keep this up and we'll be fine.

A few minutes later he returned with an old man who wore a pork pie hat and a light blue tracksuit. His name was Daniel Ngota and by all accounts, especially his own, he ran most of the business out of Kika. One of the large timber-carrying boats was his. He too spoke English.

'The boat is away at the moment but if you return at seven o'clock we will make the deal.'

'So you think I can go tomorrow?' I held my breath.

'Oh, yes, you can leave tomorrow, but first we must see the man who will take you. You return here at seven. That,' he pointed to the only building you could really call a house, 'is my home, come there.' He shook our hands and left.

'Come,' said Mojaninga, 'I take you to the compound. I think everything is okay, yes?'

'Yes, indeed, thank you.' *Thanks.*

'But first,' he said, 'we must go and see the Chief of Police.'

'What!' I exclaimed, unable to believe my ears. This was too much. To be tempted with the carrot only to be beaten by the stick. No, it couldn't be.

'Do we have to,' I pleaded, regaining some composure. 'I'm tired and want to rest.'

'It will only take a minute, I assure you,' he said happily. 'It is only for your security. Look, it is just here.'

Ahead of us was a nicotine-coloured breeze-block hut with a corrugated asbestos roof. In front of it small whitewashed stones delineated a square area of garden, though I wasn't sure why as the ground inside was as dusty and barren as the road on which we stood. I walked up the 'path' to the door but the Captain, obviously more familiar with the afternoon habits of the Chief, stepped over the rocks and rapped twice on the brittle wood of the boarded window. After a moment the shutters creaked open and a sleepy, pillow-creased face squinted out at us, the bright afternoon sun evidently causing some pain.

'Bonjour,' said the Captain, now back in French. 'I have brought this good Englishman to see you. He will be leaving for Ouesso first thing in the morning.' The Chief of Police slowly focused and looked me up and down with a truculent glare. 'In the meantime I will ask them to house him at the compound. He has a motor bike you know and is a very nice man. He has just been showing me his route acr–'

'Yes, yes, yes.' The Chief cut in so forcefully that the final word died upon the Captain's lips. He was more interested in his siesta than in me. 'Okay,' he continued a little more calmly, 'I have seen him. Now go.' And with a final withering look at the Captain, he pulled the shutters closed.

10 Christmas on the Ngoko

Kika, Cameroun

This compound was not as smart as the French one. It was more like a run-down motel, with five square rooms in a row and a shower and toilet at one end. The enormously fat manager, whose heavy paunch sagged over the edge of his tight yellow shorts like a hippo's face, agreed to the Captain's request and let me stay. There was a small wooden table in the corner of my room, a boarded window and an electric fan which hung precariously from the centre of the ceiling. Cockroaches scurried to and fro on the pale linoleum floor and the springs of the bed on which I lay squeaked a feeble protest each time I moved. At seven I wandered back through the velvet darkness to the house of Mr Ngota. The breeze had gone, the heat lay heavy.

Thomas, the owner of the pirogue, sat behind a table at the far end of the box-shaped room, a hurricane lamp at his side. The orange glow emphasised the scars on his pockmarked face and enlarged his blackened image threefold on the wall behind. He did not smile or stand but greeted me with a curt nod.

'He is wanting 14,000 CFA,' said Mr Ngota, once I was seated. He was clearly incensed by the amount. 'I tell him this is to much, far too much, but he will not come down.' It was nearly thirty pounds, a lot of money in these parts. I was hoping to get the ride for 10,000 and I said as much in English to Mr Ngota who in turn translated for Thomas.

It was hard to make out any other part of the room. The dark faces, brightened by lamplight, were all that could be seen.

'I do not care,' said Thomas, not realising that my French was just about up to his, 'he is white, he is tourist, he has money. If he want to go to Ouesso tomorrow he pay 14,000 CFA, otherwise he stay here.' Well, all that he said was true, but hardly in keeping with the Christmas spirit. What could I do though? I didn't want to hang around in Kika longer than was necessary as at any time the police might ask to see my passport. I also didn't know when the boat from Ouesso to Brazzaville would sail. If I missed it by a day because of 4,000 CFA I would be extremely angry, as the idea of riding with the rally round Angola was strengthening in my mind.

'Okay, I will pay you 14,000. What time do we leave?'

'At daybreak. You be here by six. We make Ouesso in one day.' The deal done, he managed a small smile and a shake of the hand before leaving. I sat on with Mr Ngota for some time.

I was awake long before dawn. The fan had done little to alleviate the stuffiness inside the iron-roofed room and irritating mosquitoes had whined in my ear most of the night. A row of angry bites crossed my stomach like a zip. I packed up quickly and made my way back to the river.

Away to the east, the first essence of daylight appeared. Cockerels cried and other birds sang. A few people were stirring, lighting the fires from the embers of the night before and reheating fat ready to make maize balls. The stars retreated as the sun, dull and orange like the yolk of a hard-boiled egg, lifted itself above the trees. A thick mist covered the river and hid the boats.

It wasn't long before the heat increased and banished all hint of night. I sat next to my bike at the top of the bank of hard, dry earth and waited. Eventually the mist cleared and the pirogue could be seen, which was more than could be said for its owner. It was much as the other one had been, long and thin and deep, but slightly bigger in every dimension. It had once been painted green and red, though most of the paint had peeled off, leaving it mottled. What filled my heart with a burst of optimism was the sight of the tiny outboard engine fixed to the stern. It could carry the bike, of that I was sure, though I'd have to take it to pieces again.

Children sat and watched me from large piles of ready-cut timber that lay on the bank awaiting transportation. Another policeman, one I hadn't seen before, gave me a shock by coming down to the water's edge. I told him I'd seen the Chief which seemed to put his mind at rest, though in truth he was more interested in my bike than in me.

'Can I have a go?' he asked after a minute. By this stage it had no petrol tank or seat so I had no problem in explaining that this was impossible. He seemed not to take offence and carried on inspecting it.

Thomas arrived at last, with a jerry can of petrol and a bag of food, looking a little hung-over. Well, it was Christmas morning. He grunted some half-baked apology and climbed into the pirogue. Unfortunately this was not the cue to load up and go. For the next hour he set about repairing the vessel by nailing pieces of tin over banana leaves – a process which hardly filled me with confidence.

Eventually we rolled the bike up a plank and into the dugout, this time stabilising it with large sacks of mealie meal. I placed my chair at the front and sat like a figurehead under the merciless sun, prepared for an easier, more relaxing, method of travel. Daniel Ngota, Mr Businessman, came to see me off, laden with the addresses of various relatives dotted around the world and letters for two sons, one in Ouesso and the other in Brazzaville.

'You want me to deliver these?' I asked, amused that I was being used as his personal courier.

'They are places where you can stay, if you need to. If not. post them. They are fully addressed.' I thanked him.

He pushed the pirogue's nose from the muddy bank, allowing Thomas to turn it round. 'I will see you in London,' he shouted. 'We will make business, you and I. We go to West Germany.' Daniel's Mecca. 'And tell your friends, I do business with them also.'

'But Daniel, I'm not a businessman.'

'Everyone is businessman, my friend. We will set up music company, you will see . . . Goodbye . . . Good luck.' His voice faded into the distance. I waved a final time as the bank disappeared from view and, with a heart full of hope, I settled back to enjoy this strange Christmas day.

The river was wide; a great mass of murky water moving languidly west towards the Sangha before finally entering the mighty Congo and then the sea. Giant trees stood in columns, bound together by creepers; the undergrowth, a velvet green, was almost black – thick and impenetrable. Mangrove and bush encroached on the river as it had on the tracks, thickly overhanging the water's edge. Now and again a fallen tree helped it on its way.

Every few miles islands appeared, forming lagoons and side channels. Tributaries entered from either side to join the main body of water. On a sandbank some hippos rested in the sun. A crocodile slithered down the bank and into the water, swishing his tail with extravagant vigour. Two giant birds, like pterodactyls, lifted mournfully off a tree and made for the skies, then glided effortlessly towards the interior. Dragonflies dipped and hovered along the surface of the water.

A deep contentment oozed from the trees, flowed with the river and settled upon me. There were no logging stations this far down, just Thomas, my bike and me. At last I was fulfilling one of my earliest dreams: to be an explorer. I breathed deeply and tried to take it in, to feel it, to hold it there in the hope that it would never disappear. *Yep, Jonny, like Livingstone or Burton, now you've really found it.*

Were we the only people in this prehistoric land? We would round a corner and there would be a clearing, a row of yellow reed huts and tiny black pirogues, yet, strangely, no people, as if these settlements had recently been abandoned. At the third group of dwellings I realised why. The sound of drums drifted over the river to meet us: Christmas, it seemed, had reached even here. People swayed, clapped hands, danced and sang, their spiritual chants joining the rhythms across the water. The sounds were eerie yet happy, conveying the same seasonal spirit as the sound of church bells reverberating over a snowy field.

In my mind's eye I saw my family sitting round the Christmas tree, opening presents, drinking bubbly and listening to Tom Jones records. There would be two new additions to the family this year: my sister's husband and my brother's wife. The huge meal, the Queen's speech, the James Bond movie. My little reverie made me blue but only for a moment. For *this* Christmas, I knew, I was exactly where I wanted to be . . .

The Missing
7.30 p.m. December 25th

I looked out at the cold winter moon and cursed my ill-made decision. Why the hell hadn't I gone with her? She was right, it would have made no difference at all. Behind me the fire crackled in the grate. Dad sat dozing on the sofa, Mum picked at her chocolates and Emma and Poppy, an excitable terrier, watched a tiresome magic show on the TV. The post-Christmas blues settled heavily upon me. Was she looking at the moon and thinking of me? It had been our plan. The moon was to be ours: whenever we missed each other we would look up at the same moon and be, in some way, together again. But it made little difference. Oh, how I missed her . . . what an idiot I'd been. I went to the drinks cupboard and poured myself a Scotch.

Mel's mum and stepdad had invited us to spend the holiday with them in Goa, India. Being ex-hippy, trendy types, they had rented a house there and Mel had been delighted at the prospect of the trip. At last it was her chance to see the country she most yearned to visit, not to mention getting away from cold, wet England. Naturally, she wanted me to go with her. At first I thought I might be able to. Our début record, a four-track E.P., entitled 'Cosmetics', was not due out until the following spring, but, as we'd finished the video by the end of September and had promises of subsequent television exposure, it was suggested late-November might be better.

'Come on, darling,' she'd said persuasively, 'you know how untogether these people can be . . . it's only for a month . . . or even two weeks. Besides, even if it is released, which I doubt, nothing'll happen over Christmas.'

'I want to come, sweetheart,' I answered truthfully. Going to India was hardly something I needed to be pushed into, but I felt it was impossible. 'I just can't. They've said they'll put the record out soon. We might have gigs to do . . . I don't know, anything might happen.'

Mel graciously accepted my decision. She knew how much the band meant to me and realised that at last things were starting to move. 'But,' she had added, 'I think you'll regret it.'

I did, badly. Not while she was making her preparations – I thought I was being responsible, thinking of my career – but when she got out of bed at five in the morning to go to the airport, it hit me like a train. I was shocked by the strength of my emotion. Up until that point I hadn't really imagined missing her. I thought I'd have fun, get drunk a lot, flirt a bit, maybe even have an affair – but after she walked out of the room I howled like a baby. I did get drunk – but have an affair? It never even crossed my mind.

As she'd predicted, the promise of an early release and TV shows proved to be an empty one. With Christmastime competition from Elton John, Tina Turner, George Michael and the like I should not have been surprised but, as always, I'd hoped for the best.

One week after she'd gone, the head of the small independent label, to which we were signed, told us the record would not, after all, come out until the spring. A week after that our only gig was cancelled.

I sipped my drink and looked outside again. Was she having a good time? Was she at a party, or on the beach, or would she be asleep? Was

117

she missing me the way I was missing her? Ten days later, when she burst through the door of our flat and flung her arms around me, it seemed as though she had.

We pushed on through the afternoon. The sun sank below the trees and a strip of shadow, in which we travelled, was formed down the right-hand side of the river. The heat had eased and the light softened. Suddenly, without warning, the engine died.

Thomas looked vague and took out a hammer. We drifted listlessly down the river in silence. I was not too concerned. I estimated we had about twenty-five miles to go, too much for that evening, but even without an engine we would have no problem reaching Ouesso sometime the next day. Besides, it was peaceful without the constant thumping of the outboard motor.

The hammer was not effective and soon we were pulling the nose of the pirogue up onto a patch of grass in front of an encampment. Three reed huts in various stages of disrepair sat at the top of a bank.

'We will try to fix it?' I asked Thomas.

'Yes, but we will stay here for the night . . . tomorrow we reach Ouesso.' He moved away into a hut. He was not much of a conversationalist. Three worn-out women with empty breasts sat on a wooden bench under a banana-leaf lean-to. They stared at me through vacant eyes, their children clinging nervously to their legs. A scrawny black chicken scoured the ground for its Christmas supper.

I developed a searing headache. What started out as an innocent throb soon became a tight pounding, like hammer blows to the front of my head. At first I worried that I'd caught malaria but then I noticed that my field of vision was getting narrower and realised, with considerable relief, it was only a migraine. I had no food and after lending Thomas my tools I took some pills and lay down on a grass mattress inside a stuffy, smoke-filled hut. Most of the night I drifted in and out of a fitful sleep where dreams and reality became hard to decipher. I would open my eyes and see strange shadows dancing on the wall in front of the glow of an orange fire. I'd hear laughter and singing and then a face would appear, so close to mine that I could feel the fetid breath warm against my cheek. The occasional scamper of

118

some small animal, a rat I assumed, would brush against my hair, stirring me momentarily, but I was too far gone to care.

The next morning, the world had disappeared. During the night a blanket of mist as thick as cotton wool had descended onto the river, muting all sound and vision. It looked the same as the inside of my head felt. The ache had gone and my vision had returned but I still felt decidedly wobbly. Thomas appeared before me through the opaque air, his face a mask of doom. He informed me that he had failed to mend the engine and, rather unnecessarily, that we would have to wait until the fog cleared before we could continue our journey. At nine it lifted quickly above the trees and we were immediately under way.

The river became wider the further west we travelled and the banks became harder to define. They were simply walls of green reaching high into a translucent sky, our pirogue a tiny insect crawling along a fortress floor. Behind me, Thomas and a friend he'd commandeered from the settlement were working hard with the paddles, their faces covered in sweat. I can't say I felt too sorry for them. Thomas was being paid the equivalent of a month's wages for this journey and I wondered, a little sardonically, how much he was paying his friend.

With the sun crashing down once more upon my fragile head – now bandaged in my chech – we worked our way round the bends and islands in silence until, at last, we passed from the Ngoko onto the Sangha and entered the port of Ouesso, and the People's Republic of the Congo.

11 Theirs the Darkness

Ouesso, Congo

'The boat for Brazzaville, it leave here two days ago,' the Chef du Port informed me. It was a sticky, airless day, well over a hundred degrees. A purple bougainvillaea crawled across the roof and wall of the veranda on which we stood. Insects buzzed around its flowers, foraging for pollen. I sat down.

'So when will it return?' I asked tiredly.

'Well, you know, this is hard to tell. It all depends how long they take in the capital.' He was a kind-looking man, about my age and plump, with dimples. His name was Charlie. He paused in contemplation. 'Maybe ten days.'

Lucy, his wife, and their dog sat silently at his side. He sent a boy to the bar for some beers and I did some calculations. Ten days before it would return, another two or three days here and six more back to Brazzaville. Almost three weeks, *if* everything went smoothly.

'Are there any other boats that could take me to the capital?'

'Oh no, this is the only one for passengers.' He looked uncertain, and pointed at the bike. 'But on this machine you can drive. The rains have just finished. It not rain again for some weeks . . . it take you two days, maybe three.' After a moment's pause he added: 'It will be easy.'

The beer arrived and I got my map out. It looked simple enough on paper. A thin white line cut its way through the very heart of the forest, 200 miles directly south to Makoua on the equator. Here the road to Brazzaville, 400 miles further south, began. But I also knew this had been Tony's route. 'It'll be hard.' I remembered his words, and that had been before the rains: after them it was bound to be worse. But he had also said that what I would see would be worth it. If I waited three weeks in Ouesso any chance of catching the rally would be gone. I saw myself back on the track at Mbalam, stuck, swearing at the mud and a tired shiver ran down my spine. I knew there was no choice: I would have to drive.

Charlie took me up a narrow track behind his house to a small whitewashed building. Two children pretended to drive a rusting, wheelless car which lay rotting opposite. They laughed and ran off as we approached.

'You can stay here for the night,' he said. 'It is the room for the captain of the boat . . . there is no hotel in town.'

It was in fact a suite of small rooms – living room, bedroom and bathroom. It was sparsely furnished and very dark as there was only one window. Still, I was most grateful and thanked him.

'Tell me, Charlie, do you know a man called Ashu Ngota?' I took the envelope out of my jacket pocket. 'His father asked me to give him this.'

'Ugh, that is just like Daniel to have someone running errands for him.' He chuckled to himself. 'Yes, indeed, I will send a boy to fetch him.'

It took three hours to find the right person to stamp me officially into the Congo and when I did find him he was reluctant to do so.

'What is this?' he pointed at my carnet as if he had never seen one before. My explanations met with little success and eventually I took his stamp and did it myself, just asking him to sign where necessary. He didn't seem to mind and was pleased when I handed him his piece of the form, as if I had given him a souvenir.

'I show you how many other foreigners have been here this year,' he said enthusiastically, turning the book round for me to see. 'We have been quite busy.' Twelve names were written on the page: Tony's was the last. That made me number thirteen . . . *hmmm*. At the top, next to an illegible scrawl, was the word Danish. So the guy Tony had heard of did make it through. I asked the officer about him.

'Yes, I remember, he was very ill, he come from Souanké.'

'Which way did he go when he left?'

'Oh, he have to stay in hospital here for some time, then he take the boat to Brazzaville. From there I don't know.'

If I ever meet him, I thought, I should very much like to buy him a drink.

By the time I got back to my room Ashu Ngota was outside waiting for me. He had the same proud face as his father but was considerably taller.

'Arr . . . it is a letter for my grandfather,' he said after reading the first page. Like his father he spoke very good English.

'Where is your grandfather? If you want we could take it to him.' He looked a little pensive and was quiet for a while.

'Is there a problem?' I asked, trying to put him at ease. He was looking at the floor, scuffing the dust with his feet.

'No,' he said, putting the letter in a pocket. 'My grandfather he is here in Ouesso, but . . . he has leprosy. He lives in the camp.' I knew that leprosy, far from being an extinct disease from biblical times, was very much alive and kicking in Africa. I had not knowingly seen anyone with it but I was neither frightened nor surprised in the way that Ashu seemed to think I might be.

'This does not matter, Ashu,' I said, putting a reassuring hand on his shoulder, 'we can go on my bike and take him the letter.'

'Oh, thank you.' He smiled now, looking quite keen. 'It will make him very happy. It is not contagious, you know.' I had not known.

We drove out of the docks, along a dirt track, past palms and mango trees, tall grass and bush. The sun was low and the shadows long. The town consisted of two main tracks, one running along the bank of the river and the other cutting off at right angles towards the forest. We turned left, taking the latter. People walked lazily up and down the sandy road, the heat still sapping most of their energy. On either side a single-storeyed row of concrete huts housed small shops. We passed the one-pump petrol station and the only bar.

'It is the fourth largest town in the Congo,' Ashu bellowed proudly over my shoulder. 'Everything that comes in or goes out, does so on the river. Although the track is marked on the map, it is impassable for trucks as many of the bridges are down.' No four-wheeled vehicle, he thought, had got through for some time.

'And you think I can do it?' I was sceptical.

'Of course. On this machine you have no problem.'

The camp was just like any other part of the village, for a village is all Ouesso really is. A mixture of straw huts and concrete dwellings with corrugated roofs and ill-fitting wooden doors formed a square around a dusty clearing. There were banana plants and fig trees and patches of cultivated maize. A large, red-headed hornbill pecked at the long black seed pods lying in the dirt under the far-reaching branches of an acacia tree. It hopped away as we came to a stop. The arid smell of dust and drying vegetation hung in the air.

There was great excitement upon our arrival. People of all ages came from every direction. Most of them looked perfectly healthy to me and it was only when I went to shake their hands that I realised they were not. On some the hand had gone completely, the flesh withered away to the base of the arm leaving a small stump. On others their feet were affected and they were forced to hobble on crutches. There was one girl who caught my eye. Young, no more than twenty, and exceptionally pretty, she had large dark eyes, a huge happy smile, and seemed a picture of health.

'Why is she here, Ashu?' I asked.

'She has only the first stages.' He showed me her right hand from which the little finger was missing. She was not embarrassed but giggled and turned to her friend. Her loveliness underlined the tragedy of this ugly disease.

Ashu's grandfather was sitting round the back of the square. An old man with thinning hair and sunken cheeks, he leant forward at an unnatural angle which made him look as though he had a hump. He had no fingers at all, just two shortened thumbs, and had hard calluses on his neck and feet. We sat down and Ashu read him the letter. A couple of times he chuckled with delight and was evidently pleased to see us. When, after half an hour, we came to go, I sensed a great melancholy descend upon him. He wobbled uneasily on his ruined feet and refused the indignity of an arm-shake.

On our way back, with night now upon us, we stopped off at the bar. On the road some youths, shrieking with enjoyment, played table-football, the match illuminated by a solitary yellow street light.

I asked Ashu again if trying to drive was the sensible thing to do.

'Yes, my friend. I have done it myself on small bike, Honda 125, it take me two days . . . no more.' He leant back and took a sip of his beer. 'You will be in Brazzaville on Saturday. It's a good route. No problem.'

We carried on drinking till late.

The track was firm and wide. Deep red, rust-coloured earth stretched like a carpet before me, bisecting the bush. An old man pushing a moped was coming the other way. I stopped to give him some petrol. The sun was high and the sky clear. *Perhaps this won't be so bad after all.*

No sooner had this thought flashed through my head than I passed under an arch, like an open doorway into a giant's castle made by two huge trees, and entered the forest proper. It wasn't long before the light at the entrance was nothing more than a brilliant pinprick. The track got narrower and narrower until it was not much wider than I. On either side the deep green undergrowth was thick and impenetrable, patterned with the morning dew. Sharp beams of sunlight slipped through the leaves and tangled creepers high above to brighten the murk of the forest floor. Thousands of brightly coloured butterflies, some bigger than my hand, disturbed by my passing, rose up and accompanied me or flew straight at my face only to dodge away at the last second, like cartoons in a 3-D movie. Soon I was in a dark tunnel, the roof of which was as thick as its walls. There was no breeze down here. The air was wet and stuffy, steam from the rotting vegetation hung like a fog and I was quickly wet through.

The water holes were shallow, and few and far between. If I was careful I could drive through them, keeping my feet down for balance. At some there was just enough room to scramble round the edge, but after ten miles this changed. Black stagnant water covered the entire path and stretched for great lengths into the gloomy darkness. I tried to continue driving through the water but soon discovered that this did not work. The front end of the motor cycle sank into the slimy mud and as the water covered the bike the engine cut out. I pushed it as far as I could and waited for it to dry but I realised a different approach was needed.

In order to establish the most favourable lie I decided to park the bike at the beginning of each stretch of water and test it on foot. This revealed a dilemma. Although no four-wheeled vehicles had been through here for a while their tracks still rutted the path. I could either take the bike along the deep wheel tracks on the left or right, thereby risking flooding the engine again if the water got too deep, or try to push it on the raised centre, itself a foot or two under water, and walk in the tyre trenches myself.

I began by pushing the bike along the central ridge of a stretch that was about thirty feet long, with the engine running to help pull it through. As I got further into it, the tyre track deepened until the water was almost up to my thighs and the bike so high above me that I was unable to control its immense weight. The front wheel started to slip off the ridge. I screamed to give myself more strength. To no avail – the bike slid out of my grip and plunged into the water on the far side.

Panicking, I struggled round and tried to right the machine but it was too heavy. I was just able to drag it to the side so the engine was out of the water but I could not raise it onto its wheels. I had to unpack and carry everything twenty feet to reach dry land. Then, with a Herculean effort, I got the bike up and out of the water hole. Twenty minutes later, angry and tired, I was able to continue. To add insult to my misery a large black ant bit the back of my neck.

I pushed on as hard as possible, but by now it was painfully slow. At times the ruts got so deep that the bike became grounded across a ridge. This forced me to unpack, pull the bike over onto its side, get the front wheel in the same rut as the back one and push it up again, sapping my strength still further. I imagined what this land must look like from above, a never-ending carpet of green, the track invisible. I was starting to regret not waiting for the boat.

Whenever there were water holes, which was now more often than dry track, I continued to walk the bike through. Each time I entered another stretch I sank up to my ankles in the abhorrent mud. Insects, disturbed by my presence, swarmed about my face. Only they seemed to flourish in this perpetual twilight.

Unexpectedly, the track rose, sending me out of the darkness and into the open. A village. It was positively liberating to see the sky and breathe the air, to see other human faces and know that I wasn't the only person in this godforsaken land.

A row of grass and mud huts stood back from the track, about ten on each side, in a clearing no larger than a football pitch. Three men sat on the dirt by a doorway. They were dressed in remnants of Western garb but the women, who now showed themselves by the huts with their frightened children, were not. They had made a half-hearted attempt to hide their bodies with cloth, pieces of leather and crude metal jewellery. A black cockerel cut the silence with a haunted crow but, looking embarrassed, he decided to stop halfway through. A tethered goat at the far end of the clearing scuffed up some dirt. Nothing else moved.

'Bonjour,' I said to one of the men. Apparently he did not speak French but he got up and entered a hut on the far side of the track while his two friends bade me sit down and gave me some of their drink. It tasted sharp and bitter: palm wine I assumed. The man returned a minute later with two others, one old and bent, with grey hair and hollow cheeks, and the other young and wearing a relatively smart shirt and trousers.

'My name is Joshua,' said the younger man, surprising me greatly with his English, 'and this is my father, the chief of the village.' I was a little disappointed. The Chief I'd imagined was both tall and fat, with a grand, ostrich-feathered crown and lionskin cloak, the tibia of a gorilla in one hand and a fly swat in the other. Mind you, how was I supposed to look: white flannel suit, pith helmet and cane-handled umbrella – Dr Livingstone, I presume? No, no, I pondered, these were the images of clichés; this was reality and he looked no different from any of the others.

I shook their hands.

'Can you tell me how far the next village is, please?' I was hoping to reach it before nightfall.

'It be twelve kilometres from here but road it very bad. There be much water.' Joshua paused. 'It better you stay night here.'

It was only half past two and although it had taken me nearly four hours to cover the last twenty kilometres, for some inexplicable reason, I thought I could, and should, go on.

'Thank you,' I answered, 'but I think I will make it.'

'Okay, but be many careful at the next bridge, it no good.'

The track led down from the shallow plateau, plunging me back into the forest once more. A deep gully zigzagged across it throwing me this way and that but after only a mile I came to the bridge. Spanning a ravine it was only a few metres across but the banks dropped away steeply to a clear pool fifteen feet below. Three tree trunks made up the crossing but the centre one was broken in the middle and there were alarming gaps between each of them.

I decided to do as I had been doing all day with the tyre ruts. I would walk along the crippled centre trunk while trying to keep the bike upright on an outside one. I got to within a metre of the other side when I slipped on the damp trunk and lost my balance. Purely by the grace of God the bike fell on me rather than over the edge and jammed firm between the two trunks. Had it fallen the other way, I imagine it would still be there today.

Cursing, I pulled myself up and walked back to the village with my tail very much between my legs. It took six of us to pull the bike clear and to get it back across the bridge. This time Joshua insisted I stay the night – I did not argue.

The Chief's hut was made up of three rooms and, naturally, was the biggest in the village. At the front there was an open-sided room with three home-made stools around a grass mat. There was a larger room just to the right and a small, damp, airless one behind. This, the Chief said, was for me. A bamboo mattress, bound at the corners by thongs of leather, was raised a foot off the ground. The deep brown walls were made of woven branches and mud with a tiny window cut in the far side. Cob-webs covered the walls like drapes, but, thankfully, through the gloom I could see no spiders. We sat down outside the house. I took out a packet of damp cigarettes and handed them round.

Joshua was a schoolteacher in Ouesso. He had come home to see his family for Christmas and tomorrow was going to walk out along the track on which I had just arrived. I thought he might well cover it faster.

'Where is your weapon?' he asked, once his cigarette was lit.

'I have none. It is not allowed for a foreigner to have weapons in the Congo.'

'But you must have weapon.' He was incredulous. 'There are many bad things in jungle . . . it dangerous.'

'All I have is my machete,' I said with a resigned smile, showing it to him. 'It will protect me . . . I hope.'

'Yes, I hope also, but I do not think this will do good with leopard or gorilla.'

'Let's just hope I don't meet any.'

Joshua's younger brother, Kalifa, passed round a bowl of delicious pineapple. Nothing but water and sardines (and a torrent of swear words) had passed my lips all day. The sweet tangy juices sent my taste-buds dancing. I must have eaten a whole one by myself.

While munching on the last piece, I noticed some water

dripping slowly from the right-hand box on the bike and that the ground below was stained dark. At first I was too tired to get up to investigate and thought it was only excess water from the last of the mud holes. After five minutes, when the stain had grown and the drip continued, I knew all was not well. I found to my horror that the box was three-quarters full of murky brown water. Half my medical kit – in a supposedly watertight bag – was ruined. Dressings, plasters, syringes and antibiotics were all useless. Spaghetti and rice had swollen and were unusable and the maps of the north were soaked. I salvaged what I could and hung it on a line to dry before making two small drainage holes in each box. I then sat down on the dirt and stared at the machine. It was the last slap from a frustrating and exhausting day.

At that moment Kalifa, whom I'd taken not to speak a European language, came over and put his hand on my shoulder. He looked me in the eye but seemed to see further – into the centre of my being.

'M'sieur,' he said quietly, 'vous êtes vraiment un homme.' He turned and walked away.

I leant back and smiled to myself; suddenly it all seemed worth it. Tired and apprehensive I undoubtedly was, but deep inside I couldn't help feeling that all was well. The worries about my ruined kit, the continuing hardship of the journey and the aches and bruises in my limbs began to fade. With my thumb I felt the reassuring touch of Mel's ring. I somehow knew she wasn't far away.

Twilight turned to darkness and fires were lit. We sat round the table for a dinner of bush-pig tongue and trotters, steamed in banana leaves; they were foul, but, thankful for the hospitality it represented, I ate every last piece.

I talked for a while with Joshua and stared into the glowing embers of the fire. In truth I was too shattered to hold much of a conversation. He told me that the route would be very bad for another fifty kilometres and then, at a place called Yengo, I would cross the river on a barge and conditions would improve.

'Vehicles get that far,' he said. 'You have come at bad time. After rains there is always much water.' *Thanks, Tony.*

I took off my damp clothes, lay down on the hard mattress and waited for sleep to come. The room was damp and musty, the air heavy and claustrophobic and all around me was a faint scratching noise. I lit a candle to see what was sharing my room and rather wished I hadn't. Eyes – round, bulbous, arachnid eyes – staring from motionless sockets, shone like Cat's-eyes on a road. The walls were covered in spiders. Their bodies were about the size of my hand, their shadows even bigger on the ceiling. With the candle burning they froze, transfixed, hypnotised by the light. There must have been at least thirty. So much for the mud hut of a friendly Chief!

I slept badly, drifting in and out of nightmares. The cockerel woke me long before dawn and I lay worrying about the hardships the day might bring.

I didn't leave immediately but waited for the sun to clear away the mist which crawled around the huts like an evil spirit. As I was packing up I noticed Joshua walking away into the forest carrying his weapon and I wondered whether he would really be safer. His gun, the only one in the village, was ancient – a Chassepot or Martini-Henry, or some such rifle. The chances of hitting even a gorilla with it, I figured, must be small.

By seven thirty I was back on the track and heading, once more, deep into the heart of darkness. This time I crossed the bridge successfully, only to ground the bike on the other side. The further I got, the worse the track became. Rotting pieces of vegetation half-covered by thick, black water and blanketed by tiny insects formed my route. At times, when the sun managed to penetrate the dense forest roof, the water would steam and colours formed in the vapour, but the going was too hard for me to see any beauty in it.

In addition, that morning I had another problem to deal with. In my fall on the bridge the side stand had become bent, making it hard to prop up the bike. If the ground was not slightly uphill, and lower on the left-hand side, the bike would topple over. This made it hard to leave the bike while I was walking through the water to check the best lie and I often had to head straight through. Many times I tried to guide the machine down the central ridge only to have it slip off. I would feel it going and scream with frustration as I held it for a few seconds, but invariably its weight and momentum would pull it over. Once it fell the other way, on top of me. It pressed down from above, making me slip backwards, forcing me almost entirely under the water as I fell. For a few desperate seconds I was trapped under my bike with water up to my chest.

Around midday I got really stuck. The flooded area was long and thin and I, too tired by now to bother walking through, had chanced my luck and driven at it hard and fast. The front end dipped, steam hissed as the hot-engine submerged in the water and the bike cut out. Miraculously, considering he was the first person I'd seen all day, I spotted a man some way off down the track. I called and two strange-looking figures emerged from the shadows and ran towards me: a man and a woman, both in their twenties I guessed. He wore a suede headband and an exceptional pair of shorts. They were, or at least had been, a pair of pin-stripe trousers, that could easily have started life on the legs of a merchant banker, now in shreds, cut off just above the knee. With their enthusiastic help I pushed the bike clear of the hole and walked it a hundred yards up the track to their camp.

These people were hunters. An older man, whose bald head was as shiny and black as a seven-point snooker ball, leant against a tree, whittling arrows from bamboo. There was a small grass shelter under which the girl bent to tend a boiling cauldron of food and a crude wooden bench on which I rested. We spoke no language in common and so sat in silence. In the clearing the sun cast long beams of light upon us.. Everything steamed.

It was only then that I realised just how filthy I was. All my clothes were soaked, my hair was matted to my head and my unshaven face caked in muddy sweat. I took out some cigarettes and handed them round. The girl said something and pointed at the pot. It smelled good and although I feared it would make them all a little short, I could not resist. She poured some of the grey stewed mixture into a metal bowl and handed it to me. It tasted sweet and fruity, mangoes I guessed, but the stringy meat was a lot less flavoursome.

'What is it?' I asked, pointing at my bowl. After a minute of charades it dawned on me that I was eating elephant trunk.

The bike, dried by the sun, burst into life and carried me back into the forest tunnel. If Joshua were right I would have about twelve kilometres left before Yengo. Doesn't sound too bad, does it? It was hell. There was so little dry path here that I was, in effect, driving, or rather pushing, down a narrow stream. The heat and humidity were intense and the pores on my body opened in a way they never had before, streaming sweat like a thousand tiny waterfalls. I gulped down tepid, chlorinated water, my body desperate to rehydrate, but dirt always found its way into my mouth and crunched between my teeth.

When the track dried up, which was rare, there were other problems to overcome: small fallen trees or thick bamboo blocking the path. Twice I was forced by the narrowness of the track to lay the bike down on its side in order to haul it round to face the way I had come. Then I attached a rope to the rear end and pulled the obstacle clear. Sometimes the vegetation was so thick I had to hack a hole with my machete before pushing the bike through. I was forced to draw on reserves of strength I never knew I possessed, but on I trudged through the watery hell, this jungle obstacle course.

For the umpteenth time that day, I came to a muddy submerged trench. By now almost delirious and at the absolute end of my tether, I tried to drive down the right-hand rut, praying that it wasn't too deep. Water sprayed high on either side, increasing in quantity the further I progressed. The traction was good, my balance fine and I could see the water's end through the darkness. Suddenly, the front wheel sank into an invisible dip, disappearing under the water. I pulled back on the throttle in desperation. The bike lurched, jumping forward like a coiled spring. The high revs from the engine were deafening. Further and further, nearer and nearer. I bounced up and down on the foot pegs to try to give the wheels more purchase but by now it was only going at a crawl. 'Keep going you son of a bitch. Keep going!' Just when I thought I might make it, down went the front end again, this time jamming firm into the mud, and with an horrendous dank . . . dank . . . dank . . . the engine died.

A mass of tiny black flies swarmed around my head, biting my neck as I tried in vain to push the bike to the other side. A large spider crawled up my sleeve. Two more, lanky and brown with long, furry legs, gripped onto my thighs. I was too far gone to care and swatted them off as though they were bluebottles. The bike would not start, it would not even stand up. 'OH GOD . . . PLEASE . . . HELP!'

I managed to prop the bike up on my machete and staggered out of the cursed, thigh-high water. Watching my feet move laboriously beneath me, I began to walk. How far was the next village? Three miles? Six miles? For the first time, I really thought the journey was over.

After a while I fell to my knees. *Christ Mel . . . aren't you helping me? . . . You were meant to be looking after me . . . I thought . . . Oh, for fuck's sake . . . look at me. Is this it? Jesus . . . what am I supposed to do now?* My body trembled and I felt quite faint. *I trusted you . . . you were going to see me through, remember? Shit . . . You're not bloody with me . . . WHERE ARE YOU?* Dropping my head in my hands, I began to weep.

Some way ahead, where the track wound round to the right, a crashing noise brought me to my senses. Without the sound of the engine the forest was eerily quiet; even the insects refrained from buzzing. For a moment nothing moved. The track was firm, on a slight incline and the vegetation was fractionally less dense. I wiped my eyes.

The noise again; a breaking of bamboo and scuffing of leaves. A dark shadow appears through the undergrowth, then the body that makes it. He stands in the track, trapped by a shaft of sunlight, thirty yards ahead of me. We hold each other's glance for a second; his a sublime look of indifference. He shows no surprise or anger; a docile giant. He sniffs the air and is gone, back the way he'd come, into the trees. A gorilla . . . a huge, silver-backed gorilla.

Suddenly, I found myself running. Crashing back through the jungle, I pushed haplessly at the undergrowth and splashed through puddles. Water was squelching in my boots and air rasping through my lungs. A rush of fearful adrenalin surged through my body, filling me with an all-embracing determination. A sudden realisation of where I was swept over me. I was alive again, on edge, every sense acutely aware. *You're in a bloody jungle, now start the bike and get out. It's not over yet.*

I plunged back through the dirty water, disturbing the swarm of insects and pushed on the starter button. Nothing happened . . . 'Come on you bastard.' The insects bit. 'Come on, come on . . . you fucker . . . STAAART!' And it did, spluttering and coughing, but going. Filled with a superhuman strength, the like of which I had never experienced before, I scrambled clear, out of the mud and up the other side. I pulled my goggles down, took a deep breath and raced on up the track.

It proved to be the last serious stretch of water there was and before long the path began to climb. A startled hen ran across my path with two chicks in tow, telling me a village must be nearby. A mile further on I came over a lip and there it was. A more welcome sight I could not have imagined.

In the unwalled communal shelter five people sat staring at the white embers of the dying central fire. I offered them greetings and the last of my cigarettes. I took off my boots and trousers and sat there in silence, semi-naked, exchanging glances.

'D'où venez-vous?' asked the oldest of the men, who sat at the far end of the hut. I was quite startled. Again I had not expected them to speak French; it was a nice surprise.

'I have come from Ouesso. Is the track from here good or bad?' I was painfully aware that there were still nearly 500 miles between me and Brazzaville.

'Oh, la route est bonne, après Yengo elle est bonne.' He poked a stick into the fire to give it more life. 'Il n'y a pas d'eau, m'sieur . . . pas d'eau.'

I repeated the words out loud and then to myself. What a beautiful ring they had. I'd done it, I had got through, there would be no more water. I looked down at my battered legs. They were bruised and swollen. A fat leech sucking my blood clung just above the right heel. I burnt it off with my fag. My arms were scratched and my head hurt. I knew I had achieved something tremendous but I was too tired for self-congratulation. I just sat there quietly thinking of nothing. After a while I asked if I could stay the night. He said he would see the Chief.

It was late afternoon, the shadows were lengthening and the light turning gold. Two girls sitting opposite whispered to each other and giggled. The village looked a little bigger than the one of the night before. There were the same number of huts on either side of the track, but behind those on the left were a group of ten more. Women sat clutching their babies in front of their huts. Seeing the old man returning with two others – one young, one old – I flicked my butt into the fire and stood up.

'Of course you must stay the night.' This Chief looked much the same as the last: old and wizened, with tufty grey hair and three tribal scars on each cheek. Again, he looked no different from the other villagers, except for his natural air of superiority. He wore just a sarong and was named Matonga. 'Lango will give you a hut,' he continued, gesturing to the young man at his side. 'You must stay as long as you like. Tonight we will eat.'

'Thank you ... I think I need to wash as well,' I said, looking down at myself.

'Oui. Lango will take you down to the stream. But first you will put your machine in my hut.' His jaw jutted out slightly as he said this. He was a proud man with a fine chiselled face and seemed to take a great deal of pleasure in having me as a guest. He didn't smile much though, just a vague flicker at the corners of his mouth, as if smiling were a sign of weakness, and something he could not afford. In a place as isolated as this, being Chief means being law, teacher, father and priest. He had to be strong, his position depended on it.

'Some months ago,' Chief Matonga went on, 'we had another white man here. You are the only two visitors at Doua this year ... he was on a bicycle.'

'Did he have a telephone on the front?' I asked, miming.

'Oui, oui,' said the Chief excitedly, his face at last breaking into a full smile. 'He is your brother, non?'

'Yes,' I replied, 'he *is* my brother.'

Lango, who was the Chief's youngest son, gave me his hut. I tried to persuade him that this was unnecessary but on realising that I was getting very close to causing offence changed tack and gratefully accepted it. It was essentially one mud-walled room partitioned into three. It was lighter than the room I had slept in the night before but had the same amount of cobwebs.

We walked back down the track from where I had come. Wide-eyed children stared. As I passed by, some started to cry and ran for their mothers while others followed us, murmuring inquisitively. Soon we cut off the track and into the forest. A narrow path led us between creepers and trees; the damp, pungent smell of the earth and vegetation filled my nostrils. I was light-headed, almost floating. At the bottom of a small bank, running under foliage, silent and clear, was a shallow stream. I stripped off and sat in the cool water. After a moment I covered myself in soap. Scrubbing hard soon turned it into a lather. My face, my hair, legs, groin, buttocks and arms. I rubbed and rubbed, almost losing control of myself removing the dirt from my body, trying to empty thought from my mind. It was as though I had been raped by the forest and was now being cleansed. I lay down hoping the water would wash my memory clean.

Soon after dark Lango entered the hut carrying a lantern.

'M'sieur Jon, you must come. We eat.'

He led me out onto the track. All was quiet save for the rhythmical buzz of the cicadas. Thousands of tiny fireflies drifted on the breeze which carried sweet smells from the various fires into the night. Above, the sky was teeming with a million stars and the air, for a change, felt light.

Most of the villagers sat gathered round a fire in the communal hut, the children on the floor and the elders on benches. Those who couldn't squeeze inside sat at the entrance. The smoke made a heavy blanket above their heads, seeping slowly out through the thick grass roof. Two oil lamps, hung from sticks, cast dark shadows and coloured faces orange.

At the far end sat the Chief in front of a low table; he motioned for me to join him. Though the ostrich-feathered crown and lionskin were still safely locked away, the Chief had made some effort. On his head he wore a conical-shaped animal-skin hat, a necklace of dull stones dangled loosely down his chest and he had metal bangles round his wrists and arms. He looked at me as I sat down, his face solemn and proud.

Earlier, Lango had told me that a gazelle was being killed in my honour. It was now brought in, skewered on a pole, the size of a small lamb, and placed on the table before us to excited applause. Lifting a large knife in flamboyant style the Chief began to carve. Pounded yam, cassava and fried plantain were handed out, followed by hunks of the succulent meat. It was a feast to be sure. Curious faces looked at me in silence as I put the food to my mouth, asking with their bright eyes, 'Is this white man going to like our food?' On hearing my approval they laughed and began to discuss me in their own language. I laughed and smiled with them. More and more they passed me, pleased with my contentment. Bananas and pineapple followed the meat and lastly some strong dark tobacco in a wooden pipe.

The feeling between us was one of trust and understanding, an immediate affinity of fellow human beings. Here there were no secrets to hide, no fear or worry. They did not know where I came from but I was there, in their world, enjoying their culture and that was enough. We sat, our souls as bared

135

as I'd been in the stream, our hearts as clear as the sky above.

This is it, I thought to myself, this is why I've left home and come this way. I rubbed my eyes with the palms of my hands and sank back into the shadows, a warm glow resting on my contented heart. Mel was not only helping me, she was there with me, as vividly as if she were sitting on my lap. She had brought me here to show me this. In a mud hut, sitting on a bamboo bench in one of the most impenetrable places on earth, I knew I'd found my answer.

12 Diamonds, Gorillas and a Little Black Spot

Gamboma, Congo

The exit from the forest was as vivid as its entrance. As though a curtain had been drawn, the vista widened and the trees stopped. For the first time since Nigeria, I saw open skies from horizon to horizon, and felt the rays of the sun rather than just its heat. I turned and looked back. The forest stood like a great army waiting to advance; giant trees, silent and still. At last I was free from their grasp.

At Gamboma I stayed the night in a hotel and enjoyed the luxury of a bed. I washed in a bucket of cold water and had a shave, the first for more than a week. It was bliss.

By morning the skies had clouded over, the wind had quickened and the promise of rain lingered in the air. I left early in the vain hope of avoiding the downpour but road conditions made progress slow. The forest had ripped the rear brake pads off the bike and the spring that had held them in place was lost. With only the front brakes working I had to weave my way slowly through the countless pot-holes. When the rain started things got worse still. At times I was back on dirt, as slippery as ice, but about ten miles outside the capital I hit the newly constructed 'highway' and joined the flow of vehicles moving languidly towards the centre of Brazzaville. The shanties of the suburbs closed in around me. The thin band of tarmac which cut the dirt was packed with old trucks, rusting cars and bikes. On the muddy sidewalks young men played table-football while women fanned the embers of their charcoal stoves, the fish and maize smoking gently. There was a feeling of decay, of a tired town in need of a rest. Rusting roofs were set on crumbling walls and rubbish filled the gutters.

As hotels in Brazzaville are notoriously expensive I was a little concerned as to where I might stay. Tony had given me the address of the Gorilla Orphanage where a team of British primate biologists worked. He'd only met one of them briefly but he thought they might have somewhere for me to sleep. The problem was finding them and it was already getting dark. Then, to my astonishment, I saw a battered blue and white sign on my right which read 'Ngota fils'. To tell you the truth I had had no intention of delivering Daniel's second letter – I had been going to post it – but now it seemed I had run straight into the home of his eldest son; that strange travellers' luck again. I pushed open the large metal gates and drove into the forecourt.

Smith Ngota was as charming as everyone else I'd met in his family. He was tall and lean with stylish clothes and his father's love of business. His yard was piled high with expensive hardwood from upriver and various other items he had for sale. On one side was a small brick bungalow, undergoing an extension, with a wooden shed behind.

'This is really amazing,' Smith said in excellent English, 'you must stay the night.' And so I did, in the shed, which was actually a perfectly comfortable room. It amazed me that in a country where few people speak any European language, Daniel Ngota had educated himself and his children to be trilingual. He paid for Ashu's training to become an architect, Smith had gone to university in Yaoundé and Marian, his daughter, was at college in Boston. Not bad for a wood trader from Kika. Two younger daughters lived here with Smith. They both wanted to go to England to study medicine; I wouldn't mind betting they do.

The next morning, having checked there were no more letters to take to any other relatives, and armed with a map Smith had studiously created for me, I set off for the Parc Zoologique.

It's quite a strange feeling turning up in a foreign city and saying, 'Hi, I know about you from a guy you met once for five minutes, and I was wondering if you could help me,' but in Africa it seems that a lot of the friendship and hospitality shown by its natives has rubbed off onto the Westerners who live there.

Steve sat on the floor of a small forecourt, surrounded by tiny black gorillas. He had one on his lap which he was feeding from a bottle.

'Yeah,' he said, answering my humble request, 'no problem. We can't offer you a room though because Kimu's in it, she's sick with dysentery, but I'm sure Mark and Helen won't mind if you put up your tent in the garden.' He had a strong London accent which in no way lessened when he spoke French to Albertine, a Congolese helper, who was also feeding a baby ape.

'We're just gonna take 'em for a play in the trees. D'you wanna come?'

There were twenty babies in this group, and forty in all, aged between a few months and three years. They were wonderful. They ran around dragging their lengthy arms in the leaves, stopping to beat their chests or my back, depending on how mischievous they felt. They hung from my arms, swinging to and fro, climbed round my neck and fell asleep on my chest. They were unbelievably human. When the parent gorillas are killed in the forest for food, the poachers bring the orphans into the city to sell as pets – they often fetch more than a month's wage. I could easily understand why they were in demand when, later that afternoon, I sat in the house playing with Kimu. She was not a sick maid, as I'd imagined from Steve's remark when I'd arrived, but turned out to be a nine-month-old female gorilla wearing babies' nappies.

The orphanage had been set up a year before by John Aspinall, the eccentric English millionaire, to save as many of this endangered species as possible. Mark and Helen Attwater run it. With a team of wardens, backed by the law, they confiscate the baby gorillas from the poachers and then handrear them. They teach them how to be wild apes with a view to reintroducing them to the jungle. Apparently I had been lucky to see one in its natural habitat. Sightings are fairly rare, even though there are thought to be over 50,000 of them. I'm not sure lucky was the adjective that I would have used.

I was happy to camp in the garden and not blow any money on hotels as I knew I might have to stay for some time. Not too long though – I had only a week before the Paris–Le Cap rally would arrive in Pointe Noire, 300 miles to the west. For the first time, I became fully aware of the predicament I had placed myself in. In Yaoundé I had committed myself to going through Angola, but if they were to refuse me entry and I were to get no help from the rally organisers, I would have little option but to return to Bangui and think again. The thought of going back into the forest made my skin crawl.

I asked Mark about my prospects of getting a visa.

'No chance,' he said without hesitation. 'Sorry, but I heard of a German who was here about three months ago. He was a personal friend of the ambassador – got him to intervene on his behalf – but it was still "no way". From what I've heard, the only way there is to fly to Luanda.' After a pause he added, 'And for that you've got to be a businessman . . . or Press. No tourists go to Angola.' He leaned back in his chair. 'I mean it's hardly Costa del Sol, is it?'

'No, I guess not.'

So Michael had been right – I'd have to chance my arm as an irrigation specialist – but that worry was for tomorrow. Today was New Year's Eve and I intended to have some fun.

My first hot shower since France. Dirt was ingrained in my skin like contour lines on a map of the Alps. I stood under that piping hot shower for a full half-hour being gently steamed. Afterwards, while standing over the loo having a pee, I looked with some concern at a small black spot right on the end of my penis. Well, not literally, but where the head meets the shaft, if you see what I mean. I'd noticed it for the first time a couple of days earlier at the hotel in Gamboma but then it had been only the size of a pinhead. A bizarre place for a blackhead I had thought. Now it was three or four times larger. A squidgy black piece of flesh about two millimetres in diameter, like a small button attached by a single thread. It must be a piece of dead skin or a wart, I thought to myself as I pulled to free it from my person. It hung on with grim determination. Again taking it firmly between thumb and index finger I pulled, harder this time, bringing tears to my eyes. Eventually, with a sound like a cork being pulled from a bottle, off it came. In disgust I shook my hand to throw it away and glanced down to see what damage had been caused, but, like a sticky piece of tape, the strange black spot still clung doggedly to my finger. Again I shook my hand, but it refused to go. I brought it up to my face to get a closer look, now at a loss to know what I was dealing with. To my horror I saw six tiny black legs gripping to my hand for dear life. Finally I managed to flick it off and squashed it with my boot.

Some kind of blood-sucking insect from the swamp, I assumed. I hoped it had laid no eggs.

Steve was eating with some diamond buyers so I arranged

to meet him later and went out with Mark and Helen to a fine restaurant. It was wonderful to dine on beef steak and drink red wine – a holiday for my beleaguered taste-buds. The Attwaters, as primatologists, were not at all what I had expected. Mark, a reformed punk with humour as dry as Campari, talked more about the Sex Pistols than he did about gorillas. And Helen, well, she looked just too young and pretty.

After dinner the three of us went to meet Steve. The centre of the town, all three or four blocks of it, looked fairly prosperous. There were a few high buildings, offices for the oil companies and airlines, with cafés and bars in their entrances but I was surprised to see how few black people frequented this part of town. This, it seemed, was the world of the ex-pat.

The restaurant where we found Steve was as affluent as any Brazzaville had to offer and was run by a fat Swiss couple. Steve greeted us and introduced me to the people he had been dining with. As they had finished eating we didn't stay long and were soon on our way to a night-club. Steve said it was where the children of the Europeans go. It was horrendous: smart and naff, like stepping back to Ibiza in the late seventies, I imagine. Obnoxious French kids in sequined boob-tubes, and guys with shirts undone to their navels, danced to the Bee Gees and the Commodores. The floor flashed with the same colours as the dayglow cocktails and sent my head and stomach reeling in different directions. I explained to Steve that this was not the place I wished to spend my heard-earned New Year's Eve and, slurring his words slightly, he told me he knew of another.

Leaving the others behind, the two of us staggered outside and climbed into the jeep. It was a hot and sticky night with a clear, star-filled sky. Even though it was well past two the streets were packed with joyful revellers. We drove south out of town, hugging the river, to the Congo rapids.

This place could hardly have been more different; as sleazy a dive as you're ever likely to see. It was simply an enormous, open-topped enclosure made of bamboo and bush. Hundreds of sweaty bodies writhed to the rhythm of Zairean music, replenishing themselves on Primus beer. The pungent smell of marijuana smoke filled the air. From what I could see we were the only whites. At one end was a small stage immersed in darkness. We sat down with our beers at a rickety table as the music started to fade . . . it was obvious a band was coming on.

The Deal
11.25 p.m. March 16th

'Okay guys. Two more minutes and you're on.' *The presenter's head disappeared behind the door.*

'Pass me the spliff, Guy,' *I said, getting to my feet. I took a long drag and strummed a few chords of the opening song. It was always a strange feeling just before going on stage. The dope and drink had little effect against the dramatic surges of adrenalin. Nerves, nerves, nerves. I sang a couple of lines to calm myself down. The others did not look impressed.*

Outside I could hear the crowd – all 3,000 of them, it seemed. We were at the Hammersmith Palais, the most important gig of our career – blow this crowd away and we were looking at fame and fortune.

'Come on then,' *I said to the others,* 'let's get out there and do it!'

The excitement and 'buzz' about us had started a month earlier. The record had finally been released and the promises of TV exposure had come good. First the video had been shown on Channel 4's The Chart Show *and a week later ITV had followed with a showing on a late-night entertainment programme. Suddenly we were being taken seriously. A couple of write-ups in the music press and soon we were being played on the radio, but it was at The Mean Fiddler, the venue of our first gig, that the real breakthrough came.*

We were all sitting backstage enjoying the post-gig euphoria when the door opened and a girl entered.

'Do you mind if I come in?' *she said rather unnecessarily.* 'My name's Christine. I'm a talent scout at MCA.' *And so the excitement began. A week after that we were doing another gig in East London in front of her boss and two days after that we were sitting in his office.*

Mark Dean had one of those thin faces, with narrow eyes and a small chin, that was really just an extension of his neck. Indeed, if it hadn't been for his nose giving you a rough indication of where the centre of his face was it would have been hard to tell where to direct one's gaze. He had made his name some years back for his discovery, and subsequent signing, of a certain Georgious Kyriacus Panayiotou, soon to be known as George Michael. He was young and brash but there was no denying his success. To be in his office was nothing short of a dream.

142

'It was great, guys,' he said leaning back in his chair. There was a 'Wham' gold disc on the wall behind him and two more opposite. He smiled, evidently enjoying his power.

'I won't fuck around with you, I reckon you've got a few great songs. I like the image and I like your voice. We wanna sign you. What do you reckon?'

What did we reckon? What the hell did he think we would reckon? Fantastic! Bloody fantastic! I couldn't believe it was actually happening. I expected him suddenly to say he was joking and kick us out, but he did not. After Andy had replied, with a lot more cool than I could muster, that that would be good, he went on.

'The figure will be something like three hundred grand. We'll get you some decent equipment and record the first album at Hanser Studios, Berlin. I think Chris Kimsey would be a good producer for you, he's hot at the moment. In the meantime we'll try and get you on an American tour with one of our other acts. All right?' When we floated out of his office ten minutes later our heads were spinning.

That evening a few friends came round to the flat to celebrate with us. Mel was torn two ways. She was terribly excited for us but also worried because she knew what fame might mean. I told her not to worry, that rock stars can have girlfriends too. I was too carried away to be concerned by such things. Having striven towards our goal for so long – four years now – thinking of little else but how to get a deal, it was an incredible feeling to have finally reached our dream. But had we got a deal? Our signatures were not yet on the contract.

'Merely a formality,' Mark Dean told us at a second meeting. 'Let the lawyers work it out, we'll sign within a month. You got any gigs coming up? Some people from the States might want to see you.' We told him about the Palais.

'Yeeerrrhah,' screamed Tom as we made our way back to the dressing room. It had been our best concert ever. Everything had gone right. The lights were fantastic, as was the sound, and the crowd had demanded two encores.

'That's it Tommy,' I cried, 'you can give up your day job now.'

'Tomorrow bloody morning.'

I opened the door of the dressing room and we all barged in. Mark Dean was sitting there with two fat Americans, a bottle of champagne in his hand.

'Boys,' he smiled, 'you're gonna be stars.'

About lunchtime on New Year's Day, feeling like death, Steve and I went down to see the diamond buyers. I needed to send a fax to England to ask for some spare parts to be sent to the Cape and to let people at home know the route I was hoping to take.

The diamond dealers' heavily fortified home was manned by armed guards. Security cameras scanned one way and then the other above walls topped by razor wire. Rottweilers clawed at a cage.

Phil and Gary, two Lewisham lads, sat in a small room bent over piles, literally piles, of diamonds; millions of dollars' worth, they said. Like an amazed schoolboy I asked if I might pick up a handful, imagining that I would never again have the chance to hold half a million dollars in my fist. They were uncut newly mined stones so they didn't shimmer or sparkle with beauty, but when I looked closely through the eye-glass they provided I saw each one had a centre of pure perfection.

After we'd eaten and I'd sent my fax, an Angolan came to the door with some stones. Since the trouble across the river in Kinshasa, the company Phil and Gary worked for had closed down in Zaire and because of the war had no office in northern Angola. Anyone with stones to sell brought them to Phil. He then bought them for a fraction of their final value and shipped them back to Antwerp.

I still needed to get an Angolan visa so that, if I couldn't catch the rally's boat, I would at least have a way forward. So, the next morning, once the others had gone to work, I sat in the living room with Mark's typewriter and constructed a letter. I hoped that, by some miracle, I'd get the visa, but I had been told it was impossible. Inside I sensed it would be all right, and that my luck would hold out, but what did I or anyone else really know about Angolan entry requirements? The German had tried over three months ago – a lifetime in such matters. All I could do was give it a try. The letter I wrote, on the headed paper Julius had acquired for me in Cameroun, was like this:

U.K. AGRICULTURAL LTD.
SYSTEMS

SHOWROOM
35-39 LOWLANDS RD
HARROW
MIDDX HA1 3AW

TEL : 081-864 0668
FAX : 081-864 9511

WORKSHOP & ACCOUNTS
45b BRIDGE ST
PINNER
MIDDX HA5 3HR

TEL : 081-868 2918

TO WHOM IT MAY CONCERN:

Dear sir,

    This letter is to verify that Mr. Jonathan Guy Bealby, holder of British passport No. 174855R, is in the employ of the above company.

    Mr Bealby is currently engaged in a research project looking into the possibilities of expanding our interests on the African continent - for the purposes of this visit he will be concerned with Angola, Zaire and Zambia.

    We are primarily involved in irrigation systems and have a number of successful manufacturing plants in Europe, Asia and North Africa.

    Any help and advice you can give our collegue will be gteatly appreciated. He will be returning to the United Kingdom in early February.

    We thank you for your time,

    Yours sincerely,

A. Patterson M.D.

DIRECTORS : A PATTERSON (MANAGING) — B. PHILLIPS — M. WEEDON — L. DOCHERTY/SALES ' J. G. BEALBY
REGISTERED ADDRESS : 64 AUBURY ROAD. PINNER. MIDDX.

And so, sweating profusely in my borrowed clothes, heart in mouth, I entered the austere Angolan Embassy – the fate of my journey hanging by a thread.

The room was light and cool. The monotonous drone of the air-conditioner hung in the background while three men, two black and one white, filled out forms round a small table.

What made them look like real businessmen? Was it the way they held themselves, their confidence or their clothes? My borrowed shirt and tie were okay, my hair was brushed and clean but was I one of them? I feared not. I straightened my back, placed a confident smile on my face and, still feeling like a dirty traveller, approached the desk. I knew no Portuguese so spoke in English.

'Hello, I would like to apply for a visa.' A young girl sat at the desk, a map of the country I wished to visit behind her.

'Please fill this out,' she said without surprise, taking a large four-sided questionnaire from a drawer. 'Do you have two photographs?'

'Yes,' I nodded.

'Very well, return it to me when you have finished.'

I sat down with the others and did as I was told. It was not as bad as I had expected: the usual questions – passport number, nationality, father's full name, date and place of birth, occupation (in my case irrigation specialist), places to be visited in Angola plus the name of firms one hoped to see. This was a bit of a poser: I knew no companies in Angola. All I could think of was what Michael had put, The University of Luanda, and then – a brainwave – I added The United Nations Agricultural Development Project. I knew it was a bit of a shot in the dark but I had to come up with something. I kissed Mel's ring, tapped it on the form and handed it in.

'Okay,' she said looking through it, 'You have 12,000 CFA?' I took the money eagerly from my pocket and handed it over. 'You wait here.' She walked through a door and disappeared. Would an interview be required and if so could I bring it off? I did know something about irrigation systems as there is one on my father's farm and I felt, if pushed, I could talk on the subject for a minute or so. But if anyone cross-examined me or asked to see more evidence I might very well be exposed as a fraud.

I sat nervously rubbing the sweat from the palms of my hands, fidgeting slightly. I pretended to read one of the magazines and nodded to the other men as they received their passports. Judging by the look on their faces as they rummaged through their well-worn books, it seemed that they had been successful.

After what seemed like a week, but was probably no more

than twenty minutes, the door opened and a short, fat man handed what appeared to be my passport back to the receptionist. I stood up with my stomach twisted in a knot so tight I could hardly breathe. She handed me the book and said, 'Thank you. Enjoy your stay. Goodbye.'

I could have bent down and kissed her. On page twenty-six was a twenty-one day single entry visa and, crucially, no 'by air only' stamp across it. The gateway to the south was open. The ticket to Cape Town was secure and my quest was still on. *Thank you, thank you, thank you.* I could have danced down the street.

13 Train Through the Jungle

Brazzaville, Congo

'I'll take the train,' I said to Steve. 'I really can't cope with another track of mud. It would kill me.'

It was Saturday and it had rained hard since Thursday evening, leaving my tent an inch deep in water and my sleeping-bag soaked. I had got through the forest just in time.

So I walked down the sodden streets to the station. Huge pot-holes, filled with water, crossed the roads. Even here in the city cars were up to their doors in water.

In front of the station there was a tall pillar, a cenotaph to the forgotten age of Communism. The column, topped by the star and with hammer and sickle at its base, was all that I'd noticed of the former regime which had ruled the country till only a few months before. It looked forlorn, as if it wanted to be demolished and saved any further embarrassment. The large cold frontage of the station was the hue of a sepia photograph. In the flat light and drizzle the scene was almost colourless, everything, including the few people on the platforms and in front of the façade, reduced to base, dull lifelessness.

I rapped on the window of the second-class ticket office. The black blind rolled up and a middle-aged man with greying hair stood waiting for me to make my request. I asked about the train to Pointe Noire which he informed me departed at six the following morning.

'Okay, I would like a ticket for me and my motor bike.'

'Why should you want to go on the train if you have a motor bike, m'sieur? It will be very expensive for you.'

'Too much rain and too much mud. How much will it be?' This was a real concern. West Africa had been far more expensive than I had anticipated and if the money I had got at the British Embassy in Yaoundé was to last to the Cape I should have to take care. I feared there would be no more places to get money before South Africa.

'How heavy is the bike?' he asked, pencil poised.

'About 250 kilos,' I said truthfully, adding, 'with all the luggage.'

He scratched his head and jotted down a great list of figures none of which looked too promising. In the end he vigorously underlined the bottom one and swung the pad round to face me. British Rail might be ludicrously expensive, but this was extortion. I asked him to check his figures, which he did, though unfortunately the outcome was the same: 54,000 CFA, about £125. This, no matter how I tried to work it out, was impossible. I would have to drive and leave tomorrow. I walked out into the rain with heavy spirits. I knew what this would mean: more mud, water, blood, sweat and tears. I felt as gloomy as the day.

At least the rain had stopped by the time I said goodbye to Steve, Helen and Mark. I had mended the rear brakes the day before by grinding a spare set of the larger front pads to the size of the rear ones and jamming them into position. I changed the oil and filters, bought provisions, sent another letter to Amel telling her of my progress and generally prepared myself to go. I knew the road would be better than before, it could hardly be otherwise, I just wasn't sure if I could handle even an ordinary African dirt road. I felt weak now, both mentally and physically. The rainforest had taken a lot out of me and the thought of more mud and water, even in less excessive amounts, filled me with weary resentment. Knowing there was another form of transport that could get me to my destination in half the time exacerbated the feeling, but I was developing a quality that, prior to this journey, I had seldom had need of – determination.

As I made my way out of the capital the road was asphalt and in good repair. Dark grey clouds still lingered overhead and the rain never seemed very far off. It was hot though and the muggy air was oppressive. After about forty miles the road branched in two. One continued, asphalt, to a village called Matoumbou while the other crossed a small wooden bridge and turned into a muddy quagmire. Unfortunately I knew which one I had to take.

The track was neither narrow nor pot-holed, and there was no vegetation marching across it, but the ochre-red earth was sodden; it was like driving on porridge, heavy yet slippery. The wheels were instantly caked in mud and all traction disappeared which left me sliding all over the place – I could go no faster than ten miles per hour. The night before Mark had told me that it was widely believed that the government deliberately kept the road in bad condition so that people would be forced to take the train, which is why the state railways charge so much. He had not been in the least bit surprised at the cost of getting my bike to the coast. When their animal cage was sent out from England it had cost as much to get it from Pointe Noire to Brazzaville as it had from London to Pointe Noire.

As the first droplets of rain came down I stopped, anger bubbling inside me. I looked at the map and saw that the train went right through Matoumbou. Perhaps, I thought, I could join it there. I knew I couldn't afford the ticket, and what of my determination to get my head down and keep riding? *Sod determination, I can't handle this*.

It was a quiet village that amounted to nothing more than a shabby hotel on a grassy bank overlooking the station and a row of stalls. None of these was doing much business as no train had recently arrived. A few people lingered, sheltering from the drizzle. A dog wandered aimlessly through the mud and some children played in a dead truck.

The station master and his colleague, the ticket inspector, were friendly men, both in their middle-forties, the hair of the former greying, of the latter receding, and both with beery paunches.

'Je voudrais prendre le train pour aller à Pointe Noire,' I said for the second time in two days. 'La route est très mauvaise.'

'There is no more train today but tomorrow early, is possible.'

We were standing up against the counter in the crumbling whitewashed station house. It was dark and hot and I felt weak.

'And how much will it cost for my bike and me?'

'For you it will be 4,000 CFA. How heavy is your bike?' The station master was doing all the talking while his mate stood smiling at his side. How much wool could I pull over their eyes? They looked like decent men – I decided to meet them halfway.

'M'sieur, my bike is heavy, about 150 kilos, but I am in a very bad situation. You see I have very little money left and it is imperative that I get to Pointe Noire by tomorrow night. You see I must meet the rally.' Most people had heard of the rally and I hoped it made me sound important. They nodded in unison and looked concerned. 'I am too weak to drive as I fear I am not well and may be coming down with malaria and the road is very bad.' This was only a half-lie. My head was pounding and I did feel as weak as a child, but I doubted it was malaria. I felt sure I would know if it was. 'So, I am wondering if you can say for me that it is less heavy, so I can afford it.'

I put my hands down on the counter and gave them the most pathetic, pleading look I could manage. In the end it worked. They looked at each other, discussed something in their language and nodded.

'We will say the machine is eighty kilos. This will make it not so much for you.' For the second time that week I felt like kissing a total stranger.

'Merci bien.' I shook both their rubbery hands. 'How much will this be?'

'Twelve thousand for the machine and 4,000 for you.'

It was still nearly thirty pounds which left me only £150 for the 3,000 remaining miles to the Cape. I couldn't really afford it but I had to take it. *Things will work out Jonny, they always do.*

That evening I took a double dose of Nivaquine anti-malarial tablets in the hope that it might alleviate the all-embracing lethargy I seemed to be consumed by. It was as if I had the malaria in me and only the pills were keeping it at bay. Awaking before dawn, I made my way back to the station through the mist.

A high-pitched whistle shattered the morning calm. Clouds of steam lifted above the trees and round the corner came the large black bulk of the Pointe Noire Express. The platform, which had been packed since dawn, burst into life. Sacks of maize and bundles of cane were picked up by their owners and thrust forward towards the edge. People, shouting and cursing, jostled for position with little regard for themselves or others. An upside-down chicken, feet held firmly by an albino boy, maniacally flapped its wings. Children shrieked excitedly and women, both young and old, made ready pineapples and mangoes for sale to the passengers on board who might be in need of breakfast. Any seats left would be fiercely contested.

Again the whistle blew, three short blasts, and the train slowed still further. It was obviously very old, a relic from a different age, but, like so many things in Africa, it worked so it was used. The few carriages that still possessed any paint had light brown slatted wood sides. Thick black diesel smoke belched from the one central exhaust. The brakes hissed a final time and, with the heads of its inquisitive cargo popping through the countless windows, the tired locomotive shuddered to a halt.

I had been told that the train would not wait long so had assembled a crowd to help lift the bike aboard. With consummate ease they raised it to head height and hurled it forward into the last trailer, closely followed by me and the rest of my possessions. The luggage coach, which was nothing more than a cattle-truck, was packed with people. The large sliding doors did not close and before I had time to secure the bike the train lurched forward and began to move slowly out of Matoumbou on its 300-mile journey to the coast.

It took twenty minutes to secure the bike to a rail in a corner of the wagon. The train threw me over sacks of grains and clusters of bananas, onto people's laps and almost out of the door as it jolted and bumped along. I managed to pack the rest of my luggage by the side of the bike and eventually sat uncomfortably at the open doorway, watching the countryside slip slowly by. It wasn't forest here but lush savannah; sugar cane, thick bamboo and tall grass the colour of lime. Fig, palm and mango trees divided small areas cultivated with manioc and maize and patches of pineapples. The clouds had cleared and the sun was out. The air was so hot that even the draught through the train gave no relief. The track was on a slight embankment so although the grass was high it was possible to see the wobbling heat haze above the forest far off in the distance.

After an hour the train stopped and I was persuaded to go to one of the carriages. My primary concern had been for my possessions but with a dead arse and sore back this had changed and now comfort was all that mattered. I dragged my tank bag with me and found a seat in the restaurant car. There was nothing to eat on offer here, just beer and coke and a lot of drunk men. One of them came straight over, placed his hand on my shoulder, and burped into my ear.

'Bière,' he said, now plonking himself opposite me. He was as frightening looking a person as you could imagine. Ian Fleming could not have created a more plausible baddy. Huge, with a shaven head and a crazed look in his eyes, he wore a torn one-piece military jump-suit, stained with sweat, and carried a bad smell. His cheeks bore tribal scars and his teeth, at least the front ones, were made of shiny steel. When he bared his lunatic smile they glinted like flashing blades. I refused his offer politely, not really sure if that is what it was, and pretended to read my book. I felt his hand on my arm.

'Non,' he said looking intently into my eyes. 'Bière.'

'Er. Oh . . . okay, thank you, it's very kind. Yes, please.' Again he flashed his smile of steel. He put his hand out to be shaken. Apprehensively, I placed mine in his. He stood up, and grabbing our two interlocked hands with his second, shook vigorously, almost in a trance. He then turned away, dropping my hand as though, like a child growing weary of a game, he had suddenly had enough. He staggered to the disconnected deep-freeze in the corner of the carriage and hauled out two large bottles of warm beer. It was only nine thirty a.m. I wondered how I was going to last until eleven that night.

My experience of travelling in Africa had led me to believe that if someone bought you a beer or a coke it made you their property for the duration of that drink. That's to say they buy it for you because they want to talk to you to find out where you come from and to tell you as much about themselves and their country as they can. Most of the time this is fine, as it is exactly what you want. So now I was fully expecting to endure a stilted, possibly frightening, conversation with my monster friend, which in my weakened condition, quite honestly, I did not fancy. None came. He handed me the beer, touched the glass bottles together and sat quietly watching me. When I tried to talk to him, feeling almost guilty, he just flicked away my comments with the bottom of his bottle saying in mime, 'You carry on reading, I'm all right.' At the first station we came to he bought me a hard-boiled egg, a mango and a chicken brochette and when a scrawny man with a voice like a dalek started to hassle me he made it quite clear it was not a good idea.

An hour and two more beers later there was trouble. A ticket inspector got on at a station called Mindouli and, as if knowing that this was where the fare-dodgers hang out, came straight for the restaurant car. My friend had no ticket. A heated argument ensued in a local language and the upshot was his eviction from the train. He shook my hand again before leaving, flashed his smile and turned to go. When he got to the door at the end of the carriage he turned, gave me a surreptitious wink and disappeared down the steps. The train trundled on slowly without him.

It was hot and getting hotter. Dust came in through the open windows and flies buzzed incessantly around our faces. They'd rest for a moment on my mouth or nose in search of moisture, waiting for me to swish them away with a handkerchief; it seemed I was the only one bothered by their presence.

Quite why the train was called 'Express' was mystery to me; it stopped at every village. What had been a quiet, unpopulated place before the arrival of the train would suddenly metamorphose into a thriving market. Passengers leant out of the windows and reached down for mangoes, pineapples, hard-boiled eggs and smoked fish, plastic bags of water and bundles of cane or grass. Hundreds of people jockeyed for position, some clambering in while others climbed out. Soldiers would watch from afar. It was the event of the day and nobody in the village wanted to miss it.

At Madingo a middle-aged man and his old companion got on and came to sit opposite me. Francis Jumboubo was a talkative person who seemed unused to travelling with a white man. Now that he was he seemed intent on making the most of it. On and on he rambled with vigour and enthusiasm in fast French, but the noise of the train and his deep, sticky voice made understanding difficult. The old man, Francis's father, was the spitting image of Ray Charles, right down to the black-rimmed shades. He didn't nod or shake his head to signal his agreement with his son, but shook his whole torso, usually repeating the final couple of words as though trying to lend his statements more credence. 'That last village was a leper colony,' Francis would inform me. 'Leper colony,' his father would quietly add, wobbling in his seat.

The gist of what Francis was telling me was interesting: a history lesson about the railway line on which we were travelling. It had been built in the twenties by the French and by The Belgian Trading Company who were looking for a quicker way into the interior, or, more accurately, by the labourers of the region who were treated no better than slaves. A lack of even the most basic safety standards had cost thousands their lives.

'Every sleeper and track laid, every tree cut and all the tunnels carved,' Francis told me, as we passed through the largest one, about four kilometres long, 'were done by hand.' After a moment's pause he added, 'Black hands.' He held up his own as if to say 'like these'.

154

'Umm . . . Black hands,' mumbled his father.

When we emerged from the twelfth tunnel the horizon had gone and once more I was back in the rainforest. The train carved its way along the edge of the hills and over iron suspension bridges before plunging deep into the gloom of the forest again. Twilight came and went unnoticed and left us sitting in the dark, just the red glow of cigarettes lighting up the faces in the crowded coach. There was precious little air, what there was being thick with smoke and hard to breathe.

Francis, to my eventual relief, turned his attention to an army captain sitting nearby. What began as an amicable conversation soon deteriorated into a vicious argument. In England such a violent disagreement would probably end in a fight but in Africa things are different and argument is something of a sport. Francis must have been champion of the Congo. The discussion had something to do with Communism and free trade, the old regime and the new, but they soon fell into their own tongue and I could not keep up. All the passengers in the coach joined in cursing Francis and his views, except his father who sat impassively at his side. Francis roared aggressively with anger and force, throwing his hands in all directions to emphasise a point and yelling into the faces of his enemies. Then the others would counter-attack, fifteen men screaming blue murder, but one by one they'd drop out to let a spokesman, usually the calm captain, talk for them all. It seemed as though this war on all fronts was going to be too much for Francis, who by this stage was giving me a headache. Then, like the desperate struggle of a wounded animal, just when I thought it was over and peace restored, he began again. Shouting, screaming, banging his chest, showering them with vitriol and spit he turned his aggression against them one by one. The captain and his three colleagues gave up and sat quietly, then another and another until he had silenced them all – all except one, who would have been far better advised to keep his mouth shut. For a full twenty minutes Francis metaphorically beat him to the floor, then continued relentlessly, reducing this creature to a mere shell of a man. It was truly extraordinary that anyone could feel so passionately about something, but it was also cruel, in the same way that a physical beating is cruel.

I could bear it no longer and clambered out of my seat, scrambling over the bodies sitting in the corridor, and stood next to an open window, Francis's voice still echoing in my head.

The pitch black of the forest night slipped by as the train rolled on. Occasionally I caught a glimpse of the stars in the sky, but as yet there was no moon. It seemed an age since I'd last seen the moon and I missed it. At about ten thirty I smelt the salty air and electric lights began to appear. Five minutes later we pulled into the station at Pointe Noire.

Wearily I climbed down the steps and made my way to the rear coach. The platform was long and packed with people alighting from the train, carrying their bundles and making for their homes. There was no rush now though, no panic to get the last seat, no screams and shouts; they too, it seemed, had lost their energy. Outside the small station hut a swarm of insects circled a neon light.

There was a tap on my shoulder. I spun round, startled. So he had made it after all. My monster friend stood behind me smiling proudly. In the shadows and semi-darkness his smile was about all I could see of him.

'How . . . ? Where?' I pointed at the train, but he shook his head and chose not to answer. Together we reached the rear carriage where I was pleased to find all my possessions intact. I untied the bike and with monster friend's help got it out onto the platform. I got back in to fetch the rest of my luggage, but as I did so the train began to move off. I grabbed my stuff as quickly as possible and jumped. The platform was now all but empty and as the noise from the locomotive faded into the distance it seemed eerily quiet. Four inquisitive children gathered round my bike, their voices loud, magnified by the silence. But my Bond villain had gone, disappeared without a trace.

One of the kids got great pleasure from squeezing on pillion and taking me to what he said was the only hotel in town.

'Twenty thousand CFA,' the receptionist said.

'You must be joking.' But of course he was not. It was a Novotel, part of the international chain, and although forty-five pounds does not sound like so much now, it was simply not what I had been expecting in Africa. It was gone eleven, I had been up since before dawn, I was tired and did not feel in the least bit like looking for a camping ground by the sea. I asked to see the manager.

'Yes m'sieur, can I help?' He was younger than I expected, not much older than me. He wore a black jacket and tie.

'I hope so,' I said and went into my sob story again. 'I have arrived here to meet up with the rally as I wish to catch a ride on their boat round Angola. I do not have the money to stay in your hotel so I was wondering if you would be kind enough to let me put my tent up in the grounds.'

'Um ... the rally arrives here tomorrow. They will be staying with us.' He was obviously proud of the fact. 'And you are?'

'I am British, on a rally of my own. I have just come down through your rainforests in the north.'

'Yes. I see. You know we do not normally allow this, but I expect we can make an exception ... just this once. You can stay, but only for a few days.' He turned to a junior member of staff and, probably not realising that I understood French, said, 'Make sure he puts the tent where it can't be seen.'

That proved to be at the bottom of a stairwell next to the boiler room. It was stiflingly hot, mosquito infested and extremely noisy. *Things could be worse Jonny, it's dry and free, you're in Pointe Noire and the rally is expected tomorrow.* I was asleep soon after midnight.

The Holiday
11.45 a.m. June 7th

The rich scent of the cypress trees, mixing with the hard earth and wild thyme in an invisible mist of olfactory wonder, hung in the scorching air. The narrow road ran down the hill away from a group of small, honey-coloured dwellings where three old men in black caps and pale shirts sat quietly drinking, past a larger farmhouse and on towards the sea. Where the gradient levelled out and the road swung sharply to the right to mirror the coastline, a dirt track, partially obscured by two pines, branched off to the left. It was not much wider than us, certainly no room for more than one vehicle and controlling the little bike with two of us on board was not easy. With the deal for the band still stuck with the lawyers, we'd nipped off to Greece for a week's holiday.

At the end of the track was a ramshackle taverna built of dark wood and whitewashed concrete blocks with a few wooden tables in front of it shaded by tatty parasols. We alighted from the bike and sat down in their shade, facing the sea which was less than thirty yards away. Even though it was almost midday there was no one else waiting for lunch yet.

'Arrh, good morning my friends,' came a voice from the back of the

building, 'you want the same as yesterday?' I turned to see Nikos, the establishment's fat owner, emerge from the shadows carrying a bottle of Greek rosé. He was a warm, friendly man, somewhere in his mid-fifties, with a bald head and many chins that practically obscured the knot of his tie. Having picked up two glasses he approached our table, his face split with a welcoming grin.

'Thanks, Nikos, and two sandwiches please.'

He put down the glasses on the table and started to pour. 'I am afraid that today you may not be so lucky with your little beach.' He gave me a wink and moved the bottle to fill the other glass. On registering the question in my eyes he went on, 'Yes, it is true. I am sorry to say that a French couple went off in that direction about half an hour ago. Of course they may not find it, but you did, so they might.'

'Damn,' said Mel, 'but that's our beach, Nikos, they can't go there.'

Nikos laughed, 'Well, don't worry so much, they may not stay too long – it is hot now, they will be gone by two I think.' He wandered back into the shadows towards the kitchen.

We were a little disappointed. Since stumbling across the small horseshoe cove at the beginning of the week we had been there every day – even when it had rained – and had seen no one else. We had come to think of it as our beach.

'Let's take the wine and the sandwiches and go and check it out,' I said, taking her hand. 'If they're not there we'd better take it over before someone else does and if they are . . . well, there's room for four of us I'm sure.'

Having re-corked the bottle, emptied our glasses and collected the food, we walked down towards the sea. To the right the beach ran uninterrupted for more than a mile. The far end, in front of a complex of villas and hotels, was crowded with tourists, but to the left, a few yards from where we were, the beach ended abruptly in a wall of rocks some twenty feet high. I settled the small, cotton rucksack on my back and started to climb, giving Mel my hand to help her. It was easy if you found the right route and soon we were over the ridge and onto an uneven plateau which ran for fifty feet.

As we got closer to the far edge, where the rocks fell away to the sea and the cove, we became aware of sounds of passion. I smiled to Mel and, crouching down, put my finger to my lips. We reached the edge and, hiding ourselves behind a high rock, looked down. Right in the middle of the little beach with the sun streaming down on their naked bodies and the clear blue sea just reaching their ankles, the couple were locked together. We watched and waited. It was more than an hour before they left for lunch.

We finished the wine and followed their example.

158

After waking, stiff from the hard concrete floor, I went to the bank where I was relieved to find a Mastercard sign stuck to the inside of the door. They gave me one hundred pounds at a terrible rate but at least I now had enough money to get me to South Africa. At the docks I discovered that the ship which was to ferry the rally would not arrive for another day and would leave the day after that. Everyone assumed I was taking part – it seemed my bike gave me clearance to go anywhere I liked. I set about trying to find the right person to ask for a lift.

All the teams' back-up personnel were dotted around the town wearing their sponsors' brightly coloured clothing. Seeing hundreds of smartly dressed Europeans was quite a contrast to what I'd become used to. The yellow team of Camel-Citroën sent me in one direction, only for the blue and red Rothman-Mitsubishi personnel to send me back again. At the Novotel, where things were starting to hot up in preparation for the arrival of the rally in town that afternoon, a member of the red Yamaha team sent me to the airport where there was a press conference happening.

On the runway two Hercules transport planes sat resting along with a couple of helicopters and various light aircraft. I shuddered to think how much this little jaunt from Paris to the Cape was costing.

In the airport terminal, which amounted to not much more than a small brick shack, I found a friendly Swiss official who told me that the press conference was over. If I wanted a lift on the ship, which she thought would be no problem, I would have to ask a girl called Sylvie Chevaleaux of T.S.O., the organisers. I found her a little before lunchtime at the Novotel. It was almost droll that this young girl had the power to make my life simple or hard, safe or dangerous. Since nothing had been easy so far I had no reason to think it would change now.

'Mademoiselle, j'ai une problème . . .' and I explained my predicament in as charming a manner as possible. She was really quite pretty but for some reason saw fit to hide half her face behind giant, plastic-rimmed, personality specs.

'Oui, m'sieur, c'est possible. There is room on the boat but the problem is one of security; you have not been passed.'

'Well, I could of course give you my passport and keys.'

'Oui, but this might be a problem. I will have to inform you later.'

'D'accord, merci.' There was nothing further I could add.

Tired of the hustle of the hotel, I headed for the beach. In the car-park children cheered and asked for my autograph. I obliged and let some of them sit on the bike. A TV camera crew, convinced I was a competitor, chased me down the street as I made my way out of town.

It was the first time I'd seen the sea since that miserable night in Tunis over 7,000 miles ago. It was pleasing to be near it again. Three children danced and played in the water. They would creep up on the sea, treading gingerly on the sand as the water retreated to the ocean and then flee, with peals of excited laughter, as it turned and advanced towards them. Further off two large women ran, fully clothed, straight into the foam, submerging themselves in the surf. Their thin cotton dresses clung to their extravagant bodies like vacuum-packed sausages. The sun was high and more than a match for the few audacious clouds which tried to cross its path, and the beach, which was clean but dull, ran as far as the eye could see in both directions. Far out on the horizon a row of oil platforms stood like metal monsters.

I somehow doubted the rally organisers would let me join them. They were evidently quite uninterested in my exploits and all seemed terribly self-important. Did *I* want to go with them? Did I really want to be escorted round Angola purely because of rumours and speculation? Wasn't that cheating? Originally I had said I wanted to drive to Cape Town, only banning myself from air travel, surface being okay. But it was adventure I'd wanted. If I was to ship my way around danger every time it arose, the point of the journey would be lost. Mind you, perhaps the choice wouldn't be mine. I would have to wait and see.

At four in the afternoon the first of the vehicles came roaring into town, watched by excited spectators, TV crews and police. Yellow baffle-free Citroëns, flames extruding from their exhausts, proceeded noisily down the main street. It was all a spectacle for the local residents as the race section had been completed thirty miles back. That morning they had left Ntente in Gabon 350 miles to the north but, as is always the case in such events, only a certain section is timed to determine the position of the competitors. A few minutes later came the bikes, their drivers looking more like astronauts than sportsmen – I was pleased to see how many were riding Yamahas.

Rather unexpectedly, but making no less a spectacle of itself, the bikes were followed by an ambulance, siren wailing and lights flashing: there had been an accident. One of the Yamaha team riders had been killed in a cruelly ironic way. Having finished the timed section in fourth place, looking set for a medal overall, he had come round a corner and driven straight into a medical van, apparently killing himself outright. A German biker had also had a bad accident earlier in the day, rupturing a kidney. Amazingly, he had continued for another twenty miles before fainting and falling. He was flown out by one of the helicopters and was thought to be okay. So far, three competitors had died, and of the 337 vehicles that had left Paris, only 142 would arrive in Pointe Noire.

Darkness was closing in as I made my way back to the hotel. Inside the lobby teams huddled in groups discussing the day's performance as they waited for their representative to check them in. I felt strangely alien. I knew none of these people but it felt like I should. Some were bike riders, others were mechanics or organisers; all were European and many my age. I wanted to go up to some of them and say, 'Hi, how was it today? How's the bike holding out? What was Gabon like?' But I couldn't. They were in a world of their own, concerned with nothing other than the race. I hadn't had to talk to a total stranger from my culture for quite some time, and now that I wanted to, I lacked the self-confidence. Perhaps it was me who was in a world of his own. Why should they be thinking of anything other than the race, after all that was what they were here for? Again I wondered if I really wanted to go with them. Maybe I'd be better off getting out of this strange, expensive hotel, away from these people whose hearts and minds were on a path a million miles from my own. I stood at the desk and talked to one of the receptionists, waiting to spot Sylvie Chevaleaux.

Eventually she appeared, looking a little harassed, with an older man by her side. He was about forty-five with fine brown hair hanging down over his ears, as if to make up for what was lacking on top. His grey, beady eyes were closely set and his nose was too big for his face. He too looked far from relaxed – I knew I had no chance. *Ah well, here goes.*

'Bonsoir, Sylvie, do you have an answer for me?'

'Ah, pardon.' She turned to the man, Monsieur Saben, who was the chief organiser, and explained my predicament.

'Quoi?' he said incredulously when she had finished; it was as though I had just asked to fuck his wife. 'Oh, c'est impossible. Impossible.'

'But I could give you my passport and keys,' I persisted. 'Angola is supposed to be very dangerous at the moment.'

'Non, m'sieur, c'est impossible . . . sécurité.'

'Security? What do you mean security?'

'You have not been passed.'

Passed? This is the bloody Congo, not Paris. Do you really think I've driven all the way from England just so that I can put sugar in some Kawasaki petrol tanks?

'You would represent a risk, m'sieur,' Saben went on, answering my questioning eyes. 'We do not know who you are. Sorry, but it is not my problem.' *I know it's not your problem, it's my problem and I'm asking for some help. Christ, if anyone here represents the spirit of the Paris–Le Cap rally it's me. What the hell would you know about risk.* I stood looking at this Gucci-clad lounge-lizard for a moment and then at Sylvie who had turned away embarrassed. It was no good, I could see he would not budge. *Well then, I'll damn well do it without your help.*

'D'accord.' I walked away enraged.

The bar was crowded but the beer was cold; I found an empty seat in the corner. I knew I should not be too hard on Saben. Presumably he had his rules and was not prepared to break them for me. But isn't that just it: in our world – the Western one – we've almost forgotten a thing called trust. Everyone must be up to something and nobody is prepared to take the chance that some of us, indeed most of us, are not. The lines are drawn and cannot be bent. In Africa the very opposite is true. People will bend over backwards to help without any knowledge of the person they are helping. Everyone is trustworthy until they prove themselves otherwise.

After the second or third beer my melancholy thoughts were interrupted by some young men sitting at the table next to me. They were English and discussing the two crashes of the day. With the beers inside me I felt more confident.

'Do you mind if I join you?'

'No, no, please, sit down.'

They were four journalists. Three from various motor magazines and Jeremy Bowden from the *Telegraph*.

'Is that your bike outside?' asked Jeremy, a good-looking thirty-year-old with tight curly hair. 'The one with the English number plate.'

'Yep. It is.'

'And you've driven it from London?'

I nodded. We talked for a while about my trip, the route I'd taken and about the rally. It was good to be chatting in English again and to people similar to myself. Then Jeremy asked, 'So where are you going from here? You've about run into a dead end, I think.'

'Well, almost, but I was lucky, in Brazzaville they gave me an Angolan visa, so I'll hit Cabinda tomorrow.'

'Lucky!' He looked amazed. 'You have heard about the shootings?'

'Shootings? No . . . why . . . who's been shot?' I usually prided myself on knowing what was going on. The BBC World Service with its *Focus on Africa* was a constant source of enlightenment, but since arriving in Pointe Noire I had not listened to my radio once.

'Yesterday, four English travellers were shot and killed while trying to get through Angola.'

I looked down at my beer, stunned. He carried on, 'We don't know where or by whom, only that it was somewhere in the south. They think they were the first travellers into the country.' He could see my concern. 'If I was you I'd try and get on the boat with us. It'll be bloody dangerous now . . . especially on your own.'

'I've already asked Monsieur Saben: he said no. Do you think he knew about this?'

'Of course, we were all told this morning. When did you ask?'

'Half an hour ago.' *Bastard.*

We drank and talked a while longer but one by one they left for showers or a change of clothes, leaving me to contemplate this major piece of news. I was now confused, partly through drink and partly through the fear of doom the others had put into me.

Was it worth the risk? I tried to think. To be killed in

Angola? Shot dead on a scrubby mountain side? Or should I turn round as they had urged. I could fly out of the Congo and persuade Amel to spend the rest of the winter with me in Paris. I could go to Kenya or drive back another way; there was still northern Zaire. But could I? The stakes had been raised but the journey's importance, I now realised, was greater than ever. It had taken on a new dimension, threatening the very person I perceived myself to be. What began as a journey to pack up my pain and troubles and drive them into adventure and out of my system had changed into something greater. Africa had become a challenge, a way of discovering a core belief in myself, of proving I was who I thought I was. To succeed I must ride to Cape Town. If I were to turn round now and give up it would be a foretaste of the rest of my life. I might always take the easy way, bottle out and give up, but, if I were to continue and triumph, surely then I could do anything. As I stood in the gents, staring into my hazy eyes reflected in the mirror, I knew that this was it. I could not go back.

14 Tourist Number Two
Cabinda, Angola

Emerald hills and cane fields cascaded down to the ocean's edge where breakers kissed the virgin beach. Thin, dark wooden pirogues sat in line like the black keys of a giant piano while two small children played on the sand. The sun was high and the sky clear. Something seemed to be saying 'Forget the Congo, forget the rally. You're the lucky one . . . this is Cabinda'.

In front of me, at a check-point, a blue Nissan stopped and a young man in his late twenties jumped out. There was a conversation in Portuguese, the young man occasionally pointing back in my direction. After a couple of minutes, smiling at me, he got back into the car and the soldiers waved us through. I passed Angolan customs, again having to show the soldiers how and where to stamp my documents, to find the young man waiting for me. He introduced himself as Fernando and treated me as though his very life depended on making my time in Cabinda run as smoothly as possible.

'You must follow me to town,' he shouted over the crowd which had gathered round the bike. His English was excellent. 'You must stay close behind. We will not go fast. The town is about an hour away.'

Small villages of quixotic Portuguese architecture enhanced the beauty of this forgotten paradise – though only from afar. As I got closer I saw that the large white mansions and elegantly steepled churches were peppered with the ugly scars of war. Plaster, torn from the houses, lay in heaps on the deserted streets, shutters hung limply from a single hinge, the windows had no glass and political graffiti, demanding Cabindan independence, decorated the surviving walls.

Leaving his friend to concentrate on the driving, Fernando talked us through each of the army road blocks and, as promised, within the hour we arrived in Cabinda Town.

By far the most important thing on my mind was getting to the port. I had to find out about a boat to take me the thirty

165

miles round the mouth of the Congo river, which separates the northern enclave from its southern parent. Fernando had other ideas. Our first call was to be on the police followed by the local television station. Who was I to argue?

As we drove through the centre of town the contrasts brought about by oil were apparent. Looking one way, across a grassy square, the affluence was unmistakable. I could see a tall Fina building and a DHL office with a Toyota Landcruiser in the car-park behind. The wide, well-conditioned streets were lined with European-style bungalows. The pavements were shaded by mango and fig trees and purple bougainvillaea sprawled across the mottled walls. But out across the bay the rusting roofs of the shanty towns glinted in the sun, their crumbling mud walls home for most Cabindans. It was mid-afternoon and the heat had increased appreciably. There was no one around.

The police station looked more like a middle-class home than a place to hold criminals. It was a deep green, wooden house on a leafy side street with two Russian-made cars parked outside. The visit didn't take long. The Chief was so surprised at seeing me that he called all his staff to the windows to have a look.

'You are only the second tourist to Cabinda,' he said while studying my passport.

'For how long?' I asked, a certain pride in my voice.

'For how long?' he chuckled. 'For ever. We had a Brazilian here last year . . . he was on a bicycle. But that is all.'

The second tourist ever, that was really something . . . but I couldn't help thinking how nice it would have been to be the first. . . . *Maybe if I could manage to drive all the way round Africa and back to London I might have a first. Yes, I bet no one's done that, at least on this route.* The thought excited me. I smiled and shook the Chief's hand.

Ten minutes later we pulled up outside a yellow-walled building opposite the school. Fernando jumped from his car like a bodyguard looking after royalty.

'Come, we will go and see them.'

It was refreshingly cool inside the glass-fronted TV station. A receptionist sitting behind a desk asked us to wait while she telephoned through. We sat on two sofas divided by a coffee table.

Fernando carried a serious expression most of the time, his

dark eyes were sunk deep in his head and his skin was badly scarred by smallpox but it was obvious he was extremely kind. He was the English teacher at the school across the way. I was thankful to have met him.

A short man came through a door behind the reception desk and introduced himself as head of programming. Fernando had to translate. Yes, they would be very pleased to interview me if I wouldn't mind waiting five minutes. I didn't, so we did. Ten minutes later he reappeared with a taller man carrying a large video camera.

'We will do the interview outside,' the boss said excitedly. 'With the motor bike, it will be better.'

On the street an extraordinary transformation had taken place. The road, which had been totally deserted not ten minutes back, was now thick with children. Hundreds of them blocked the road, hustling for position round the bike. Evidently Fernando's school had been let out.

'He wants you to drive round the block so that they can film you arriving,' Fernando said, at last allowing himself a smile as the children closed ranks around us. 'He will then ask you some questions which I will translate. Then you will go again.'

'I'll try, Fernando, but it won't be easy with all these kids.'

'I will tell them to keep out of your way.' And with that he bellowed an instruction in Portuguese which caused the crowd to open and allow me through.

I did as I was told. I drove round the block, up the street into the mass of bodies standing round the camera, and came to a halt. The interviewer asked such questions as how far had I been? When had I left? What did I eat? Did I have a wife back in England? Why was I doing it? What had I learnt? (To this I answered 'Don't believe all you are told until you have seen it for yourself' . . . *Bonne route indeed!*) What countries had I seen? And what did I think of Cabinda?

The ages of the children stretched from about four to sixteen years old and hundreds of bright eyes watched me closely. A particularly cute little boy, no more than five, chewing on a stick of sugar cane, stood at my side. He clung with his free hand to my trousers and each time I was asked a question he pulled gently, seeking my attention. I answered the questions as accurately as possible, stating, truthfully, that Cabinda was the most beautiful place I'd seen so far.

167

The filming concluded, the interviewer shook my hand and then said something to Fernando, who again translated: 'He says it has been a pleasure to interview you – the tourist number two.'

I turned on the engine, making many of the children leap out of their skins, and pulled away. Far from staying where it was, this time the crowd, in a frenzy, charged down the street behind me. Cheering and waving they danced with excitement, flailing their hands, clapping and singing; I felt like the Pied Piper. Bit by bit the multitude turned to a trickle and, as I hit the main road where Fernando had told me to wait, it petered out completely. I was truly moved. It was a wonderful feeling to bring entertainment to so many people. Still, in a country where tourists come around less often than Halley's comet, it was not, I suppose, a surprising reaction. Tourist number two . . . I liked that.

Much to my relief, all went smoothly at the docks. Via a three-way conversation I gathered from the Chef du Port that the twice-weekly boat was leaving in the morning for Soyo, the northern point of the mainland, and, if I wanted, I could have a lift. The next boat would be leaving four days later and although I had hoped to stay a day or two in Cabinda I could not afford to spend four. A price was worked out and I left.

By this stage I had gathered quite an entourage. Fernando and his friend now had an armed policeman on their back seat, followed by two customs men, three from immigration, one of the Russian police cars containing two officers and the Chef du Port – four cars, a moped and me. We finally arrived at a hotel on the beach, and seeing a thatched circular bar I thought it was only right that I should offer them all a beer. Although I was one of only two tourists to have seen this beautiful enclave I could quite clearly hear Madonna's voice echoing from a tape-recorder somewhere down the beach. Fernando changed me some money and, as the sun disappeared, we sat and drank.

'Was the war as bad here as it was on the mainland, Fernando?'

'The war was bad everywhere,' he said, looking out across the sea. On the far horizon excess gases from the oil platforms burned like Olympic torches. Darkness was falling quickly. 'But it is true it was worse in the south.'

168

'And now,' I asked, 'is it safe? Why do you think those English people were killed?'

'No one knows why they were killed or by whom. This country will not be safe for years – there are still many problems. These people I think they drive at night. This is not good. But you can get through . . . if you take good care.' He took a swig of beer then added with a wry smile, 'And if you have luck. But I think you have this. I am a Christian. I think God is with you.'

Although I was thankful for his optimism and belief in divine assistance, I was unconvinced.

'I wish I spoke some Portuguese; it would be useful in a bad situation.'

'I will write a letter for you to show the police and military. It will not be perfect but it may be better than nothing.'

The rest of the gang finished their beers and departed. A large, drunk, laughing woman brought us a leg of chicken each, some sweet potatoes and another beer. Cicadas buzzed and mosquitoes started to bite.

'What about Cabinda,' I asked, once we'd finished, 'will she get her independence?'

'I hope, but I do not think so.' He looked sad. 'You see, Cabinda is very rich. We have many diamonds, we have minerals in the hills and,' pointing out to sea, 'we have the oil. If we were independent we would have very much money and all our problems would be over. We could built better schools, we could have better hospitals and better homes. You have seen yourself how beautiful it is. We could have tourism. But as it is at the moment all the money goes to Luanda and we see nothing. They will never let us go, they would lose too much.' I knew he was right. The crude oil from the offshore drilling around Cabinda and Soyo accounts for nearly ninety per cent of Angola's export earnings. They would never give that up. 'But this is not your problem my friend.' He forced a smile onto his thoughtful face. 'Come. We will keep my class waiting if we do not go soon.'

'Your class?'

'Oh yes, did I not tell you? I have told my top English class you will give them a talk. They have never met an Englishman before.'

The classroom was much like any other: twenty or so desks, arranged in rows of five, with a table and chair in front of a square blackboard. A map of the world hung on one wall while a poster of Big Ben and the Houses of Parliament was stuck to another. There were equal numbers of well-dressed boys and girls, all aged about sixteen.

I had never done anything like this before and wasn't sure quite what to say or where to start. They looked at me expectantly. I began to recount my trip . . . They were attentive and interested. They were shocked at the correct times and laughed in the right places. I kept it short and simple, using the map on the wall to illustrate my route. Fernando sat in the corner looking proud – of me or of his pupils I was not sure.

After about fifteen minutes something crashed to the floor at the back of the class. An embarrassed boy in a short-sleeved blue shirt scrambled around and eventually came up with a transistor radio, an ear-piece attached. Everyone laughed. All, that is, except Fernando. Being on this side of the teacher's table was an unfamiliar situation for me – at school I was usually the embarrassed boy. I had been kicked out of many a lesson for listening to a test match or football game and he had my sympathy.

'What's on the radio?' I asked.

'Oh, it is a basketball match,' he said sheepishly, his eyes darting between Fernando and me, wondering no doubt how much trouble he was in. 'Between Angola and Sierra Leone. It is the African Championships.'

'Who's winning?' I asked.

'Angola, 77–73.' The class let out a unified whoop of pleasure. 'It only two minute to go.' I corrected his English and added, 'Then perhaps we should all listen. I can imagine how important this is.'

Fernando didn't seem to mind. I expect he was as interested as the rest of them. So the boy, whose name was Miguel, brought the radio up to the table.

The commentary was in Portuguese and had to compete with a lot of static but it was obvious that things were very close. By now, so Miguel translated, Sierra Leone had come back to 77–75. The classroom was quiet, then Angola scored, two more points, and the students cheered. One more minute to go Angola leading 79–75, then disaster. Sierra Leone was awarded a penalty – meaning they got two free shots at the basket. They got the first, closing the gap to two points. All was quiet but for the metallic fizz of the radio. The second, worth one point . . .

scored. The atmosphere inside the room was electric. Angola was now winning by only a single point with about forty seconds on the clock. Fortunately they didn't need it. They scored twice more to run out comfortable winners. Both scores were greeted with shouts of joy; I couldn't help joining in.

This rather deflated the mood of the rest of my talk and I cut it as short as possible. In the question period at the end the children seemed more interested in Gary Lineker than they were in my tales.

15 The Angolan Princess

Cabinda Town, Angola

The Angolan Princess was a shabby old tub. A grandiloquent name indeed for a vessel in a bad state of repair with more rust than paint. She was flat-bottomed, about thirty feet long, carrying amidships a single funnel high enough to reach just above the forward cabin and out of which black smoke continually belched. She reeked of age and decay, but also carried a certain charm and, after all, what did it matter what she looked like so long as she delivered me safely to Soyo.

The day was grey. A thin fog hung over the sea, muffling all colour and sound. The gentle breeze blowing off the ocean carried with it a hint of impending rain. I stood with the Chef du Port and Fernando at the end of an L-shaped jetty, looking down at the boat.

'How long will it take?' I asked.

'Oh, about four hours,' answered the Chef. 'It is not far, but this boat is not fast.' He chuckled to himself. 'Not fast but reliable, it has been doing this journey for more than thirty years.' That I could believe.

To our right, two old navy frigates, second-hand favours from a defunct Soviet backer, their hulls and guns looking tired and out of date, bobbed up and down in the grey water. At the end of the jetty next to them stood a crane. Its one long arm circled round and lowered its heavy chain to hang over the bike. We found a thick net, wheeled the bike onto it and secured the four corners to the hook. Making sure nothing was trapped I watched with trepidation as my best friend was lifted up into the air, swung round over the ocean and lowered safely onto the back end of the boat.

Fernando took a letter out of his back pocket. In it he stated that I was a harmless tourist and should therefore be given all the help and protection anyone reading the letter could give me. I was thankful to him for making the effort but quite how much good it would be I wasn't sure. I fancied the soldiers would look at it and say 'Fernando who?' Still, it was better than nothing.

I shook his hand, thanked him for everything and climbed down into the boat. Dock workers loaded up the stern with hessian sacks of mealie flour and salt which the other five passengers used for seats. I lit a cigarette and waited for the off. It didn't come. I'd had no breakfast that morning and I began to feel very hungry. Along with about thirty others on the jetty above us, Fernando sat doing nothing but watching us watching them and waiting for the cast-off. He had done so much for me already I really didn't want to ask another favour but in the end my stomach overcame my conscience.

'Fernando,' I asked, 'is there anywhere near here you can get me some bread?'

'I don't think so but I will try.'

Ten minutes later he was back with three cans of drink, six bananas, a packet of stale biscuits and four small bread rolls. No matter how hard I insisted, he would accept no payment.

'No, you are my guest. It is my mission.'

As he waved farewell, when we did finally leave, the Christian spirit that shone from his face was a lesson to me. His unselfishness and goodwill are characteristics seldom met with in the West. The longer I travelled through Africa the more aware I became of the generosity and kindness of its people. Poor in material wealth, their richness of spirit was a revelation.

In Soyo I headed for the only hotel in town. When I reached a large pair of steel gates in a high wire-mesh fence I wondered if I had followed the directions I'd been given correctly. This was a compound on a mammoth scale. A metal barrier at the gatehouse barred the entrance but not the exit. As there was no one manning it I decided to take a closer look at what I was now sure was an oil complex.

Perfect asphalt roads, lit up by orange street lamps ran between immaculate grass lawns. The rows of bungalows and the other large buildings seemed to glow in the crepuscular light. Some way off, towards the sea, the industrial side of the plant was situated – workshops and heli-pads and huge oil containers displaying Exxon, Fina and Agip logos. I pulled up at reception next to a white UN jeep.

Inside a man sat behind a semicircular bank of lights and telephones. He looked up when I came in.

'Good evening, I have been told there's a hotel here.'

'Well . . . er . . . yes, but it's never been used by travellers. You wish to stay the night?'

'Yes, or I could put my tent up in the grounds if it is all right with you.' A UN soldier in a sky-blue beret entered the room from two swing doors behind the desk.

'I don't know,' the receptionist was saying, 'I will get someone to take you to the Chief.'

'Where are you going?' asked the soldier. He was Portuguese.

'I've just arrived from Cabinda on the boat. I am hoping to get through Angola to Namibia.'

A wry smile appeared on his face; he took a step back from the desk. 'You know the dangers I suppose?'

'Some of them,' I answered. 'No one seems to know very much . . . especially about the shootings.'

'In Angola it is hard to know anything. We think it was UNITA but it might just have been bandits or,' he threw his arms in the air, 'it could have been troops of the MPLA disguised as UNITA.' I looked confused. 'Trying to discredit them,' he explained, 'to lose them support in the elections.' I had read that the country's first elections in fifteen years were due to take place in September; these were tense times. He put his hands back on the desk. 'As I say, it is hard to tell, but my guess would be UNITA. There is some talk of them starting an offensive. If that happens . . . ugh . . . I hope for your mother's sake you are out of this country. It is no place for the tourist.'

The receptionist returned with another man.

'Pierre will take you to see the Chief.'

We found the Chief with some friends in one of the bungalows. When the door opened I noticed a half-finished bottle of J&B on the table.

'Of course you may stay.' He was French, about forty and obviously much the better for the whisky. 'Pierre, give this man a room in the hotel and some meal tickets. If you have driven this far it is the least we can do. But where are you going?' he looked puzzled, his eyes not quite in focus.

'South Africa.'

'Mon Dieu. But you know this is crazy. It is very dangerous. Only four days ago . . .'

'Yes, yes, I know . . .' I interrupted, but it didn't stop him

174

putting the fear of God into me for a full five minutes. In the end he clasped me by the hand.

'You have much courage my friend. Anything in the mini-bar is yours. Please enjoy yourself and bonne chance, bonne chance.' He certainly restored my faith in Frenchmen: what a contrast to Monsieur Saben. Though I wasn't sure if my courage was as strong as he thought.

The room was fabulous. I helped myself to a vodka and had a steaming hot shower. Pierre returned with tickets for dinner and breakfast and offered to take my clothes to the laundry – worrying that they might fall to pieces in a washing machine, I declined the offer. In the canteen I had roast beef and Yorkshire pudding followed by crême caramel. I felt like a condemned man being given his final meal. A rotund little Geordie called Steve, who'd seen my bike, came over and invited me to the compound bar. I found it bizarre: here I was in a Western bar in Angola drinking Heineken beer and playing pool with my own country-men. A European oasis in the middle of darkest Africa.

'It's amazing,' Steve said, after hearing a brief account of my journey.

'Well, thanks . . . but I don't like the sound of the next bit.'

'Aye,' he said, pushing a hand through his thinning hair, 'maybe Jan here can help you. His ship runs from here to Luanda, he might give you a lift.'

Jan was a Dutch Glaswegian whose English was almost incomprehensible. His ship would be going to Luanda on Tuesday, but it was now Thursday, longer than I could wait.

'Boot ya don' wonna cume on ma' boat, ya cume thes far, ya'll meck et. Ya gotta teck sume resks ain't ya?'

'Aye,' said Steve again, evidently used to his mate's drawl, 'you'll do it. I bloody know you will. Just take care and trust no one.'

I went to bed drunk and confused. If UNITA did launch a new campaign, my journey would almost certainly be suicide. My route went right through their heartland and if my luckless compatriots had been killed by them they could kill me just as easily. There were bound to be check-points – should I stop or drive through them? But if, on the other hand, the troublemakers were simply bandits I had every chance of getting through. The other travellers might just have been in the wrong place at the wrong time. My problem was lack of information. I was asleep before I could reach a conclusion.

Outside the compound there was little evidence of oil wealth. A crumbling asphalt road ran out of the town through decaying streets and tired homes. It wove its way through low barren hills, the rusty earth peppered with scrubby bush and thorn trees. After fifteen minutes the tarmac died and left a rough dirt track cut like a channel through the coarse vegetation. It was hot and overcast.

I had been given directions by an African at the camp. 'You will come to a T-junction, you must turn right then straight on. Straight on all the way.' How many times had I heard that before? The first part of the information was accurate but had I gone 'straight on all the way' I would, within a few minutes, have ended up in the Atlantic ocean. African 'straight ons' normally involve a few T-junctions and forks: all I could do was follow my nose. I knew that if I drove south for one hundred miles close to the sea, with the sun on my left, I would eventually come to N'zeto, the town where the road starts again.

The track I chose soon became a footpath of deep white sand. Short pine trees pressed in around me and the wheels struggled to grip. I came to a gathering of creosoted wooden huts, some lived in, others burnt out. At one a young man turned and fled at the sight of me, obviously fearing for his life. And why shouldn't he? For the last twenty years, indeed for all his life, he'd been hiding from strangers who might turn out to be killers. So why stop now, just because two people had signed a peace accord in a foreign city many miles away, to him as worthless as any scrap of paper. I had wanted to check the route but no one would come near me. I pushed on.

The track widened. It was now firm and straight, evidently the right one. I passed through another village where giant palms swayed in the breeze that came gliding up off the sea. Thatched mud and wattle huts separated the track from the long white beach which ran parallel to my path. Tethered goats bleated and scuffed the earth while their owners stared from doorways with wary eyes.

After an hour I came to the first of two natural obstacles I'd been warned about. It was a river, thirty metres wide. The bridge, blown up in the war, had not yet been mended.

176

I waded down the gentle slope into the water which soon rose above my waist. It was too deep for the bike to drive through: I would have to find another solution. It presented itself almost immediately in the form of a crowd of young men who, after a little persuasion, rallied to the cry and came over to help. Ten of the largest and strongest lifted the bike to shoulder height and walked it into the water. Children, too small to help, insisted on carrying something: a boot, my helmet, my sleeping bag. One little boy swam with one hand while holding my goggles aloft with the other. In the middle the water came up to the young men's chests but laughing and chanting, with me wading beside them, they marched across and up the bank on the far side.

The track continued along the beach where a herd of cattle wandered on the sand. Twenty humpbacked cows with drooping horns and soft folds of skin under their necks, moved lethargically at the water's edge. A young boy carrying a stick neglected his drove and stared out to sea. The waves rolled in and the hazy sun climbed. This was as old a tropical paradise as I'd ever seen.

By early afternoon I'd reached the second bridgeless river. This time it was wider and deeper, an estuary that reached the sea only a few yards away. Drooping palms sprouted at acute angles from the thin soil and battered wooden fishing boats rested on the sandbanks, their nets drying in the breeze. A queue of vehicles had built up on either side of the estuary and crowds of anxious people waited.

I had been told that there was a barge here to ferry the vehicles across, but that the man in charge was completely unreliable. I was lucky, for evidently today he was working. It was a large flat-bottomed yellow platform and was secured by metal ropes to the other side. I was immediately set upon by an inquisitive group who packed in around me so tightly that I could barely dismount. A man in a peaked cap sent me to the front; I could go with the next crossing.

Two large green trucks moved down the ramp onto the barge, and I pulled in behind. What space wasn't taken up by the vehicles was quickly seized by people. They were a dishevelled, poorly dressed group and carried their possessions in large bundles which they now used for seats. The more fortunate ones had a goat, a chicken or a sack of corn to sell in N'zeto on the other side. Many had heard of the possible new offensive and were looking for safety in the town. Most had already been displaced several times by the fighting.

Once across, I reported to the MPLA barracks. It took an hour to see all the right people, none of whom seemed quite sure what I was doing there, but all were cordial. 'You should stay here tonight and go on in the morning,' they said, but I decided that three o'clock was too early to stop.

The road was thin, crumbling at the edges, and with vicious pot-holes every few yards. It cut through a dry land of thorn trees, coarse grass, chalk-white boulders and termite mounds. Large brown eagles glided on the thermals high above, their shadows crossing my own as they swooped down low looking for food. A dark snake slithered across my path, the front wheel clipping its rubbery tail. I jerked my right leg out of the way of its lethal reaction and glanced in the rear-view mirror. The front third of the snake was bolt upright, its deadly, diamond-shaped head heaving with anger: a cobra. There were no villages and no people; the only living beings were either slithering on their bellies or circling the skies. It was a land accustomed to death.

It was now late afternoon and away to the west the sky began to darken and a warm wind blew off the sea. I was heading for the port of Ambriz, sixty miles to the south, but the road was slow. I started to go faster, concentrating hard to miss the holes, some of which were so big and deep they must have been formed by landmines.

Up ahead, a mile or so in the distance, I noticed a plume of dust. As I got closer I saw that it was made by two trucks packed with people and goods. I could not sit in their wake as the stones they threw up peppered me in the usual way. I moved out to the side, found a clear route and zipped past the rear one while the people on top waved and shouted. As I came alongside the leader it veered sharply to avoid a pot-hole and almost knocked me off my bike. I fell back blinded by the dust and waited to try again. The truck moved over to the left giving me a glimpse of the road ahead and, pulling back on the throttle, I took the chance. I had failed to mend the horn so could still only flash my lights in a vain attempt to let the driver know I was coming through. It seemed to work for within a second my sight was restored as I moved up alongside and eventually past the laden truck. A passenger in the front had a gun. I accelerated down the clear track.

Then the road just stopped; as suddenly as if I'd come to

178

a bridgeless river, a void or chasm. I was no doubt going too fast and must have lost my concentration after the strain of passing the lorries. It was too late to take evasive action, I simply had to accept I was on a collision course with a mine crater. The front wheel fell over the edge and spurred on by momentum, raced up and out the other side; it was as though I'd taken a ski-jump. Suddenly I was flying. Everything went quiet and time slowed to half-speed. I could hear the exaggerated beat of my heart and see the sky. 'You prick, Jonny,' I thought as I flew through the air, 'how many times have you told yourself, when you're tired at the end of the day, slow down, don't speed up.' I lost contact with the bike and seemed to be freefalling towards the ground which I eventually hit with such force that the wind was knocked from my lungs. The bike skidded along the road beside me.

The Near-Miss
11.50 a.m. June 20th

Junction five of the M4 looped round in a large arch, rising steadily to join an elevated section of the M25. The concrete walls and pillars seemed to merge in the dull June day, only the bright blue signs and coloured chevrons standing out. I pulled the car into the inside filter lane and indicated my intention to join the flow heading south. It was Sunday, about midday, a time not normally associated with traffic congestion, but the London orbital had scant regard for such things: a constant stream of cars, coaches and lorries sped along – a three-lane traffic jam travelling at over seventy miles an hour. I moved onto the motorway and then into the faster-moving middle lane. The MGB was an old car and seventy-five was quite fast enough, besides we were in no hurry, the cricket match was not due to start until two.

The springs in the passenger seat had almost entirely gone, which left Mel struggling to see out of the window. Before she passed her driving test it never seemed to bother her but ever since she had insisted on sitting up and checking how I was doing. But now she sat contentedly, listening to the music while I, a little preoccupied with the worry of still not signing the band's deal, concentrated on driving.

We both enjoyed these cricket days, though I suppose I was the one who pushed for them. If the weather wasn't too bad and there were friends to chat to while we were out fielding, Mel did not get too bored. The Rascals, our team, had been formed a couple of years earlier by a good friend who,

179

very sadly, had since died. We played on partly in his memory and partly because we loved the game and it was fun meeting up with friends outside London at the weekends. Generally we played in Tunbridge Wells and it was there that we were heading.

The car in front of ours, a blue saloon of some sort, had slowed to seventy and I was now too close behind it. It always annoys me when a car pulls out in front only to slow up in my path and I checked my wing mirror before moving towards the outside lane to overtake. A horn blasted close up on my right. I turned my head and saw that a large black Merc had been sitting in my blind spot and I was about to hit it. I swung the wheel too far to the left causing the car to veer sharply towards the inside lane, into the path of another car. Trying to compensate I turned the wheel too far again, to the right, and the car went up on its side, on two wheels – I was out of control. Mel gripped her seat as I turned the wheel to the left again and this time the car spun. We had four wheels on the ground once more but we were now facing the wrong direction. I saw the surprised faces of the people in the car which had been behind us – they appeared to be braking. Then, a miracle. What I did or did not do at that point I cannot say but within the blink of an eye the car was back facing the right way, still doing seventy miles an hour and completely untouched.

We carried on in silence for a moment, then Mel asked me to stop. She climbed out onto the hard shoulder and threw up. I started to shake. It was hard to believe what had just happened. By all that's normal we should have been dead. Rolling an open-top sports car of that kind leaves little room for survival, especially at seventy, surrounded by other cars. There were marks on the tyres halfway up their outside walls: the car must have been nearly at forty-five degrees.

I went round to where Mel was wiping her mouth. She was white, her eyes wide open. As I threw my arms around her she started to cry.

'I really thought we were going to die,' she sobbed, her precious arms tightening round my back as she squeezed me to her.

For a moment I lay in confusion, fighting for air, wondering which parts of my body were broken. I could feel no pain; was I in shock or was I unharmed? I could hardly believe it. My breath restored, I staggered to my feet and rushed for the bike, suddenly aware that it was losing petrol. I turned off the taps and tried to right it; I could not. I tried again, air rasping through my teeth. This time I managed it. I was starting to shake. *Come on, Jonny, start the bike, let's go.* It looked undamaged. The jerry-can holders had done their job and protected the engine, and the wheels seemed to be straight, but all my strength had gone. I could hear the trucks approaching from behind. *Come on, come on, you don't know who these people might be. Pull yourself together, let's go.*

I turned the ignition key and pressed the button . . . nothing. *Get it into neutral, quickly.* I shook my head trying to regain my composure and fumbled with the gear lever . . . no light showed. I tried the button again . . . still nothing. I checked the headlights; there was no power at all. The bike was dead.

I pulled it to the edge of the road and looked up. The trucks were now coming up the hill towards me, only a hundred yards off. The sky was ominously dark with heavy clouds. The breeze stirred the dying grass. Nothing else moved save the trucks and me; the only life in this forgotten valley.

Trust no one, Steve had said, but how could I? I could hardly run and hide, they had surely seen me by now. Besides, where to? It was getting late and the last thing I wanted was to stay out here all night. That definitely would be dangerous. *Try and fix the bike, keep calm.*

I took a deep breath and crouched down to look at the electrics. *Think, Jonny, think.* I heard the first of the trucks stop ten yards from where I squatted and then the second also pulled up. Two men jumped out of the first, one carrying a Russian machine gun. Sweat dripping from my forehead stung my eyes. I wiped it away with a shaking hand. Keeping my head down I heard steps. There was a tap on my shoulder.

Towering above me like a granite statue, silhouetted by the glare of the sinking sun, was a large, fat African. He was handing me something pink, pushing it towards my face. I pulled the hair back from my eyes and saw, to my confounded amazement, a perfectly cooked lobster.

Where am I? What the hell is this? Am I really here or is this some kind of surreal nightmare? I had been so affected by the constant talk of danger, the thought that round any corner a gunman might be waiting, that for a moment I couldn't quite work out what was going on. I expected bullets not food, aggression rather than friendship. *Is this man really trying to give me a boiled lobster? Pinch yourself and wake up.* I did, and he was.

I realised that I had said nothing to this man, only stared in incomprehension. He spoke in Portuguese and again thrust the cooked crustacean towards my face. This time I thanked him but declined and got to my feet. *Turning down lobster?* I was too nervous to eat – my stomach in knots. He shrugged and turned away, tearing a large piece of rich, white flesh from the tail and putting it in his mouth.

Soon most of the thirty or so passengers from the two trucks had scrambled down and were watching me trying to fix the bike. I checked the fuel line, the wiring, the cut-out switch on the side stand and the battery connection. Nothing helped; the bike had done all the driving it was going to do that day.

A young man wearing large glasses and carrying a bundle of books was the only person to speak English. I asked him to find out if I might put my bike on the back of the truck and catch a lift. He passed on the request to Arius, the lobster-giver, who, it appeared, was also the truck driver. He slapped me on the back affectionately, mimed the lifting of the bike, and nodded enthusiastically before throwing the empty lobster shell into the bush. It took the best part of an hour to get the bike on board. To help them cope with rutted tracks, trucks in Africa are built with a much higher ground clearance than those in Europe. Consequently, hauling the bike up into the vehicle proved a mighty task. First all the manioc, pineapples, goats and chickens had to be moved forward – heaped on top of other manioc, pineapples, goats and chickens – then the top half of the tailgate let down. The bike was lifted by six men below and three above, including me, dragged it over the side and propped it against some sacks of corn. I sat on the seat of the bike, leaning against the piles of produce. With a toot of the horn we were under way.

I probably incurred more harm in the next few hours than I sustained in the crash. Sitting over the rear axle I was thrown all over the place, at some points having to hang on to a rope to stop myself being jettisoned altogether. A lot of the time we were weaving our way down the gutted road at walking pace and if we did speed up it was only a sign to hang on tighter and brace myself for more bumps and bruises.

It was nice, however, not to have to concentrate. For the first time since the train to Pointe Noire I was travelling under someone else's guidance and could enjoy what was left of the day. The sun had now reached the far horizon. It was large and orange, scratched by the scrawny leafless trees and wild grass that passed before it. As we wound our way through the folds of the valley it would disappear for a second behind a rock, casting us into refreshing shadow, only to emerge again the other side like a child playing peekaboo. Soon the hungry earth swallowed it up and the dark clouds dispersed, leaving the sky a tranquil shade of deepest blue, studded with the first smattering of stars.

Once again I was filled with an overwhelming feeling of wonder and joy. By rights I should be sick with torment. I was in a war-torn, irrational country with a broken machine and no real idea of where I was heading. But no, I was peaceful and content. Turning my eyes to the west I found the reason. A new moon was lying on its back looking down on me for the first time since the Cameroun; a tiny silver bow resting above the sunset. None of my problems seemed to matter: I was alive and heading south. Things would work out, they always did. My companion was back and, if the gods were willing, would now carry me all the way to the bottom of this exhilarating continent.

At about one thirty in the morning I spotted the lights of Caxito. There were three or four road-blocks on the way into town but as no one noticed me perched on the back, all were passed with a minimum of fuss. The streets were eerily quiet. A few lamps emitted a pale light which cast long shadows over the shabby houses and broken walls. The moon had long gone, carrying with it my euphoria. I was too tired to feel anything. All I wanted to do was get my head down and sleep.

The truck rounded a corner and entered a grassy square. It was a football pitch with badly ripped nets attached to each goal. At the far end of the square was a high wall with razor wire running along the top and an archway in the centre formed by two giant crossed sabres under which we drove. Tall lookout posts, manned by soldiers staring down from behind their automatic weapons, towered above the floodlit compound we had entered. The truck came to a halt outside a long, thin, single-storey building. It appeared to be a soldiers' mess but once I had climbed down, I realised it was a jail. Tired, scared faces appeared at cracks in the boarded-up windows. A low-pitched murmuring came from within.

'Come with us,' said Arius, 'we must see the Commandant.'

One sleepy soldier led us to another who eventually presented us to the Captain on duty. I knew his rank, not by his uniform, for he wore only shorts, but because Arius told me. We stood on a porch outside the guard house while my situation was explained. Thousands of insects circled the pale light. One rested on the Captain's chest; he flicked it away.

'You are to go with him,' Arius explained, 'he will find you a bed. Tomorrow we will mend the machine: there is a man in town who can help.'

In silence the Captain led me down a narrow corridor and into a small room. The paint was peeling from the walls and cobwebs clung to the corners of the ceiling. It was stuffy and hot and held the pungent smell of human sweat. Well-used Kalashnikovs were piled in a corner like a bundle of firewood. The light was on and a radio played. There were four bunks pressed against the walls with semi-naked men asleep on all but one of them. I'd have much preferred to sleep outside than in this airless pit but the Captain was doing his best to secure my safety so I thanked him and crawled behind the mosquito net. I lay back on the dank mattress and was asleep within seconds.

16 Fork Right for Hell!

Caxito, Angola

Fuse. I seemed to wake with the word on my lips. I opened my eyes and, looking around, remembered with a start exactly where I was. The light was still on and a thin Portuguese commentary continued to flow from the battered radio in the centre of the floor. Through the uncurtained windows I could see the first rays of the sun creeping over the eastern horizon. The room was now empty except for me. I looked at my clock, it was a quarter past five.

Lying back, I thought again, *Yes, it must have blown a fuse in the crash.* It was the only explanation for the utter deadness of the bike. Why on earth hadn't I thought of that before? I sat up and rubbed my eyes. I felt stiff and dirty and had a musty dryness at the back of my throat. I reached for my water and got up.

Outside, slovenly soldiers appeared to wander aimlessly in the misty half-light that engulfed the compound. At a flagpole in the centre of the dry parade ground two privates raised the Angolan flag. One attached a crumpled piece of cloth to the rope and pulled while the other squeezed a sequence of strangled notes from a dented bugle. Most of my fellow travellers slept on, some on the truck and others under a corrugated-iron awning behind the wall of the prison. Obviously nothing very much was going to happen for a while. I couldn't get my bike down alone and I couldn't fix it on the truck so I sat leaning against a post and waited.

Soon after eight, with the ferocious heat already bearing down, the Captain appeared and assigned five soldiers to help me with the machine. Much to my relief the fuse was indeed burnt out. Surrounded by the usual crowd of inquisitive onlookers I replaced it with a new one. I said goodbye to Arius, who categorically refused to take any payment for his services, and left feeling sweaty, tired and hungry. I had not eaten for twenty-four hours.

The road to Luanda from Caxito was under construction. Dumper trucks and earth levellers moved up and down the left-hand side, flattening the deep red soil to prepare it for a covering of tarmac. It was busy with traffic compared to the roads I had been used to: lorries, cars and small motor bikes all bound for the capital. In the maize fields, on either side, women worked and their children played. I was driving in the dirt, when, not five miles down the road, the back wheel wobbled and sank to its rim. A blow-out! I could hardly believe it. Extremely vexed, I sat staring at the bike for a full five minutes before I could summon up the energy to do what had to be done.

At noon I reached the capital which sat in a bowl surrounded by barren hills. The earth had turned from red to yellow as I'd driven further west and now, by the sea, it was almost white; hard and dry like a cornflour biscuit. A procession of military trucks swept past me as they climbed the ridge on the way out of town. The smiling driver of the last one tooted his horn and waved me a greeting. A white UN jeep was dragged in their wake.

As I rounded a sharp hairpin corner, still a little way above the city, the ground to my right fell away steeply giving a spectacular view of the harbour below. I pulled up onto a ledge beside the drop and watched. The horseshoe cove was busy with commerce. Ships of various sizes and class seemed welded to the surface of the metallic sea, waiting for their turn to dock and unload. Cranes on the quayside swung the cargoes in and out and the rooftops of the warehouses glinted in the noonday sun. Wispy cirrus clouds hung high above the ocean, forming a ceiling above the swooping gulls. It made a fantastic picture and, worried that I still had precious few shots of this photogenic country, I decided, like the tourist I was, to take a photo. I pulled the camera from the tank bag, attached a lens and pointed it in the general direction of the port.

No sooner had I clicked a few times than I heard someone shouting at me from behind. I turned to see a bus driver gesticulating angrily towards me though his glassless windscreen. I could not understand what he was saying but obviously other people did and three or four pedestrians came over and joined in.

Never having set foot in Portugal I spoke fewer than five

words of the language but my travelling Spanish was not bad. I had been finding that if I talked in Spanish I could usually get across what I wanted: they understood me even if I could not understand them. So, shrugging my shoulders, I asked, 'Que es la problema?' No one answered, they just stood there shouting. With great animation the driver explained the situation to new-comers while the others – who by now numbered at least ten – kept shouting a single word. Whatever the problem, it was obvious that I was better off away from here so I packed away my camera as fast as possible and started the bike.

Espiao . . . espiao . . . what the hell does that mean? It suddenly dawned on me.

The bus driver, seeing that I was planning to make my escape, pulled his shabby coach forward in an attempt to block my path but he was unable to see how far he could go before losing his front end over the edge. Luckily he erred on the side of caution and left just enough space for me to squeeze the bike through. As I came out on the other side I saw him pointing after me as he said something to a man on a scooter; evidently 'Follow that man!', which he duly did. It was a phase of the game which I had not bargained for . . . being chased as a spy in the capital of Angola.

The narrow streets were clogged with traffic, spewing fumes into the baking air, making slow progress to the centre of the city. I fell back on my experience as a dispatch rider and wove my way as quickly as possible through the throng, driving down the outside of the descending lane, into the oncoming traffic. A car crossing my path as it emerged from a side street saw me just in time and screeched to an abrupt halt. I waved an apology and carried on. My pursuer was a hundred yards behind when he failed to make it across a set of changing lights and was forced to stop. I entered a cobbled square from a small side street. In the centre, surrounded by four defaced statues, an ornate fountain leaked greenish water. The route to the left seemed to be the only exit south so I took it and urgently pulled back on the throttle. I was gone before I saw my pursuer enter the square, which gave him a one in four chance of choosing my route, though how keen he was to catch me I was beginning to wonder.

I didn't slow down though, and soon came to the seafront where a wide thoroughfare lined with palms circled the sea. Imposing government buildings with grandiose façades and orange-tiled roofs reflected a vanished colonial life but, like everything else in this disturbed country, reeked of decay and disintegration. There was rubbish and filth on every corner. Ragged figures, some crashed out on grassy verges, others glaring with sinister eyes, gave the place a crazed feel. There was tension in the air, a kind of tangible expectation, as though it was about to explode.

At the far side of the port I came to a roundabout. Two booted policemen wearing starched blue shirts and black jodhpurs sat astride their motor bikes, fiddling with their pistols. As I entered the junction one of them put up his hand signalling me to stop. *Oh hell, did that little bastard not fancy the chase and tell a policeman instead?* It suddenly seemed highly probable. I thought I'd lost him a bit too easily. There would be no point trying to outrun these guys, their Honda 750s were the fastest bikes I'd seen in Africa.

'Papers,' said one of them in English while the other studied my bike. They both wore pear-shaped sunglasses.

'Where are you going?'

'To Lobito, but I'm trying to find the coast road via Porto Amboim.'

His face was expressionless. I could not tell if he had been told about me on his radio or not.

'You are lost, no?'

'No sir, I'm heading for Lobito.'

'But everyone else they catch the boat.'

The boat? Everyone else? What's he talking about? My mind raced. *Ah . . . that boat. He thinks I'm with the rally. Well, that's a lot better than being thought of as a spy. In fact it may be helpful . . .*

'Yes, I was with them in the Congo, I hope to catch up with them again in Namibia,' I said, telling only a half-lie.

He was another who seemed more interested in the bike than in me. Handing back my papers he joined his friend in studying it from every angle. They discussed it in low professional tones. After a pause, he said, 'My friend want to have a go.' What do you say to that? Up to this point I had not let anyone drive the bike, though I'd had quite a few requests. Fully laden, it is quite hard to ride and if somebody else fell and damaged it irrevocably . . . well, it would have been too much. What, however, I wondered, might happen if I said no.

'Okay, but please, not too far. I still have a long way to go

188

today.' I got off and he got on with an expression like that of an excited child. He started the engine and drove away while his friend handed me a cigarette. We made a certain amount of small talk of which I was the instigator, keeping the subject away from the rally as much as possible. He told me I should be okay to Lobito but to take care from there. From Lobito to the border was the danger zone. Much to my relief his partner returned quickly and handed back the machine.

'The road to Porto Amboim is here,' he said, pointing down the right-hand exit, 'it is straight on.' I shook their hands and left, greatly relieved to be leaving Luanda.

The policeman was right and the next twenty-four hours went surprisingly smoothly. The road, which cut along the coast through the Quicama National Park, was in an excellent state of repair, making progress quick. At about two I stopped at a restaurant by the sea and, thinking of the lobster I'd turned down the previous day, asked how much they were.

'Five hundred kwanzas, sir,' the waiter said.

'Is that all?' He nodded with a lofty smile. 'In that case I'll have two.' What joy. I was so hungry my stomach was beginning to think that my throat had been cut.

When they arrived on a steel tray there were three.

'Excuse me, but I only ordered two.'

'There are only two here, senhor,' replied the waiter, pointing at the tray.

Quite how six halves made up two lobsters I wasn't sure but the prospect of getting an extra one of those succulent shellfish was a little too much; I decided to let it be. Having eaten two with voracious delight I was presented with the bill. Even in this country of hyper inflation and devalued currency – the exchange rate had gone from forty to 1,100 kwanzas to the dollar in six months – the bill of 31,000 kwanzas seemed well over the top. I checked it again and saw that the lobsters were 15,500 kwanzas each. I had obviously not heard the first part of the figure when the waiter told me the price. Five hundred kwanzas is a little under fifty cents, and nowhere, not even in Angola, does lobster come that cheap. I mused that Mel must have deafened me for a second, knowing that I would have gone for something cheaper had I understood. She obviously thought I deserved the feast. The only problem was that it would now be touch and go as to whether I would have enough kwanzas to see me through, and I only had a fifty-pound travellers' cheque left to cash. I wrapped up the third lobster for supper.

The Grand Hotel, Lobito, as its name suggests, was another survivor from the bygone age of colonial ascendancy. It stood, all seven floors of it, on Avenida Lenin, just behind Independence Square, and was once the best hotel in town. It might still be for all I knew, as the Continental, so the excited receptionist of the Grand informed me, had been shot up in a battle between UNITA and government troops three weeks before my arrival. I'm not sure it was exactly the news I wanted to hear. Thirty keys hung above empty cubby-holes behind a dark mahogany reception desk, which ran all the way along one wall. The man ran his hand along them deciding which one would fall to my lot. It came to rest upon number thirty. To judge by the smile and nod I received with the key, I had evidently hit the jackpot.

A heavily made-up Portuguese woman sitting on a sofa in the lobby bellowed at a boy to come and help with my luggage. I crossed the room and made towards the gold-meshed elevator but she shook her head with a sorrowful glance and displayed seven beringed, clawlike fingers. I'd evidently been given the penthouse. The stairs went round and round and up and up. Fraying burgundy carpets led from one landing to the next and peeling wallpaper hung limply from the walls. By the time I reached the top my legs were trembling. I hoped the room would make up for it.

It was indeed the penthouse; not just a single room but a suite of four. The air inside was dank and stuffy, in need of a change. Sunlight fell in stripes through the shuttered French windows and across a huge double bed. I forced the shutters open and let the refreshing sea breeze fill the rooms. There was a spectacular view from the balcony which led round to a shabby brown sitting room. The bathroom had a shower, bidet, bath and sink, all made elaborately in porcelain and next door there was a small lavatory. But as I looked more closely, moving from one room to the next, I saw that nothing had been used for years. A thick layer of dust rested on every surface. No water came from the taps, there was none in the loo and on checking the light switch I found there was no electricity. Well, what did I expect for two pounds fifty, the Hilton? It was fine, after all I wasn't used to electricity and a bucket of water would get me clean.

As I looked out over the rooftops of the dilapidated town that stretched away to the sea I knew the climb had been worth it. Down a quiet street, away from the harbour, I noticed a crowd of well-dressed people emerging from a doorway. There was a small metal cross on the roof of the building which sparkled in the afternoon sun. More and more people came out, breaking the calm with their songs and laughter. A moment later a tired sedan, draped in decorations, came slowly round the corner. It tooted its horn a number of times and pulled up next to the church. The bride, dressed in pink, appeared with her groom. They were showered with rice as they made for the car. Their entourage then formed a guard of honour and followed the couple up the street, past the hotel, and turned out of sight towards the sea, leaving the town in silence once more.

I lay back on the bed, losing myself in a cloud of dust, and drifted into a peaceful doze.

The Wedding
2.32 p.m. August 27th

It was a nasty English summer's day. The sky was grey and a strong wind blew from the west. The sun occasionally broke through the clouds but it made little impression on those guests who'd arrived in silk dresses and thin cotton frocks; they entered the church shivering. Guy and I were the only two left outside when the black horse-drawn carriage pulled up, late by the traditional two minutes. The coachman got down and opened the door for the bride's father, who in turn helped his daughter to alight. A Japanese tourist snapped a few photos and a small crowd watched as Tania, looking nothing short of fabulous, calmly entered the building on her father's arm.

We found the last of the ushers' seats and waited for her to reach the altar. Mel, who was standing some rows in front of me, turned to look at her friend; in doing so she caught my eye. Although she smiled, I noticed a minute difference in her eyes, a look I didn't recognise, but I had other things on my mind and pushed it from my thoughts.

It had been nearly two months now since the deal had fallen through. Had I been surprised? I don't suppose I should have been . . . I'm not even sure I was. When you're hot the phone keeps ringing, when you're not it stops. It had stopped about a month after the Palais gig but it took another week for us to know for sure.

Our management called on a hot July day to say that MCA had decided to 'pass on us', and out of the window had flown our dreams. While they had been interested word had got around and three of the other major record companies had started to bid but once the news broke that we'd been dropped by MCA the others pulled out just as fast.

It had been hard to know what to think. We all speculated as to why it had gone wrong – another band, a dodgy gig, a greedy lawyer – but we also knew that whatever the reason it made no difference. So fickle is the music industry that things like this just happen. Bands are chewed up and spat out every day of the week – we were just another. None of us, though, was prepared to see it as the fatal blow it would ultimately prove to be. We rehearsed, recorded demos and kept on gigging, refusing to give up, but the heart of the band had stopped beating. Everything we did was done with a little less energy, a little less care.

Although I didn't really see it myself, my spirit had been broken. My enthusiasm, which had largely kept the band going, had been crushed. But it's always hard to know when it's the right time to quit. Those bright lights still seemed to be waiting just around the corner. I couldn't believe we'd been beaten. I'd put too much into it for that. So, doggedly, we all pushed on.

If I'd bothered to pay attention I would have noticed that this blind struggle was affecting the one thing that meant more to me than anything. The more lost I became in the struggle, the larger the waves it made. Mel tried to talk to me about it, to encourage me, but ultimately I felt she was not involved. It was my problem and I wasn't quite sure how to cope. The bright-eyed optimist was turning into a sceptic. I was retreating into myself and little by little letting Mel slip away.

On the other side of our quartet things were very different.

'Do you, Tania, take this man, John, to be your lawful, wedded husband?' The priest asked, bringing my thoughts back to the present.

'I do,' replied Tania.

I was awoken from my snooze by the sound of gunfire. Three short cracks echoed in the distance. I got up and went out onto the balcony. The heat of the day had passed and a refreshing breeze carried the lilting beat of local music up from the street. There were many people outside now, better dressed than those I'd seen in the countryside, sitting in doorways or walking by.

No one seemed concerned – I wondered whether the shots had been part of a dream.

Downstairs, the concierge told me they were real but nothing to worry about, probably someone just having fun. It was dark and gloomy in the lobby, even though the late-afternoon sun was still shining brightly outside. A small boy in a tracksuit who'd been standing in the doorway came over. He was no more than twelve years old with a big bush of frizzy black hair.

'Your name is Mr John, yes?'

I was quite taken aback, not only by this unexpected use of my name but also by his excellent accent. Before I could answer he continued.

'I see you on the TV . . . two days ago . . . you were in Cabinda.' So the interview had been shown on nationwide television. I had thought it was only for the northern enclave. Well, Andy Warhol had promised us all fifteen minutes of fame, though Angola seemed a strange place for me to be granted mine. 'I know Mr Sanenan,' the boy was saying, 'he work for the United Nations. I think you want to see him, yes? He can help you.' Although I'd never heard of this particular man I'd been hoping the UN might be able to give me some assistance.

'You know where we can find him?'

'Yes, I know. We can go on your bike. Is not far.'

I was a little sceptical. This wasn't the first time that young boys had invented stories purely to enjoy a ride and impress their friends as they got me to drive past their homes. I didn't usually mind too much but today I was feeling a bit tense and the gunfire, the first I'd heard, had done nothing to ease my mood. I agreed with some reluctance and after retrieving the bike from the storeroom under the hotel we set off in search of Mr Sanenan.

We found him almost at once. His white Landcruiser was parked outside a colonial bungalow on the main road which ran along the harbour's edge. As we approached the house a grey-haired man with a kind face and clear blue eyes opened the door and came down the steps to meet us, evidently a little surprised. He was of medium height and broad physique, and the shorts and long white socks he wore gave him the appearance of a PE teacher. He was Dutch.

'I am sorry,' he said after a friendly greeting, 'but I'm afraid I'm in a hurry. If you tell me where you're staying

193

I'll try to come and see you later. When do you leave?' I told him the next day. 'Very well, but I will show you the route you must take now, in case I don't have time to see you tonight. Do you have a map?'

I opened it out and we bent over it.

'Here, you must take this route by the sea.' He pointed to a thin track which led south-west over the mountains. 'You must not take the main road – it is very dangerous. Especially here at Quillengues, where the English were killed last week. You will avoid it if you take this route to Namibe where you can stay the night. Then drive to Lubango, from where you can reach the border in a day.' With a smile he added, 'You will be okay. At the moment the conditions are good.'

I thanked him.

'You say you are staying at the Grand?' I nodded. 'Okay, I will try and see you there for supper . . . about seven . . . the fish is good.' And with a wave he climbed into his jeep and was away.

At eight, as Jack Sanenan had still not turned up, I decided to eat alone. The spacious dining room was on the first floor and was as grand as my chambers. In one corner, which was lit by a number of smoking oil lamps, five of the fifty or so tables had been laid. Any worries I may have had about what to order from a Portuguese menu were dispelled when a bowl of yellowish fish soup was placed in front of me the moment I sat down. I would eat what I was given. As soon as the bowl was empty it was unceremoniously whisked away and replaced by a plate of what I suspected were the same fish, only grilled. They were sardines, I think, though it was hard to taste anything other than the throat-burning chilli and tomato sauce. Jack arrived just as I was swallowing the last dregs of my semi-flat beer.

'Sorry, have I kept you waiting?'

'No, I'm afraid I ate without you,' I said. 'I wasn't sure if you were coming or not.'

'Oh, ja, good for you. I got held up at the office trying to organise some things. It's been a busy day.' At this point the soup was thrust in front of him and a beer placed at its side. I ordered another.

'What is it that you do for the UN?' I asked, once he had settled himself. 'You're obviously nothing to do with the military.'

194

'No, no, I work for UNHCR, for refugees. I'm in charge of relief aid to the south of the country. It's a job that can be very frustrating and I suppose . . .' he shrugged his shoulders, 'rewarding as well. But it's a hard place to work.'

'Aren't they all? I mean, wherever aid is needed it's bound to be pretty hard.'

'Ja, of course that is true,' he said wistfully. 'Maybe I'm just getting too old for it. My wife would like that I retire early and go home but I feel I must finish at the right time. I only have eighteen months to go.'

'Well done. I don't blame your wife though. I must be hard for her.'

'Ja . . .' he mused, taking a bone from between his teeth. 'she used to stay out here with me. Lobito was not so bad during the war, but no more. She had enough. She is now back in Holland . . . it is best.' He took a sip of beer and continued on a lighter tone. 'But enough of this, what on earth is a young Englishman doing in Lobito?'

'To tell you the truth I'm not entirely sure. When I left England I never dreamt I'd pass through here. It just sort of happened. Is there anything you can tell me which might improve my chances of getting out again . . . in one piece I mean.'

He grunted, dabbing his mouth with a paper napkin, 'You will get through, so long as you don't drive after dark. That, I'm afraid, is what killed your countrymen, but I suppose you know this?'

I nodded.

'How long is your visa for?' he asked.

'Twenty-one days . . . I arrived in Cabinda a week ago.'

'Then you are lucky. Your friends had only three days.'

No wonder they felt they had to travel at night. Driving through Angola in three days would be almost impossible.

'Do *you* know who killed them?'

'No, we're trying to find out at the moment. It was only 300 yards from a UNITA assembly point so we must assume it's them, but . . .' He stopped talking as the waiter took away his empty bowl and replaced it with a plate of sardines. A wry smile formed on his face as he recognised the fish, '. . . but is not at all like them. They are normally very organised and disciplined. I see no reason for this.'

'What about bandits,' I prompted, 'could it simply be them?'

'Bandits . . . ? ugh, bandits, soldiers, they are all the same. They still carry the same weapons they used in the war. Some still wear the same uniform – a beret or an armband. If you mean was it people doing it for their own gain, I should think it highly unlikely, but it makes no difference – a bullet kills no matter who shoots it.'

I was up early the next morning determined to get a good start. It was a day, I felt sure, that would be full of excitement. It was over 300 miles to Namibe and, looking at the map, I guessed that each mile would feel like two.

In Benguela the road crossed a railway track and started to climb. The parched land was yellow and dry and as hard as flint. Small, thatched huts appeared to be stacked on top of each other, clinging precariously to the hillsides. The gravel track began to climb quite steeply, darkening in colour the higher it got. Away to the left a carpet of green stretched along the valley floor, giant palms and flooded paddy fields standing out like birthmarks on the side of the earth. After a while the land levelled out onto a plateau where the going was easier. There was precious little vegetation up here, only scraggly thorn bushes and cacti. I saw no birds or animals; it became obvious I was leaving the living world behind.

Towards noon, to my dismay, the weather closed in from the sea. Thick dark clouds engulfed the sky, shutting off the sun. A light drizzle started to fall, making the track slippery and hard to see. A few times I nearly lost my balance as I fought with the front wheel to hold the bike up. The track was narrow and difficult to define, threading its way around boulders and rocks, over gullies and craters and through patches of sand both hard and soft. It felt like driving on the moon.

My difficulties increased as the path again began to climb. The bike slid on the steep gradient and loose stones and rocks battered the suspension and cracked up hard against the engine guard. The higher I got the thicker the mist became, bringing visibility down to less than fifty yards. All traces of vegetation had now disappeared, leaving only dark brown earth climbing into the descending heavens. The track was now nothing more than a shadow on the ground, one of many criss-crossing in all directions. With mounting concern I realised that I really had no idea if I was following the right path or not. As I searched in vain for the invisible sun, I was no longer sure which way was south.

I came to a fork where the track split in two, one way more worn than the other. After taking the more used road I realised that I should have passed a village a few miles back and so, starting to worry, I turned round to check. The path here was of soft sand, built up in ruts. The front wheel went over the centre ridge and as the back one tried to follow the bike reared up and sent me somersaulting over the top. I came down with a thud and hit the side of my head hard against a rock, stunning myself for a moment. Cursing, I climbed back on, reluctant to accept the inescapable fact that I was lost.

The rain was now getting heavier, falling in large, cold drops through the mist that swirled around me. Panic grew as I realised that far from avoiding Quillengues, which was the whole idea, I could actually be heading straight for it. I was high up in the mountains of Benguela Province, in a land known to be frequented by bandits, only a few miles from the very spot where my compatriots had been slaughterd and, for all I knew, getting closer to danger every second. I began to wish I'd never seen Jack. Surely I would have been safer on the main road. I could hardly imagine a more fitting place for a murder. I tried to breathe deeply and concentrate on driving.

The track rounded a corner over a slight incline before dipping into a bowl with a ford of muddy water at the bottom. As I came out of the water my heart sank; on a flat piece of ground a little way ahead, by a thorn tree, the path again split in two. This time both tracks looked as used, or unused, as the other. I stopped the bike and got off. I had taken such a roundabout route that without the help of the sun it was impossible to tell in which direction either path led. One way I felt sure would lead to Quillengues and danger while the other would take me to the village of Lucira and the main road to Namibe.

Suddenly it seemed as though the entire journey had been condensed to this stark choice. Getting it right would lead to deliverance but if I chose badly, hell would be waiting. I looked around in desperation, hoping to find something to give me a clue. There was nothing.

It seemed too absurd, too surreal, too unfair. One choice,

that was all, yet how could I make it? I crouched down by the thorn tree and put my head in my hands, 'For Christ sake . . . which way?'

'Ugghh!'

My heart missed a beat as I heard the shout behind me. So this was it, there was no choice to be made after all. They had found me. Fully expecting to see bandits aiming AK47s at my gut, I turned slowly to face the call.

A gnarled old man, with a face of wizened parchment, stood staring at me; I'm not sure who was the most surprised. He had a dirty cloth tied round his head, wore an old brown greatcoat and was using a thick branch as a crutch to help support his diminutive weight. The features of his face were sharp and angled, more Arab than African, and a tuft of greying hair sprouted from his chin. He closely resembled the six withered goats which stood by his side.

'Lucira?' I exclaimed having got to my feet. I pointed first down one track and then down the other. The old man merely looked at me and cried something while flailing his one available arm towards the mountains which I'd come from.

'Si, si,' I replied and pointed again down the two tracks saying, 'Lucira?' But he was not watching me. He stared at the ground, kicking at it and shaking his head, seemingly in bewilderment. He looked up and cried something in a manner which frightened me. His eyes were clear and edged with crow's-feet and they carried the haunted look of a man who has seen too much. When I pointed to the right-hand track again he shook his arms vehemently, letting the staff fall to the ground. Allowing the goats to follow him, he hobbled over to block the path.

'Namibe, Namibe,' he said urgently, pointing down the other track. Glancing over his shoulder at the route his goats had now sealed off he added, 'Impulo.'

Looking at the map I saw the Impulo was a village only a few miles from Quillengues. So I had been right to be worried about the choice. I thanked the old man who waved the gratitude away and stared at the ground, mumbling to himself. I clambered aboard the bike and hurried off down the left-hand track.

Fifteen minutes later, having wound my way down from the top of the mountains, I saw far below me the thin black line of the main road running like a lifeline in the eerie mist. When I reached it some time later I turned back and looked up. The peaks of the dark brown cliffs were lost in cloud, only the foothills could still be seen. Had I really just come through there? Was the old man real or imagined? Where had he come from and why had he arrived at that moment when I'd seen not a soul all day? A shepherd appearing from nowhere to show me the way, it seemed so strange, like a biblical fable. I turned away and let out the clutch.

17 Desolation Road

Namibe, Angola

It was six fifteen in the morning and I saw with tired resentment that the rear wheel of the bike was flat again, not totally, but about two-thirds of the way down. It was no way to start the day, especially when I had hopes of driving the full 370 miles to the border. I debated just pumping the tyre up and hoping for the best but thought better of it. I got the wheel off, took out the damaged inner tube and put the new one in, but being too hasty as usual I caught it with the tyre lever and tore an inch-long gash in it just below the valve. Cursing to myself I took it out again, got my patches from the box and stuck one over the hole. This time, taking a good deal more care, I put it back in and pumped it up. Oily and sweaty I set off, crossing my fingers that I had been served my quota of trouble for the day. But only a few miles out of town that familiar sensation of riding on jelly hit me again. Another blow-out. I discovered that I had actually put the patch on the wrong way up.

As I sat on the ground changing the patch an army truck approached from the direction of the town. It stopped just in front of the bike and ten or so red-bereted UNITA soldiers alighted and gathered round. I was too pissed off to be afraid; besides, they were all smiling and, as far as any African soldier can, they looked benign.

Their Captain was a very large man with a round flat face as black as his combat boots. The soldiers' camouflage uniforms were clean and pressed, their backs were straight and, as Jack had said, they appeared to be well-disciplined and professional. I got it across that I was going to the border via Lubango and they offered to escort me some of the way, telling me in mime and Portuguese that I had inadvertently taken a wrong turning in town and was actually heading back to Lobito. The second puncture fixed, more oily and sweaty than ever, I set off behind my personal armed escort feeling fairly confident that those arms would not be turned on me.

The road started to climb from sea level back onto the sandstone plateau. My good Samaritans moved slowly before me and at last I managed to enjoy the day. A few more miles down the road and the wheel blew again. My cup of misery was full.

'FUUUCK!' I swore as I slithered to the side of the road. Three punctures in ten miles was too much to bear, but bear it I had to for short of putting the bike on the soldiers' truck, there was nothing else to do.

To my relief the soldiers stopped and came back, all sympathy. It was a dangerous place to be stuck, at the mercy of any passerby, and I was thankful for their protection. The rip in the inner tube had now reached the valve and was beyond repair, leaving me no option but to replace it with the one I'd found semi-deflated earlier that morning.

Forty minutes later we were under way again. Then the drive chain started to slip, missing every few turns on the front sprocket and so losing me power. Was this going to be a stage of the journey blighted by ghosts in the machinery? Not yet, I prayed, at least hold together to see me into safer territory.

The dark mountains, jutting almost vertically out of the earth, became larger the further east we travelled. Nestling in their lee, there were more homesteads, mud and wooden kraals set back off the road, though it was hard to see what was actually farmed. At Caraculo the soldiers explained they could go no further. They all shook my hand ceremoniously and wished me luck, with the Captain advising me to stay at Lubango, on top of the escarpment, rather than risk driving at night to the border; this time I vowed to take the advice. It was impossible for me to believe that any of these men could be connected with murder. They had gone about 150 miles out of their way to see me safely through their area. I only wished I could keep them with me to the frontier.

Since Namibe the road had been flat and straight; it now began its serpentine climb into the clouds, coiling powerfully one way then the other through looping hairpin bends. Two large trucks crawled painfully up the steep incline in bottom gear, swinging out wide, using what limited space there was to see their long back-ends safely round the corners. Here the chain slip became more of a problem. As I arched round each of the bends the front cog slipped through the chain leaving momentum my only form of propulsion. On the straight stretches its bite was better and I was able to push past the trucks. To my surprise they were driven by whites.

The mountainside was thick with vegetation. Exquisite red flowers on long, elegant stems, orchids perhaps, nodded their heads in the breeze as I passed. Up and up I went, ever closer to the distant mist. A few hundred feet before the top, just below the clouds, the road levelled out and ran along a ledge. Looking back, the view was unbroken, holding no buildings, no people. A place that was as old as the earth itself.

Soon after one o'clock I came over a ridge and found Lubango nestling in a valley below me, guarded by an effigy of the Madonna, high on the opposite hill. After some difficulty I found a place to stay and store my bike. When I looked at the chain to check its strength I realised that the slippage was because I hadn't replaced the wheel correctly after the last puncture. I fixed it before going to rest in the hotel.

Sitting on my musty bed going through my wallet I realised that, after all, I did not have enough local currency to see me out of Angola. I had of course been keeping an eye on the situation as I knew it would be close, but, in short, I'd got it wrong. I had enough to pay for the hotel and to buy some supper but even if I went without that, I would still be a couple of thousand kwanzas short of what I needed for petrol. This was a problem as I only had one fifty-pound travellers' cheque left. I was fairly confident that I would be able to cash it, but not so confident that I would be able to change into rand the sixty or seventy thousand kwanzas I would have left when I reached Namibia. This would leave me in a new country without so much as a bent penny until I could find a bank to give me some cash on my Mastercard. The lobsters had cost me dear.

The first couple of banks would not accept travellers' cheques but at the third, the Bank of Agriculture, I had more luck. It being a Friday, the bank was packed inside and out and I had some trouble getting in at all. The guard insisted that the bank was now closed but after I'd pleaded and begged, and taken the gamble of slipping him a 1,000-kwanza note, he finally allowed me entry. Inside, the noise and smoke from a thousand cigarettes made it feel more like a pub at last orders than a bank. I was taken round the back, away from the throng of punters

202

clamouring at the tills, to a quiet small office. An attractive lady appeared and informed me that the official rate was 1,500 to the pound and gave me, after bank charges, over 70,000 kwanzas. I couldn't imagine how I would spend even half of it. A reasonable dinner would be a start . . .

The Surprise
8.15 p.m. October 10th

All along the rue de Rivoli leaves were falling, dancing along the stone pavement, floating down to the darkness to drift along the Seine. Street lights lit up the Pont D'Arcole which stretched away towards the Ile de la Cité, where the dramatic outline of Nôtre Dame glowed orange against the night sky. At the Hôtel de Ville a long line of people waited at a taxi rank but as it was a warm evening we decided to walk. I took Mel's hand in mine as we strolled along the right bank.

'So, come on,' she said, smiling, 'you can tell me now – where are we going?' A breeze blew her hair across her face and with her free hand she pushed it back behind her ear. The pavement was busy with people and we had to part as a group of five laughing youths pushed between us. I took her hand again and looked at her.

'You'll see in a minute.' She turned her face towards me and smirked mischievously. I imagined she had already guessed where we were going and was really only pretending for my sake. After all, how many amazing restaurants could I know in Paris? Only one – the one everyone must know.

Paris was Mel's favourite city. It was the first place we had come to as a couple and she had loved it. She loved the narrow streets of the Marais, the shops and stalls of rue Saint Denis, the galleries, the exhibitions, the churches and restaurants. When I finally realised that I had not been giving Mel as much attention as perhaps I should have, I decided to treat her. A surprise long weekend in Paris seemed the right idea. So for three weeks I worked doubly hard on my bike, driving like a maniac from eight in the morning till seven at night, risking life and limb in the pursuit of a few extra pounds. It was hard to keep it all from Mel. When she sat at home, bored by some rubbish on the TV, I wanted desperately to tell her, 'Don't worry, next week we'll be in Paris,' but I also knew how much she would enjoy the surprise. I rang her place of work and arranged for her to have the Friday and Monday off, collected the tickets and on the Thursday night told her of my plan. She was delighted. There was one part of the trip I still kept from her and for which I had had to borrow Tania's smartest dress – the black velvet number – which Mel now wore with a few pieces of jewellery and a small amount of make-up. She looked terrific.

It was only a short walk from the Hôtel de Ville and before long we rounded the corner into the Place Vendôme. There, on the left-hand side, lit up by pale spotlights was the Ritz Hotel.

'Wow!' was all Melanie could think of to say.

We passed the doorman and entered the lobby. Crystal chandeliers hung from the ceiling. Bell-boys, porters, and the concierge, all in uniforms from an earlier century, rushed about. Mel looked up and grinned as one of them took her coat. We were led down a corridor, past boutiques offering products from Chanel, Gucci and Hermès and into the restaurant where the head waiter showed us to our table.

The meal was out of this world and Mel's pleasure at the whole experience was as easy to read as it had been earlier in the afternoon when buying clothes and presents on the Champs Elysées. But, for some inexplicable reason, I just couldn't seem to share in her enjoyment – a part of me simply wasn't there. I was in Paris having dinner at the Ritz Hotel, opposite the girl I loved and yet no matter how hard I tried not to, I couldn't help feeling in some way removed. I tried so hard to be jolly and to hide it from her but I could tell that, deep down, she knew. The fire that had burned so brightly between us was in danger of going out and no matter how hard I tried, I seemed unable to do anything about it. Why, I kept asking myself, why can't I be happy? I still didn't understand and neither, it seemed, did Mel.

The road south from Lubango to the border had been almost destroyed by the sixteen years of fighting. What was marked on my map as a smooth-surfaced road had been turned by bombs, landmines and strafing jets into a battleground of rubble and craters. At times even the suggestion of an asphalt surface was gone. A thick layer of mud, pocked with deep pot-holes, was all that remained of the only route south. It was agonisingly slow work weaving around the craters, like trying to stay on the ridges of a honeycomb. At times I missed the line completely, plunging myself into ankle-deep water, and once I was thrown off-balance by a particularly large hole and forced off the road down a steep bank to a boggy marsh below. I held my breath while I scrambled the bike back up to the track.

'Oh ja, there's still plenty of active mines out there,' Rolf, one of the Afrikaner truck drivers I'd seen coming from Namibe, had happily informed me in a restaurant the previous evening, 'so be sure to stick to the tracks. Only three days ago I saw a cow get it. Blew the fuckin' thing sky high.' He had laughed maniacally at the memory and slapped his hand on the frail table. He told me the drivers had christened it Desolation Road.

'What about bandits,' I'd asked, 'are there any?'

'Jesus man, are you green? Of course there are fuckin' bandits. Why do you think they pay me 25,000 rand a trip?' While he'd downed half the contents of his can in one gulp I worked it out. Five thousand pounds for a ten-day journey. I could barely believe it. ' 'Struth man, these guys would fuckin' kill you for a packet of Marlboro. I'm telling you for nothing, get your bloody head down and go for it . . . Ugh . . . it's no place for sightseeing.'

And that's exactly what I did, but it was far from easy. Rain had been coming down most of the night and started again soon after I had left the town. At Chibia I tried to fill up with petrol as there had been another of the frequent power cuts in Lubango. Unfortunately the same was true here so the pumps didn't work. The lanky attendant told me he had fifteen litres stashed away which I could have at a black market price. As money was one thing I was not short of I accepted but I doubted it would be enough fuel to see me through to Namibia.

For thirty miles the road improved and I managed to make up some time. On top of the plateau dense stretches of thorn and acacia, grass and baobabs sprouted prosperously from the deep red earth. I passed Rolf's empty truck, its cargo of Castle beer safely deposited in the bars of Namibe. Two more such journeys and he would have the money to buy the ranch he wanted up here.

'I don't want no fuckin' Communist ruling me,' he had said in reference to the ANC. 'I'll buy my land, fence in the cattle and get the fuckin' kaffirs to work for shit.' If that was all Angola had to look forward to after the elections I wondered how long it would be till the next war.

For the next fifty miles the roads could not have been in worse condition. The way was brown with mud, not grey with tar, slippery and wet. Some of the craters were so large you could lose a car in them, and all were full of muddy water.

Up and down I'd go through the filth, stopping every few miles to pump up my ever-deflating tyre, all the while paranoid that I might meet bandits. I would have tried driving through the bush at the bottom of the road's grassy bank had it not been for the warning about unexploded mines. There was nothing to do but battle on. Not knowing how long it would last I kept looking hopefully into the distance for clear grey patches of asphalt. Sometimes they materialised but they were always short-lived and soon returned me to the gauntlet of Desolation Road.

At least the rain had stopped, allowing the sun to beat its way through the retreating clouds. Every so often, near a village, I'd pass some cattle and a herdsman walking next to the road. 'Go home,' I'd think. But the cattle had to be grazed and the herdsman had to be with them. Mines or no mines.

Most of the once-picturesque villages were now bombed-out shells, some completely deserted. Walls, painted with murals of Castro and Lenin, were smashed, the heavy concrete and twisted girders looking as though they'd been dumped there by trucks and had never formed homes. At Xangongo the bridge over the Cunene river had been destroyed in an air-raid. All that remained, trailing pathetically in the brown torrent, was tangled metal and shattered stone. A makeshift pontoon bridge had been placed further along and I trundled over it and up the other side, where I found a tumbledown bar. Spent shell cases served as flower pots outside and inside was dark and dusty. It belonged to a middle-aged woman with a mild manner who said I would find no petrol in this town, but maybe in Ondjiva a further fifty kilometres on. Throughout the war she had kept the bar open, she told me, catering for the Cubans and now for UN officials and the truck drivers.

South of Xangongo the road, a thin corridor through the now receding bush, improved enormously. This was surprising as the signs of war were more evident than ever. Burnt-out tanks, trucks, armoured personnel carriers, fuel bowsers, even helicopters lay rusting where they had died or been pushed to clear the road. The jagged metal and torn shapes took on hideous forms – ugly beasts from an evil world left to rot in the scorching heat.

I almost laughed when I reached Ondjiva, an hour or so later. This was where I wanted to stay the night? There was barely a building left standing and those few that were were so badly scarred by bullets and crippled by mortars or bombs as to be practically useless. Countless civilians must have died in this destroyed town. It was a damning indictment of the South Africans and exposed their lie that 'our boys' only hit military targets. In a ruined church a young female teacher defied the conditions and led her class through a lesson. The children sat on the rubble under the open sky. What future, I wondered, did they have?

In the street nothing moved save the wind and the dust. Thin, war-weary faces looked out of glassless windows. Girders creaked. There was no hotel, no petrol, and no food. A ghost town full of ghosts. How long would it take to get that community back to some semblance of normality? One thing was for sure, whoever did get power in the elections would have a mighty job on their hands. There was nothing for me to do but carry on to the border in the vain hope that my petrol supply would last the thirty miles.

The track now was white with chalky stones and still pot-holed. The verdure had disappeared once more, leaving dry sparse bush. I turned on the reserve petrol as I left the town and drove as steadily as possible in an attempt to conserve what fuel I had. It was not enough though and about five miles before the frontier the engine cut out. Still high, the sun was beating down from a clear sky and the slight breeze brought little relief. But there was no alternative, I had to push.

After a few minutes, with sweat already dripping off my face, I heard a vehicle approaching from behind. I stopped, welcoming the rest, and turned to see a white Range Rover pulling up alongside.

'Howzit, you got a problem?' I could tell by the trapped nasal accent that he was an Afrikaner. He was about fifty and was travelling with a boy, who might have been his son, and an old, smiling African with greying hair.

'You could say that,' I panted, 'I need some petrol to get me to the border.'

'Well then, it's your lucky day,' he said, getting out of the car. 'You don't want to hang around here you know, it might not be so good for your health.' He smiled and took a twenty-litre jerry can from the boot, along with a large plastic funnel, and made towards the bike.

'I should warn you, I don't have any rand or dollars, only kwanzas.'

'Ah, don't sweat it, I can spare a few litres.'

I undid the petrol tank and he started to pour.

'You'll need enough to get to Ondangwa,' he said reflectively, 'you'll not find any at the border. It's quite a machine you got there. How many ks does she do?'

'Oh . . . quite a few, six or seven to the litre. A gallon should be enough.' I was very thankful for this show of generosity and I couldn't help wondering if I might be able to push it a little further. 'I don't suppose you would swap my kwanzas for a few rand would you? Make it worth your while . . . I mean, anything would be good. They're useless to me and, like I say, I've no hard cash.'

'I'm afraid they'd be just about as useless to me, too,' he said, returning to the rear of his car. 'I don't think I'll be back up here for a while, but I'll see.' He threw the can into the boot and climbed back in. 'We'll see you at the border, maybe I can help you there. It's no good hanging around out here.' With a short wave and a smile he moved the long gearstick into first and left in a cloud of dust.

Such was the state of the road it took me twenty minutes to reach the customs post where I found the white car parked outside the immigration office. After the formalities were completed the kindly Afrikaner handed me fifty rand, about a tenner, for the 50,000 kwanzas I had left. Even though the rate of exchange was diabolical I was extremely grateful.

'How are the roads from here?' I asked wearily, once the transaction was complete. 'I hope they're better than these.'

They looked at me with mocking astonishment, the father placing a hand on my shoulder. 'Are you joking? . . . the roads? . . . better? I don't know how long you've been stuck up there in the bush fella, but you're about to rejoin civilisation. And, if you don't mind me saying so,' he turned to the others, 'you look as though you could use some!'

While they laughed I pondered the word. *Civilisation . . . yes.* I tossed it around in my head for a moment, lingering on each syllable: what a wonderful sound it had. It would mean a road, straight and flat, without pot-holes. It would mean shops with provisions that I actually wanted and food that was pleasant to eat. It would mean hotels with electricity, showers with hot water and bedrooms without insects or rats. It would mean people not wearied by war and aggression, and it meant the Cape and the completion of my original journey. In short, it meant everything.

'There's a hotel in town called the Three A's,' the father was saying, 'you can't miss it. It's cheap and clean. Do yourself a favour and stay the night.' Smiling they wished me luck and drifted back to their car.

An hour later as I studied my reflection in the hotel mirror I realised that his remarks had been justified. I looked a mess. I hadn't shaved since Soyo, the venue of my last proper wash. My skin was both stained with dirt and burnt by the sun. My lips were cracked and my hair lank. Little more than oily rags were left of my jeans and my T-shirt had fared no better. However, when I looked into my eyes I saw a sparkle I had not seen for many a day. They seemed bluer – as though a cloud had been lifted – full of energy and life. Even if it was still a little bruised, my body beneath the rags was lean and fit. Not only had I almost achieved my initial goal, but I knew I'd actually enjoyed doing it. All that aggro: the endurance across the desert, the seemingly endless fight through the jungle and the constant fear of attack in the land I'd just passed through were what I had wanted. I had left England for adventure and I had found it.

My hotel room had an electric fan and clean cotton sheets. The shower was hot and the taste of the succulent fillet steak indescribable. I sat on the veranda afterwards, *real* scotch whisky in hand, looking up at the moon, and tried to take it all in. I had put myself in the hands of something bigger and had been rewarded. Wherever I decided to go, whichever route I took, I now felt I'd make it. It seemed I had been chosen.

Holding the drink up to my far-off friend I swirled it round, enjoying the moment of anticipation as the ice clinked gently against the glass. I took a long pull and let the smooth, fiery liquid rest on my tongue, the flavour filling my mouth as it reached each taste-bud in turn. I held it there for an age, reluctant to let it go. Then, with a final swish through my teeth, I let it slip down my throat. It tingled sweetly all the way down. 'Yes,' I thought, 'civilisation . . . hello there.'

18 Reflections Under the Mountain

Cape Town, South Africa

Eighteen Dunkley Street was a small, whitewashed, turn-of-the-century town house which nestled in the middle of a row of twenty or so similar dwellings. It had black, wrought-iron bars on the windows, and with its heavy wooden door and grey-tiled roof it was quaint in the manner of a Chelsea mews house. As the street was close to the city centre, most of the other buildings had been turned into offices. Posters advertising investment broking and assurance policies beckoned customers from the window of the house next door and each of the street corners was occupied by a quiet restaurant. On the other side of the road there was a large square of rough grass and rubbish. Half of it had been turned into an impromptu car-park while the other half, furthest from the house, was occupied by five or six hobos, crashed out on the grass, their empty bottles discarded beside them. I parked the bike in front of the house, gave it a pat of congratulatory thanks and rang the doorbell.

After a minute the door was opened by a tiny woman wearing a large woollen beret and a pink nylon smock. She looked about sixty and had a tired face but a beautiful smile with which she welcomed me inside.

'Marius, no here,' she said, first pointing upstairs and then signalling back to the door, as though this was the only route he ever took. 'You wait.' She gestured towards a sofa at the end of the living room and bid me sit down. I wasn't actually there to see Marius. That's to say I'd never met him and only knew him through a telephone call I'd made a day or two earlier. I was there to see a friend of mine from England, Richard, with whom he shared the house. The problem was that Richard had gone with his father up the coast for a few days to visit his sister. 'That doesn't matter,' Marius had said on the phone, 'come on down. If I'm not around I soon will be. Make yourself at home.'

After an hour the front door swung open, rather taking me

by surprise for I had fallen asleep, and a young man, a little older than me, walked in.

'Hey, so you made it!' he exclaimed, thrusting one hand before him while removing his sunglasses with the other. He was of average height, just erring on the wrong side of well-fed, with a thick mop of curly red hair swept back from a pale face. He wore a long green T-shirt, faded black jeans and baseball boots and had a leather thong wrapped round each of his wrists; he looked cool, trendy.

'I'm Marius,' he said. 'It's really amazing what you've just done. You know, we're not even allowed in half those countries. Still, things are changing . . . so maybe soon.' He moved on into the kitchen. 'I spoke to Richard this morning, he says he's sorry not to be here, told me to look after you. He'll be back on Thursday.' It was now Monday. ' "Look after him?" I said. "The man's just driven from London. I'll get him to look after me." ' He stuck his head back round the doorway, a wide grin creasing his face. 'You just help yourself to anything you want. The dope we keep here, the beers are in the fridge and I'll show you the spare bedroom where you can crash.'

I barely knew what to say, except thanks.

'Ah, forget it. We want you to relax and enjoy yourself while you're here . . . have a good time.' I couldn't see that there'd be a problem with that.

'How was the journey down from Namibia?' he asked.

'Oh, very easy, best roads I've seen in Africa. I just went for it. I was too tired to bother with any sightseeing or anything. I just wanted to get here.'

'Yeah, I don't blame you. So how long has it taken you . . . the whole thing I mean?'

'Exactly one hundred days,' I said proudly. 'Ten countries and 10,000 miles . . . well, as near as damn it.'

'Wow! And what now?'

'After I've rested here for a while, I think I'll drive back . . . up the other side.'

'You mad bastard.'

I heard the clink of glasses.

'After you telephoned, I put a bottle of champagne in the fridge – reckoned you deserved it.' He came back into the living room with two champagne flutes and a dark green bottle. 'You open it up, I'll be back in a second.' He put them down on the table and bolted up the stairs.

Cape Town! Yes, Cape Town. Jonny you made it! I hadn't had champagne since the night before I'd left London and didn't that feel like a lifetime ago. Suddenly a vision of Paul and Van in a little Battersea restaurant made it all come flooding back. It was as though I'd been suppressing any thoughts of home and friends but now that I was just a phone call away I was filled with an overwhelming desire to talk to them all. How the hell was Neil? Had his leg healed? What about John and Tans, had she had her baby yet? There was Ann, Robert, Guy, Andy, my parents . . . Oh damn, I bet they're worried sick. The last they would have heard was that I was going into Angola. After a while drinking and chatting, which really consisted of me answering a barrage of questions, I asked:

'Marius, do you think I could use the phone? Nobody will have heard from me in months. I must call home.'

'Sure you can, all night if you like.' He climbed to his feet. 'But not just now. If they've waited this long another few hours won't hurt. We've got to go over to my girlfriend's place and hang some pictures. Come on. Afterwards I'll show you Cape Town.'

Table Mountain climbed vertically through the rich blue sky into a white, viscous cloud which poured over the mountain's edge like dry ice seeping off a stage. In his magnificent off-white and burgundy 1966 Merc 220SE, Marius drove us over the ridge next to Signal Point and down to Clifton where his girlfriend lived. After a short wait, Bronwyn arrived and invited us up to the flat. She was extremely pretty with a nice, slim figure, shown off by a short skirt and T-shirt. Immediately I felt myself clam up. The living room was spacious with large windows facing the sea and the setting sun. It was sparsely furnished with a wicker sofa and chairs. I was handed a beer and sat down. Bronwyn excused herself and went off to change.

A little while later another girl arrived; this was Vanessa. From their affectionate greeting I realised that she, and not Bronwyn, was Marius's girlfriend. She was even prettier than her friend: in a word, gorgeous. She had huge, deep blue eyes, a soft, kind face and a wide mouth that often creased into a mischievous smile. Her hair was short and dark and under her shirt and jeans her figure was the kind most women – or men come to that – can only dream of having; a cartoon caricature of the perfect body. This did nothing to help my confidence and I sat gawking stupidly around the room while she and Marius discussed her day.

Bronwyn came back carrying a large picture wrapped in brown paper.

'Oh great!' Vanessa exclaimed. 'You got it back. Do you like it? Let's see.'

Bronwyn, although obviously pleased by her friend's enthusiasm, seemed a little less excited. 'I really don't know,' she said, removing the paper, 'I'm not sure if the colour's right.'

Apparently she had had the painting for some time and had just picked it up from the framer that morning. To be honest, once it had been fully revealed, I was far from sure about the painting, never mind the frame. It was a poster print, by Rubens I think, of a small boy sitting in a field of corn. Still, it wasn't me who would have to look at it.

'Ah, it's lovely,' said Vanessa reassuringly. 'It looks good in gold. Black, I think, would have been too . . .' she chose her words as though plucking them from the air, '. . . too heavy, too intense.'

'Umm, do you think so?'

'Definitely,' concurred Marius. 'How much did it cost?'

'Quite a lot actually,' reflected Bronwyn, 'about . . .'

As they continued discussing the pros and cons of this new acquisition I nervously sipped my beer, at a loss to know what to say. Bronwyn still seemed quite a distance from being truly content with her choice, so the others did their best to convince her: 'Black or red would have been too boring.' 'The gold looks nice, it goes with the corn.' 'It makes the picture stand out better.' 'It's more unusual.' 'I don't think that's expensive.' All the while gazing at the picture intently.

Aware that I'd said very little, I tried hard to think of something constructive to add, but whatever I thought of seemed stupid or inane. I kept the stem of the beer bottle firmly implanted in my mouth and tried not to be noticed.

In truth I was paranoid. I seemed to have completely forgotten how to respond to a perfectly normal social situation. Confronted by these two beautiful girls and a trendy Cape Town socialite, I was all at sea. As if reading my mind, Marius said:

'This must be a bit strange for you, Jonny ... something of a reverse culture shock.' He was absolutely right. It was probably as bizarre to me as my rainforest friends in the Congo would have been to them. My brain seemed unable to engage any of the social tools we all use, like tact, small-talk or fake enthusiasm. I couldn't even conjure up a good old fib. My drive from London on a route seldom, if ever, travelled had been the greatest achievement of my life. I should have been elated but I wasn't, I felt only hideously self-conscious. Having been stuck up in the bush for so long, away from 'civilisation', concentrating on other, more basic problems, I really found it impossible to have any ideas or give any encouragement to Bronwyn on the subject of her frame. It wasn't so much that it was trivial, it was just, to me, so different, as indeed was the whole situation. I tried to explain this.

'You can go and sit in an uncomfortable position on the balcony if it makes you feel any better,' said Bronwyn, with a mocking but friendly smile.

'Yeah, we could throw cold water over you every few minutes,' added Vanessa in the same joking manner. 'Make it really nasty, then bring you some burnt food.'

'Oh, don't be too hard on him, girls,' said Marius. 'The poor boy's tired, probably hasn't had a decent meal in months – he looks half-starved. Come on, let's give him a real Cape Town welcome. We'll take him down The Key for dinner.'

The Split
8.30 p.m. January 21st

It was a chic, ethnic restaurant in Fulham, West London. Elegant waiters wearing turbans and sashed tunics strutted around tables and a small rock-pool full of bright orange carp. There were enough plants and vegetation to give the place its own ecosystem. We'd wanted very much to come to this restaurant but because of the price we had never actually managed it before. It amused me that now we were separated we were finally there. I spotted Mel sitting at the bamboo bar sipping on a vodka and tonic. Nervously I made my way towards her.

The actual break had happened three weeks earlier and had come as a total surprise to me. I had taken the weekend off from the studio where we were recording an album for a dodgy independent record company and had gone to meet Mel at a friend's house in the country. As soon as I arrived I knew all was not well. We acted out the first night as if nothing was wrong but by early the next morning I'd had enough. I mean you can't have a four-year relationship with someone and not realise when something like this is afoot. So it was I who said:

'You want to break up, don't you?' I was angry. I just couldn't believe she was prepared to throw it all away. But then, as blind as I'd been, I hadn't seen it from her point of view.

'I don't know, Jonny,' she said sadly, her eyes cast down. 'I just can't live like this any longer. We don't seem to have fun any more. We never have any money. We never go anywhere . . . we just don't do things like we used to. My life is going nowhere. I want to go away . . . I want to travel.'

I had talked many times of my exploits in Australia and the Far East, where I'd travelled after leaving school; such talk had got her very excited. 'Can't we go away together?' she used to say. 'Please, let's go travelling.'

'Soon, darling, soon,' I'd cheatingly replied. 'You know I can't at the moment.' Deep down I had suspected that one day it would come back to haunt me.

'Sweetheart, please don't go without me,' I pleaded. 'It'll be all right, the band's practically finished anyway . . . I'll quit. In a couple of months I'll have the money. Come on, let's go together like we always planned. You and me in paradise.'

But it was too late. She'd lost her belief in us as an entity and no longer wanted me to go with her. She'd made up her mind.

'I have to do this alone now, Jonny . . . for myself.'

A week later, when I got back from the studio at the end of recording, she'd moved out of the flat; all her possessions were gone.

At first I'd been angry, then devastated, then angry again. To my eye it was as if she had tried to remove all trace of our life together. The bedroom was totally bare of anything belonging to her: her clothes, toiletries and trinkets. She had even taken our photographs, leaving me nothing to remember her by. All that remained was her faint, but distinctive, smell and a huge emptiness descended upon me. For two weeks I drank too much and slept too little but in the end the darkness lifted and I became calm. Her leaving and the consequent soul-searching of my lonely mind made me realise what I had been doing with my life for the last nine months. I'd been drifting, reaching for a dream that was beyond me. We'd got a very small deal to record an album but even that was going badly – we'd been forced to sack Tom and hire another drummer and any last vestige of spirit we'd *had left had gone with him. My misery also made me think about what it must have been like for her, being cut out of such a large part of my life for so long. It made me realise that she was right – the spark between us did seem to have faded – but within I also knew that she and I were bound by infrangible links. Just because I'd fucked up and lost my way did not mean that our fundamental togetherness had gone. This was not some six-month fling we were talking about. I was sure it was still the real thing. If Mel had to go abroad for a while to rediscover this, so be it. If our relationship was to survive, I knew I had to let her go without argument.*

So I hadn't contacted her. I knew it would make her life harder if I did. I set about putting my own house in order. A week before she was due to leave – for India again – I invited her out to dinner.

Neither of us ate a thing. I expected her to be happier, after all I was the one being dumped, but she was sad. She told me she had expected her emotional state to improve once she had left me, but it hadn't. She had become physically sick and had lost a lot of weight. She just didn't know if she was doing the right thing, she said. The two voices inside her head, one saying 'stay' and the other saying 'go', were as loud as each other. I'd never seen her confused in such a way; she usually knew exactly what she wanted. Ironically, it came down to me to tell her that what she was doing was right, that it really was the only way forward.

We left the restaurant just before eleven and walked into a park. We sat on a bench for an hour, talking and hugging, and, in the end, kissing more passionately than we had in ages.

'I'll start saving now,' I told her, 'and if ever you want me to join you, just give me a call and I'll be on the first plane out.'

We walked back to the road and hailed a cab. We embraced for a last time and she climbed in. As the taxi pulled away she turned and put her thumbs up: 'It'll be okay,' she mimed.

A face full of excellent wine and I soon came out of my shell, but the culture shock did not end there. I spent the whole of the next day wandering about the city centre looking in amazement at this strange new Africa of giant buildings and shops full of goods. I was under the impression that South Africa had had sanctions imposed upon it; they seemed to have made little difference. What they couldn't import – which didn't seem to be much – they made for themselves. This was not Africa – Angola, Congo, Algeria are Africa – this, as far as I could tell, was another planet.

Outside, bronzed, beautiful, well-dressed people occupied the paved trafficless streets. They stopped to buy ice-cream or fresh orange juice from a giant orange kiosk and to sit in the shade by ornamental fountains. Smiling buskers, faces painted like clowns, entertained white children in pretty frocks while their parents invited each other to dinner. Some say South Africa is a country of the third world disguised as one of the first; from what I could see the disguise was a good one.

I did finally put through a call to my parents. Understandably, they were delighted to hear from me. Two days after they had received word that I was going into Angola the English press had been splashed with the story of the dead Britons. It had taken them twenty-four hours to find out that I was not among them.

After that the telephone did not stop ringing, bringing me news of all my friends and family. I spoke to Neil and learnt that by the time he had got to a hospital in France his leg had started to go off. He had developed thrombosis and had had to spend the next six weeks on a Heparin drip. Indeed he was still on crutches and was regularly visiting a London clinic. Had he not gone home when he did, the outcome might have proved very different.

With the phone calls came the elation. Talking to family and friends back in England, receiving their congratulations and praise, finally brought it home to me that I really had done something quite special. Not in terms of making the world a better place, making my fortune or becoming a star but just by proving to myself that I could do it. I was filled with a sense of achievement.

On my third full day in Cape Town Richard returned as promised, the first familiar face I'd seen since leaving England; it was extremely pleasing. By way of a second celebration, that night the three of us went out on a clubbing binge. The next morning, realising that what I felt was not a simple hangover, I went to see a doctor.

'This is going to hurt me a lot more than it does you!' he said as I bent over his surgery table with my pants and trousers round my ankles, ready to accept a begloved finger where the sun don't shine. I doubted it. He took some urine and blood and told me that I was simply suffering from

217

fatigue. He gave me a vitamin injection and told me to rest.

So that's exactly what I did – ate, drank and slept. Most days I walked down to one of the beaches, swam, and soaked up some rays. At night I watched TV, went to the cinema or had a few drinks at a café Marius ran, slowly acclimatising to Western life. It seemed unusual that a city could be like this. Normally they're hard work, a hassle – I know London is. Countless grey-faced people barge their way in innumerable cars to jobs they'd rather not have, causing congestion and pollution as they go; expensive rents are paid for tiny flats and there's barely a blade of grass to be seen. Cape Town could not have been less like that. Some nights I'd sit on the cliffs with my new-found friends, eating lobster and drinking Chablis while watching the sun set. It offered all the fun of a beach resort plus the spaciousness of country life while still managing to boast the conveniences of a modern metropolis.

Now that I had time on my hands I was starting to think more and more about Amel. I had written three letters to her over the course of my journey and had been extremely disappointed not to receive any from her at the Cape. After a couple of weeks however I received a package from a friend which contained a new pair of jeans and a letter from Amel. On reading her letter it became obvious that she had not received any of mine. Later that afternoon, in the General Post Office, I discovered why.

'We don't have an air service with Algeria, sir,' said the girl behind the glass screen as I handed her a birthday card for Amel. 'I doubt whether many African countries do. If I was you I'd send it via London. Take a while, but at least it'll get there.'

So I sent it to a friend and asked him to send it on to Amel in Algiers, telling Amel to send any further correspondence via him. Her letter explained that she had now left her job at the hotel in Tamanrasset and was back living with her family. Although she didn't actually say so, I could tell by her tone that she was disappointed not to have heard from me. At that moment I would have given anything to let her know about my letters and my feelings. How, although my mind had been largely preoccupied with the struggle of fighting my way south, I was now thinking about little else but seeing her. I would often find myself lost in a reverie about meeting her again. I'd fantasise about taking her back to England and introducing her to my family and friends, lying in bed with her and making love to her. I'd sit on the beach and remember her face, her voice, her funny bouncy walk and of course her beautiful smile. Like Mel, it seemed to me as though Amel had some part in the greater context of the journey – perhaps, of my life. Her character, her looks, and her name, made me feel that I hadn't simply stumbled upon her by chance, but certain powers had been guiding me, had led me to her deliberately. When I started waking each morning with her firmly ensconced in my brain, I knew something had to be done. My journey would be incomplete if I did not see Amel again. All I could think of was asking her to meet me in Cairo.

It did seem a little crazy to suggest a rendezvous in Egypt while I was still over 10,000 miles away in South Africa but I could think of no alternative. To get Amel to Nairobi would cost a fortune and be impossible to arrange in time, and getting back to Algeria would be totally impractical for me. But would she be able to come? Amel was a Muslim girl after all, living in a deeply religious country. Back in Tamanrasset she had talked of the love and respect she and her father had for each other, that she felt she was the apple of his eye and how he always wanted what was best for her. Even so, I doubted many fathers, let alone Islamic ones, would allow their young daughters to roam the world in search of a man they had never met. He would probably be persuading her to get married to someone local – the thought appalled me. Instinctively though, something told me that this girl would do her damnedest to get there. She was a risk-taker, a romantic, just like me. In her letter she said that when we had met she had fallen in love for the first time – I hoped she intended it to be the last.

Feeling both excited and nervous, I returned to the General Post Office and sent another letter telling her of my feelings and my plan. I asked her to write to Nairobi with an answer.

PART THREE

Silent Savannah
Cape Town – Nairobi

19 Back in Africa

Pitsane, Botswana

I sat on the raised veranda staring west towards the sinking sun. It was still and hot and the vast African sky was an unending sea of blue. On the edge of the Kalahari desert there was little in the way of vegetation and my view across the burnt plains was uninterrupted.

A mule and trap rattled slowly down the dirt track between the railway line and the main road. The driver, a young man with a large brown hat, smiled and waved. Some children, calm now after the excitement of a game of tag, sat quietly in the shade of a msasa tree and a fat woman, as pretty as a sunbird in her bright red clothes and head-dress, walked by, a baby on her back, beautiful and serene. It was peaceful enough for me to be aware of the creaking wooden floorboards beneath my chair. At last I was back.

The sense of liberation I'd experienced as I'd crossed the border into Botswana two hours earlier had been exceptional, as though storm clouds had finally moved away. From Cape Town I had driven down to Cape Agulhas – the southernmost point of the continent – from where I had turned the bike north for the first time in over 10,000 miles. Unfortunately, the prospect of travelling the same distance again, all the way home, didn't seem to appeal to the machine and it promptly developed a loud clanking noise inside the engine.

Snapped piston ring had been the verdict of a podgy Afrikaner mechanic in Bloemfontien. He had been able to fix it but not before I had spent an eye-opening weekend with his family and friends, all staunch AWB-Terre'Blanche supporters. Generous they undoubtedly were, but by the time I'd left my head had been fit to explode with their extraordinary views of social justice. I had driven hard and fast to escape from a country where, away from the Cape, I had seen little in its people but ignorance and pain.

Now I was back in the Africa I loved. Once more children

223

ran to the roadside to wave joyfully. They were healthy and fit and in their eyes they carried that precious spark of freedom. Here the population seemed content. There was no conflict or unrest, the government, democratically elected, was stable and sincere and, for the most part, everyone had what they needed. Keen to remake this Africa's acquaintance, I'd stopped for a beer and a chat at a pale blue bottle store.

One beer had soon become three, and then four, and now I realised, with little concern, that I had done all the driving I was going to do that day. Victor and Charles, two young schoolteachers, sat talking and laughing with me while the sun disappeared behind the plain. That warm feeling of contentment drifted over me again. It was a sensation which had been missing for quite some time and I welcomed it back with a smile.

By nine the next morning I was past the capital, Gaborone, and making good progress north. A dead straight road, both smooth and flat, skirted the edge of the desert all the way to Francistown. Here I stayed the night, crossed the border into Zimbabwe early the next morning, cashed some money at Barclays, Bulawayo, and pushed on towards Hwange National Park.

As soon as I left the town the verdure increased and again I was back in deep bush. Animals grazing by the roadside became a problem. Goats that seemed not to notice me would suddenly bolt as I passed. One rushed into my path and I knocked it over onto its back but thankfully I saw it stagger away. The cattle were more of a worry as hitting one at forty miles per hour would have been a disaster. After a few near-misses I worked out how to avoid them. When startled, a cow would bolt only in the direction its head was already facing, so if it was pointing towards the centre of the road extreme caution had to be taken. If, on the other hand, the head was facing directly down the road or slightly into the bush, the animal would shy away.

Beautiful Matabeleland slipped slowly by. Gathered in clusters, rondavels crowned the tips of the low hills. There were well-worked fields of maize but the leaves had wilted, scorched by the sun. A plume of black smoke appeared above the trees on a railway embankment next to the road. A minute later it was followed by an ancient steam engine, black and red, which lumbered slowly along pulling goods carriages. It tooted its whistle and the driver waved.

I arrived at Hwange National Park soon after five and in excellent spirits. A chalet, complete with fridge, fan and barbecue area was less than two pounds a night. I took it for the weekend.

I spent Saturday morning sitting quietly on a large wooden platform which overlooked the ever-decreasing watering hole, watching a small herd of zebra, wildebeest, warthog, buck, kudu and two elegant giraffes come to drink. The snouts of a couple of crocodiles could just be seen above the water and various birds picked at the mud. Other groups of tourists came and went, including the first overland truck I'd seen since Cameroun.

In the early afternoon I found old Mr Stubbs sitting in the shade of a weeping acacia, whisky in hand, talking to three Dutch women. I had been told by the manager of the park that he would drive me around for a few dollars and that with him I would have as good a chance as any of seeing a lion or, my real desire, a herd of elephant.

'Yes,' said the old man, 'I'll take you into the park.' His hair was white rather than grey, swept back from his angled face. He was slight of build and had an extremely smart Surrey voice. A silk cravat was tied around his neck. 'I doubt we'll see any lion, though. Don't seem to be many about. Mind, I'm sure we can find you some elephant.' I assured him this was all I really wanted. He drained his glass, made his apologies to the women and led me off in the direction of his van.

Find some elephants? They practically charged the van. It happened when we came round a corner – a little too fast – and almost ran into a herd crossing the road. Twenty or so, ranging from tiny ten-week-old calves to full-grown adults, crashed out of the bush on one side of the track and re-entered it on the other. Two large males raised their trunks, letting out blood-curdling screeches. They stamped their feet and flapped their ears. Mr Stubbs seemed quite unperturbed by this show of aggression and merely told me to take some photos as that's what I'd come for. What neither of us noticed was that more elephants were crossing the road behind us.

Suddenly the tusked head of a young male emerged from the bush on the old man's side, less than ten feet from the van. It too raised its head and trumpeted. Mr Stubbs put the van into reverse and turned, only to see his way blocked. He still looked remarkably calm.

'Okay, we'll just sit it out, they'll go eventually. I doubt they'll charge, they seldom do.' He turned the engine off and tapped his fingers on the top of the steering wheel.

He was right, of course, and within a few minutes the path ahead cleared. The elephants once again seemed more interested in consuming vast amounts of fodder than in us and slowly we moved forward, slipping away up the track. He told me that two weeks earlier an American woman had got out of one of the safari Landrovers and, 'Seeing as they looked so cute an' all,' had patted a full-grown male on the rump. It had swung round, picked her up with its trunk and hurled her against a tree. She had been lucky to survive.

That evening groups of tourists sat drinking and laughing on the forecourt outside the lodge restaurant and bar. They were holidaymakers, in this part of the world for a few weeks only, with chosen companions, and gave no indication of wanting to meet anyone else. I soon became very lonely.

The high adventure of the Congo and Angola had left me no time for feeling down, my mind too absorbed in the challenge of what I was doing, but here, with more time and fewer problems, alone in a crowd of happy faces, I felt alienated and unhappy. I was reminded of holidays with Mel, in Greece or France or Spain – the setting was different but the expressions on the faces of the happy couples were just the same as ours must have been. On reaching Cape Town a part of me had felt that I had this grief thing licked, that I was 'over it' – but I wasn't; like the journey, I now realised there was still a long way to go. The feelings of pain and loss, unlike the miles of my trip, weren't constants that diminished logically over time, rather they changed shape and moved about within me.

The prospect of what lay ahead made me feel no better. Would Tanzania let me in? If Tanzanian customs officers suspect you've been to South Africa they are entitled to refuse you entry. For this reason I had not had my carnet stamped at the border and intended to get a new passport in Lusaka. However, officials are usually wise to such ploys. It would be touch and go. And would my bike last the distance? Would I get visas for Ethiopia and Sudan and if so how dangerous would it be? An escalation in fighting in the Sudan and skirmishes in Ethiopia were being reported almost daily on the World Service. I took a long pull on my vodka and tonic and tried not to dwell on these matters.

With this loneliness came an urge to be home. It was Saturday night and what I really wanted was to be in the pub with friends, to debate who was going to win the forthcoming election, to discuss the chances of Manchester United's winning the league (the fact that that day they'd only managed to draw with Coventry did nothing to improve my spirits). But at the same time I knew that if I'd been there I would have been wishing I was in Africa. *Come on, Jonny, it's only boredom that's making you feel this way. Keep moving on. Yes. Tomorrow I'll head for Victoria Falls – tomorrow I'll feel okay.*

The cloud of mist which hung above the falls could be seen from more than five miles away. The locals call them Mosi-O-Tunya, 'The Smoke That Thunders', and it's this spray – or smoke – that drew Livingstone to them more than a hundred years ago. I was lucky, for unknown to me this was about the best time of the year to see them.

I found the camp site, changed into my shorts and, deliberately leaving my camera behind, I wandered off to see this gargantuan sight. As I walked down the street I speculated about Livingstone's thoughts if he could have seen the place now. There was a Wimpy burger bar, a pizzeria, shops and a museum. On the vibrant lawns of the Victoria Falls Hotel well-stocked buffet tables were surrounded by overfed package tourists. Next to a shop which offered bicycles for rent was a large sign advertising 'The Flight of the Angels'. For about thirty pounds you could swoop down over the falls in one of two twin-prop planes. One buzzed over my head as I read. A coach packed with sightseers let out a toot on its horn as it swung round the corner and entered the car-park. At the entrance there were ice-cream sellers, guides, and people renting waterproof clothing. It was a far cry from the sight enjoyed by my fellow Briton.

I followed a footpath through the undergrowth. The noise – indeed like thunder – got louder all the time. The air was thick with tiny particles of spray and there were puddles beneath my feet. With excitement rising, I rounded a corner and found myself standing beside a statue of the great Doctor himself, looking out over a deep gash in the surface of the earth. Upstream, to my right, the languid waters of the Zambesi flowed gently along until, with startling suddenness, they crashed 250 feet into the gaping void. The foaming waters accelerated as they fell into a maelstrom of power and chaos. As they hit the sides of the basalt rock they were hurled forward to smash violently into the blackened canyon wall opposite, where they were repulsed and flung back again, sending the spray high into the sky. A bright prismatic rainbow arching above the mist linked the two sides like a magic bridge. Moved by this powerful sight, I stood and watched until the sun went down.

That evening while drinking in the camp-site bar I overheard three guys talking in English. They looked more like travellers than holidaymakers, so, summoning up my courage to talk to strangers again, I asked if I might join them. One was Dutch, one a Finn and the other English, all travelling around Southern Africa. After a brief résumé of our various journeys I asked the Dutch guy, whose name was Frank, where he was heading next.

'I go back to Harare and then head up to Malawi.' He was short and thin with cropped dark hair and small round glasses. A crystal on a chain hung round his neck.

'How will you do that?' I asked. 'Will you fly?'

'No, I go through Tete, it is now open. I'll hitch a ride on one of the trucks.'

'Tete is open!' I was amazed. 'Are you sure?'

'Yes, I met two Swedes who came through last week.' He looked excited. 'Their truck got shot at.'

The Tete corridor, or Gun Run as it is more infamously known, is a 150 miles of narrow, cratered road which stretches through the Mozambique bush connecting Zimbabwe to Malawi. It is the most direct route from Harare to Blantyre and once carried most of the goods and commerce between the two. Each day at dawn at least sixty, and sometimes more than a hundred, trucks would line up in a convoy and, accompanied by a unit from the Zimbabwe Army, would start the perilous twenty-hour journey. Often the stragglers from these convoys, victims of breakdown or puncture, were attacked by the MNR – Renamo rebels – which has been at war with the government of Mozambique for years. Goods were stolen and occasionally people killed, but protected by the Zim Army it was usually fairly safe. At least it had been. But the previous December a massive ambush had resulted in over fifty trucks being hijacked or destroyed, the goods stolen and many of the soldiers and drivers killed. Since then the Zimbabwean government had pulled out its protecting troops and the road had been closed, leaving the trucks with a far longer journey via Lusaka.

'Are the convoys protected?' A little buzz of adrenalin stirred in my stomach.

'No. The Army no longer goes with the trucks, it's just down to you.'

I had first heard about this route and how exhilarating it could be when I was in the Sahara. Then, before I had changed my route, I had planned to do it on my way down to the Cape. But in Yaoundé Tony had informed me of the ambush and massacre and subsequent closure of the road and since then I had given it little thought. Now I was being told it was open again, and spurred on by the drink, I felt a sense of excitement. I could get my new passport in Lusaka and a visa from the Mozambique Embassy, cut back to Harare and do the Gun Run!

20 Vagabond Blues

Lusaka, Zambia

Lusaka seemed vaguely familiar, reminiscent of many other African cities. The same confusion of crowds and vehicles barged their way down grimy streets, filling the air with a cacophony of noise and fumes. Grey concrete office blocks, many looking derelict or unfinished, climbed out of the honey-coloured smog. Groups of men loitered on the pavements, dogs scavenged through rubbish and children, hoping for a sale, thrust cheap cigarette lighters into the faces of passersby. I sat back against the hot plastic seat and waited for the taxi driver to deliver me to the Mozambique Embassy.

I had arrived in the city earlier that day, after an easy drive up from Livingstone, and had been pleasantly surprised to discover that the new passport I needed would take only a few minutes to issue. In fact the British Embassy staff were so quick to oblige that they failed to fill in any of the relevant information or even to stick in the photo. It occurred to me that a blank British passport would be worth a considerable sum of money in such a place. On reflection, the hassle involved didn't seem worth it so I handed it back, much to the relief of the young girl who'd issued it, and five minutes later it was correctly filled out.

As the taxi moved out of the centre of town into the suburbs the streets widened and became less congested. We turned down a smaller road and then into a walled compound where I asked the driver to wait. Outside one of the garages to the side of the embassy, a man was lovingly washing a big black Mercedes. He nodded towards a door that was slightly ajar.

Inside it was dark and cool and it took a few seconds for my eyes to adjust. The hall led straight down the centre of the bungalow to a desk at which a young girl sat humming. Behind her a curtain partitioned off a small office. There were plants in pots on the tiled floor and a picture of the President hung on the wall. The girl's tune faded as I approached her desk.

'I would like to apply for a visa, please.'

230

She looked surprised. 'A visa?' she asked. 'Why?'

'Well, I heard that it's now possible to drive through Tete,' I said. 'I have a bike, a motor bike. If it's possible I'd like to do this journey.'

'I don't know. You will have to wait. I go and see.' She got up and walked behind the drape where I could see two men working. After a mumbled conversation she emerged with one of them, a young man whose right ear was missing its lobe.

'So you want to go on the corridor?' Our hands met in a firm grip. I wasn't sure how to read the strange smile on his face. Was it friendly or condescending?

'I'd like to. Is it possible?'

'Yes, it is possible, I think we can give you the visa. Where is your motor bike? I would like to see it.'

'So the route is open?'

'Yes, it is so, but not really for the tourist. The trucks they go again but it is still some dangerous. And on a motor bike . . . this I don't know. Where is it?'

'I have left it at the Brit—'

'Excuse me . . .' I was cut short by a gentle voice behind me, 'but what can we do for you?' I turned to find a large middle-aged man directing the question at me. He was impeccably dressed in grey striped morning-suit trousers, black waistcoat, tie and jacket and a crisp white shirt. His receding hair revealed a domed forehead and his thin mouth curled in a helpful smile.

'This man, he is English. He want visa to go through Tete, Mr Ambassador . . . on a motor bike.' The lobeless attaché wriggled nervously in the presence of his boss.

'Um, I see,' mumbled the ambassador. 'Will you come this way, please, for I do not think this is a very good idea.'

I followed him down the passage. *What the hell do you call an ambassador . . . Your Excellency? Sir?* He opened a large wooden door and ushered me into his office. It was brighter here, for a window ran the length of the far wall and overlooked a small inner courtyard. Two flags, swaying slightly in the breeze of a whirling ceiling fan, hung behind the desk at which the ambassador seated himself.

'Tell me,' he said, sitting forward with his arms resting on the desk, 'what journey are you making?'

'I have driven from London to Cape Town, sir, and now I am going back.' His formality made me nervous. He said nothing,

231

expecting more. 'I am driving from here to Kenya and then, if I can, through Ethiopia and Sudan to Egypt and home.'

'So why do you wish to go through Tete? From here to Malawi is only 600 kilometres but if you go via Mozambique it is more than a thousand.'

'Yes, sir, I am aware of that but I thought it would be an exciting trip.'

'Exciting . . .' he sat back, chuckling. 'Oh, yes, I think we can promise you that. Renamo now hold more than fifty per cent of the land around Tete, you know. They regularly stop and kill people on this road, sometimes simply for a cigarette. Last week, near Maputo, forty-seven bodies were found, and when I say bodies, my friend, I mean only the body, there were no legs, arms or heads on any of them. These people are animals.' If he was trying to scare me he was doing a very good job. He continued: 'And you say you want to get through on a motor bike?' He shook his head pityingly and looked out of the window. 'This is really crazy . . . you would not even reach Tete. Let me explain. You see they place one man on the roadside a kilometre before the ambush. When you go past he shoots some rounds into the air to let them know you are coming and then, when you round the corner, they will be waiting for you. You will not stand a chance. They will shoot you like a dog!' He crashed his hands down firmly on the table to emphasise the point, holding my eyes with his.

'Is it really this dangerous?' I asked. 'I mean, why is it open in that case?'

'It is open for the truck drivers. If they wish to take this risk it is one thing, they have some safety in numbers and no one wants to steal a truck . . . and the goods on board are mainly fertilisers and things like this that MNR do not want . . . but you, on a motor bike, I really do not believe you would get through. These men would do anything for such a machine. It is my duty to tell you this.'

'Yes, thank you, sir. I appreciate your frankness.'

'The only way would be to put your bike on one of the trucks and hope they don't hit it.' He looked at me in a friendlier manner. 'But is it really worth it? From what you tell me you still have some hard places to go. This one you can avoid . . . I think you should.'

Of course he was right. Suddenly it all seemed rather stupid.

Was my life worth so little that I was prepared to risk it on a throw of the dice? No. Not now. No longer. To risk all for the sake of the journey was one thing, but to risk it when I really didn't have to, just for the sake of excitement, that was mad. That I had made it so far showed luck was on my side but, as the ambassador had pointed out, if I was going to make it all the way home I would still need a lot more. I should not waste it on a whim. I looked again at his considerate face which seemed benign, almost fatherly, and wondered why I had been so nervous of him.

'Yes, you're right, it's not worth it. I'll leave for Malawi tomorrow. And thank you for your advice.'

'Oh, you need not mention it,' he said, getting to his feet. 'It is what we are here for. If I have saved one man I am pleased.'

Ambassador Khan opened the door and led me back into the hall. The lobeless attaché was still there talking to the girl but he hurried back to his tasks when he noticed us coming. We walked outside into the forecourt. The man had finished cleaning the car and now stood chatting to my taxi driver. The late afternoon was quiet and peaceful and I realised that a self-imposed burden had been lifted from my shoulders. I turned and shook the ambassador's hand, thanking him again.

'It's okay. Good luck on the rest of your journey.'

'Thank you and good luck to you.' I climbed back into the cab and with a wave we drove away.

I picked up the bike from outside the British Embassy and made my way to the Salvation Army hostel, which I found on the outskirts of town. There were no beds available but I was told I could put up my tent on the grass lawn at the back of the compound. As I was doing this I noticed an old white man walking slowly towards me. He stopped some way off and stared but his look went past me into space, a vacant expression in his pale eyes. His clothes looked as old as he did and were badly worn but of good cut. The detachable collar was coming away from his shirt and there was a dark stain in the centre of his tie. He moved forward again, towards me. Feeling he was summoning up the courage to address me, I thought I'd pre-empt him.

'Hello, Jonny Bealby, how do you do?' I offered my hand to be shaken.

'Eh . . . what? Oh, yes, yes, quite so, quite so . . . John de

Paravicini, but . . . but . . . I don't believe the rest of the family . . . use the "de" any more.' His voice was tremulous and he left long spaces between each word. There were shaving cuts across his thin face; his sunken eyes still avoided mine.

'Hampshire,' he said, still holding my hand. 'Andover, do you know it? You are English, aren't you?' He was shaking slightly, unsteady on his narrow legs.

'Yes, yes, I am English but I'm afraid I don't know Andover. Is that where you're from?'

'What? Umm . . . , Thomas, my younger brother, only he lives there now. I haven't been back since '66. Saw the Cup Final you know, great day, great day.' At last he let my hand drop. He turned away and walked off towards a corrugated iron lean-to in the corner of the garden. Was that where this man lived?

Grabbing my cooker and a saucepan of water I approached the shack. A rectangle of breeze-block walls reached to about waist height and wooden poles at each corner supported the sloping iron roof. The floor was unlevelled concrete. Oblivious of my presence, the old man stood in the middle of this hut, gazing down at his meagre possessions.

'Would you like a cup of tea?' I asked. 'I'm just about to make one.' He turned, at first quite startled, but he regained his composure as he recognised me and nodded.

What was this man doing here? For, now, I could tell that this was indeed his home. A mattress of flattened cardboard lay on the floor surrounded by jars of butter, jam, sugar and medical supplies. Two old leather school trunks with his name and number painted on them were propped against a central support pole. Boxes crammed with books, some of which had spilled out into the dust, lay on their sides. A dirty blanket was crumpled in the corner. There was no chair or pillow.

The old man sat down on a concrete block, took his teeth from an empty yogurt pot, placed them in his mouth and started to eat his evening meal. He had no plate or surface on which to prepare his supper, therefore his mouth was the first place in which the ingredients could meet. First he placed a knob of butter on his shaking tongue, then he added a piece of bread followed by a slice of leek. Once all these were in place he began to munch. He was a pitiful sight. I gave him his tea – with seven sugars – which he seemed to enjoy greatly.

'Tell me, John, how old are you?'

'Eighty-nine,' he said instantly. 'I was born in Andover in 1902, August ninth . . . the day they crowned the King . . . Aunt Annie used to look after us then, my mother could be terribly ill you see but . . . but she emigrated to Canada after the first war . . . became a postman . . . died of cancer.' His words were quiet and hard to hear, but what he said made perfect sense. There was no senility, the voice was simply slowed by age. 'Aunt Emily,' he continued, 'my father's sister, she stayed with us most of the time, she was so very beautiful . . . a real character, you know . . . used to hunt in breeches.' He tried to chuckle at the memory but found the effort too great.

'Where did you go to school?' I asked, trying to bring him back to his own story.

'What? Oh, Marlborough,' he said proudly, pulled from his reverie. 'Passed with distinction. I was in the same dormitory as Lord Rothermere you know, got the VC in Burma. Nice boy, one of my friends. Damn good sportsman as well, as I recall . . . Can't remember how he died.' Between each sentence were long pauses. I often had to jog his mind back into life or help him retrace the line of his thoughts.

'What about university, did you go to one?'

'Of course,' he said indignantly. 'I was a scholar at Cambridge, Emmanuel College, a mathematician . . . and my brother Tom . . . uh, but I believe I was a little better than he. We were both Blues at athletics as well, ran against Abrahams, you know, but we never beat him. He was a fine fellow . . . a great runner, a little older than us, of course . . . something of a hero, I suppose.' His glazed eyes stared into the middle-distance, looking at nothing. The day had died and darkness had fallen. By the pale orange light which hung on the compound wall John's thin face looked haunted and ancient. I set about making another cup of tea.

'So how long have you been in Africa?'

'Since 1927.'

'All that time?' I asked.

'Like I told you, I went back in '66 but that was the last time. I moved out to Jos in Nigeria as a geologist working for the government, lived there for more than thirty years. Then I came out here to build the international airport runway and have been here ever since.'

I handed him the tea.

'Were you ever married?' I realised that this might be intrusive, but I still couldn't understand how a Cambridge Blue and a person of obvious intelligence and a certain amount of wealth could be living out his days as a dignified tramp in Lusaka.

'Yes . . .' he mumbled. He took a long time to continue. 'I was married . . . an English girl. We lived in Jos.'

'Did you have any children?'

'Two boys. They're in England.'

'Do they know that you are here, living like this? Surely if they . . .'

'Do not ask such things,' he said angrily. 'It is not your concern. How could you know . . .' He coughed deeply and got to his feet mumbling to himself, clearly incensed. Had there been some family row? So big that his sons had seen fit to abandon him out here, or was it his pride that refused to allow him to make contact? I couldn't know.

'I'm truly sorry,' I said. 'I had no wish to be indiscreet.' But he didn't hear me and started to remove his clothes. His yellow skin hung off his body like an oversized suit. His back was hunched with age and his legs were like pins. He put on a pair of dirty red and white striped pyjamas and lay down on the cardboard, wrapping himself in a blanket with immense difficulty. Still mumbling, he placed a cloth over his face and tried to find solace in sleep.

I rose with the dawn and was soon packed up and ready to go; with luck I would make the Malawi border that evening. The old man stirred and staggered to his feet, the bitter thoughts of the night before lost to his fading memory.

'Goodbye and good luck,' he said whilst shaking my hand. 'Do send me a postcard . . . I should like that.' I assured him I would and feeling more than just a little concerned for this poor man I climbed on the bike. Destroying the morning calm the engine shrilled into life and carried me up to the compound gates.

'I'll see you again,' said the guard as he pulled himself from his chair.

'You won't,' I replied with confidence, 'I'm on my way to Malawi.' He just grinned and opened the gates. I passed through them, over a ditch and onto the streets of the city centre. At the roundabout next to the railway station I turned right and joined the main highway east.

The early morning sun soon started to break up the clouds, giving the promise of another fine day. Circular thatched huts sat back from the road, almost obscured by the long, coarse tussock grass. Healthy red cattle grazed the verge and people loitered. Without having to worry about the dangers of Mozambique, I felt wonderfully free. The fresh, clear water of Lake Malawi was waiting at the end of my drive. I couldn't help smiling.

Some way ahead I noticed a young man walking along the road, in the same direction as me, pushing a toy. It was a small metal-frame car which he controlled via a steering wheel at the end of a waist-high pole. All over Africa one sees these amazing toys made of wire and tin. They are often vehicles of an extremely intricate design: not only do the front wheels steer but they can also have quite sophisticated suspension systems.

I moved out to give him more room. It was not enough. Just as I was a few yards off he turned the wheels on the machine and steered it, and himself, right into my path. His face turned in horror as he saw me nearly upon him. He froze. I swerved as much as I could, just enough not to hit him straight on, but not enough to avoid him altogether. I caught his left leg with the front wheel and down we all went. I slid along the road with bright lights – sparks from the rack which was saving my legs – flashing in my face. There was an angry noise of scraping metal. My head crashed hard against the asphalt and everything went still.

When I opened my eyes I was staring at the sky. I could hear the sound of running feet approaching from behind. I felt no pain; was nothing wrong? I started to stagger to my feet. Two or three men were around me, talking at me, making no sense.

'I'm okay, I'm okay,' I told them and hurried over to the youth. He was almost on the other side of the road, sitting up with a blank expression on his face, evidently suffering from shock. I looked down at his foot which was twisted badly; the leg was surely broken. Beside him was the upturned toy.

'Are you all right?' I asked, but he said nothing and just looked at me questioningly. My mind went back to the bike. Was it smashed up? Was the journey over? As I turned and limped back across the road towards it, one of the bystanders came up to me.

'Mister, I think you please sit down now.'

'No, I'm fine, we must get the bike up.' I could see it was losing petrol.

'No, sir, you are not so fine.' He pointed at my left shoulder. I touched it crudely and a searing shot of pain rippled through my body. Suddenly the arm seemed unbelievably heavy as though nothing was carrying its weight. I held it with the other arm and looked. The collar bone had snapped and although the fracture had not punctured the skin, the bone stuck out in a nasty lump. My legs felt like consommé and I started to shake.

Two men had got the bike up and were trying to start it with the kick start.

'No, no,' I said through clenched teeth, 'use the ignition button.' At first nothing happened save the dry whirring sound of the starter motor, but after a minute the bike spluttered into life. It coughed a little and let out a belch of grey smoke. Looking from the front the forks seemed straight and although the plastic fairing was smashed slightly I realised with relief that it was I who had fared worse.

'We walk to Changwe,' said the man who'd pointed out my misfortune, 'it is only a mile away. Here there is clinic and police.' So one man drove the bike, another two carried the young man and I walked holding my arm. *Bollocks*, I kept thinking, *what the hell am I going to do now*.

At the police station there were various formalities to be sorted out. I was relieved that two of the witnesses backed me to the effect that it hadn't been my fault, for I could have landed in serious trouble had it been otherwise. I asked if we could get back into Lusaka as I was sure we both needed a hospital and they assured me that an ambulance had been called.

In the meantime we were sent to the clinic. This was a thatched concrete hut in a cluster of tall palms. A crowd of mothers and babies sat outside on the veranda waiting patiently to be seen. I felt quite awkward as I was ushered to the front of the queue but my pain was such that my scruples were quickly overcome. I was told to sit on a couch and given two paracetamol. Moments later a laughing doctor called Minyoi Munalula confirmed that the collar bone was broken and that the young man's leg had suffered the same fate.

He made the lad, whose name was Boyd, as comfortable as possible by splinting his leg before he turned his attention to me. Crowds gathered round the doorway to see if the pain of

238

a white man was the same as theirs. The truth was this white man seemed far more pathetic than any of them would have been in the same circumstances, at least if Boyd's reaction was anything to go by. He lay quietly the whole time with the same non-expression on his sorry face while I, with a break far less serious, found it impossible not to crease mine in an agonised grimace. Taking off my leather jacket was the worst part as it meant lifting my arms. All the while the doctor kept laughing and smiling. I assume he thought this show of good humour might rub off onto his patient but on this one, I'm afraid, it did not. When it came to my long-sleeved T-shirt, even though it was my favourite, I pointed to the scissors and asked him to cut. Once the clothes were removed, he bound my shoulders tightly using two bandages in a figure of eight, criss-crossing just below the back of my neck. Each armpit he packed with cotton wool to stop sores forming and then he sent me through to another room to wait for the ambulance.

At once the pain was reduced by this support and I could sit in relative comfort to contemplate the meaning of this new twist. Every so often a face would appear at the window or doorway, sometimes two or three stacked on top of each other. They'd look for a second, then get embarrassed and shy away. Flies buzzed and rested on the mattress; as always it was hot and sticky.

It was hard to know what to do. The doctor had said it would take three weeks to heal so that was how long I'd have to stay in Lusaka, but where? The Salvation Army was the only place I knew and could afford. I supposed it might be possible to travel north by train but with a useless arm I would have to rely totally on others to move the bike. If only this had happened in Malawi, I could have just relaxed by the lake for a while – but it hadn't. I would have to camp at the hostel that night and try to think of something else thereafter.

With still no sign of the ambulance after two hours of waiting, I got painfully to my feet and went to ask the doctor for news.

'Yes, I am so very sorry but it is apparent that they have no petrol in Lusaka . . . The ambulance – I am most afraid that it will not come.'

I looked down at Boyd who was still lying in the same position, the expression on his face unchanged. His mother and father were at his side. Was it anger and blame I saw in their eyes? Did they hold me responsible? Was I responsible? I knew the accident wasn't my fault, but I couldn't help feeling guilty. If I had not been in his country, driving on his roads, he would still be fine, steering his little wire car.

'Look doctor, I'm all right but this man must get to hospital. Can't I hire a vehicle to take us back?'

'Yes, this might be possible, I will see if it is so.'

Ten minutes later he returned with a rough-looking man who said that for a hundred kwachas he would take us to the hospital in his Landrover. It was robbery, a taxi would have done it for half the cost, but having little choice we bundled Boyd into the back and I, after claiming my tank bag and clothes from the police, climbed into the front.

The journey was a painful one. We bumped over countless pot-holes, swerved out of the way of kamikaze cattle and a lot of the time drove on the dirt where the going was easier. The driver seemed intent on gaining his reward as quickly as possible and it wasn't long before we entered the gates of the University Teaching Hospital.

The UTH was just like any National Health hospital in the UK. In the reception area rows of worried-looking relatives and friends of the ill sat patiently waiting for news. Countless grey corridors reeking of disinfectant led dejected patients from one department to another. Pretty nurses swooped like angels to help the ill and wounded on their way; one took my better arm and led me towards the X-ray department. The results were as suspected: a broken collar bone for me and a snapped tibia for Boyd. He was wheeled off to the operating theatre while I was sent back to reception and again asked to wait.

Another hour passed. I asked a nurse if she could help find out what was going on and whether I could see a doctor. Mrs Simwanza was something of a saviour. She was huge, with a heart to match. First she led me through the labyrinth of staircases and hallways to her office, where I deposited my bags, then she got me a bottle of painkillers from the pharmacy and lastly presented me to a doctor. He was an Englishman from Manchester called Dr Keyhole. Perhaps it was wrong of me, but the relief I felt when I saw that he was English was colossal, especially when I thought of what had happened to Neil. His verdict was the same, however: three weeks and then I should be fine. The figure of eight was okay and there was nothing else he could do.

'Have you seen the guy I hit?' I asked. 'I'd like to be sure that he's okay.'

'Yes, as a matter of fact I've just come from theatre. They're going to operate in an hour or so.'

'What will they do? Is it bad?'

'No, it's a clean break. They'll put a plate in to hold it together and then plaster over that.' He looked at me and smiled. 'Don't worry, we'll keep him in here to see that it doesn't get infected. He's young enough to heal . . . he'll be fine.'

Outside, the hot afternoon sun had started its descent towards the shanty towns and rubbish dumps of the western city. I bought a Coke from a refreshment stall and hailed a cab. It took me out of the hospital gates and back down the Cairo Road.

At the Salvation Army the same guard welcomed me back without surprise.

'Oh dear, you have had accident, I think.' It was almost as if he had known all along what fate had held in store for me. 'There are still no beds, but I will see if I can get you a blanket.' He trotted off in the direction of the main building and returned a few minutes later with a bundle of goodies and a happy smile on his face.

'Look what I get you, two blankets and a mosquito net! You can sleep under the metal. Tonight it might rain.'

There was no one around, just the old man's hut and his possessions, the remnants of his strange, sad life looking very out of place in their current surroundings. With great difficulty I managed to hang the net over a piece of cardboard, put the blankets below it and, having left my bags with the guard, wandered off to find something to eat. By the time I returned the sun had given up on the day and night was taking over. John de Paravicini was there and greeted me like a long-lost son.

As I was lying down preparing for sleep – having taken a handful of painkillers – he turned, and, looking quite ridiculous in his worn-out pyjamas, quoted to me something that he must have told himself a thousand times: 'Do not laugh and do not cry but try to understand.'

The Phone Call

6.35 p.m. May 2nd

'This is a person to person call for Mr Jonny Be– ' Bleep . . . bleep . . .
bleerrrrr . . . The line went dead. I removed my jacket, positioned myself
more comfortably on the floor and, with a racing heart, stared at the phone.
A moment later it rang again.

'Mel, is that you?'

'Jonny? Oh, sweetheart . . . Hi . . . how are you?' She sounded as
though she were at the bottom of a stone well. There was a bad echo
on the line.

'I'm fine. What about you? How's it all going. Where are you?'

'I'm at the tourist camp in Delhi. I got here yesterday from Jaipur.
I'm okay, babe, but . . . but I miss you.'

'Ah . . . I miss you too, darling . . . badly.'

What a relief that was. Before leaving she'd said, 'I just want to
think,' and told me that she probably wouldn't write. She'd been as good
as her word. I had no clear idea where she was or how she was feeling
about things. Evidently she had now made up her mind.

'So, when are you coming out?' she asked excitedly, as if it had been
planned all along. My cheeks stretched into a huge grin. It was the perfect
call. I started to relax.

'Well . . . when would you like me to come?'

'Yesterday.'

I laughed.

'No, really, darling, please. As soon as possible.'

'But, sweetheart, when I said the next flight out I didn't imagine
you'd actually hold me to it . . . There are things I have to do before
I can get away.'

'Umm . . . when then?' She sounded disappointed.

'Soon, sweetheart. Believe me, I want to be there as quickly as possible
but you know how it is . . . I have to get someone to rent the flat. I have
to tell the band . . . you know.'

'Yeah, I'm sorry.' Putting cheer in her voice, she said, 'How was
the album. Will you send me a copy?'

'Of course, but it didn't turn out as well as we'd hoped. We're all
a little disappointed.' The record, for one reason or another, had never
really sparked and now we were just biding time, waiting for the release
– a release that in itself was far from certain. The record company was
having problems with paying the studio and the producer, which left a
bundle of unmixed tapes in limbo. As we didn't have a drummer we

242

*couldn't gig or rehearse, and so, on a day to day basis, we had very
little to do.*

*'What about money, darling?' she asked. 'Have you managed to
save any?'*

*'Over a grand,' I said proudly, 'but I'll need another if we want
to stay for six months. I'm working my backside off dispatch riding.'*

'Oh, do be careful.'

*'I will.' That was a half-truth. It was only three weeks since I'd
had my crash. My left knee had blown up to the size and colour of
a rotten grapefruit, but so determined was I to save money in case I
received this phone call, that I'd been back on the bike as soon as I could
walk. 'Anyway,' I said, changing the subject, 'I thought you wanted to do
Australia on your own.'*

'I did, but . . . you know, I miss you.'

*When Mel had left England she had intended spending three months in
India followed by a spell in Australia. She needed, she'd said, to prove to
herself that she could live and work in a strange new place – on her own.
I had no desire to go back to Australia and although, given Mel's slightly
lonely state of mind, I felt I could have persuaded her not to bother going
there and to meet me instead in Bangkok, I didn't want her, later on, to
feel that I'd robbed her of an adventure. Australia, I felt, was the heart
of the matter. If she really loved me after that, I felt sure our lives would
always be together. It was important that she went on her own.*

*'You'll be all right, darling,' I said. 'Besides, I really need more
money. I can save it quickly here. If I were to come to Australia I'd
blow it in a week.'*

'Yeah, you're right. So how long . . . when shall we meet?'

*'Maybe . . . beginning of August?' I said, making a quick calculation.
'In Bangkok. That'll give you three months in Oz.'*

'Okay. That's fine. First week in August then.'

'I'll book my ticket tomorrow.'

*'Oh, babe,' she said in the softest tone, 'it's so good to hear your
little voice again . . . I just miss you so much.'*

*'I miss you too. It's just not the sa– ' I heard her laugh down the other
end of the line. She said something while covering up the mouthpiece.*

'So what's so funny?' I asked.

'The man here has just asked if I'm talking to my husband.'

'What did you tell him?'

*'I told him you soon wi– ' Bleep, bleep, bleerrr . . . Again the
line went dead.*

The night was hell. Lying on my back with little between me and the concrete floor, unable to move much, it seemed to drag on and on for ever. I must have drifted in and out of sleep, for I remember waking from dreams to hear the old man's snoring. In one dream I was dressed up to the nines at a great ball. I was dancing with a beautiful girl in a black velvet dress, but each time I looked into her face it dissolved into a blur – was it Mel or Amel? I couldn't tell. When I was awake, my body, except for my shoulder which throbbed and ached, seemed to be floating, not really attached to me at all, as if the painkillers had affected every bit of me except the part they were supposed to. By four in the morning I knew I would sleep no more.

It was then that I started to think about my situation and what to do about it. I knew I could not last three weeks like this. I would have to find somewhere better to recover, but the problem was where. Hotels were no use and I doubted the Embassy would help . . . Then it suddenly hit me. So excited was I by this sudden flash of inspiration that I heaved myself up and fumbled in the dark for the torch. *That address. Was it Lusaka? I bloody well think it was!* Propping myself against the wall I rummaged feverishly with my good hand through my tank bag. I found my diary and pulled it out. As I rested it on my lap and opened the front sleeve a loose piece of paper fell out. I held the torch in my mouth and opened the paper up. Sure enough, there was the name: Mr Jaap Garos. P.O. Box 7514, Lusaka, Zambia. Under the address was a note from an old schoolfriend, Christiaan: 'If you need help, this man will give it to you; we were at college together. Try not to get killed. See you when you get back.' *Well, you little beauty!*

21 A Very African Death

Lusaka, Zambia

A huge man, Jaap Garos came striding into the bar as though he owned the place. All his facial features were slightly exaggerated, like those of a caricature: large puffy lips, a long nose and wide, sparkling eyes. Only his chin was small and fell away sharply to a thick neck as wide as his head. He wore khaki shorts, covered in oil, a pale blue short-sleeved shirt, long socks and heavy working boots. Despite his size and grimy appearance he bore the pleasant, affable look of a gentle giant.

I had been lucky. Finding him had been easier than I had expected. At the General Post Office two delightful women had traced the owner of the P.O. Box and via a series of short informative telephone calls I had tracked him down to his farm in, would you believe it, Changwe. His was the only address I had outside Cape Town. It was a good place to have had my crash.

It had been a bit difficult on the phone having to swallow my pride again and ask a total stranger if I might stay, but as I'd already discovered, if you need help in Africa you generally get it.

'So you took one out, uh?' he said once we were heading back to Changwe in his pick-up truck. 'Did you kill him? I did mine.' He laughed without humour.

'What!'

'Yeah, I hit a guy about six months ago not far from where you had your accident. Same thing I expect, guy just walked straight out in front of me. Problem is a lot of them don't realise that roads are for vehicles, not for them and their cattle. He was dead instantly and I was in hospital for a week, so I should say you've got away lightly.'

'Phew . . .' I exclaimed slowly. 'No, I didn't kill him. I just managed to swerve at the last second . . . only broke his leg. He was young, I guess he'll be okay.'

'Yeah, well don't blame yourself. In Zambia things like this happen all the time. It's just the way things go. Remember, he's lucky to be alive.'

A short distance before the accident spot we turned off the main road and onto a dirt track. It cut through the bush for about a mile, past fields of wilting maize, a bottle store and a tin-roofed church, before coming to an abrupt end at a group of nyumba huts. The farmhouse stood behind a fence of tall grass and a metal gate, which was opened as we approached by a small toothless man. It was a large single-storey house covered in creamy honeysuckle and shaded by large, thick-leaved mukua trees. A '30s Chevrolet rested on blocks in the forecourt and Idi Amin, Jaap's faithful mongrel, lay panting under a lean-to. He got up and wagged his tail as we alighted.

Inside it was bright and clean, floored with cool stone from the kitchen to the living room and through to the bedrooms.

'I'm sorry,' apologised Jaap, 'but I haven't been here long so there's no spare bed, only a mattress . . . and I haven't painted the room yet either. I was meaning to do it before my father gets here next month; I wasn't expecting visitors before.'

'To me Jaap this is a five-star hotel. I really am extremely grateful.'

'Ah, don't worry, this is Africa . . . I have to go out now. You relax. If you want anything, ask Pedro, the man at the gate. He's also the cook. Make yourself at home. I'll be back around six. I'll get some beers.'

Jonny – you're a lucky bastard.

Shortly before Jaap returned that evening I turned on the television and sat back in the comfort of a large armchair. As the picture slowly emerged to settle on the flickering screen I was surprised to see the face of Ambassador Khan. What the voice of the reporter was saying made my mouth go dry.

'. . . whose strangled and beaten body was found today tied to a chair. It is not yet known why the ambassador was killed or by whom but it is suspected that Renamo had infiltrated the embassy staff.' His benign face disappeared from the screen to be replaced by that of the news-reader. 'His death comes on a day when heavy fighting has been reported between the rebels and government forces near both Maputo and Tete, with some reports suggesting that as many as 200 people may have been killed. Peace efforts in Rome seem to have reached a stalemate.

'At home now, and in Ndola . . .'

Shocked, I sat for a while staring blankly at the screen. It seemed incredible. Only two days before this compassionate man had persuaded me not to risk my life. Now he had lost his, perhaps at the hands of the very people he had been protecting me from. *Two days . . . Yes, I would have been on the corridor today had he given me the visa.* 'Good luck' had been our final words to one another. Even with a broken shoulder it seemed as though I'd had mine.

I spent my time at Changwe quietly reading, writing letters and relaxing. Jaap's jeep had broken down and was waiting for spare parts to be sent from Holland, so we didn't go out very often. When he wasn't working on the farm he managed for a European company, Jaap would be punching clumsily on his little computer, putting together some sort of feasibility study on a paprika processing plant in Malawi – a scheme that he was sure would catapult him to riches within five years. With his natural enthusiasm and love of life we had little difficulty in getting on. Often we'd sit up late into the night, either alone or with a few of his friends, playing cards or just drinking too much and trying to put the world to rights. He was generous too, expecting no payment for the room and a good deal less than I perhaps should have paid for the groceries and drink. (The only criticism I could make of Jaap was the schoolboy delight he seemed to extract from releasing gases through whichever orifice he could muster. If girls were present, it merely heightened his enjoyment.)

The farm lay on a slight ridge overlooking fields of drought-ruined maize and irrigated paprika which ran all the way to the main road. As my shoulder began to feel stronger I ventured out on walks. I'd follow a line of mukua trees that stretched away from the house into the distance. Their bright orange flowers stood out like fairy-lights in the dusty sun-bleached land. Jaap told me their path indicated an underground river and it was here that boreholes were dropped for the irrigation system. This year had been so dry though that even the underground river was in danger of drying out, which left only enough water for the more precious, because exportable, paprika. I'd walk all the way down to the road and sit at the bottle store drinking beer and watching the odd vehicle go slowly by before returning to the farm.

On one afternoon, coming up a track I had not walked before, I came across a great gathering of people and cattle. A corral had been built which held about forty animals. It had a funnel-like exit down which the animals were pushed twelve at a time. They were then led by their owners up a ramp to the killing ground, a large concrete platform with metal bars above, like goal posts. The animals' hooves and horns were bound with ropes and, in two rows of six, they were pushed onto their sides. Two strong men held each quivering animal down while a third, one looking no more than ten years old, stood at the head of each animal, cutlass drawn. On a count of three from the master of ceremonies down went the knives into the flesh and a minute later all was quiet. The ropes binding the beasts were then tossed over the metal posts and the carcasses hauled upside-down off the ground. The thick red blood, warm and slightly pungent, drained down the ramp and into the soil.

After ten days Jaap decided it would be a good idea to get the bike back. This was something that should have been extremely easy but, as always, there was a problem. On checking my paperwork I found to my distress that the insurance Julius had acquired for me in Cameroun had run out three days before the accident, a fact that could land me in considerable trouble. But Jaap, who knew the Chief of Police quite well, had an idea.

It was a Sunday morning, and the day of the local police versus the village football match, when we set off for the police station in a borrowed van. Jaap walked into the building with the same confidence with which he did most things and asked to see the Chief. After a minute the latter came out smiling, his yellow and green tracksuit dazzling in the sun.

'Good morning, Chief Ndeliki,' Jaap thrust his hand forward and matched the policeman's grin. 'I have come this morning with my very good friend Mr Bealby to collect his motor bike so that we can fix it at my place. He's staying with me to convalesce after his crash, and . . .' Before the officer had a chance to respond he continued quickly, '. . . in view of the important match being played this afternoon I thought it would be in order if we were to give you and your fellow players some refreshments.' From the back of the van, Jaap hauled out four crates of Lion lager. 'It's for all the tireless work you do in protecting my farm.'

248

The Chief's face was a picture: pride and pleasure beamed from every pore.

'Mr Gaaaros, this is most kind of you and indeed you too, Mr, Mr . . . ?'

'Bealby,' I prompted.

'Yes, Bilby, quite so. We were all so very sorry to learn about your unfortunate accident. It is most regrettable. Tell me how is it feeling now?'

'Oh, much better, thank you. Another ten days and it'll be as good as new.'

'Good, I am most pleased to hear of it. Of course you may take the bike and your possessions. You will be staying with Mr Garos until you leave?'

I nodded.

'Good. I will try to come and see you before you go.' I wasn't sure if he meant socially or otherwise. 'But, Mr Garos, I think it is very fortuitous that you have come. You see our referee fell very ill this morning and is unable to participate. I wonder if you would be so kind?'

What could the poor man say?

I spent my last week in Changwe itching to get going again. I knew that by now a letter should be waiting for me in Nairobi from Amel and I was getting more and more anxious to learn its contents. What would she have made of my ridiculous suggestion? Would she think me mad or was she as foolishly romantic as I was? I could only hope she was.

The day before I left I ventured back into town to buy provisions and to have my arm checked by Dr Keyhole. I saw Boyd, who looked a good deal more cheerful. His operation had gone well and he was due to be discharged in four days' time. I also dropped by the hostel but John was not there. I left him my fishing chair and a note saying goodbye.

Having bid farewell to Jaap, at last I climbed aboard the bike and headed down towards the Great East Road. I was pleased to be on my way again but, in truth, I was extremely nervous. The bike seemed to wobble more than usual, as though it too was unsure of itself. My shoulder ached from the start and I had set myself the rather ludicrous task of reaching the border that night. However, as the miles ticked slowly by, fifty turning to a hundred and then to 200, I realised that I hadn't actually lost my nerve, just mislaid it for a while. Soon I entered the highlands of the Eastern Province, settled down and began to enjoy the freedom of being back on the road.

I entered Malawi and drove along the coast of beautiful Lake Malawi stopping off at Nkata Bay. There I had the pleasant surprise of running into Frank and Iliana. It's strange the bonding that occurs between travellers who are roaming around a continent like Africa. I spent only a few days with them in the desert but when we saw each other across an empty beach it was as though we were the oldest of friends. Again Iliana cooked a delicious spaghetti bolognese. Again we got drunk.

That night I lay awake, my mind preoccupied with the problem of crossing the border between Malawi and Tanzania. Ever since Yaoundé, when I'd made the decision to attempt a full circuit of Africa, I knew the day would come when I would have to deal with this. I had taken every precaution I could – new passport and no South African stamps in my carnet – but these facts were in themselves heavy hints that I'd been to S.A. If the Tanzanians were to refuse me entry it would mean returning to Zambia, travelling up Lake Tanganyika, crossing somehow into Zaire and Ruanda, then into Uganda and finally down through Kenya to Nairobi. A journey of many weeks, through some of Africa's hardest country. I knew the Tanzanian border officials would suspect I'd been to South Africa. I pinned my hopes on a bribe.

The perfect undulating road moved away from the lake to weave its way through the Miombo woodlands and open rolling grassland of the northern plateau. Rivers and streams flowed from the hillsides and here at last the square patches of crops looked healthy and plentiful. I drove on hard and fast making good time and reached the Malawi customs with the sun still high in the sky. The formalities took a lot longer than expected and it was well past four by the time I arrived at the Tanzanian entry point.

A creosoted wooden shed sat by the side of the road with three raised concrete huts behind it. Dark clouds moved in from the west bringing the promise of rain and a breeze started to stir the dust. I parked the bike on the gravel, took my papers from the tank bag and apprehensively entered the shed.

It was dark and stuffy and as quiet as a church on a

Saturday night. A drop of sweat ran down my back. I took a deep breath and approached the desk, uttering words of greeting in my limited Swahili.

'Habari gani?'

'Mzuri,' the official replied, looking up suspiciously, surprised but not impressed. I wished I hadn't said it. He had a cruel little face with a small mouth, two tribal scars across each cheek, a sunken chin and a bandit moustache. There was another scar, of a type I hadn't seen before, running right the way across his forehead. It looked as though someone had tried to scalp him. He wore large peardrop sun-glasses and, auspiciously for the bribery plan, a large gold watch.

'Where are you going?' he asked drily, without looking up.

'I am on my way to Nairobi, sir. Tonight I will stay in Mbeya.' This was a town about seventy miles away over a mountain pass.

'And why do you have a new passport?'

'Because the old one was full.' He looked dubiously at me, expecting more. 'I have been on a trip round Africa. You get many stamps.'

'And where has this trip taken you?' He seemed bored as if he knew damned well where I'd been and was simply playing with me.

'I went down the west of Africa to Namibia and then cut through the Caprivi strip to Botswana before continuing north.'

'Let me see your carnet.' I handed it over and he studied it hard.

'Why have you not got stamp out of Namibia or,' he turned the page, 'an entry stamp to Botswana?' The answer was obvious, because they both bordered South Africa. I had already thought out an excuse.

'Because both of these countries are part of the Southern African Union, sir. It is not necessary to get stamps while you are in the Union, only when you enter or leave.' I didn't really expect him to swallow it but it was the best I could manage. He called over a colleague. They spoke for a few seconds in Swahili. The question that followed took me totally by surprise.

'Where is your diary? We would like to see it.' I looked at them blankly for a moment too long. Another drop of sweat rolled off my forehead.

'I don't keep a diary, only photographs.' I'd blown it. They knew.

'Why don't you stop lying to us?' he said disdainfully. 'Do you think we are stupid?'

I looked at them nervously. They had me. No question. If they searched the bike they'd find my journals. I took my passport back from the counter and, turning to the wall, placed a twenty-pound note inside the front page. With my heart in my mouth I handed it back. The colleague had walked away.

'Mr Jonathan Guy, it is a long way back to Lilongwe do you not think?'

'*A long way back*' – *what the hell does that mean?* He wasn't going to accept the bribe? I couldn't believe it. The other route flashed through my mind . . . Oh no, surely not. He had taken the twenty pounds from the passport and was holding it up to the light. Smirking, he turned to me. 'This is not enough.'

Thank God. It was a bloody cheek, though. I thought twenty pounds was far too much. His grin widened. Evidently he enjoyed his authority. I felt sure now that I could sit it out and eventually he would let me pass for the amount already offered, but time was against me. We had jumped a time zone and it was now half past five. Outside it had started to spit rain. I knew the road would be bad, almost impossible in the dark. I must get on. I handed him a ten-dollar note, this time not bothering to hide it.

'That's all the cash I have.'

He put them both in his pocket. 'Okay, this will do.' And with as large a smile as his sour mouth could muster he stamped me into his country.

I comforted myself with the thought that it was only the price of a visa.

For the most part the road through Tanzania was smooth and fast. It ran along the southern plateau cutting through a land of rolling peaks and depressions and scattered bush peopled by Bantu tribesmen. Armies of rough grey baobabs marched in endless columns towards the road. There were herds of cattle, zebra and kudu as well as hyenas and snakes.

South of Mbuyuni I came to a narrow bend where the road was blocked by an upturned truck. A group of people were gathered around three dead bodies. A middle-aged woman was crying over one, banging her head with the palm of her hand. I stopped and tried to offer help but when I realised there was nothing I could do, I pushed the bike through a gap and continued on my way.

At Chalinze, where the road forks north to Kenya, I found a shabby hotel which doubled as a brothel. I couldn't have been there more than a few minutes when an ugly old hag, tired and gaunt and only kept going by the whisky she consumed, came over and demanded: 'Hey mzungu (foreigner). You . . . me jig-jig?' Before I had time to reply she placed her right index finger on her left nostril and, without looking away or trying in any way to be discreet, blew an ungodly amount of green phlegm out of her other nostril onto the wall and floor. She wiped what remained on her sleeve and registering my emphatic 'No', staggered back outside.

I drove around the base of Kilimanjaro, across the flat agricultural plains of coffee, wheat and maize to the beautifully lush Arusha and north again to the border. By the time I reached Nairobi a storm had really set in: it was the first of the long rains. On Kenyatta Avenue hundreds of umbrellas marched along the pavements and water filled the gutters. Even in these conditions there were tourists everywhere, huddled into the curio shops, buying safaris from agencies or having tea in one of the many restaurants. Jam-packed minibuses played tunes on their horns. The traffic pushed steadily through.

In the north of the city I found Ma Roche's guest house without much difficulty and by luck secured myself the last bed in the dormitory. This is a legendary stopover for budget travellers, though I never did find out why. The conditions were far worse than those of the downtown hotels and the price no better. The advantage for me was that my bike would be safe there. I was wet through, all my bags were soaked and I could do nothing but wait for time to dry me. Still, as I looked out over the tents surrounded by pools of water in the camping area, I didn't feel I had things too bad.

It continued to rain with equal vigour throughout the night, finally ceasing just after dawn. The tents now floated on a lake like a tiny armada cast adrift on a becalmed sea. Most of their occupants had abandoned ship at some point during the night and now lay in awkward positions on the floors of the dorm and the veranda. With the sun breaking

253

up the heavy sky I made my way back to the town centre.

The General Post Office was an imposing building situated about halfway down Haile Selassie Avenue. It was built in post-colonial times with little attention to elegance. Outside, men sat behind ancient typewriters attacking the keys with a single finger, mottled umbrellas protecting their heads from the sun. Countless unwashed windows offered light but little air to the thousands of people who worked within, where giant propeller-like fans whirled from the grimy ceiling, forcing the reluctant air to circulate. Crowds of people queued in lines behind each of the counters or wrote in cubicles set against the wall.

It was easy to spot the poste restante pick-up point as it had the only white-skinned queue. Anxious travellers searched through bundles of mail, some retreating with a handful, others without any at all. I reached the front, presented my passport and was handed the pile of Bs. I had letters from Mum and several from friends in Britain, a postcard from Tony saying he'd reached the Mediterranean, but none from Amel. I checked again. Nothing. My heart hit my boots.

'Are you sure these are all the Bs?' I asked the clerk.

'I don't know. I shall look again.' He came back with another, smaller pile.

'These have not been in so long . . .' But before he had finished I was grabbing for the letters. The top envelope was covered in handwriting I recognised. Not even bothering to go through the rest of the pile, I tore open the letter. It was enormous – at least six sides. I scanned it as fast as I could, trying to find the important bit. I found it. My sweaty hands were smudging the ink.

Yes. Yes. Yes. She says she will.
What? . . . But only with her mother?

PART FOUR

Farewell to Shadowlands
Nairobi – Home

22 Night Ride to the Border

Dida Galgalu – the plains of darkness – Kenya

The truck bumped and bounced down the gravel track. The suspension squeaked and the body shook. Next to me an old man stirred and pulled his blanket closer to his chest. I wrapped my chech a little tighter round my face and stared out across the desert plains.

There had been no twilight that evening – there seldom is in the desert – day and night simply swap places like scene shifts in a play. It was moonless but the scrub and rocks of the desert floor could still be seen, lit up by a million stars. It was as if we were travelling through a huge planetarium, the domed sky, encrusted with tiny diamonds, reaching far away on every side.

In Europe we tend not to notice the moon and stars and are often ignorant of their movements; horizons are frequently obscured and nights either too cold to observe or too pale to heed, but out here on the equator, where the heat of the day can be fatal, night becomes a time to work and move. The stars and their names are known to most and their patterns give guidance, friends of the traveller since the beginning. The Plough stood ahead with the Southern Cross behind. Away to the west, just above the horizon, Orion lay on his back waiting for time to raise him to his feet. The sudden flash of a shooting star sped across the heavens, dissolving into the streaky blur of the Milky Way which rested like a cloud directly above us.

As I looked east my eyes were greeted by lights of a different kind. Tiny orange specks, like fireflies, zipped through the darkness. At first I did not realise their significance but as another arc appeared and died I realised that this beautiful display held a sinister sting – tracer bullets.

'Shifta,' said a quiet voice beside me. 'It be the Shifta . . . bandit from Ethiopia.' I could hardly make out the face in the darkness. He prodded my arm with a packet of cigarettes. I took one and crouched down out of the wind. The fire from the match flared in his eyes which were big and brown, moist from the cold night air. Then a gust extinguished the flame and his face was cast once more into shadow.

From the little I had read about the Shifta I had no desire to be as close to them as this. The Shifta warrior is famed for removing the private parts of those he had killed – or, even worse, has injured – as a present for his intended bride. Mine twitched at the thought.

'Are you sure?' I pulled hard on the reassuring cigarette. 'How do you know?'

'If it not them, it be Army patrol, drunk. Whichever, we be okay. Them shots are a long way away.' I hoped he was right.

'Are there many bandits up here?'

'Oh yes, all the way from here to the border, and after if you go on.' The cigarette glow lit up his face. He was young, with frizzy hair and pale skin. He certainly wasn't Kenyan – Ethiopian, I presumed. 'Further north it get worse. We will have to take Army convoy for last hundred miles.'

I crawled back into the hold of the truck and lay down on the dusty boxes it was carrying to the border. The harnessed bike bounced up and down next to me, crunching against the side with every pot-hole we hit. I was on a truck in the dead of night moving once again towards the unknown. In all my life I had never felt more alive.

The time spent in the south had been for the most part uneventful. I had left my bike and taken the train to the coast where I'd spent a week giving my shoulder another chance to strengthen and the various embassies time to issue my visas. Sitting on a white beach under a palm tree in Malindi should have been idyllic, but I was impatient to get on. The route north through Ethiopia and the Sudan was the only viable one, but everyone I spoke to told me I was mad to contemplate it, and that it couldn't be done. Marauding tribes were said to be on the rampage in southern Ethiopia and the war in the Sudan was as bad as it had been at any time in the last fifteen years. But after 17,000 miles I was reluctant to give up with only 3,000 left to go. Besides my funds were running short and the rains in Ethiopia would be falling by the end of May which would cut off my route if I hadn't got through by then. Also, I had now sent another letter to Amel committing myself to a firm plan – I must be in Cairo by 5 p.m. on the fifth of June. Just over one month hence.

At least her letter had cheered me. She had been delighted, if a little amazed, to receive such an offer, but as I had suspected it was one she had been determined to accept. She had pleaded with her father who, on the condition that she was chaperoned by her mother, eventually agreed to her going. Apparently Amel's mother was almost as excited as she was at the prospect of going to Egypt, but Amel assured me we would have plenty of time to ourselves. As much as I was looking forward to seeing Amel again, knowing that they would be waiting for me in Cairo did nothing to relieve my anxieties. What if something should happen to me and I couldn't get through in time? It was a long way, taking me through dangerous territories – anything might happen. The thought of them hanging around in Cairo, waiting for me, was not a pleasant one. Would any girl forgive a man for dragging her a couple of thousand miles across North Africa, at considerable expense, only to be stood up, humiliated in front of her mother? I feared not. I had to make it there in time or I'd have blown it.

My visit to the Ethiopian Embassy in Nairobi in no way allayed my fears. I was not going to get a visa; no chance. The border with Kenya had been closed for a long while. My mental picture of a closed border was vague: guns and tanks? Road blocks and barbed wire? Whether I'd get through or not I hadn't a clue. I liked to think that the eyes of my guardian would not blink now but there was still a nagging worry in the pit of my stomach. So much so that I investigated a different route – by dhow, an Arab fishing boat, from Mombasa to Yemen and up to Egypt. But the price of £500 and the duration of the journey, at least eight weeks, made this impossible.

The Egyptian visa had at least been easy to get but for the Sudan I had been extremely lucky. On my arrival at the embassy I was told that the visa section had been closed for a month but if I waited until one p.m. they would see. At one, on the dot, I was given a one-month visa, albeit entry by air only. The only problem was that the entry date expired on the fifteenth of May. Suddenly I was in a hurry.

I did some maintenance on the bike: a new set of tyres (fourth in all), plug and filter, adjusted the carburettor for the mountains and changed the oil again. I dumped all non-essential items – tent, bed sponge and books – and on the morning of the twenty-fifth, hung over and with chronic diarrhoea, I set off north. It took me two days to reach Marsabit where I had secured the lift after warnings about trouble ahead.

The truck shuddered and stopped. Rising awkwardly to my feet I moved to the front where the others were alighting. The wind had freshened, bringing in a layer of clouds which obscured the stars and turned the night black. Fifteen yards away a kerosene lamp hung above an entrance to a shack.

'Chai,' I recognised the voice from below. 'We are stopping for chai.'

I climbed over the edge and down the metal steps, jumping the last few feet. Through the darkness I could just discern the outline of other huts in an area cleared of scrub.

'Where are we?' I asked.

'Turbi. It three o'clock. Come, we take chai. We will be here for some time.'

The hut was gloomy and dank inside. Another lamp flickered on a rough wooden table and a wizened old man stood bent over a smouldering low fire, willing a kettle to boil. The walls and ceiling were black with smoke, the air acrid and stale. We sat down on stools and introduced ourselves.

'So where are you going?' I asked.

'I am travelling to Sololo, to the camp there.' Now that I could see more of his face I could tell that Dawit was definitely Ethiopian. His skin was light and his features sharp: thin lips and angled nose – more semitic-looking than negroid. He had soft, dark eyes but a creased forehead bore the scars of worry.

'What camp is that?'

'There is a camp for the refugees there.' He moved back to allow the old man to fill two dirty glasses with hot, sugary tea. 'People from Somalia, Sudan and Ethiopia.'

'Why do you want to go there?'

'I have a friend who is there. I must see him.'

I took out a packet of cigarettes and handed him one. 'And you, you are from Ethiopia?'

'Yes. From Addis, but I too am a refugee.'

'Why? Have you been caught by fighting ... or famine?'

260

'No. I had to leave the country some time ago, when Mengistu was still in power. I got in big trouble.'

Other voices murmured quietly in the shadows. The old man stirred the embers of the fire and the wind whistled through the thatch. I took a sip of tea and leant back against the fragile wall.

'So what happened?'

He began: 'It start near three years ago. Mengistu, he was very bad man you know. He had fourteen of his generals executed because they try to overthrow him. Nobody want this man as president, everyone hate him, everyone want change. I was in my first year at the university then . . . I study English,' he smiled proudly.

'I can tell, it's very good.'

'Thank you.' He continued. 'We had to strike to demonstrate against this . . .' he searched for the word, '. . . atrocity. Three hundred students. We lock ourselves in with enough food for a few days. It was fantastic at first. At last we were there having our say, defying this regime we hate so. But after three day the riot police attack. They fire tear-gas into main building where we occupy and smash down doors. Some of us arrested and others run but myself and some friends manage to barricade ourselves into sports hall.' He spoke slowly, his voice full of emotion. I was enthralled. 'From windows at top we could see what was going on outside but we not know that they filming us. They have a video camera and photo man catching us as we look. When food finish we get very hungry.' He took a last drag on his cigarette, dropping it on the earth floor and blew the smoke out slowly.

'After seven days the police attack again, this time with guns. They killed some of us but me and two friends, Solomn and Kebede, managed to escape through the toilets. I went home where my father say I must leave. The police already been once. He gave me all the money he could which was not much and told me to go. I met Solomn and Kebede and we get a bus south.

'That first day we were lucky. We reach Shashemene by afternoon, and Dila by night, but next morning we see our pictures in the paper and it say police look for us.'

The old man hobbled over and refilled our cups. Outside a dog howled.

'I found nomad in the town later that day who said he can take us to Duro. The journey was very hard. It take more than one week. Over the mountains near Gidole and down into the valley. We have very little food, water only from streams, but the nomads were good to us, they treat us well. We stay with them. Look they give me this.' He pointed to a dark wooden coptic cross on a string tied round his neck. 'It supposed to be good luck. I think it is.

'After a week a nomad with big jeep say he take us over the border to Kenya. But he want 1,000 birr each*. This very too much for me and Kebede but Solomn he has the money so he go. We not mind, we tell him he must go. After two more week the nomads say they take us round by camel through the desert of the south-west. This journey is very bad also. Kebede he get thorn in his foot, it go very bad. He must ride most of the way. I have to walk. Here there very little water or food.' He shuddered at the memory. 'We cross the border at Jabisa and travel round to Moyale.

'But here it no better, the police they treat us very wrong. For two weeks we locked up. They beat us with pole and all time say they will send us back. They take all money and possession and send us to refugee camp in Marsabit.'

The wooden door creaked open and the driver of the truck came in. He said something to Dawit in Swahili.

'He say we have hole in tyre. We still stay here for the rest of night and move on in morning after they have mend it.'

It must have gone four, I thought, not long till dawn. I got another cup of chai and lit two more cigarettes.

'So how long did you spend in that camp?'

'Nearly nine month. There were five in each tent, one maize meal a day. Water, it be carried from five kilometres away. Many people die each day. But for me the more bad thing is to have nothing to do. For nine month I sit and do nothing.'

'So what happened?'

'I was lucky. One day I walk the ten kilometres to town and saw tourist truck. I thought they are English so I go and try to talk with them. They are French but they are good and

---

*One thousand Ethiopian birr would officially cost roughly £350 *or seventy-five pounds on the black market.*

ask me to show them camp. Kenyan Red Cross get very angry with me for taking them and showing them the conditions but I do not care. Peoples from outside should know. The leader, he ask if I want to go with them to Nairobi. Of course I say yes.'

'When was this?'

'In July last year.'

'And now you live in Nairobi?'

'Yes, but I have just been granted asylum in Australia.'

'You have!' I was astonished. 'But that's fantastic!'

'I know. They not take me in Canada but United States and Australia they both accept me. Look, I show you.' From a little leather pouch round his waist he took out a much-folded piece of paper and handed it across the table to me. Sure enough it was a letter from the Australian High Commission acceding to his request for asylum.

'I get new passport next week and leave at end of May.'

'It's fantastic,' I said, staring at the letter in the dim half-light. 'What about Solomn, did you find out what happened to him?'

'He is now in America,' he replied with a grin.

'And Kebede is up here? He is your friend in the camp?'

'Yes, but I am not sure. In Marsabit they tell me that they move him to Sololo but he might have got away himself. I not know. The problem is he speak no English. I want to see him before I go.'

'Yes, I can understand . . . you must try.'

Outside dawn was breaking. A thin line of red lay along the eastern horizon. The wind still blew, stirring the dust. In the gloom I could see that they had taken off the offending wheel but seemed to be doing little to fix it. I climbed back up onto the truck and lay down, thinking of the strange story I had just heard. It was a tale that must have been told over a million times on this continent. His had a happy ending, but I wondered how many others had not. When I closed my eyes I saw Mel's face . . .

The Reunion
3.20 p.m. August 7th

'We are now starting our descent into Bangkok's Don Muang International Airport,' the Captain informed us. 'There's some low cloud cover so the landing might be a little bumpy . . . The ground temperature is currently thirty degrees. Thank you. I hope you have enjoyed your flight.'

I took a deep breath and tried to loosen the knots in my stomach. They had been getting tighter and tighter the further east we'd flown. Mel and paradise were only minutes away. I closed my eyes and tried to relax.

The three months since she'd phoned had passed surprisingly quickly. The day after the call I started counting down and soon found myself with only a few weeks to go. Realising my enthusiasm for the band had gone, Andy and Guy greeted my decision to quit calmly and without surprise. Considering how little was happening and how remote the chance of success now seemed, neither of them could blame me for leaving. It was highly unlikely that the album was ever going to be released and even though a new drummer was doing a few rehearsals with us, they knew as well as I did that we were flogging a dead horse.

Guy, and his girlfriend Lindsay, agreed to move into our flat and with two weeks to go I had doubled my savings to over two grand. By the first of August I was itching to be away.

The wheels of the plane screeched along the runway, eventually coming to a stop. I collected my rucksack from the baggage hall, passed customs and secured myself a taxi to the city centre. The heavy afternoon rain had just relented but the sky was still dark. The air was so thick and heavy it was hard to breathe, and moments after leaving the terminal building I was covered in sweat.

For some reason I had imagined the airport close to the centre of town and that my journey to the hotel would be a short one. One hour later my cab was still crawling slowly down a five-lane 'express' way. Would she have got there safely? I wondered. She should have arrived from Sydney the day before. How will she be? How will she look? I hope the flowers I ordered for the room arrived okay.

The buildings grew taller as the suburbs gave way to the city centre. At last we came to a stop. Dwarfed by its more illustrious neighbours, the Oriental and the Meridian, the Swan Hotel nestled in a quiet back street a hundred yards from the river. I paid the taxi driver and walked towards the reception area.

'Could you tell me which room Miss Akroyd is in, please?'

The concierge smiled and stood up. 'Certainly,' he said, 'she is in room

201. It is on the second floor at the end.' I thanked him and made my way up the stairs.

I stood outside the door for a few seconds, composing myself. It was the beginning of a new chapter – the last one. I wasn't going to screw up again. I'd learnt my lesson . . . this time was for ever. I ran my hand through my hair and took a deep breath. One knock was all it took. She flung the door open and threw her arms around me – we collapsed on the bed in a heap.

She looked more beautiful than I'd ever seen her. Her skin was tanned and her hair long – evidently the Aussie climate had agreed with her.

'Look what I got at Singapore Airport,' she said after a minute, pulling something from the bedside table. It was a bottle of wine . . . Château Margaux! I opened it up immediately and filled two plastic beakers.

'To us, sweetheart,' I cried, bumping them together.

She leant back against the headboard and took a sip. 'So,' she said with a mischievous smile, 'when are we going to get married? In Goa at Christmas or back home in the spring?'

I couldn't stop myself from bursting out laughing. It was a long way from the romantic proposal I'd planned, but what the hell . . . In Goa at Christmas sounded good.

I woke to the sound of a baby's cry. The mother squatted in the corner, hiding her child behind her cotton veil. She stared vacantly, unresponsive to the discomfort of the infant. She was pitifully thin, with skeletal face and arms and bent legs like the wishbone of a chicken. She was not Kenyan – a Somali, I guessed – another refugee from another war. I got up and climbed out of the truck.

The sky was grey and depressing, hanging over the land like a blanket of lead. The promise of rain lingered in the air and a cutting wind still blew. Slovenly soldiers sat outside the hide shacks and wattled huts. Crows scavenged and goats bleated. During the night-time journey the desert had given way to a scrub plain of pale green bush which stretched away in all directions, broken only by the Huri hills which hovered like a distant cloud on the western horizon.

I walked over to the shack where Dawit was sitting and got some chai and a fried dough ball. 'How long will we be?' I asked.

'The wheel is fixed but we must wait for more soldiers. They say there are bandits about.'

Looking around at the soldiers we did have, I wasn't filled with instant relief. They looked tired and depressed. After a few minutes an order was shouted and the engine on their truck broke into life. They picked themselves up, dragging their guns behind them, and made their way across the dirt to climb aboard.

'They have been called to help some other soldiers,' Dawit informed me. 'They are fighting ten miles away. It means we will lose our escort, but I do not think this will matter.'

When the soldiers were assembled they looked a good deal more cheerful, spurred on perhaps by the prospect of a fight. The horn blasted and off they went, due west, straight into the wind.

It started to rain as we climbed aboard our own mended truck. We pulled the plastic tarpaulin up to the cab and continued our journey north.

The baby seemed to be getting weaker. At first it had cried, now it didn't even have the energy for that. The air, trapped between the boxes and the plastic sheet, was stuffy and hot. We sat, huddled together, trying to limit the bruising from the bouncing truck.

'Where do you think they are going?' I asked Dawit, nodding at the woman and child.

'They will be going to the camp as well. It is very big, maybe 50,000 people.'

The baby's eyes were glazed and unfocused. Its naked stomach was stretched with gases, fit to pop. The skin on its arms looked like a covering of thin brown leather. Its mouth and nose were encircled by flies and I wondered if it would last the journey. It shook with a spasm of pain and coughed. A thick, dark green sludge, the consistency of tar, oozed from its mouth onto its chest. The mother stirred and wiped it away. For a moment the baby seemed not to breathe, as silent and still as the land through which we passed, but then an arm flinched and again it coughed.

I crawled across the boxes towards my bike. In an inside pocket of the tank bag I found a couple of sachets of powdered rehydrant and got out the chipped enamel mug. I poured some chlorine-cleaned water into the mug and added the powder.

'Dawit, we must get her to feed this to the baby.' She could tell I was talking about her and looked at me nervously. 'Can you tell her it is good for him.'

'I can try but I no think I speak her language.' He was right, the explanation was not understood. So I mimed, then handed her the cup. She tried to make the baby drink but it was a long way gone and unable to respond. With the continuous jolting of the truck much of the liquid spilt over its chest, but with constant coaxing it stirred enough to take down some of the life-saving draught. I worried that it would just throw it back up, but it did not. It lay in its mother's arms, unconscious or asleep, I wasn't sure. I mixed another drink for the mother who drank the contents in one gulp.

Soon after eleven we reached the refugee camp, ten kilometres short of Sololo, where a crowd of men swarmed around the truck to unload the sacks of sugar and flour and carry them to safe-keeping. I gave the woman, who by now could barely stand, a few more sachets of the rehydrant and said goodbye and good luck to Dawit.

Once they had gone I pulled back a small part of the tarpaulin and poked my head out. A more depressing sight was hard to imagine. As far as I could see in all directions were miserable hovels and worn-out tents. Domed branch frames were covered in pieces of plastic, hides or hessian sacking. The land between seemed dead. Withered thorn trees and rough bush united these woeful dwellings whose occupants, themselves clothed in sacking, wandered aimlessly in the drizzle, their sole consolation being that here, at least, nothing was trying to kill them, except perhaps nature.

We reached Sololo a little while later and joined the thirty or so other trucks waiting for the army escort which would take us to the border. It was greener here, more alive, as though the land itself had been depressed by the camp and now felt cheered and optimistic. There was a gathering of mud shacks and a breeze-block hut. I climbed down and bought some more chai.

We waited and waited. The clouds parted and the sun came out and the smell of wet earth filled the air. Eventually soldiers arrived and took up positions on each of the trucks. A green Landrover with a huge machine-gun mounted on the back headed the column. Three burly soldiers, far more fighting-fit than the ones I'd seen earlier that morning, sat beside me, above the cab. They looked tough and well-trained and carried their MI6s with pride. 'There be no problem,' one of them said, 'last attack over two week ago . . . We kill them all.'

The trucks moved slowly down the red, puddle-ridden track without incident. Besides us the only things moving in that silent wilderness were the graceful eagles soaring high above. The truck climbed into Moyale as the dying sun disappeared behind the rooftops.

Moyale is a town of two halves, divided by a border stream. The Kenyan side was a pit: muddy streets lined with ramshackle dwellings and messy shops. People seemed to shout rather than talk and played their music incredibly loudly. It had a debauched roughness and simmering aggression common to most frontier towns, and reminded me of Arlit.

A great crowd assembled at the back of the truck and helped lift my bike to the ground. They all wanted paying and grew angry when I refused. Rather than pay twenty-five people a few shillings each, I gave the biggest, angriest man a hundred shillings and told him to share it out.

I was exhausted. My head hurt and my body ached. I made my bike as safe as possible in the courtyard of the thatched hotel-cum-brothel, and, avoiding the advances of a number of girls, secured myself a cell. When I did leave the room I was immediately set upon by a group of rowdy opportunists. I was one of those strange things they'd heard of but seldom seen: a tourist. They knew nothing much about us except that we had money and they wanted mine. Stretching out their upturned palms, tugging on my shirt, they straightforwardly demanded anything they could think of. I quickly ate a bowl of rice and with my head fit to explode returned to the room and slammed the door.

What the hell's going to happen now? I somehow had to talk my way across the closed border and secure safe passage to Addis. If I achieved this, there was only one more tricky crossing to go. If not, I would have had it. A radio was screaming on one side of my room and a dog began to bark on the other. I lay on the bed, played with Mel's ring and prayed that I hadn't been forgotten.

Once again the rain teemed down. I checked out of Kenya, rolled down the hill to cross the stream and rode up the other side into Ethiopia and back in time seven years: here they use the Julian calendar, not the Gregorian.

Tanks, barbed wire, roadblocks and guns? The flimsy metal pole crossing the road was unmanned. I drove around it wondering whether anyone in Moyale would have enough clout with the new boys in power to give me the *laissez-passer* and if such a person existed, where I might find him.

The town looked as shabby as its Kenyan brother; sad and grey, disconsolate in the morning rain. Yet it also appeared calmer, less chaotic and the people less frenetic. A few stared but no one hassled or begged as I pulled my bike up out of the rain and entered a large circular bar.

It was warm and stuffy. Men sat at tables round the edges of the room, drinking coffee and tea from miniature glasses. Most wore shammas, the traditional dress of Ethiopia for both sexes. Essentially a long piece of cloth, ranging in material from finely woven cotton to thick wool, occasionally beautifully embroidered, it is wrapped around the shoulders and head. Smoke from cigarettes spiralled towards the domed ceiling. Faded posters were stuck to the walls. I was cold and wet and needed something hot.

'Coffee, please.'

The man behind the central bar didn't understand and called over one of the waitresses.

'Do you speak English?'

She was short and slim and pretty. Her features were Semitic and her skin dark. Her hair was braided into a thousand beaded plaits and she wore a bright pink jacket with faded jeans. Her name was Helen.

'Some,' she answered coyly, 'it depends what I must say.'

'I would like a coffee, please.'

'Buna or Nescafé?'

'What is buna?'

She smiled at my pronunciation. 'Buna, it be Ethiopian coffee. Very strong, very good.'

'I'd better have that then. Thank you.'

I sat down against a wall and took off my wet leather jacket. The gentle murmur of Hamitic voices was quietly pleasing and though I wasn't officially in Ethiopia yet I was delighted to be out of Kenya.

Helen returned with the drink, not much more than a couple

269

of sips, but oh, what sips they were. Ethiopia is supposedly the home of the bean and if you agree, as I do, with the old Greek proverb that coffee should be drunk 'as black as hell, as strong as death and as sweet as love', you will find here the greatest coffee in the world.

Helen sat on a chair opposite me to find out if I liked it and was clearly pleased to discover that I did.

'I need to see someone about stamping my passport,' I said to her after I'd finished. 'The person who can give me permission to enter Ethiopia. Do you know where they might be.'

'You must see the OPDO.' She said it so fast I barely caught the letters.

'What does that stand for?'

'The Oromo People's Democratic Organisation,' she frowned as she fought to say the words. 'They be in charge now.'

'Where can I find them?'

'They have council just on road.' She pointed up the street. 'But it better for you wait. Masfin be here soon. He is friend of the head. It better you wait for him, he can help.'

There was no great rush I concluded. While I was in the bar, which I now realised was also a hotel, I was out of harm's way. The place was warm and the people friendly. I asked Helen to give me a room.

There was a row of eight motel-style rooms across a muddy courtyard. The rancid smell of the squat loo at one end lingered in the air. Helen gave me the key to number six. It was small and dark, not much bigger than the bed it housed, which was damp, but the light worked and there was a bucket of cold water to wash with.

Soon after two o'clock, warm and dry, I returned to the restaurant by the bar. I sat down at a chipped formica table and, rather than ordering a meal, was told, very charmingly, what I was going to have. Wat and injera. I smiled and agreed.

Helen came over with another girl of a similar age, about twenty, called Elizabeth. She was more negroid-looking, very dark and, like her friend, attractive. They sat down and watched with interest as I battled my way through their national dish. Wat is a fiery stew of any meat that happens to be handy, in this case goat, and injera is a sour bread with the texture of pancake and the flavour of Guinness. You use no knife or fork but scoop the meat up in large folds of the bread. Once I'd got over the excruciating pain of burning lips it was very good. There was beer to wash it all down.

My company was charming. I think they were 'professional' girls as well as waitresses but there was none of the coarse vulgarity of the whores in Arlit. They were sweet and demure with good manners and kindly dispositions. From what I could see, these girls were respected and liked by all in the place.

After a while, as promised, Masfin entered the bar. He was a guy of about my age with a plump round face and a pleasant smile. He wore jeans and a long-sleeved shirt. The girls called him over.

'Yes, Isegaye Ragasa is my friend . . . He is my best friend,' he said proudly, answering my question. 'We were in same class at school.'

'Do you think you could help me see him, to try and get clearance to Addis.' I explained that the border was officially closed.

'Oh, yes, I'm sure there will be no problem. He can do this. He can do anything . . . He is head of the interim government you know.' A good best friend to have. 'But it is better that I see him first. You know, he is very busy and if, like you say, it is not allowed really, it may be better that you see him here . . . away from the others. He comes here for breakfast each day.'

The evening passed quickly in a welter of beer and laughter and it was well after nine the next morning by the time I woke up. My head hurt and my mouth was dry. Black flies buzzed annoyingly round the room and the bad smell had intensified . . . but at least I was on my own.

There was a knock at the door.

'Jon, are you awake? He is here.' I recognised Masfin's voice.

'Yes, yes. Give me a minute and I'll be out.'

'I have told him about your situation and he is not sure. Do you have something you can give him? It might be useful.'

'Okay, I'll find something. Thanks.' *Good.*

I went to the shower cubicle behind the bed, poured the bucket of water over my head, had a quick, painful shave, dressed, found the 'gift' I wanted and made my way back to the bar. *Take a bribe, take a bribe, please, please, please take a bribe!* Once again the fate of the journey rested on the shoulders of a single man. With or without integrity? I would soon find out.

271

He didn't fit my image of an interim-government leader. Sitting next to Masfin on the veranda outside the bar he wore sneakers, jeans and a faded denim jacket. He had long black frizzy hair, a thick moustache and at least a day's stubble. He was drinking buna and smoking. I shook his hand and sat down next to them. I had expected the 'interview' to start immediately but it did not. We sat in silence. Various people came and went, asked him questions, shook his hand or simply bowed respectfully before him. I ordered two coffees and waited patiently, getting more and more nervous. At last he spoke, not to me, but to Masfin who translated.

'He want to see your passport.' I had it on me and took it out. He examined its contents and put it on the table. Elizabeth threw me an encouraging smile as she put my coffee down next to it. Again he spoke to Masfin.

'He says you have no visa.'

'No. I don't. I was told I could get one here from the OPDO.' It was a lie of course, but a relatively plausible one. I took out a cigarette and offered one to each of them. Masfin refused but Mr Ragasa accepted. I lit it with my hastily polished Zippo lighter and placed it on the table. It caught his eye.

'The problem,' Masfin went on translating, 'is that you can only cross the border with permission from Addis. It has been closed for long time and it is only the Internal Ministry who can authorise this.'

'But how long will permission take to come through?' I asked, knowing that the chances of getting it, should I apply, were almost non-existent.

'Three weeks . . . maybe more.'

'But I cannot possibly wait that long. I have to get out of Ethiopia before the rains start, otherwise I'll be trapped. If he can give me a letter of clearance to Addis, I'll get a visa from the ministry when I arrive.'

I drank the coffee while they talked. Dark clouds still lingered over Kenya but here the sky was clear and the sun hot. A slight breeze rustled the pale blue jacaranda trees which lined the street opposite. A battered truck crawled slowly up the hill, passed the bar and disappeared. Again Mr Ragasa browsed through my passport in deep contemplation. Then he picked up the lighter and started to play with it.

'He can have it, if he wants . . . a present,' I said to Masfin.

It needed no translation. Ragasa smiled but said nothing. We sat for an age.

Come on, babe . . . do something.

Finally he stood up, cupping the lighter in his large right hand. He said something to Masfin and left.

Hundreds gathered on the compound forecourt under the feeble drizzle; the clouds from Kenya had now moved north. The speaker stood on the bonnet of a defunct military jeep in a rough woollen shamma, his henchman at his side, holding a torn umbrella above his head. The damp crowd murmured and shuffled restlessly on the pale yellow earth, jeering at one comment, agreeing with another. The flagpole stood naked, the guards without uniform. This was democracy in its foetal stage. In the grey half-light it could almost have been Cromwell stirring up support against the Crown. The occasion was a meeting called by the OPDO. We stood for a while under the sheltering leaves of a giant fig and watched the proceedings. Masfin explained to me something of the country's recent history.

In the spring of 1991 the Ethiopian People's Revolutionary Democratic Front (EPRDF), mainly consisting of the people of Tigre and independent-minded Eritreans from the north, plus, to a lesser extent, the Oromo Liberation Front (OLF) from the south, swept through the country and toppled Mengistu's thirteen-year-long, Soviet-backed, totalitarian regime. Meles Zenawiy, a young Tigrean, had been the first off the blocks and quickly formed a government – for a while all seemed well. But the post-revolution euphoria did not last long and now, almost exactly a year later, with elections around the corner, the country was once again on the brink of civil war. Zenawiy was trying hard to keep this impoverished, multi-ethnic state (there are over a hundred tribes and languages in Ethiopia) together but the OLF thought he was doing so at their expense, filling the cabinet with northerners and disregarding their views.

The OPDO had been set up by the main EPRDF party in order to give them a loyal local powerbase in the south, and extra seats in the government. Through meetings like this they were trying to drum up support for themselves and take it away from the more radical OLF faction. By the look of discontent on some of the faces in the crowd it seemed many were far from convinced.

273

The fact was however that the EPRDF held the trump card in the form of a 120,000-strong, highly skilled force which in effect doubled as the national army. They backed OPDO, therefore OPDO were in charge. The fringe OLF, while retaining their seats on the interim government, with less than 20,000 troops had to make themselves heard by engaging in banditry and guerrilla activities. This, in a nutshell, was the problem in the south.

The rain was getting heavier but it didn't deter the crowd from listening or the speaker from shouting. On a barren patch of wasteland behind the speaker, sandwiched between some dismal dome-shaped huts and a row of eucalyptus, there was a mass of rusting army vehicles. They had been the means of escape for a handful of Mengistu's 500,000 troops who had had the sense to bolt across the border after the President himself had fled to Zimbabwe. Two hundred thousand men were still thought to be in detention.

To the left of the crowd was a long iron-roofed hut. The red paint was peeling off its walls revealing the grey concrete beneath, and by the steps a goat foraged for invisible nourishment. It had just gone three. In the gloomy hallway people, old and young, standing or squatting, waited patiently to put their questions to the council which was in session behind the wooden door. We leant against the wall. People came and went as the door opened and closed. Masfin managed to get the attention of the doorman and soon we were admitted.

The room was small and shabby with two wooden tables forming a T. The three council members sat along the length of the top table with their backs to the wall, a man with an automatic rifle stood at their side. Stuck by sellotape above them was a handmade OPDO poster depicting an AK47, a shield and a spear with the inscription: 'One People, One Nation: One Ethiopia.' I took a seat facing them at the end of the other table.

'Why you travel in Ethiopia?' It was the one in the middle who asked the question. He was older than Ragasa, who was seated to his left, and was dressed in a strange assortment of clothing. His pale shamma covered a brown Western jacket and blue shirt and on his bald head he wore a small red kofia – or beret – which gave me the impression he was a Muslim. He had a straggly beard and thick eyebrows which arched above a pair of pale, intense eyes. I held one hand with the other to stop them from shaking.

'I am driving my motor bike round Africa, sir,' I answered respectfully. 'I have driven down the west and now I have only to get through Ethiopia and Sudan and into Egypt to complete my mission.' It was dark and stuffy in the room, a pall of blue smoke from their cigarettes hanging above our heads. Outside the rain battered hard against the roof. The three men regarded me curiously. It felt as if I were on trial.

'Why you do this?' Again it was the middle one who spoke.

'Umm . . . many reasons, sir.' I managed a smile and shrugged my shoulders, '. . . to learn something of life, I suppose.' He muttered something in Amharic at which the others laughed. I was pleased to see his humour and began to breathe a little easier.

'And what have you learnt?' he asked.

'Many things, sir . . . many things.' I was unable to think of a better reply.

He seemed satisfied and lowered his head to write in the large tome that was in front of him on the table. Masfin gave me an encouraging nod.

'Okay,' he said after a moment's deliberation, and a brief look at the others, 'we give you letter to travel to Addis. You must see government there to get visa.'

I grinned at Masfin, unable to contain my delight.

'How much petrol you need?' the leader asked.

'Oh, umm . . . thirty-five litres, please.'

'For a motor bike?'

I nodded. 'Very well. Ragasa will write out chit and the letter. But be careful, not everyone will be as pleasant as us. To Dila may be hard, but from there you will have no problem.' He smiled. 'I give you my luck . . .'

Ten minutes later I walked out into the rain, the permit to travel north safely placed in my inside pocket. I looked at the ring and wondered how I could ever have doubted I'd get it.

23 Mr Jon, There is War!

Moyale, Ethiopia

The road climbed steadily from the border. Although the first stretch was notoriously dangerous I saw nothing move save a brace of guinea-fowl. Here the land was rough semi-desert with phallic white termite mounds rising like statues from the hard-baked earth and on either side, in the distance, wild mountains shimmered purple.

At the check-point in Mega the minibus I was following came to a halt. Ghalib, the driver, a kind-looking man who had been asked by Masfin to keep me in his sights, jumped out, a rifle slung across his back. My letter was examined and seemed satisfactory. We'd done a hundred kilometres and it was time for some tea.

Ghalib and I sat ourselves down on the veranda of a concrete hut. It was still overcast but without the threat of rain. A gentle breeze ruffled the dust.

'Welcome in my country,' said a wild-looking man, approaching the hut. 'I like your machine.' He was wearing a torn khaki jacket, stained with oil, and was carrying a Kalashnikov AK47. A leather thong fought a losing battle to hold down his bush of hair. 'You give me go, friend?'

'I'd rather not,' I answered bravely.

'I know. You think I fall and break it, ugh?' His smile displayed an enormous set of ivory-white teeth. 'You probably right, I never drive before.' He laughed and sat down next to us. I looked at his gun.

'Where is your weapon? You let me see.' It was a demand, not a request.

'I don't have one.'

'Why not, this is most crazy. You must have gun. Here,' he thrust his into my hand, 'you buy this one. I have two more.'

'No, no, I can't,' I laughed nervously, surprised by the offer. 'I'm not allowed.'

'This is Ethiopia, you do as you will.' He was smiling

276

but definitely not joking. 'It is not expensive, you give me one hundred dollar . . . U.S.'

I looked down at the killing machine. What is it that makes them so thrilling? It was made of dark brown wood and grey metal with a short stumpy barrel and was exceptionally heavy. The stock could swivel round to turn it into a rifle fired from the shoulder or could be positioned under the gun, which made it possible to shoot from the hip. The pistol grip was worn and the wood scratched. It had obviously been well used. A hundred dollars did not seem like much for such a gun, even in a country like Ethiopia where weapons are easily found. In the frantic cold-war fight to gain control of the horn of Africa millions of such armaments had been poured into the area. If he was offering it to me for a hundred dollars I could probably get it for twenty. For a crazy moment I was quite tempted.

'I give you spare clip,' he said encouragingly, pointing to the curved magazine that jutted out below. I held the gun up in mock aggression and imitated the sound of firing.

'You not want.' Ghalib spoke for the first time and brought me back to reality. I turned in his direction. He was shaking his head. 'Is no good.'

He's right. Wake up, you're not bloody Rambo.

'No thanks,' I said, handing it back. 'He's right. I think it would be more likely to get me killed than save my life. Thank you, but I can't.'

He looked at me as though I were mad.

A youth, no more than sixteen, wearing a floppy green hat with an AC Milan badge stitched to its side stood astride my front wheel. Stick grenades hung from the belt around his waist and in his hands he held a gun. The barrel pointed at my chest.

We were a few miles short of Agere Maryam when bullets started to fly, not directly at us but close enough to make me start. On a shallow hillside, a few hundred yards away to the right, a skirmish was going on. A piece of earth was pulverised as a mortar struck the ground. Thin plumes of smoke drifted skyward and above the noise of my whining engine I could hear the distant crackle of gunfire. I put my head down and tucked myself in behind the minibus. The back row of passengers turned. Their faces were smiling, hands pointing. Was this their idea of fun?

As we entered the village the sight that greeted us was one of mayhem. People were running in panic. Almost everyone, including the children, had guns and those that didn't held spears. Mostly they had Russian-made assault rifles like the one I'd been offered but some had much larger weapons and carried belts of ammunition across their chests. At a rope barrier we were forced to stop and I was surrounded by a nervous crowd.

'I am English,' I said, and tried to smile. 'English ... British.' The AC Milan fan seemed not to understand and held his weapon steady. Only sixteen, maybe less; how much adrenalin must be charging round his body, I wondered. If the threatener had been a man – with a conscience and experience of life, knowing its value – it might not have been so bad. But sixteen! He might panic or fire the gun just to see what it did. My mouth went dry. To my right another man in khaki fatigues was beating people away with a bamboo cane. He was short and thin and looked rather weak, but he evidently held some authority. The noise was deafening, a hundred faces shouting. A dark sea of bodies writhed around me. It was impossible to know what was going on.

The OPDO had written my pass on behalf of the interim government. By them or any of their allies it would be honoured but if any of these villages were being held by the OLF it wouldn't be worth the paper it was written on. Given to the wrong person it might very well invite a kidnapping, or worse.

The man with the cane was now next to me, demanding my papers, his hand outstretched. The youth moved the barrel of his gun impatiently, indicating that I should hurry up. Realising that I had no choice, I took them out of my pocket and handed them over. For a moment nothing happened. He looked through the passport and read the letter. I could feel the exaggerated pounding of my heart and the blood thumping in my ears. He finished reading and looked up, then shouted out a question. My head began to spin.

'I am English, I don't speak Amharic. Sorry.'

He shouted again more fiercely and his friend, once more, thrust with his gun.

'What do you want? I am British. Addis Ababa, I go to Addis.' I pointed up the road. 'Tourist. Tourist.'

The boom of a distant explosion sounded from behind with

a renewed volley of gunfire. His questioning eyes stared past me in the direction of the fighting – he seemed undecided. At that moment Ghalib pushed through the crowd. He smiled nervously as he attempted to explain who I was and why I was there. My presence was attracting more and more interest and the numbers around the bike were increasing. Their faces were tense and drawn.

A moment later the problem seemed to have been resolved. 'We go,' said Ghalib, turning to me urgently. He took my papers from the soldier and handed them back. The soldier seemed pleased that the situation had been settled and the cane went rigorously to work again clearing the crowd. The AC Milan fan looked disappointed but he stood aside and let down the rope. Ahead, the road was clear. Ghalib got back behind his wheel, started up the engine and stuck his head round the sliding door to check I was ready. On my wave of confirmation he sped off up the hill out of Agere Maryam with me close in his wake.

If I'd had a gun the outcome might have been very different. I had two reasons to be very grateful to Ghalib.

The road to Dila was magnificent. We were now high up on the mountain plateau that runs like a spinal cord, broken only by the great Rift Valley, all the way to the Red Sea coast. Forests of pine, fresh eucalyptus, wild olive and massive juniper trees lined the road, which was in excellent repair. The verges buzzed with vibrant life. Squatting people laid their peanuts out to dry on the hot tarmac, the wood sellers and charcoal vendors sat beside their stock and tiny children thrust sugar-cane into the path of those who passed. Healthy sheep and cattle were herded towards the weekend market and overloaded carts trundled by. Once more people waved happily as I passed. Even the wooden huts seemed cheerful. They were far better made than anything I'd seen for some time, with fine thatched roofs, framed windows and even colourful, hedged-in gardens. The sun shone through a shimmering haze. Perhaps the taste of fear had made my senses more acute for my eyes seemed to see more and my brain was more receptive. This land was stunning, the most beautiful I'd seen in all Africa. The pictures we see on our television screens had led me to expect barren hills and dusty plains with famine rife and poverty extreme but this could hardly have been more different; this was the Garden of Eden.

In each shallow valley, Galla tribesmen stood like storks, balanced on one leg, leaning against their spears. They had guns too, thrown over their shoulders, but the threat of aggression had gone; they stood with their herds, calm and relaxed. We motored along through the trees in the dappled sunlight, dodging the multitude, the only vehicles on the crowded road.

We arrived in Dila just before five. Having said goodbye to my escort, I set about finding petrol. This meant having to pester an official at the council offices for a chit. Since the revolution imported commodities had become scarce in Ethiopia and therefore anybody wanting them had to show just cause. Was mine worthy enough? It seemed so. Having read Ragasa's letter a sour-faced soldier asked me how much fuel I needed. This time I thought I'd take all I could carry as even with a chit petrol was becoming hard to find. I had already asked at two filling stations on the way into town, hoping that the attendants might be up for a bribe, but both had said they had nothing to give. There was plenty of water around so I figured I could convert my water-carrying jerry can to petrol and make do with a one-litre water bottle. I asked for forty-five litres, enough to get to Addis Ababa and a long way beyond.

Across the hills the day had started to die. The sun, an orange disc, was falling behind the trees and the light was fading. Having filled up I found a tumbledown hotel off a dusty sand track and sat quietly on the veranda watching the pale blue smoke from the eucalyptus fires drift in spirals towards the sky and a bright crescent moon. The worst part was now behind me, from here on the government was in charge. There could be banditry, of course, but I would have to be unlucky to be caught by that. I should reach Addis the following day, which would leave me a full two weeks to get to the Sudanese border. I went to sleep extremely content.

'Mr Jon, there is war!' There was a banging at my door. 'Mr Jon, Mr Jon, you wake . . . there is war.' I jumped out of bed and, pulling on my jeans, opened the door to find an excited Asfa, one of the houseboys, outside. I was still half asleep and far from sure what he was talking about.

'Where is there war?' I asked, rubbing my eyes. The glare of the sun was making them sting. 'Here, in Dila?' I could hear no shooting.

'No, no . . . is on radio. You come listen.' He dragged me outside into the forecourt. It was not late, a little after eight, and the air still carried a chill. Next to a large wild fig on the other side of the veranda the rest of the employees stood listening intently to the crackle hissing from a little black box.

'Good morning,' one of them said, turning to me, 'I think you were good sleeping have?'

'Yes, fine, thank you. Now where is there war?'

'Oh, well. The news it finish now,' Asfa explained, 'but I think you very lucky. War it break out bad in Agere Maryam in evening, yesterday. They say many people hurt bad – killed. The national armies have been sent to stop it. They close road, maybe for some times.'

'Who was fighting whom?'

'I no know. The government think it be OLF but maybe it just bandit. Mostly they are same.'

'But from here to Addis?'

'Oh no,' he smiled, 'this very fine. You have no problem.'

The day and the place were exquisitely beautiful: above the pretty thatched roofs clouds rose like mountains behind the emerald hills, and the calm waters of Lake Abaya glistened in the distance. The buna and dabo – a delicious sweet bread, almost a cake – tasted better than ever. My luck had held out once again – one more day in Moyale trying to secure the travel pass could have cost me dear. Having packed and paid, I made ready to go.

'Hey, Mr Jon, you looks like gladiator,' Asfa said, referring to my strange attire of knee- and shin-guards, helmet and leather jacket, gloves, face mask and goggles. I wondered how the word had entered his vocabulary.

'Sometimes, Asfa,' I said, smiling, 'I feel like one.'

The road was a constant procession of people and their animals. Mules, donkeys, men and women, all piled high with hay and firewood, wandered listlessly along under their huge loads. More of the land was now being cultivated. Oxen and camels pulled ploughs through the fertile soil. It seemed incredible that this country could have had famine on such a massive scale. Yet nearly all those working the land are subsistence farmers, growing only enough for themselves. This means that if there is a bad year and some crops fail there is no surplus from which to make up the shortfall. By providing bonuses for excess produce, with the help of aid agencies, the government is trying to put this right.

The road descended from the plateau into the Rift Valley where the land was drier. Baobabs and tamarisk took the place of the pines but the ubiquitous acacia continued unaffected. North of Awusa the great lakes appeared. Buzzards and kites circled on the thermals, and on either side the pale escarpments climbed through the haze.

Suddenly the road was blocked. A mass of people were marching straight towards me, many hundreds, thousands perhaps, barring my path. Some held crosses or strangely inscribed banners while others carried spears or colourful umbrellas. All their clothes were brilliantly embroidered in reds and yellows, greens and blues. They were chanting and beating drums, making quite a noise. At first I was petrified and did not know what to do. There was no way past them, I had to stop and wait. They marched round me as though I wasn't there. Not one of them even gave me a glance. Later I remembered the date. Despite using the Julian calendar it seems the Ethiopians celebrate May Day on the same day as everyone else.

On the outskirts of the capital, next to a burnt-out tank, the bike coughed and died. The bright sun of the morning had given way to a leaden sky and heavy rain was falling. The traffic heading into the city centre was dense and slow-moving. On either side of the road were grey factories and warehouses. I hadn't really noticed the bike losing power until I'd started to climb back up the escarpment, but then it had deteriorated fast. I had crawled the last ten miles not much faster than walking pace. I couldn't imagine what the problem might be, but whatever it was I knew I could do little about it there. I needed more luck.

Within minutes it presented itself in the form of a white pick-up truck driven by a man of about forty, dressed in Western clothes, with the usual bushy hair and soft, honey-coloured, inquisitive eyes. I explained that my bike had broken down and promised him my eternal gratitude if he could just get us both to a hotel and out of the tiresome rain.

'Oh, I can do better than that,' he said in near-perfect English, 'I can take you to Hagbes. They're the Yamaha dealers in town.' Short of meeting a travelling Ténéré mechanic, I could not have sought better fortune. I made a mental note never to take my luck for granted – it was a feature of my travels I could ill afford to lose.

With the help of some kids we got the bike on the back and secured it tightly with ropes. I climbed into the front and off we went. It turned out that the driver, Makonnen Ketsala, had studied civil engineering at Loughborough University and was a big fan of the English. He liked our writers and Royals and was a keen fan of our football. In fact he held the rather dubious honour of being chairman of the Liverpool Supporters' Club of Ethiopia – though, to date, I was pleased to learn, there were only twenty-three members. He gave me a quick guided tour of the city centre, which, in the drab half-light, looked much like any other, and then delivered me, as promised, to the Yamaha specialist. Unfortunately, being May Day, they were closed.

'This is not a problem,' said my new friend. 'I have a cousin who lives just up the hill a little way. We will leave the bike there and take it in the morning. They will be open until lunch I believe.'

After dropping off the bike he took me to a hotel just off Churchill Road (another of his heroes) and secured me a room. It was a smarter place than I had intended to stay at but it was getting late, I was cold and wet and I felt I could hardly exploit Makonnen's generous nature any more. I tried to offer him something for his trouble – we had taken more than an hour – but he politely refused and promised to come the next morning to take me back to Hagbes.

The room was a decent size with an *en suite* bathroom and a huge tiled bath. I immediately filled it with piping-hot water and wallowed in it for an hour. After a Western dinner of veal and chips in the hotel restaurant I turned in early.

The explosion of gunfire, loud and close by, punched a hole through the tranquil night. I don't suppose there is any noise in the world that will bring you to your senses as quickly. I was at once covered in a frightened sweat. I pulled the blankets over my head and looked for security under my pillow. A few seconds later the return fire came, from up the hill just behind the hotel, and then all hell broke loose. The retort of the guns, the high-pitched whine of ricocheting bullets and the sound of breaking glass filled my ears. The majority of the shooting seemed to be coming from the front of the hotel. My room was three storeys up facing the oncoming slugs.

My main concern was whether or not the perpetrators of the fighting were trying to take over the hotel. If they were, which by the closeness of the shooting seemed likely, and they succeeded, I felt sure that a fat Dane, the only other Westerner in the hotel, and I would be taken hostage. In the previous few weeks there had been a number of terrorist attacks on hotels frequented by Tigreans and one had been blown up simply because an Eritrean band was playing there. The attacks had been blamed on the OLF. I had little way of knowing if this was such a hotel, or whether or not they were Oromos fighting outside. It was a little after three. I quietly cursed Makonnen's choice of hotel.

The shooting continued in sporadic bursts, sounding like the sharp crack of a thousand whips or the splitting of a mighty tree. The anger and aggression that flew with each potentially deadly bullet made my heart thump and my hands shake. At Agere Maryam and in Lobito the noise had been far off, but here it was just outside my window and it was deafening. How on earth did people survive this for weeks or even months on end without going quite mad, I wondered. I remembered a character in some book I'd read, who had found himself in a similar situation and who had sought safety between the solid sides of a bathtub. It seemed like a good idea.

I slid out of bed and crawled along the wall, hoping it was thick. As I made my way towards the bathroom, a window shattered in the room next door. I had a strange desire to look out through the glass to see the battle in progress but suppressed the urge. Shutting the door behind me, I climbed into the dried-out tub. I stayed there until long after the fighting had stopped. When I finally looked outside, soon after four, the night was as peaceful and quiet as it had been the previous evening.

In the morning the manager proudly displayed the bullet holes in the wall as if this was all part of the entertainment, a hotel perk at no extra charge. He had no idea who it had been — thieves, curfew breakers or the OLF — but he was sure they had not been after the hotel. In Addis Ababa, he told me, it happens all the time. I thanked him for the night but said I would not be needing the room any longer.

Makonnen kept his word and came to collect me. We picked up the bike from his cousin and delivered it to Hagbes. It seemed incredible to me that there should be a Yamaha dealership in Addis Ababa but there was and an invaluable help they proved to be. It was a Saturday and their chief mechanic was not in. They would start work on Monday. Having taken me to his home to change some money at the black-market rate – nearly four times the official rate – Makonnen found me a new hotel. It was not as grand as that of the previous night but I hoped I might get a little more sleep. I lay down on the large wooden bed to rest, stared at the ceiling and listened to the sound of the street.

The Visitor
1.35 a.m. August 20th

'What the hell was that . . . ?' Mel sat up, brushing her head against the mosquito net. It was pitch-black and the middle of the night. I could hear nothing but the sea lapping gently against the shore and a light breeze stirring the palms.

'What, sweetheart?'

She was silent for a while. 'There . . . that scraping sound.'

This time I heard it too, a high-pitched squeak, like nails on a blackboard. It seemed to be coming from under the bed.

'I don't know . . . maybe a rat?'

'Oh shit, don't say that.'

'Well, whatever it is I think it's trying to get into bed with us.'
The squeak was getting louder as it climbed the bamboo frame. I sat up too.

'Where's the torch?'

Mel felt under her pillow and after a moment handed it to me. I could feel the thing now, putting pressure on the frail cotton mosquito net. I turned on the torch and a huge black shadow, pincers snapping, was suddenly projected onto the wall behind. An orange crab, about the size of my hands, was crawling along the edge of our bed.

'You'll have to catch it and put it outside,' Mel said.

'Yeah,' I replied, without enthusiasm, 'right.'

I got out of bed and encouraged the crab onto the floor while Mel held the torch.

'Come on, you bastard, don't be a nuisance, let me pick you up.' It

seemed as scared of me as I was of it and cowered back into the corner of the bamboo hut, its angry pincers waving.

'Don't be so pathetic,' said Mel, after a few minutes' jousting. 'Throw your jacket over it. Do you want me to get up and catch it.'

I did not. I could, should, handle it. Come on don't be a wimp. I threw my jean jacket over it, scooped it up and hurried to the door, my heart thumping fast.

'Right, there we are,' I said, feeling rather butch. 'He won't be troubling us again tonight.' I climbed back into bed and Mel turned off the torch.

A horde of bungalow touts had greeted us at the jetty in Koh Phangan after our journey by night train from Bangkok. All except one, the youngest and quietest, had thrown themselves at us in the hope of securing our custom. His name was Ping; we'd hoped his resort would reflect his manner and we were not disappointed. A row of thatched huts, shaded by palms, lined the calm turquoise sea.

The first couple of nights had been quiet, this was the third. The unwelcome visitor didn't disturb us again that night but after finding him in our rucksack the next evening, and again in our bed the night after that, something really had to be done. After all, we were paying for the accommodation; he was only squatting. We blocked all the holes around the base of the hut and when we went to bed that night secured the door with a stool. So pleased was I by the peaceful night and a good sleep that when I went to crouch over the 'en suite' squat loo to go about my morning business I had relaxed my vigilance. As I lowered my naked bum over the hole in the concrete a sharp claw whipped up and grabbed hard at my soft white flesh. He must have been waiting, eagle-eyed, pincers drawn. He certainly got his own back. I should think my scream could have been heard on the mainland. As I leapt up he fell to the floor and scurried away.

Mel rushed in. 'What's happened? Are you all right?'

'The fucking thing has just bitten my arse,' I cried in a rage, and turned my bum to show her. She burst out laughing.

'Where is it now?' she asked when she was able.

'I don't know . . . it just disappeared through that hole. If I see it again, I'll bloody . . . !'

'Wait,' she said. 'Look, it's still there. I'll go and get one of the guys to catch it.' She disappeared, still chuckling. A moment later a Thai appeared and picked it up as though it were tame and held it high for us to see. It seemed to be smiling.

'Tie it up,' I said, still rubbing my bum, 'and we'll have him for supper.'

That evening, though, Mel persuaded me to have mercy on it and as *it was still securely fastened I went to sleep content. The next morning as we were leaving Mel cut its rope and let it go.*

Two new backpackers arrived while we were paying our bill.

'Ah,' said the Thai, 'you can have their hut. It is the nicest on the beach.'

Mel looked at me and smiled.

I woke early on Monday and made my way up the hill towards the bike shop. It was a clear day with the sharp light of a place of high altitude. Rusting iron-roofed shacks leant uncertainly against once another, continuing over the mounds and hollows up the hillside all the way to the edge of town. The ones by the road offered peanuts and fizzy drinks at their doorways.

Johnnie, the chief mechanic, was a good-looking, well-off Armenian. So well-off, in fact, that he was planning a holiday in the States. He was a thickset man with excellent teeth and dark eyes that creased when he smiled. I liked him at once. He was not only the chief mechanic for Hagbes but he had been the Ethiopian Moto Cross champion. The excited expression that erupted on his face when he saw my bike was understandable when I looked around the workshop. There wasn't a motor bike there that was over 200cc.

We discussed the various implications of the power loss and sudden breakdown and both decided that the carburettor and fuel line should be the first things to be examined. If this brought us no reward we would have to take the engine to pieces to check, once again, on the piston. He went to work. I made my apologies and headed back into town. There was still the little matter of my visa.

Addis Ababa, meaning New Flower, was made the capital just over a hundred years ago by Emperor Menelik II – the only African leader to repel a European force: the Italians in 1896. At an altitude of nearly 8,000 feet, it lies in a bowl spectacularly surrounded by pale mountains. The buildings of the city reach to the foot of the mountains which then rise abruptly to dissolve into the sky. On the whole it is a city of nondescript grey buildings with little in the way of architectural splendour. Remnants of its Communist past still linger in the form of arches made from giant sabres and starred columns surrounded by machine-gun waving soldiers cast in bronze.

As I walked down Churchill Road towards the centre

children thrust their hands out at me and shouted 'Money . . . money', and limbless men, casualties of the war with Eritrea, sat with photographs of themselves in military uniform, begging for coins. In the heat, fumes from the traffic mingled with the stench of faeces and urine which flowed in the open drains.

I joined a small crowd climbing the steps to the sprawling offices of the Interior Ministry. Having been sent away from four offices I was finally guided to the one belonging to the Secretary for Immigration and was told to wait. An old man, sitting in the corner of the office, offered me some buna.

After I'd waited about fifteen minutes the Secretary came in and sat at his desk. He listened to my request and read the letter. Then he became quite angry.

'How did you get this letter? Why do you not seek permission in Nairobi, through the proper channels?' Like everyone in charge of this country, he was very young. He glanced back at the paper. 'I can't believe they give you this!'

'Yes, sir, they did. You see I'm in a hurry. If I don't get through Ethiopia before the rains take hold I'll be stuck. The man who gave me this letter said that he would give it to me only if I came to see you to get a proper visa.'

'You should have stayed in Nairobi to apply,' he remarked, calming a little.

'Oh, I'm sorry, sir, I didn't know this.' I tried to look as dumb as possible. 'I was told to get a visa at the border.'

His eyebrows arched. 'Who told you this?'

'Some Ethiopians in Nairobi.'

He shook his head. 'How long you want to stay here?'

'Well, the problem is, sir, that my motor bike has broken down. At the moment they're trying to mend it at Hagbes, but my visa for the Sudan expires on the fifteenth, so two weeks should be enough.'

'Umm . . . and which way you go to Sudan?' I was pleased to see the temper receding from his cautious eyes. He knew that save deporting me, he really had no choice.

'I will drive up through Gojjam to Tana, then to Gondar and cross the border at Metema. I have been told this is the best way.'

He stood up and thought for a moment. 'You know this is very bad. This is how you should have applied.' He held up a telex. 'This is from Nairobi. An Austrian man, on a motor bike, same as you.'

I had heard of this guy while waiting in Nairobi, but had no idea he had been applying for an Ethiopian visa. I had been told by the British Council that it takes weeks to get through to the officials in Addis and, as far as they knew, such requests were always turned down. Few people they'd heard of travelled north of Marsabit. I was therefore amazed that a telex sent to this government, so young in its life, had actually found its way onto the right desk, and was about to be dealt with.

'Will you give him permission?'

'I am not sure. It is a dangerous road, you know. It has only just reopened. But maybe.'

'I am really sorry, sir. I didn't know.'

'Okay, you wait outside.' He took my passport and left the room. Half an hour later I left the offices with a one-month visa.

Back at Hagbes, Johnnie was looking concerned. The bike was once again stripped to a frame and the engine sat on a work bench.

'It is not the carbs or the fuel line,' he informed me gravely. 'I have checked them all quite thoroughly. I think we must now take the engine to bits to check the piston rings.'

I was disappointed. I now had my visa and had hoped that the bike would be mended so I could leave Addis with some time in hand to spend at the ancient monasteries on Lake Tana. Sadly, it was not to be.

Tuesday came and went with us only managing to confirm that the piston and rings were in remarkably good condition and that the ignition coil was fine. On Wednesday I turned up early only to be told the Johnnie was at the American Embassy trying to get a visa and that it would probably take all day. By Thursday evening we were still no nearer to tracing the cause of the problem, and I was starting to panic. Twice that day I'd been to the Sudanese Embassy in an attempt to get an extension on the entry date of my visa but had been refused. They found it incredible that I had been given one at all. I now had only six days left before it expired – the drive would take at least four. I had established that it was possible through TNT to receive packages from London and I knew I could rely on a friend to get me whatever I needed, but I didn't have a clue what that was.

Even when I did it would take over a week to arrive. Without a valid Sudanese visa I didn't fancy my chances of getting in: the Sudanese are famously hard to bribe. Moreover the rains were fast approaching and just twenty-seven days remained before I was due in Cairo, well over 2,000 miles away. That night I tossed and turned in bed, wondering if I was to be thwarted at this stage, beaten at the last. *Have faith, Jonny, what's guided you this far won't give up on you now.* But how long could I keep relying on faith and hope, praying that fate would see me right? Surely my luck must run out at some point . . . it couldn't last for ever. After nearly a week of disappointment, I felt drained, my optimism spent. From the window above my bed I saw the moon climbing over the city. Once again I found myself asking for a miracle.

The following morning, while walking up the hill to the workshop for the umpteenth time, tired and depressed, I saw a small moped struggling up the road beside me, a thin jet of pale smoke seeping from its tired exhaust. The driver made an angry face and rotated the pedals to give it more power. A thought suddenly came to me. When I'd been waiting in Yaoundé, all those months ago, a German riding a bike similar to mine had told me of a problem he had had. I quickened my pace and entered the shop in a state of high excitement. Johnnie was crouched over the bike with the concerned expression of a father watching his son in a hospital bed. I told him of my revelation.

The exhaust is in two parts, the rear half housing the baffles. With a little struggle, as the bolts had rusted, he took this section off. I held my breath as he pressed the starter button. The engine ripped into life with a deafening roar. He pulled back on the accelerator, taking the revs into the red. It worked! The power was fully back. At first I expected the sound to wither and die but it kept on running. The other mechanics gathered round and there was much smiling and shaking of hands. So that was it – a blocked exhaust caused by months of poor quality petrol. It was hard to believe it was something so trivial. We sawed the section in half, bashed a hole straight through the baffles – rendering the silencer useless, but who cared? – and welded it back together. It was Friday the eighth. It was too late in the day and I was too ill-prepared to leave but if I left the next morning I would still have five days in which to reach the border.

24 An Ancient Land

Koro, Ethiopia

Outside thunder rolled and night suddenly descended as the sun was engulfed by a vast black cloud. Soon it started to rain. I took out a cigarette and sipped at my drink. It was thick and brown with corn husks floating on the surface and tasted extremely bitter.

I had stopped at a small group of thatched mud huts at the top of the Blue Nile gorge. Children wearing an assortment of traditional and Western clothing had gathered round me and a man who spoke a little English had invited me into one of the huts.

The earth floor was dry but the lack of windows kept the room in perpetual gloom. Goat skins and dried grass lined the walls. There was a small fire in the middle of the room where a woman was preparing wat.

'How far is it to Debre Markos?' I asked the man.

'Is no far . . . no many time.' I estimated that the town I had planned to stay at was at least thirty miles away. Through the entrance I could see the rain coming down in torrents.

'Do you think I could sleep here . . . stay for the night?' The man translated and the woman nodded her consent. She gave me a bowl of the wat and a rolled up piece of injera, then lit two old oil lamps and hung them from the ceiling. A couple of goats settled down in the corner and my interpreter left. Having eaten, I rolled out my sleeping-bag and lay down.

Sleep did not come quickly. I lay staring into the darkness, listening to the rain. I knew the track would be bad anyway but after this downpour I feared it would be hell, the rivers swollen and the fords too deep. The rainy season was starting early. I prayed for the rain to stop but it did not. Never had I heard it rain so hard . . . except once, perhaps, and that had been a monsoon many moons ago.

The Storm

At first the rain fell in thin, transparent streaks but then increased to a deluge of grey, solid and impenetrable like a sheet of steel. The horseshoe cove below the mountain became invisible, lost behind a curtain of water. Parting the foliage before us we scrambled hurriedly back down the rocky path. It had taken us over an hour to reach the top. I hoped the descent would be quicker.

'Come on, sweetheart,' I yelled back to Mel who seemed to be slowing her pace.

'Ah, it doesn't matter,' she cried, 'we're soaked already. Anyway, I'm rather enjoying it.' The rain ran off her cheeks and her hair was sodden. Stretching out her arms in a crucifixion pose, she turned her face to the sky and began to laugh. It was rather wonderful, I had to concede, to be high up on a tropical mountain in a monsoon storm, but then I saw her shiver.

'Come on, darling, let's get down.'

The day had started as beautifully as all the others on that heavenly island. I had risen a little earlier than usual, leaving Mel asleep in the thatched hut, and walked the twenty paces across the sand to the coral sea. There was no one around so I stripped off and swam out towards the centre of the bay. Limestone cliffs, jutting straight out of the water, encircled the inlet. Palms, pelicans and little wooden boats; what a wonderful place to spend a birthday, I thought.

Travelling together had been even better than I'd imagined it would be. Having left the islands on the east of the mainland we'd gone north to trek on the Burmese border for a couple of weeks. Realising our time in Thailand was fast running out, we'd decided to see paradise one more time. We were now on Koh Pee Pee, an island off the west coast.

Mel stirred a little while after I returned from my swim and over our breakfast of pineapple and poached eggs informed me that she had hired snorkelling equipment, fishing gear and a long thin boat, captained by a youth called Hud. We spent the day pottering round the island, diving through shoals of multicoloured fish, studying their beauty and then catching them. We never had the heart to keep any. We spent an hour having lunch on a deserted beach on the far side of the island and returned to our hut in mid-afternoon. After a short rest we decided to set off up the mountain to view the island from above.

By the time we reached the bottom again the storm had cleared but we were both pretty cold. We dried off, changed our clothes and, with the sun turning the sky brilliant shades of orange, wandered off to get supper and a celebratory drink.

Between rows of tall palms, open-sided restaurants, lit up by dim electric light bulbs and oil lamps, lined the sandy pathway. An array of fine seafood tempted the taste-buds of those who passed: lobster, tiger prawns and ten-foot marlin or shark. We sat down and ordered two beers.

'Happy birthday in paradise, darling,' said Mel, holding my hand. We clinked the bottles together. It had been the happiest day I could remember. She shivered, then sneezed . . . and again . . . and again. She always sneezed in threes. She picked up her inhaler and had a little blast.

'Are you okay?'

'Oh yeah, probably just getting a cold.'

'Well, next birthday will be yours, in Goa.'

She smiled and gave me a kiss.

By morning my prayers had been answered and the rain had stopped but dark clouds still loomed above. I packed up quickly, had two cups of buna, and was on my way, journeying along a sodden track accompanied by herdsmen wearing animal skins. Some travelled on horseback, their lithe, compact mounts harnessed in colourful bridles and breastplates, tassels hanging from their long manes.

As I passed small encampments and villages, grubby, wide-eyed children stopped playing and stared, looking confused. What must they all make of me, I wondered, this strange vision zooming through their lives for two or three seconds. Did I seem like a visitor from another planet, an evil spirit, or even a god? Perhaps the storytellers amongst them would make up tales about the apparition they saw. In time, I supposed, more bikes would come through and even the camera-happy overland truckers – wondering, no doubt, where to buy Vegemite – and I would be forgotten. Or perhaps I was simply in their minds for as long as I was in their sights. I hoped, however, that there was a child somewhere telling another, 'You mean you didn't see that space man?'

I was pulled from my fantasy by as chilling a sight as I'd seen on the continent. A hundred yards ahead, at the top of the right-hand bank, a large man, wearing a maroon beret, khaki trousers, brown boots and bullet belts draped across his

293

chest, was aiming his rifle at me. He began to run down the slope towards the road.

My God, so this is it! My heartbeat doubled its speed.

Bandits. All through my journey I had been warned about and was constantly on the look-out for bandits – the Tuareg in the Sahara, the maniacs in Nigeria, the bored ex-soldiers of Angola, the Shifta in northern Kenya. However, leaving aside the warring factions in the Ethiopian south, I had not yet encountered any. I had begun to believe that perhaps I was invincible, that such strong powers were acting on my behalf that nothing so devastating could happen, that these desperadoes were being kept out of my way. Evidently I was wrong.

I had thought many times about what I would do if such a situation presented itself, whether I'd stop or place myself in the hands of the Gods and drive straight on. I had come to no concrete conclusions. I felt I would have more of a chance of survival taking the latter option as, even if the bandits did decide to shoot, their aim might not necessarily be accurate. But here I was, face to face with the real thing, and any action seemed impossible.

I got closer and closer, still unable to make the decision. He stood in the middle of the road now, his gun unwavering. At any moment he might pull the trigger; he made no gesture that he wanted me to stop. What was he going to do? What was *I* going to do? When I was no more than twenty yards off, still undecided whether to stop or accelerate, he lifted his head and a different expression crossed his eyes. Stamping his feet together, he swivelled his gun round to present arms, and, with his face exploding into a gigantic grin, gave me a salute worthy of the Guards. I returned the gesture and sped past, leaving him choking in a cloud of dust.

When I arrived at the Lake Tana Hotel twenty minutes later I was still shaking.

Set on the southern bank of the lake, overlooking the tranquil waters, the Lake Tana Hotel is probably the most famous hotel in Ethiopia. In front of the whitewashed building, which was almost entirely covered in purple bougainvillaea, a swimming pool and a brightly coloured garden of hibiscus and sweet-smelling frangipani led down to the water's edge. The hotel's custom had been stopped dead by the war. I had the whole place to myself.

I had a bath in my room – the water obviously came straight out of the lake: there was an inch of mud in it – and sat outside in the garden with a whisky and a cigarette, watching the sun disappear. A full moon rose from the east and papyrus fishing boats floated slowly by. It was uplifting to see the moon in such splendour, shimmering orange across the pitch-black lake. I thought about what lay ahead of me. Crossing into Sudan would not be a mere formality, even if I did arrive in time. My visa quite clearly stated 'by air only, entry point Khartoum'. But I was also aware that if I did get through, provided there weren't any unexpected disasters, I was home free; this was the last difficult border to cross. It seemed right that my old friend should be at its grandest now, ready to help me complete this last tricky stage. I realised it would be almost full again by the time I reached Cairo. A smile formed on my lips as I thought of the city that lay at the end of my journey, and the person who would be waiting there to greet me. I knew that when the time came I'd be as nervous as hell, but for now, with only the sound of the lake's gentle water caressing the night, the thought of Amel filled me with warmth.

25 Under a Sweltering Sky

Gondar, Ethiopia

'You mean you won't change me any money?' The anxious-looking receptionist squirmed behind the desk. The previous evening, when I had arrived in Gondar from Lake Tana, he had promised he would. He shook his head.

'And what about the petrol? You can't get me that either?'

The response was the same. It was not the start I'd been hoping for.

I had to wait an hour for the bank to open before setting off up the grimy streets. An excited gaggle of schoolchildren ran at my side, eager to relieve me of anything I was prepared to give. When I arrived at the bank it was still closed but after twenty minutes the large wooden doors opened and I was admitted. They changed my money at an excruciatingly bad rate, and at the petrol station, where they were awaiting the arrival of a tanker from Addis, the attendant wanted double the normal rate for his black-market petrol.

At least the day was fine. Wispy cirrus clouds grazed a blue-white sky, the chill was receding, and there was no wind: a perfect day for a drive. I packed up, collected the fuel – surrounded by a crowd of over a hundred – and made my way down from the town to rejoin the route to the border.

The stony track ran along the highlands, skirting the contours of the mountains, dipping through valleys and scaling heights. There was still some agriculture here. Wizened old men draped in animal skins encouraged oxen to pull wooden ploughs through the hard, coarse land where goats grazed and teff grew. I passed through the occasional settlement and forded streams, which were now much deeper, as there were no bridges at all.

Just past one ford, which I must have taken too fast, I misjudged my line and hit a dip. The front tyre pinched against a rock which tore a hole in the inner tube. Three farmers left their work to come and watch me mend the puncture. They stood staring silently at the machine, their faces as old and rutted as the land they tilled. After an hour I was on my way again.

The heat increased as the track began to descend. All vegetation quickly disappeared and with it any other form of life. The mountainsides turned to pale yellow, hard and burnt, the stones on the track like razors. I started to regret not carrying spare tyres: one more bad front puncture and I would be stranded for I had no more inner tubes.

The rocky path plunged down thousands of feet, carrying me off the escarpment. The wheels skidded, the suspension squeaked and from the now clear sky the punishing sun beat down on my back. At last the ground levelled out, taking me along a deeply rutted track, covered in scrub and thorn which scraped the sides of my jerry cans and tried to catch my legs. It was obvious that in a month, once the rains had really taken hold, this land would become a bog and travelling impossible. Twice the track dropped down the side of dusty river banks to run across their beds. Now the rivers were small and shallow, easy to cross, but, if the banks were anything to go by, before too long they would be twenty feet deep.

By mid-afternoon I was nearly at the border and the knots in my stomach tightened. An army truck coming towards me, packed with troops, stopped and asked for my papers. The stern-faced soldiers seemed annoyed by my presence. Before climbing back aboard their commander said something to me in Amharic and pointed the way they were going. I wasn't sure if it had been an order to follow them or the clearance to carry on. Realising the enormous difficulty they would have in turning the truck round to chase me, I put my head down and continued on my way, double-speed. Fifteen miles to go, I guessed.

After a couple of minutes I entered a village of domed thatch huts. The place was dirty, the people curious. I drove down a shallow hill, past a pile of wheat sacks and over a stagnant creek. Suddenly a large man in a white djellaba stood in my path putting up his hand to stop me.

'Where are you going?' he demanded.

'To the Sudan. How far is it to the border?'

'You have just crossed it,' he signalled back towards the creek. 'That is the border. You are now in the Sudan.'

He led me to a small dusty corral where five soldiers in bright green uniforms sat drinking tea. The air was oppressive, the heat overpowering. A tattered flag hung limply from a bent pole, and behind the soldiers a dirty sign read: 'Democratic Republic of Sudan.' I accepted a drink and sat down.

'You show me your passport,' said the Captain. I took it out and passed it to him. He was fat and extremely black, reminding me of Idi Amin. Flies buzzing around his face seemed not to bother him. I held my breath.

'This is fine,' he said after a moment's pause, 'but you were cutting it a little fine, no? This visa is only valid until tomorrow.'

'Yes, sir, I know. My bike broke down in Addis. I had to hurry.'

'Well, you have made it – welcome to the Sudan.' So that was it, I'd done it. Whether he'd chosen not to notice the permitted entry point on my visa or had simply missed it, I didn't know. It didn't matter, he'd let me in. I smiled and shook his podgy hand. 'But,' he went on, 'you will have to go to Gadaref tomorrow to get your passport stamped and clearance to Khartoum. There is no immigration until there. You can leave as soon as it's light; avoid the heat.'

Damn, almost made it! Still, I thought, if I manage to get to Gadaref, a hundred miles into Sudan, I doubt they'll send me back. 'Okay, thank you. Where might I stay the night . . . is there a hotel here?'

'No,' he replied, 'you must go back to Metema across the border. There is a hotel there.' He looked at one of his subordinates and chuckled.

I couldn't believe I was being told to return to Ethiopia. What about the next day, how could I be sure they'd let me in then?

'Can I not stay here, sir?' I whimpered. 'Sleep on the floor somewhere?'

'No, no. You can leave your machine here if you like. Don't be worried, there will not be a problem tomorrow. I will get Mustaf to take you back.' He called to a young boy. 'You be here at six . . . you reach Gadaref by ten.'

I followed the boy back over the stagnant creek, past the piles of wheat, and into Ethiopia again, at each step collecting a few more feral children. At once three ugly-looking militia men, AK47s dangling at their hips, stopped me and searched my tank bag. On finding nothing of any value they demanded to know why I was entering their country illegally. With my passport, and help from Mustaf, I managed to explain my situation. They then wanted to know where I was staying the night. They too chuckled when Mustaf told them. When we got there I understood why.

The 'hotel', if it could really be called such a thing, was the local brothel. Having left my excited reception committee outside the straw hut I was greeted by an attractive middle-aged lady called Miss Tafarina. She led me behind the hut, smiling and talking – though I understood none of it – to a small sandy courtyard where two longer shacks, each partitioned into six, faced each other. She showed me to a cubicle with paper-thin reed walls which was only a foot bigger than the bamboo cot it held. Outside, five or six girls sat round a table, all, it seemed, excited by my presence. I was almost certainly the first white man to stay in their establishment. A chicken was knocked off the bench so I could sit down. They gave me a warm beer, some hot food and plenty of friendly invitations.

As the sun went down the place filled up. The local militia were the first to show, leaving their guns in a pile by the door. They drank their beer and ate their food, laughing and chatting with the girls. Only one spoke any English and he used it to make me take his photograph while he posed with his gun and three women. Next came the locals and lastly the Sudanese officials, using the cover of darkness to sneak across the border for an alcoholic drink – forbidden under Sudanese Islamic law – and some carnal delights. There was a good atmosphere, full of fun and enjoyment.

My opinion of the place soon changed once I disappeared to my 'room' to try to get some sleep. Three portable cassette players blasted out different tuneless music most of the night. A goat, three rats, a chicken and a woman all tried at some point to gain entry to my cell, and a multitude of mosquitoes succeeded. In the cubicle next to mine a couple went at it longer than is humanly decent, grunting and groaning hour after hour. I must have dozed off at some point for I remember waking to the sound, or smell, I'm not sure which, of a person crapping on the other side of the wafer-thin partition, next to my head. When his partner did the same I knew I had to leave. I got up and, carefully stepping over many bodies, left the 'hotel' and made once more for the Sudanese border.

There was only a faint glow along the eastern horizon but already people were up and collecting water from the well. Down the track I walked, past mules, donkeys and camels, past the unmanned corrugated-iron Ethiopian customs shed, over the concrete bridge once more and up the other side to the Sudan. In the pale dawn light I secured the tank bag to its harness and accepted a glass of mint tea from the sentry on duty. Having drunk it, I filled up my water bottle, wondering if it had been so clever to convert my jerry can to petrol, and climbed aboard the bike. At that moment the Captain entered the corral.

'You cannot go now. You must wait for the convoy.' The Captain read my frustrated expression and continued, 'It is for your own safety . . . there is rebel activity in the area. To go now would be very bad. You are lucky I have caught you.'

I had hoped that I'd left all that behind me in Ethiopia, that the fighting in this country's civil war was many miles away to the south. It seemed I was wrong.

'What time does the convoy leave?' I asked, dismounting.

'Oh, at about ten o'clock. Have some tea,' he slapped me on the shoulder. 'There is no problem.'

Looking at his watch I realised that by crossing this border I had also crossed a time zone. It was five to five and not five to six. A wait of five hours in Gallabat. *I suppose he's right. Pull up a chair and drink more tea.*

Before long the sun was up and hammering us with its brutal heat. It climbed quickly, destroying the shade, dissolving the shadows. There was no breeze at all. The only things to show any sign of energy on this scorched land were the flies swarming around my face. After two hours I was told to report to an office at the other end of the village where I would be issued with my pass to travel to Gadaref.

In a thatched hut, much like the brothel, a stern-faced official filled in a form which he stamped with a big, round seal before copying the information it contained into a large book. Once he'd finished he turned the book to face me and pointed at the page. He said something I didn't understand and held up four fingers. As I studied the writing I realised, if their records were accurate, that I was only the fourth Westerner to cross this way into the Sudan in eleven years. An Australian had done it four weeks before, the other two were years back. (Ironically, a few days later I discovered that Michael Palin and an entire BBC film crew had crossed this border in the other direction only a few months before.)

Slowly the convoy began to take shape. Battered multicoloured trucks cumbersomely manoeuvred themselves into line along the sandy street. Passengers started to form groups and the soldiers arrived. Three of them climbed aboard each truck. They placed their bipod-supported machine guns above the cab at the front and lay out behind them on the cargo. Still we didn't leave. The temperature soared with every minute we waited. It was well into the forties by now, maybe even more. I feared that the oil in my engine would thin to such a degree that it might break the seals and render the bike unusable. I had only to get to Khartoum; from there I could carry the bike home.

It was past eleven when a whistle blew and the engines ticked stubbornly into life. I filled my water bottle for the third time that morning and pulled the bike into line, about halfway along the column. The whistle blew again and we rolled forward at last.

The track climbed out of the village through a dusty bowl of coarse grass and leafless trees where broken rolls of barbed wire poked above the earth. The path became as hard as flint, weaving up and down through canyons of rock, which made progress for the trucks frustratingly slow. We moved on through the sweltering air at little more than walking pace.

We had only been going half an hour when shots were heard over the hillside in the neighbouring valley. Again we were ordered to a stop. Six soldiers remained with the convoy while thirty others fanned out on both sides of the track and marched reluctantly over the craggy ridgetops. We waited and waited, hearing nothing save the buzzing of flies and the restless sound of human sighs. Half an hour later the soldiers returned and we were ordered to continue.

At a small encampment of Bedouin tents two miles on we stopped again. 'Rebels in the area,' one of the soldiers told us. I sat with the others under a sideless tent drinking my second gallon of sweet mint tea. It was hotter now than anything I'd ever known. The sun, beating down from a clear white sky, created a heat so intense you could actually see it undulating against the brittle yellow bush. I sat cross-legged and tried not to move. It was ten to one and we had covered only six miles. The others seemed unconcerned, patience personified. I tried to follow their example.

After a while I noticed two soldiers talking over my bike. It seemed they were discussing me, pointing in my direction. They both came over. One of them spoke some English.

'You can go now,' he said matter-of-factly. I wasn't sure whether to be pleased or not. If it was dangerous before, how come it was suddenly safe? I got to my feet.

'Is it safe?' I asked. 'Have the bandits gone?'

'Yes, it be okay. You follow jeep, they take you to Doka.' He pointed a few yards down the track to an open-backed pick-up with five soldiers sitting in the back. 'From there no problem.'

'They're going now?' I asked. He nodded and walked off. I asked a youth, who I knew spoke some English, to come with me and check with the driver. Without the cover of the thick canvas shelter the sledge-hammer rays were almost unbearable. I knew it was crazy to drive at such a time but I had no option. The driver confirmed I should follow them. I went back to my bike, zipped up my leather jacket, pulled down my goggles and started up the engine.

I stayed close on their tail, eating their dust all the way. Without having to wait for the convoy we could drive at a decent speed. A brown powder track, at times degenerating to bull dust, cut its way through a bleak and hopeless land. Nothing much grew and what had grown before now looked dead. The temperature and terrain were sapping my strength but we neither saw nor heard any rebels. At Doka, when we stopped, I was questioned by the military but after a while told I could go on, alone. It would be safe from here they said. *Safe from bandits, but what about the elements?*

The parched brown earth turned yellow and then white; I was suddenly back in the desert. Scorched dead trees, their burnt branches seemingly gripped in spasms of pain, wobbled in the haze before me, but they, too, soon fell away leaving nothing but rocks and sand. Driving in the torrid heat, now at its strongest, was like riding into the mouth of a blast furnace. I was dehydrating fast – faster than I knew. I stopped every few miles to drink from the water bottle but soon it became too hot to touch.

I came across more Bedouin lying in the shade of a tent. I stopped and they offered me water. I didn't care about the germs it might contain, it was drink or collapse. Nothing seemed real or felt solid. All around the heat haze was so pronounced that when I walked back to the bike it must have appeared to the Bedouin as though I were stepping on water.

Every ten miles I'd pat the bike. *Come on, only sixty left to go ... fifty ... forty ... thirty.* On the sandy track the bike was sliding. The strength in my arms had gone, my mouth was parched and the back of my throat felt raw and painful. I put the hot water on my bandana and put it in my mouth but within seconds it was like chewing cotton wool. *Twenty-five ... twenty ... fifteen ... Come on, come on, we're so nearly there. Please, please keep going.* Was I shouting out aloud or in my head? Now there were vicious corrugations which shook us badly. I couldn't believe the bike could survive such punishment. I started to see more tents, then a truck ahead in the distance, and another in front of that. *Twelve ... ten ... eight ... What am I going to drink when I get there? A Coke? A Fanta? No, there probably won't be any of that. I don't care ... anything'll do, just something cool. Seven ... six ... five ... Is that a building on that hill? Oh please, God, say it is.* It was, a black and white water tower away to the left. Then more buildings, small stone huts in the valley beyond: a village, but not Gadaref. The track led past a water hole where three youths were filling containers strapped to the sides of their mules.

'Gadaref?' I mumbled. The tallest youth pointed straight ahead towards the sun, which had started its fall to the west. I dropped the bike into gear and headed towards it feeling as though I were floating, disconnected from the world. Women carried water in earthenware zirs; goats lay in newly formed shade. A tall sand-coloured minaret climbed from a mosque, looking, through the haze, like a rocket about to take off. A minute later I entered the town walls. *You old beauty, we made it ... !* I slapped the petrol tank hard. It was the last bit of non-surfaced road I would have to negotiate.

The first hotel I found was a large pale building situated at the north end of the main street, next to the railway line. There were three steps leading up to an open green door which revealed a large room the size of a gym. Rows of paintless, iron beds stretched its length, listless bodies resting on most of them. To one side, next to the wall, was a desk with a djellaba-clad man behind it. I staggered across.

'Do you have a bed?'

He answered me with a sullen shake of his head. There were so many beds I found it hard to believe him.

'Please, just one bed.' My speech was slurred and my balance failing, I leant against the wall. 'What about a Coke, you have Coke or cold water?' The response was the same, though this time he did at least look at me. I was getting pissed off. I couldn't think why, but I was sure he was lying.

'Okay,' I panted, realising I wasn't getting anywhere, 'what about another hotel? Where is another hotel?' He pointed out of the door to the other side of the road. I found the place he meant in a block opposite, but the answer here was the same: no beds available. I was starting to panic.

On the street the heat was still suffocating and I wasn't sure how much longer my legs could carry me. I needed to drink and lie down. I needed a bed. On the main road there were few people about, the town still taking its afternoon rest. I really didn't know which way to go. Just as I was climbing wearily back onto the bike a young man dressed in an old brown suit approached me.

'Hello, friend. Where you come from?'

'England. Where's a hotel?'

'Why, here. This is hotel, just here.' He pointed to the green door. I explained that there was no room in either hotel, I had checked, and asked if he knew of another.

'Oh,' he said, 'well there is only one more. I take you there. It is just up the road. Come. My name is Yacine.'

He clambered onto the machine behind me and directed me back down the road the way I'd come. Halfway along we turned left between a couple of three-storeyed buildings and into a large sandy courtyard. Groups of men in turbans and thin white djellabas lay on the floor under the balconies, drinking tea and pulling smoke from hubble-bubbles. They looked at me blankly. Kids played in a broken car among piles of rotting refuse.

'Here. We go this way.'

I left the bike and followed Yacine up some rickety iron steps to the second floor. On the wall next to the open doorway was an old thermometer: it read fifty-four degrees. Inside the room a wizened man with a white beard stood behind a desk. At first, to my amazement and despair, he too said he had no beds. In the end Yacine persuaded him to find me one and we were led down a corridor to a glass door beyond which was a room with five filthy but empty beds. The windows had been painted over to keep out the sun; it was dark and cool.

Once the old man had gone I said to Yacine, 'I need drink, fast. Can you get me any Coke or something? . . . I'm really desperate.' I unzipped my bum-bag and took out some money.

'Oh no, it is not necessary. I will get you drink and some food. It is very hot, yes? May and June always hottest months.'

He left and I collapsed on the bed. Five minutes later he returned with four bottles of fizzy orange and some biscuits. If I'd had any moisture left in my body I would have cried with joy.

'There is more of this than water,' he said, handing me the bottles. 'We must all drink it. This is why the hotels are so full. The people from the land have come for drink. There is none out there.' He didn't need to tell me that. I drank the first two bottles without noticing, savoured the third and sipped the fourth. I doubt I will ever have a more pleasurable drink but it did little to improve the way I was feeling. I was sick, as weak as a child. After Yacine had gone I just lay there, inert, and stared at the blistered ceiling, my mind empty, thinking of nothing. I didn't want to move for a week.

The Bus to Shangri-La
2.35 p.m. October 6th

Mel sat up on the bed and wiped her eyes. She looked so sad, like a little girl of four not twenty-four. I put my arm round her shoulder and pulled her to my chest.

'Don't worry, sweetheart. There might be a perfectly good reason for why they can't come. You know Tania . . . India is hardly her scene.'

'I know,' she said, resignation in her voice, 'it's just that I'd been so looking forward to them coming to Goa. It won't really be the same now.' She snivelled. I felt a warm tear run down her cheek, and wiped it away.

This wasn't the only reason for Mel's blues. Having arrived in Delhi late the previous evening, she had been convinced that the receptionist at the hotel had ripped us off. Following that, on our way into town in the morning, she had left her wallet on the bus with fifty pounds and my emergency credit card in it. While I was trying to cancel the card she had gone to poste restante and got the letter telling us of John's and Tania's decision. Added to the intense heat and hassle of India's capital it had been the final straw at the end of a depressing few hours. Normally such disappointments would not have affected her – such lows are part and parcel of travelling – but she was still a little weak. She was brown and looked fine but her skin had lost its sheen. The bronchitis she'd picked up thanks to the storm in Thailand had improved but her strength had not fully returned. What she needed was a place to relax. I sat up.

'Look, sweetheart, we don't need to stay here for a week like we planned. Sod Delhi and Agra, we can see them later, let's go to Kashmir . . . today.' The look on her face changed. 'We could get the bus this evening and be relaxing on the lakes by this time tomorrow. What do you reckon?'

She sat up and smiled, the look of excitement back on her face. 'I'll pack, you go and get the tickets.'

I agreed and set off.

We arrived at the Interstate Bus Terminal at Kashmiri Gate with plenty of time to spare. Long and white with a metallic brown stripe running down its sides, the bus was in surprisingly good condition for Indian public transport. Surrounding the driver's seat were garlands of brightly coloured flowers, written prayers and an effigy of Vishnu; on Indian roads, Mel explained, it was always worth having the gods on your side. Golden light from the hot evening sun cut through the shadows to brighten the crumbling dwellings. Two cows wandered in the rubble and an excited child showered under a broken water main. We found our seats at the front behind the driver, boarding just before the bus pulled away.

It would not be a comfortable journey, we both knew that, but at its end would be the place we both most wanted to see: the Kashmir valley, the lakes, the beautiful houseboats, the forests, the eagles and the white-peaked Himalayas, all lost to the tranquil shades of autumn. If the islands of Thailand had been paradise, we were both sure Kashmir would be heaven. Mel slipped her arm through mine and looked at me with beaming eyes.

'Thank you, sweetheart,' she said.

'Mister . . . Mister Inglish,' it was the voice of Yacine, 'are you there?'

'Yes, hang on a second.' I moved for the first time in

nearly five hours. It wasn't easy. When I opened the door the sight which greeted me was not a pretty one. Yacine stood next to two soldiers, an apologetic look on his face.

'Ah, I am most sorry,' he said, 'but you must come with us.'

'Why?' I asked tiredly. 'Where to?'

'We must go to immigration. Do you not remember? You tell me that your visa it no good after today. We must see them tonight.'

'But I have my travel pass to prove I was in the country on time,' I complained. 'I'm really so tired . . . must I?'

He looked at the two soldiers and assured me I must. 'They like to know who is in town.'

The night was dark with the waning moon falling to the west. The heat had subsided slightly but it was still hot. At the bottom of the steps a jeep was waiting and we all climbed in.

All this bother seemed a little extreme to me. It had gone ten o'clock, couldn't it all wait till morning? *Can they still send me back? I doubt it. Will they just stamp my passport? . . . I doubt that too.*

In the distance a fluorescent light hung above a small whitewashed building. The jeep turned through an unmanned sentry post and pulled up outside it. Three men sat in the small office, all smoking. Young and official-looking, they had neat moustaches and tidy hair. They were out of uniform, dressed in Western clothes. The President stared down from the wall above. I sat opposite them and handed over my passport and travel pass.

They understood the Arabic permit, grunting their approval, but the passport was more of a problem. In turn each of them studied the pages with extreme concentration, holding on to it for more than a minute each, but it was obvious that none of them understood it. Half the time he was looking at it, the oldest, a thickset man with stubble growing almost visibly, held it upside down. In the end it was he who asked Yacine a question.

'He want to know your name,' Yacine translated, 'and why you entered Sudan this way.'

I pointed to the back of my passport and showed them the information they required. Then I said to Yacine: 'Tell them I am doing a motor-cycle journey round Africa. I am now heading for Khartoum and Egypt. I need a stamp in my

307

passport and a travel pass to the capital.' He did as I asked. After much muttering and general uncertainty one of them opened a large ledger, like so many I'd seen in the past nine months, and started to copy.

'Josman Bibi?' the official asked, turning the passport towards me to check this was my name.

'Yes,' I said, 'Josman Bibi.' He wrote it down in Arabic.

And so began my crash course in Sudanese bureaucracy. It was more than an hour later when I returned to my room without any stamp in my passport or permission to travel to Khartoum.

Practically all the following day was spent tired, frustrated and scorched, getting these important things. At about eight a.m. I returned through the sand-coloured streets, under the already brutal sun, to the immigration office, only to be sent, an hour later, to the police station. Here, after three officials passed me on to three different offices, I finally ended up in the room belonging to the Chief of Police. He, I was told, was still at breakfast. Breakfast obviously turned to lunch and by two I was wondering if he would ever show up. Sudanese officialdom, I was beginning to realise, was tortuously slow even by the normal African standards. At about three, the Chief sauntered into the dusty square carrying a cane and his huge round belly. A general murmur greeted his arrival: salutations from other officers and head-bowing from skull-capped civilians. His beaming face chuckled acknowledgment to most, he stopped to talk to some, and took messages and papers from others. When I finally got to see him half an hour later the process was quick and efficient. Without any questions he stamped my passport and filled in half the opposite page in Arabic writing. I was then sent back to the immigration office where they issued my new travel pass to Khartoum. By four I was back in my room, lying on the bed, too exhausted for self-congratulation.

Less than five minutes later, Yacine entered.

'We must now go to bank,' he said. 'You need currency declaration form for to get money. Don't worry, it will be easy, my friend he work there.' If I'd had more energy I think I would have throttled him for his helpfulness. Back out into the heat, down a couple of side streets and into the air-conditioned Bank of Sudan – the temperature inside was only thirty degrees! *Easy?* Two more offices, two more interviews and more than an hour of waiting. But eventually the problems were solved.

'You must come to eat with us tonight,' Yacine said as we left. All I wanted to do was lie down and rest. I knew I would have to be up before dawn if I were to reach Khartoum before the heat became too great and I was very worried about the bike which had developed starting problems. Yacine had been invaluable, though. Without his help what had been a tiresome hassle might well have proved too much for me. It was a kind offer and one I knew I must accept.

Yacine lived with his friend from the bank and three other young men in a small, sparsely furnished, bare-walled bunga-low just behind the mosque. He was the only one who could really speak any English, though the others all thought they could. They were pleasant, and generous too, but I was more tired than I'd ever been in my life. I'd taken rehydrants to try to recover some of my body salts, but it didn't seem to have done much good. I wasn't just tired. I felt sick, dizzy. I tried to be polite, to talk about their country and the situation there but, not understanding me, they thought it better to laugh, as if everything I said was a joke, when actually I'd been talking about the famine or the civil war. I gave up and let them continue in Arabic. There were only hard wooden stools to sit on and when after two hours no food had been forthcoming, I really thought I must leave or faint. Just as I was about to make my apologies, Yacine came into the room with a bowl of foul (pronounced fool), a dish which contains mushy red beans with, if you're lucky, onions and tomatoes.

We sat around the communal bowl scooping up the food with folds of thin unleavened bread. It didn't make me feel any better, worse if anything. Just when I thought I'd had enough my stomach told me I'd had too much. I rushed to the corner of the forecourt and threw it all back up – the first time I'd been sick in ten years. The others looked at me in some confusion.

'Are you okay?' Yacine asked, handing me some water.

'I think so, thank you. It's probably just the heat. But I'd like to go back to the hotel.'

'Of course,' he said, 'I will take you, and don't worry, tomorrow you can rest. You will be in Khartoum.'

'Insh' Allah,' I replied. 'Insh' Allah.'

Again the others laughed.

26 The Last Frontier

Khartoum, Sudan

Four Western travellers sat dejectedly round a table in the centre of the room. A Sudanese houseboy loitered in the corner. The paint was blistering from the walls and the pale linoleum floor was cracked and worn. I nodded an acknowledgment to the man facing me and put my bags down.

'Which way've you come from?' He was English.

'Er, south,' I answered. They were the first whites I'd spoken to since Nairobi and their presence had taken me quite by surprise. Regaining my composure, I continued, 'I've come up from Kenya, via Ethiopia. Just arrived from Gadaref. It was a good drive, but my God this country's hot.' I pulled up a chair and sat tiredly upon it. 'What about you guys . . . did you all come down from the north?' They nodded. 'On the train?' The houseboy handed me some water.

'Only me.' Again it was the Englishman who spoke. 'The others travelled by truck.'

'Right. How was the train? I want to catch it myself.'

'Fifty hours of utter hell,' he said, smiling. He was only in his mid-thirties, I guessed, but his face was creased with lines. 'Oh, it's not so bad,' he continued, 'if you go first class. At least it gets you there. But why do you want to take it? Aren't you going to drive?'

He pointed at my helmet.

'Ah, no. At least not if I can help it. My bike's about knackered and so am I. Another 600 miles of desert would be too much for both of us I think. If I can, I'll take the train.' This wasn't the only reason. The Nile Valley Express, the line built by Lord Kitchener to retake Khartoum after General Gordon's last stand, was once the pride of the empire and must still be one of the most famous tracks in the world. As soon as I had realised my route home would take me through Sudan, I wanted to travel on it.

'How often does it go?' I asked.

'Not very, I'm afraid. Once every two or three weeks . . . depends on breakdowns.'

'And you don't know when it last went I suppose?'

'Well, I've been stuck in this shit-hole for over two weeks, so I should say if it's not back here now it soon will be. You'd best check at the station tomorrow.'

'What about permission to travel? Is it easy to get, here in Khartoum?'

'Easy? Ugh! You're joking? Nothing is easy in this country. How long have you been in the Sudan?' Tim asked.

'One day, officially, but three really.'

'And how many offices have you been to just to get here?'

'Umm,' I tried to work it out, 'about seven, I think.'

'Well, tomorrow be prepared to double it. They don't like people moving round, not even if they're foreigners trying to leave. You might be lucky and do it in a day, but I doubt it.'

'Yeah . . . well, hopefully, the train won't be leaving for a while. Should give me plenty of time to get it.' The thought of doing it all in a day was not very appealing anyway. I was still feeling weak.

'It leaves tomorrow morning.'

'Tomorrow morning! Are you sure?' It was a stupid question and deserved the condescending nod it received. I stared into the dark hole in the wall at the station, the early morning sun burning down on the back of my neck. 'And no tickets! Do you really not have any . . . even first class?'

'Especially first class.' He was a short, fat, balding man with beads of sweat dribbling off his forehead. His white robes were brown with dust. 'The only chance you have is to be at Khartoum North by six tomorrow . . . maybe you get ticket there . . . third class.'

My God!

'Okay,' said Pete, a wild Australian. (Apparently it was his name I'd seen in the entrance book at Gallabat.) 'If you really want to catch the train it's possible to get all the right permission in a day. I've done it myself, but you'll have to hurry. Have you got your map?' I showed it to him. 'Right, first thing you'll have to do is go to the tourist information office.' I was amazed such a place existed; surely it must be one of the quietest offices in the world.

'Register with them,' he was saying, 'they then give you permission to get permission.' He smirked and marked their location on the map, then pointed out of the window. 'It's just across the road. Now, have you got any passport photos?'

I shook my head. The ministry in Addis had taken my last ones.

'Okay, well you'll need at least four of them. I need some as well so we'll go together in a minute. Once you've got those you start at the Ministry of Information . . .'

Out on the street Khartoum had come alive. The shops were all open, the cars in jams and there were people everywhere. Having been to the tourist office, where, as you might expect, the only worker was fast asleep with his feet on the desk, we walked down Baladaya Avenue and into UN Square.

At stalls on the corners men, some in djellabas and turbans, others in Western clothes, stood drinking freshly squeezed fruit juice from dirty glasses. Students with satchels talked in groups. Veiled women hurried about their business. The air was dry, the day hot, already well into the forties. An Army truck roared round the corner into the square, victorious soldiers standing in the back waving their guns and singing. The government forces had done well over the past few months.

We walked down the northern side of the square and into a photographer's shop. Half an hour later we were back on the street, going our separate ways. I was concerned. *What the hell will I do if I can't get permission quickly? It's the nineteenth today, so if I wait for the next train I've no chance of making Cairo by the fifth . . . Shit, I'll have no choice. I'll have to drive and hope the bike makes it.* Again I kissed the ring . . . *Give me a hand, sweetheart.*

I found the Ministry of Information and in a small white-washed office a friendly man gave me five forms, three white, two blue. After I'd filled these out and waited a while he stamped them all, pinned a photo to each, kept a white one and handed back the others.

'Okay,' he said happily, 'now you go Ministry of Interior.'

And so this strange, if not sadistic, bureaucratic obstacle course began. At the next ministry the process took a little longer but was essentially the same. Again the officials were charming, but slow. After an hour they sent me to the Ministry of the Exterior. On the southern edge of town, behind the railway line, this building was more like a suburban house than a

312

government office. I handed in my forms and passport and was sent to wait in a converted, grass-sided garage where, much to my surprise, I found a sweet-looking European girl reading. I sat down next to her.

'Have you been waiting long?'

She was surprised and looked up with a start. 'Oh, sorry. Umm . . . yes, an hour at least.'

'Oh dear. Are you hoping to go on the train tomorrow as well?'

'No, I'm afraid I don't have the money. I'll hitch a ride on one of the trucks.' She had wavy auburn hair tied up behind her head and wore round John Lennon specs. Her accent was Germanic but soft and she had a lovely smile. Next to her, propped against the wall, were seven enormous swords, all elaborately engraved. I picked one up.

'What are you doing with these?' I asked curiously. They were very beautiful but must have been immensely difficult for her to carry for they were nearly as long as she was tall.

'I bought them from the market here. They only cost 600 Sudanese pounds each [about six pounds sterling]. I'm sure I can sell them for ten times that in Berlin.'

'But how will you get them back . . . send them?'

'I'm not sure, maybe from Cairo, otherwise I'll carry them.'

'All the way home?'

'If I have to.'

I was amazed. They're extraordinary, some of the scams travellers get up to: she'd bought so many she couldn't afford a ticket for the train.

'Do you think there's anything we can do to speed this up?' I asked after we had chatted for a while. 'If they don't do mine soon I'll have no chance.'

'I don't know. We can try.'

'Have you stamped my forms yet?' she asked politely, once back inside the house.

'We are about to,' said the same man who'd greeted me earlier. He was giving her papers to a secretary.

'Oh good, thank you, but do you think you could do my friend's at the same time. We are travelling together. It would make it much easier for us.'

He looked at me suspiciously but nodded after a moment and handed over my documents as well. Five minutes later we left. She'd saved me an hour at least. I was starting to get quite

313

confident.

At the Ministry of Transport, next on the list, we were directed to a wooden shutter which covered a small hole in the side of the building. It was slightly ajar. We knocked, pushed it open and optimistically held out our forms. An officious man in a dark green uniform told us the office was closed.

'No you are not,' said Christina matter-of-factly. 'It is not yet two. That is when the government offices close. We have to get these forms stamped so that we can go on the train tomorrow. Where is your superior, I wish to see him.'

I expected instant arrest, or at least to have the shutter slammed in our faces, but the man withered before her. He stared at us for a second, grabbed the forms and then stamped them. I was amazed. If I'd been on my own I would almost certainly have given up but, despite her petite physique and gentle disposition, Christina, it seemed, was not one to be messed around.

'They are told to make it hard . . .' she said as we walked away '. . . to discourage people from travelling. I've been in this country now nearly two months. If you are stern with them you usually get what you want.'

With only five minutes to spare we arrived back at the Ministry of Information with all our chits and forms in order and were immediately issued with our passes. Back outside we had a congratulatory drink and, bonded by the shared experience, hugged farewell. On reflection, it was a dangerous thing to have done. The penalty for public displays of affection between the sexes, I found out later, is a few nights in jail. As she disappeared into the crowded streets I hoped I might see her again, if only to help with the ridiculous swords.

Now, provided I could get a ticket for the train, I was really on my way home.

'ALLAHHH OU'AKBARRRR . . .' The microphoned voice of the muezzin reverberated through the town like the opening bars of a Hendrix solo. Across the street a dog joined in, raising his head to howl at the fading stars. To the east the sky was red, still purple-black to the west. One by one the doorways opened as the faithful obeyed the call.

At the third attempt the engine broke into life and carried me back to the square. I turned left towards the river and then right along the corniche. The brilliant white of the People's Palace was turned to pink by the rising sun. Minibuses and taxis started to appear, bringing their cargoes of workers to town. Khartoum was waking up.

At an iron bridge I was questioned by two bored soldiers but soon allowed to continue. The road hugged the edge of the Blue Nile until the confluence with the White, where it branched away towards Khartoum North. I stopped and got off my bike. It wasn't actually very spectacular. I don't know why I'd expected it to be, but at least here they held their colour. The White bubbled over small rapids to the left and merging with it the gentler Blue flowed in from the right. I picked up a stone and threw it into the Blue Nile – I'd seen it at its source, now I'd seen its middle and I knew that soon I would see it at its end.

A few miles on I turned right and there she was, all twenty-three tatty, pale brown carriages, with a smart green Pullman leading the column.

To my amazement, and annoyance, the train already seemed to be full. Through the open windows I could see entire families, and what seemed to be all their worldly goods, squeezed into the corridors, never mind compartments. Outside, all along its length, relatives and friends waited for the off. The last three carriages were rusty red iron, obviously for carrying goods.

'I want to put my bike on the train,' I shouted to a man packing sacks of grain in the middle one. He pointed to a hut behind me. At that moment there was a tap on my shoulder.

'You want ticket, mister?'

I turned round sharply to find a large, negroid man smiling at me, his face only inches from mine. I pulled away.

'Yes, for me and my bike, can you help?'

'Oh . . . yes, yes, sure. You are lucky man. You see my brother he was to be travelling on train but now he no go so I have ticket to sell.' He smiled again and flashed the ticket in front of my face. 'Very nice. Second class, you know.' Of course, a good old ticket tout. He must have thought it was his lucky day finding a European to sell to.

'How much?'

'Well, you know I am very honourable man. I am Christian like yourself so you know my price it is fair. I . . .'

'Yes, yes, I'm sure it will be. How much?'

'Only thirty dollar US.' I didn't know how much the ticket

315

would normally cost. I didn't care. Either way it was not as much as I'd expected. I agreed without fuss.

'What about the bike, can you help me get the ticket for that?'

'Oh sure, it is very no problem. We get it here.' He led me to the hut.

The tout was right and half an hour later the bike was strapped up in the last of the carriages. I collected all I thought I might need for the journey and followed the tout back up the train. We came to a carriage where three young Arab men were leaning out of the window. Inside, the compartment seemed packed.

'Here. This it.' He shouted something to the men and passed them my bags. As there was no way in through the blocked doors, the window was the only form of entrance. He gave me a leg up, the others pulled and through it I flew, crashing hard onto the floor. Almost at once the train pulled away.

I stood up and looked around. There was no spare seat of course. Ten men, all Arab except for one old black, sat squashed along both sides of the compartment, their luggage and possessions all around them. However, this was the Sudan and although the country may be a hassle its people are generous and kind. Three passengers on the bench to the left edged nearer to the window while two others squeezed closer to the door and I was left with a foot of bench on which to sit. Happy to be aboard I tried to forget how long the journey would take.

The industry and suburbs of Khartoum soon gave way to irrigated fields and desert scrub. I wrapped my chech tightly around my head to keep out the dust, picked up my Le Carré and tried to lose myself in a cold Berlin day.

'Where are you going?' asked one of the men who'd helped me in. He was sitting at the end of my bench next to the window. The train, five hours into the journey, had just passed Shendi, a hundred miles north of Khartoum.

'To Egypt, then home. England. What about you?'

'Myself and Mohammed,' he gestured to his friend sitting opposite, 'have just finished our exams at university so now we can go on holiday to Cairo. We study to be doctors.' They were both in their early twenties with strong Arab features and wore Western clothes.

'Fantastic. For how long?'

'We must be back in three weeks.' He leant forward and pulled a basket from below his seat. 'So I hope we get on the boat quickly. We don't want to stay in Wadi Halfa for too long. Where is your food? It is time for lunch I think.'

'I stupidly forgot to bring any,' I said, rather feebly, 'but it doesn't matter, I can wait till Atbara.'

'Arh, no. Of course you will share ours.' That didn't just mean me, they started to feed the whole compartment.

'What did you mean about staying in Wadi Halfa so long?' I asked. 'Won't you go as soon as you can?'

'Oh yes, we will, but there is a problem. How many people you think there are travelling with us on the train?'

It was a tricky question. I guessed: 'About a thousand.'

He laughed and slapped his friend on the leg. 'It is more like 5,000.' I was agog. 'And do you know how many people the ferry can take to Egypt?' Again I did not. 'Six hundred and it only go two, maybe three time a week. You see the problem.' I did, but he spelled it out for me anyway. 'If you are unlucky and don't get in queue for ticket quickly you can be waiting in Halfa for weeks.' By the way he said it I could tell it was not a pleasant prospect. 'The race for the line will be a fast one.'

I munched contentedly on an egg sandwich and tried not to worry. It was still over two weeks before I was due in Cairo.

With the sun at its height it was sweltering inside the carriage. Through the window the pale land merged invisibly into a brilliant white sky. Mud buildings, palms and the odd animal gave evidence of a human presence but there were few people to be seen. It was hard to believe that one of the earth's longest rivers was less than a mile away.

The sun went down and the stars came out and still the train trundled on. I tried for a while to find comfort in sleep but soon realised this would be impossible; without a corner to lean against I was permanently being thrown by the momentum of the train. There was nothing to do but bear it. How envious I am of people who can sleep anywhere – the man on my right really pissed me off, he seemed to be unconscious.

We arrived in Atbara soon after ten. I climbed out of the compartment window and jumped down. Railway sidings and a few discarded carriages, lit up by the tenuous glow of some pale security lamps, stretched away towards a row of warehouses in the distance.

I crossed a couple of tracks moving innocently in and out of the shadows and made towards a row of abandoned cattle trucks. We had been on the move for nearly fourteen hours and once this stop was over I didn't know when the next one might come. Nature told me I'd better do my business now. There seemed to be no one around but I turned to check I was not being followed. As I crawled under one of the carriages a dog began to bark. *What a palaver, just to take a shit . . . why couldn't you just find the loo?* When I came up on the other side I got quite a shock – evidently I had. Extending in a line on either side were two rows of squatting figures, some silhouetted, others clearly lit, their djellabas pulled up around their waists. I felt rather foolish sneaking in halfway down the row, but luckily there was no one just in front.

The second day continued much the same as the first in a plethora of dust, sweat and discomfort. We were soon well into the Nubian Desert where the heat turned the carriage to a crucible. At each of the identical stations – numbered not named – the train stopped and people would jump off.

At four o'clock we stopped at station Number Five and I, like others, jumped out to stretch my legs and have a pee. I was musing on the reasons for building the line, trying not to think how many lives it must have cost, when I was pulled from my thoughts by the startling sight of the train already on its way. I ran, with the others, back to the moving carriages. I missed my own and was hauled aboard a few further on. There was no way back to my seat so, as the heat was subsiding, I climbed up to the roof.

Flat orange sand stretched away on either side to a shimmering horizon where distant rocks, piled in pyramids, appeared through the haze like islands in a lake. That was it. There was nothing else at all save the long, straight single-line track, carrying 5,000 people towards the horizon.

Little by little the sun went down, losing intensity as it did so. The time between day and night in the desert, although brief, is the most beautiful of all. The colours are surreal, almost transparent, an essence of themselves. To be sitting in the cooling breeze on the roof of the train only made it more pleasing.

At two the following afternoon – ten hours late – the Nile Valley Express reached Wadi Halfa, the end of its line, and the race began. Before the train had even stopped hundreds of people jumped frenziedly from the windows and the roof. There was no ceremony here, no rights for women or old men. I didn't take part.

By the time I had collected my bike the queue was enormous; hundreds, maybe thousands, of people pushing and barging towards two small windows in a whitewashed wall. I found Khalim and Mohammed from my compartment a long way back. It seemed they too had been slow.

'You must go to the front,' said Khalim. 'You are foreigner, you will get preference.'

'But I can't, that wouldn't be fair.'

Around us bodies vied for position. It wouldn't be long before people started to faint for there was no cover from the sun.

'You must,' agreed Mohammed. 'Don't be afraid, it is our way in the Sudan . . . foreigners come first.'

With trepidation I walked to the front, thinking the crowd did not look friendly. To my surprise, however, they immediately opened up and let me in about three from the window. A minute later I was staring at a hard-faced Nubian. He had frizzy hair and a dirty white shirt. I started to take the money from my belt.

'How did you get there?' He was angry. 'You did not wait in the line . . . why? Because you are foreign you think you can go first? Get to the back.' He looked over my shoulder and shouted what I assumed was the Arabic for 'Next'. Feeling embarrassed and not just a little sorry for myself I walked slowly away. Looking at all the people I knew that things were bad. Tomorrow's ferry was already full, Monday's was filling up fast and the one after that would be oversubscribed. A week at least, maybe two, in Wadi Halfa. Looking around me, the thought was not a pleasant one.

Over twenty years ago this town was elegant and prosperous. Wooden-balconied houses of two or three storeys enjoyed waterfront views, tall palms shaded the steets and minarets climbed to the sky. No longer. Since the Aswan High Dam was built, 250 miles to the north, Lake Nasser's waters have slowly risen to engulf almost all of central Nubia, including the old town. Still uncertain as to the final height the water will reach, Wadi Halfa is now an unassured mess of mud, tin and hessian dwellings

319

sandwiched between the lake and low, barren hills. There are no streets as such, just expanses of sand; on one was the Nile Hotel – the only hotel.

'Do you have any beds?' I knew before I asked it was a ludicrous question. The man behind the counter simply shook his head. Dejected, I went round the corner, got a cup of mint tea and sat down to ponder the situation. I had no ticket, no bed and no likelihood of getting either. Just to compound matters, when I had retrieved my motor bike from the train my sleeping-bag had gone. The desert nights are cold; things did not look good. But how often on this journey had things looked bad? And how often had a miracle occurred? This time was no exception. Lady Luck stuck out her head from the heavens and kissed me on the cheek once again.

'Salaam alaikum.'

Four Arab men in their early twenties sat down next to me. They all wore Western clothes but two had skullcaps on their heads. I returned their greeting and shook each one by the hand.

'We see what happen to you at ticket office.' The one who spoke was fat and bearded. He smiled as he talked. 'This is no good. In our country we respect the foreigner. He treat you very wrong.'

'Well, thanks, but I'm not sure that he did.' I answered apathetically.

'Oh, well we think so.' They all nodded their agreement. 'What is your name?'

'Jonny.'

'Okay, Mister Jon, you see, we can help you.' Suddenly I was interested. Their spokesman noticed the difference. 'Oh yes, you see Hakim here,' he pointed to the man opposite me, who again insisted on shaking my hand, 'has to go home on train. We have been waiting here nearly two weeks. We now have tickets for ferry on Monday, but this be too late for him.'

'I am sorry,' I said to Hakim, trying to suppress my utter delight at this poor man's misfortune.

'It is of no importance,' said Hakim resignedly. 'We have had fun here in Wadi.' That I found hard to believe.

The fat man went on: 'So Hakim can give you his ticket. If you like and you can travel with us on Monday.'

I couldn't believe it . . . yet somehow I could.

'If Hakim really doesn't mind, that would be fantastic,' I said. We exchanged the ticket for the price he'd paid for it and I left, my passage out of that godforsaken place finally assured.

Those five days were painfully slow and the nights punishingly cold. I slept on the sand with Khalim and Mohammed and a group of others but without the warmth of my sleeping-bag I could only manage a few hours a night. My two cheerful friends were happy that I had been so fortunate. They'd missed Monday's ferry but were confident about being on the one after that. I passed the days swatting flies in the shade and swimming in the Nile. For lunch and supper we ate Nile perch from a stall near the hotel.

On the Sunday, as you might expect, I had to get clearance to be allowed to take the boat: the ticket was not enough. This was possibly the most tedious and tiring day of all in the Sudan. From eight in the morning until six at night I was passed from the police station to the customs office, to immigration and the office of information, back to the police and finally returned to the ticket office. At each bureau there was a queue of a hundred or more. At the ticket office I told the Nubian man that I was not jumping the line but had simply been lucky. He accepted the explanation and became surprisingly charming, telling me that as nobody knew how much they should charge for the bike I could take it for nothing. He checked I had all the right forms – a red one, two blue, a green, a yellow and a white – stamped the ticket and wished me 'Bon voyage'.

'It will start boarding at eight and leave around three,' he said. I told him I'd be there at seven.

That evening as the sun went down behind the sandy hills even Wadi Halfa seemed pleasant.

The Sinai, as was her name, was a pale brown, trusty-looking vessel, bobbing up and down at the end of a thin wooden jetty. She was about 150 feet long with a large central funnel and thick ropes protruding at either end to secure her to the mooring. Quite how 600 people fitted into her I had still to find out.

The morning was bright, the sun already high in the east and the air was still and dry. Sellers of karkadi – a drink made from water and hibiscus flowers, which tastes like Ribena – were setting up their stalls. People and their possessions were starting to collect. Soon after nine the customs and immigration officials arrived and an hour later the queue began to move.

I had been there early and was near the front. I was excited, the buzz of success bubbling in my chest. At last I was leaving this chaotic country to complete my dream. During my twelve-day stay in the Sudan I had been to twenty-five offices and filled in sixteen forms to make three journeys. The step I would take to leave would be one of the happiest I'd taken in all Africa. At eleven I took it, climbed onto the jetty and greeted the official with a smile.

'Your passport please.' He didn't look mean, just bored by the prospect of the day which lay ahead. 'Papers.' I confidently handed them over.

'Where is your blue form?'

I pulled the two blue chits from the pile in his hand and put them on top. 'These ones?'

'Not these,' he said, taking me to one side. 'Your customs import licence,' he gestured to the bike, '. . . for the machine.'

Oh God. Stay calm, stay calm . . .

'They should have given you one at the border when you entered Sudan.'

'But they didn't.' I answered, fear rising. 'Have you been to Gallabat? There are only a few grass huts. There is no customs and no immigration, let alone blue forms. They gave me nothing.'

'So how do we know you not buy this machine here in the Sudan and have not paid duty.'

I was incredulous. 'Look,' I said in near desperation, my hands starting to shake, 'I have my carnet which proves that I brought the bike into the country.' I got it from the tank bag and showed it to him. 'Here, you can see . . . Cameroun, Angola, Malawi, Tanzania. I've been driving the bike round Africa.'

'This is not blue form. You must go back.'

My God! No! Please! I was on the gangway, the ship to home and freedom only a few feet away. I felt physically sick and my head started to spin.

I begged: 'Please don't make me go back.'

'You have no blue form. You will have to go back to the customs office in town. We cannot let you board without one.' The official shouted an order to a younger man in civilian

322

clothes, telling him to go with me. On their instructions I left the bike where it was and walked back onto Sudanese soil. So near and yet . . .

Back at the customs offices I was shown to a room and told to wait. Dark and airless it contained four chairs and three desks but no one sat behind them. Eleven o'clock gave way to twelve and twelve to one. By quarter to two, when the official finally entered, I was fit to explode.

'How do you like our country?' he asked unwisely.

'Delightful, sir,' I answered.

He asked to see the carnet and questioned me about my journey. In the end he seemed satisfied and started to fill out the all-important blue form, but time was rapidly running out.

'Sir, do you think you could hurry up, the ship is due to leave at three.'

'Ah, do not you worry, the ship never go before six. You will make it. Insh' Allah . . . Insh' Allah.' He put down his pen and stood up, smiling. He was a tall man in traditional clothes, a dirty turban falling from his head. I stood up too, hoping it might speed things up . . . it did not.

'You know some time ago we have very famous man here,' he said happily, rubbing his chin. 'He was English, too. Yes, Mister Palpin I think . . . you know him? Famous man . . . television . . . many people with him.'

'Michael Palin, I think you mean.'

'Arh yes, very funny, very nice man.' At last he walked to the door, chuckling to himself. *Funny, yes; nice, I'm sure . . . but I'll bet he never had to deal with any bloody blue forms!*

Two offices later, two more officials and two more stamps and at last I really was on my way. It had gone four o'clock. My escort from the ship drove me in a jeep the three miles back to the jetty. The boat was still there. Seldom has a sight been so cherished.

An hour later I was the last one on. There was no hold as such and I had to move a group of veiled old women to park the bike in the passageway. By the time I got out on deck the land was receding. I stood against the guardrail looking out across the peaceful waters and watched the sun sink slowly behind the darkening hills.

At last I knew I'd done it. At the end of the lake, twenty-four hours to the north, lay Aswan and 600 miles of surfaced road to

Cairo. Tourism would begin again and with it 'civilisation' – a beer, a good, large meal . . . and no more blue forms. Looking down at myself I realised I needed some decent food – a month of injera and foul had taken its toll and I was really quite thin.

Behind me the deck had become a mosque. Even here the muezzin cried. As many as could be fitted on the deck lined up in rows and bowed their heads towards the softening eastern skies. I found myself saying a prayer . . .

The Dream Palace
9.00 p.m. October 15th

'*Do you believe in God?*' *Ahmed Nadroo, the owner of the houseboat, sat cross-legged in the centre of the floor, his weathered face creased with lines, his eyes sunk deep in his head. It wasn't that it was a strange question to ask Mel, after all, he was a devout Muslim, I just wondered how she would answer. Before her travels it would have been one word, 'No'. But now she had to think.*

'*I don't believe in a God in terms of an old man with a long grey beard sitting in the clouds,*' *she said, staring at the ceiling, as she worked out her views, 'but I do believe in something.*' *She was lying on the wooden sofa, her legs across my lap. 'I'm sure that there is something bigger than all this, a kind of entity, I suppose, that governs us all . . . you know.*' *She sat up a little and leaned on her elbow to look at him. 'Something that makes us good or bad, that makes our life easy or hard and that ultimately decides when we've been here long enough.*' *She lay back again. 'Yes, I do believe in something. I don't see the point otherwise.*'

Ahmed smiled, pleased by her response. He took a glowing ember from the stove and lit his hubble-bubble. Outside it was dark and cold, a thick mist settling on the lake, the first snows of winter not far away, but inside the temperature was warm. The newly arrived guest had already gone to bed. We had just finished eating and were both content.

I was also pleased. This was exactly my philosophy: not so much God with a capital 'G', but some greater force shaping our lives and actions. It wasn't that Mel had categorically refused to believe in such things before, it was just that she had enjoyed life and people too much to dwell for long on other-worldly matters. Kashmir, though, was the most beautiful place we'd ever seen and drifting around the lakes on shakaras, watching eagles climb through the clear blue sky above the snowy Himalayas, it was hard not to think about spirituality and one's own beliefs. Mel had worked

324

out her own faith and seemed content with it.

'And do you believe in paradise?' Ahmed asked, disappearing behind a cloud of smoke.

'Of course, Ahmed,' Mel replied, freely. 'We're on board the Dream Palace, after all, and I've never been happier. If you gave me a wish I wouldn't know what to do with it . . . except perhaps ask to stay here for ever. Paradise?' She squeezed my hand as a smile danced across her lips, '. . . I think I've found it.'

27 Shadows Passed

Cairo, Egypt

I got out of the shower and wrapped a towel around my waist. My clock showed twenty to five. On the other side of the room sunlight poured through the open french windows. I crossed the floor, leaving a trail of small puddles on the terracotta tiles, and walked out onto the balcony.

On the fifth floor the heat was still strong. The sun, just above the roofs, cast golden light along the top half of the ornate buildings, but further below, down on the street, the shadows had already fallen. Talaat Harb was blocked solid with four lanes of cars honking like a demented orchestra and conducted by a wildly gesticulating fat policeman. As the clock downtown pealed quarter to five I went back into the room.

Cairo. June fifth.

I felt sick with nervousness. I took a deep breath and put on my clothes. My rendezvous with Amel was only fifteen minutes away.

The Sinai had docked at Aswan one week earlier and with no major problems I passed into my nineteenth, and last, African country. The town was quiet, pleasantly subdued after the hassles of the Sudan. I spent the days relaxing by the swimming pool of a multi-starred hotel before returning at sunset to my one pound a night hostel. Along the corniche in the evenings persistent felucca owners tried to persuade me to travel with them up river: 'It okay,' they'd say, 'I have beer . . . I have hashish. My felucca very nice. For you no backsheesh . . . only hundred pounds.'

After four days I started off north and discovered there was still another danger to negotiate: the horrendous driving of the Egyptians. Twice I was driven right off the road and once almost involved in a fatal accident. Just before Daraw I came round a corner to find a car and truck blocking the road and had to swerve hard to avoid them. The driver of the car had obviously taken the bend too fast and skidded out of control. He'd hit the lorry broadside on and been sent through the windscreen and on into oblivion. His crumpled body still lay on the bonnet.

In every town and village crazy youths on mopeds would swoop out of side roads into my path, doing little to avoid me: their ability to stop depending totally on the thickness of their flip-flops. This kamikaze driving was a shame. I'd wanted to take it easy and enjoy my ride along the lush, green banks of the Nile, watching my last rural African scenes. It was impossible, though. I had to concentrate as hard as ever. After ten o'clock the roads themselves became treacherous – they melted. It was a bit like being back in the rainforest, only this time I was struggling with molten tar. I had two more punctures and the bike was still going badly but, after all, it had done 20,000 miles.

I stayed for a couple of days in Luxor to see the Valley of the Kings and on the evening of the fourth, accompanied by a generous moon high in the sky, I reached Cairo. My arrival was something of an anticlimax. Celebrating an achievement alone is okay up to a point but patting oneself on the back soon gets a little boring. My pleasure was also mixed with sadness. The journey that had absorbed me for nearly two years was finally nearing its end. I was pleased therefore when an Englishman in his mid-thirties asked if he could join me as I sat on the terrace of the Meridian Hotel, a vodka and tonic in hand, watching the Nile slip slowly by. I accepted his drinks and conversation in the same manner as I had accepted everyone else's on my journey. It was only when he said how attractive he found Egyptian men, adding that my eyes were as blue as the Nile at noon – it looked gungy grey to me – that I realised he wanted more than just dialogue. I finished my drink and left muttering vaguely about Amel.

Leaving the lift, I walked out onto the street and joined the flow of pedestrians on Talaat Harb heading for the Midan. If I walked fast I'd be there in five minutes . . . I slowed my pace. Past the fruit bars and kebab stalls I sauntered, moving in and out of the tourists and locals, my mind far away from my surroundings. *What the hell are you going to say to her, Jonny? Hi! I realise it's nearly a year since we met, and I know we never really kissed or anything, but I just wondered if we still loved each other.* I hoped I couldn't say that. We'd think of something, I felt sure. *You're crazy, how do you know you'll still find her attractive . . . or nice for that matter . . . You don't even know the girl.* If it was a disaster and we really didn't get on, I figured I could always just leave. At least I'd know for sure and not be carrying her in my heart for ever. Anyway, I reflected, she might not even be here today. The letter I'd sent from Nairobi, explaining the rendezvous, had said that for one week from the fifth of June I'd be waiting at the Tulip Hotel between five and six and between twelve and one. Her flight might not get in for a couple of days. I had no way of knowing. The thought did little to lessen my anxiety.

On the corner of Kasr El Nil an old man selling papers thrust an English-language *Egyptian Times* into my hand. While he foraged for change I glanced towards the square. It was less than fifty yards away, the large clock in the centre showing five to five. I crossed the road, looking around. From here on I knew I might see her.

The Midan was busy. Three policemen in pale blue shirts and white armbands stood in the middle directing the traffic which entered the square from four main roads. At street level the shops were crowded. Above, elegantly formed, grey-brown buildings climbed high to merge with an azure sky. I waited for a policeman to stop the cars then crossed to the hotel.

In Kenya, when I'd searched my guide book for a suitable place to meet Amel, the Tulip Hotel had sounded a lot grander than it turned out to be. I'd imagined sitting at an open bar, sipping on a beer, watching her arrive through some tinted-glass door. Even from the entrance I could tell it was a dump. Disappointment set in.

'You want hotel?' said a teenage boy, sitting on a chair outside. Even he looked unpleasing. His djellaba was dirty and his hairline almost reached his too closely set eyes.

'Not to stay at,' I replied. 'I've arranged to meet someone here.'

'Is okay . . . you go four floor.' I walked up the chipped marble steps and entered the grimy one-man lift. I pressed button four as the clock struck five.

When I opened the door I was greeted by a one-armed man who looked as seedy as his co-worker downstairs. Amel was nowhere to be seen. I fled back to the street, hoping I could catch her before she came in. Sitting on the steps, I took out my newspaper and started to wait.

At a quarter past five there was still no sign. I finished the paper and watched the passersby. My heart lurched as suddenly I saw her. She was cutting through the traffic on the other side of the square, her long dark hair flowing out behind her. To my considerable relief she was without her mother. I jumped up, my stomach in knots, and stood ready to receive her. *Should I take her in my arms or just kiss her cheek? Should I speak in French or English?* It didn't matter . . . for it wasn't her. The girl turned right down Moh Bassiuni and disappeared into the crowd.

'Do not worry,' said the leery boy, who had watched the scene, 'she will turn up, you will see.' But that evening she didn't. At six, feeling positively worn out from the expenditure of so much nervous energy, I returned to the Nile – this time to the Sheraton – and consoled myself with another vodka and tonic.

At one the next afternoon, when Amel had still not shown, I decided to try the airline offices. Air France was just across the square.

'There are no direct flights from Algiers to Cairo, m'sieur,' said the girl behind the counter. 'She could fly via Marseilles and arrive here on Saturday or . . .' she tapped a few more keys on her computer, '. . . with Tunisian Airways, via Tunis, on Friday . . . tomorrow. That flight lands at twelve fifteen.' I thanked her and left. There was nothing more I could do that day. It seemed most likely that Amel would be coming from Tunis. I hailed a cab and went to see the Pyramids.

When she hadn't turned up by one o'clock on Friday I put it down to slow clearance at the airport but by six it was dawning on me that perhaps she wasn't coming. On Saturday morning I checked with the post office to see if she had written, but there was nothing, and at the embassy, where I went looking for messages, the story was the same. The flight from Marseilles had now landed and still she hadn't come. I found the Tunisian Airways offices and asked if her name was on any of the flight lists. Reluctantly they gave me the information – it was not – and back at Air France they told me the same. I had to face it . . . she wasn't coming.

That afternoon I bought a ticket for the only ship that could take me back to Europe; it sailed the following Tuesday. In the evening I returned to the Tulip and left a note saying where I was, should she arrive by some other means of transport. I knew now, however, she would not.

'Don't be too disappointed, Jonny,' I told myself and I'm really not sure that I was. It's true I'd wanted, even thought I'd deserved, the fairytale ending. I'd reached the end of the game and wanted my princess. But this was life, not a game, and things like that seldom happen. I was disappointed but not unhappy. After all, there might be a perfectly reasonable explanation for why she hadn't come. It didn't necessarily mean I'd never see her again. Once more I went to the Nile Sheraton, got myself a drink and watched the sun and moon gracefully swap places. *Things could be worse, Jonny . . . oh yes, they definitely could . . .*

The Magic Ring
7.35 p.m. October 21st

It was the finest hotel I'd ever stayed at. Marble floors and colonnades separated boutiques from bars, restaurants from lounges. Well-dressed men and beautiful women strolled through reception area attended by uniformed waiters. I felt distinctly out of place. The Oberoi Hilton, downtown Delhi.

It had taken far longer than I had anticipated to sort things out with the authorities in Srinagar: for eight hours I had been held by suspicious police while an autopsy had been carried out. Once it had been established that Mel had died of natural causes, I had expected to get her on a flight back to England immediately; but, for reasons I never did quite understand – the hospital was having some sort of a row with the police – nobody would embalm her. For three days, constantly surrounded by police and Urdu-speaking officials, I carried her body between the morgue, the hospital and the police station on the back of an open-sided, 1950s truck, only to be met at every point by stifling bureaucracy. Eventually, they told me that it was too late, that the only way to get Mel home now would be to cremate her. So, under soaring eagles and a crystal sky, with the help of a priest, that's what I did. It was a relief. Early the next day I collected her ashes and flew south.

At the British Embassy I was told that a kind uncle of Mel's had arranged for me to stay at the Oberoi before catching the morning flight to London. I showered, called home and went to the bar to wait for the main restaurant to open. I could have been waiting at the gates of hell for all I cared – nothing was real, nothing mattered.

I got a whisky and sat down in one of the comfortable leather chairs.

*In front of me on the table, next to a bowl of nuts, was a smart yellow
card. I picked it up and started to read. 'If you have a favourite song you
would be liking to hear, please ask the pianist and he will play it for you.'
In the corner of the room was a shiny black grand piano, but no musician
to play it. The only music I could hear was drifting quietly through the
ceiling speakers.*

*What song would I most like to listen to, I wondered. Nothing
immediately sprang to mind. After all, what song could possibly sum
up how I felt now my world was at an end. Asphyxiation caused by
an asthma attack was what the death certificate said. The doctor had
added that the altitude and bronchitis hadn't helped. But the explanation
made little difference – Mel was dead, end of story. Then it came to me:
'Yesterday'. Yes, if I could have anything it would be to have yesterday
back. For the first time I kissed Mel's golden ring. A moment later one
track ended and the Beatles' classic began to play. I vowed then to wear
her ring for ever.*

*I finished my whisky and went to the restaurant. The first thing
I ordered was a bottle of Château Margaux.*

Eventually Tuesday came and my spirits rose – I was going
home. I packed the bike up for the final time and with the
help of a young Egyptian pushed it out onto Talaat Harb. The
bike looked a lot different from the gleaming fantasy machine
in Dover all those months ago. The seat was ripped, the fairing
smashed and both front indicators were hanging limply from
a single strand of wire. I felt stupidly affectionate towards it,
though, in the way a cowboy might feel about his horse. After
all, it had never really let me down. The early morning traffic
was as dense as usual, the crisp air singed slightly brown by the
fumes. I drove round the Midan, full of thoughts of what might
have been, and onto Abdul Aziz to join the main road northeast
to Port Said and the coast.

At the entrance to the Suez Canal a continuous flow of
enormous ships moved in line on the lazy waters, their green
and red lights flashing. Moored to the dock was a giant white
cruiser, the *Princesa Marissa*, my passage to Europe.

It was gone five by the time I got the bike into the hold and
reached the packed upper deck. Across a floating pontoon jetty
a constant stream of holidaymakers were boarding, their time at
the pyramids now at an end.

The African sun sank into a copper sky as a huge moon rose from the horizon. As I turned to look into its familiar face I knew that I'd been wrong. This had, after all, been one of our journeys, just the same as the others. It wasn't so much that Mel had been travelling with me, or even watching over me, though I'm sure she had. It was more that she was actually within me, in my heart and in my mind, and now in the place where she would always remain – at the very centre of my being. All I'd done and everything I'd ever do would be affected by knowing her, loving her and ultimately watching her die. The determination I'd needed to see me through I'm sure had come from her, the smile on my face was hers. I realised then that I'd never really miss Melanie again, for how can you miss what you are? I hadn't lost her after all. She'd be with me till the end of time.

Was my journey a 'first'? I'd probably never know and it didn't really matter. I hadn't set out to break a record. Before I left, it had been one of my dreams to find myself in a situation where I could save a life, perhaps to make up for the utter helplessness I'd experienced at the time when I could not. I realised now that I had saved a life – I had saved my own.

The foghorn blasted and the ship slipped away from the dock. In a few days' time I'd be home and all that had happened would become memories. I wasn't sad, for I knew they would always be more than that. Over the loudspeakers came a crackling announcement: 'This evening's bingo will be taking place in the Churchill lounge in five minutes' time, and the cabaret, starring our very own Elvis, will be taking place at nine . . .' I could hardly wait.

The shadows of Africa faded into darkness, the last lights snuffed out by the night. Only the moon and the stars were left shining . . . Game over player two.

Epilogue

Florence, Italy. Sometime later.

The plaza was crowded. Groups of tourists and schoolchildren stood outside the Duomo posing for photos, licking ice-creams and listening to bored tour-guides. Around the edges of the square, cafés brimmed with activity and blocked traffic idled on the narrow streets behind. For the most part the sky was blue and a bright sun shone, but the heavy grey clouds that had burst only minutes before, still lingered above the city to the west. I bought a packet of cigarettes and made towards the cathedral. Amel was there, standing on the third step, leaning slightly against a rolled umbrella. I stopped, hidden behind a postcard stand, and watched her. She was even more beautiful than I had remembered.

On my arrival home from Africa a letter had been waiting for me. Amel's father had changed his mind about letting her come to Cairo. She apologised at great length and told me that she was planning to take a job in Italy. We kept in contact through correspondence but when, after a gap of six weeks, I'd heard nothing, I assumed she had lost interest. As fate would have it, three days before I was due to drive with Neil to see some friends in France, I received a letter telling me where she was. There was no hesitation or doubt in my mind that I would travel to see her. Neil understood completely.

On his way round to my place to hitch a ride to Paris, Neil once again fell off his bike, this time breaking his arm, but we still made it there that day. I sent a telegram to Amel, simply saying, 'Meet me on the steps of the Duomo, Saturday, four o'clock,' and headed off south alone.

So that she wouldn't see me, I walked up the steps from the left and with a thumping heart tapped on her shoulder. She spun round, her huge eyes laughing, and leant forward to kiss my cheeks. It was instantly fantastic. All the nerves I'd felt waiting in the hotel disappeared. Hand-in-hand we wandered off to a bar.

The next day we drove to Sienna where, under an umbrella and a drenching thunderstorm, at last we really kissed. For a week we toured Tuscany, staying in hotels, taking in sights and walking on the beach. The love between us was as real and powerful as anything I'd experienced. It was as if we had known each other for a hundred years – a chemistry that bound us inexorably into one. When I lost myself in her deep brown eyes I knew I had at last come home. On the final night of our holiday, at the spectacular Villa di Corliano, just outside Pisa, I asked Amel to be my wife. And Amel, as crazy as me, said 'oui'.

'*Farewell to Shadowlands . . . the term is over; the holidays have begun.*' Fairytales be damned, I thought, if anyone's going to write the ending to my story it's going to be me. But then again, it's probably already been written . . . Insh' Allah.

Acknowledgments

As anyone who has undertaken a journey will know, its success often depends on the people encountered along the way. Some may be frightening, others frustrating, but the vast majority are extremely helpful. You have read my story and know the names of some of these people, my thanks to them is unbounded. But there are others whose names, for one reason or another, have either not worked their way into my tale, have been changed to save their identity, or have been cut by the editor's sword. I'm sure you know who you are – though I doubt many of you will read this – and my thanks to you is equally great.

I would like to thank Robert Farren, a brilliant mechanic, for his help in preparing the bikes and Irvin Naylor in America for his generosity at a time when I needed some help. In terms of writing the book I should like to thank Kate Thorne for the use of her cottage, John and Tania Keeling for a similar reason, Paul and Vanessa Keeling for lending me a bedroom in London and all my other friends whose encouragement and support has been fantastic. I would like to thank my brother Chris and Robert Tasher for help on the computer and my parents for giving me the space to write most of this book and their patience in always sticking by me. Very special thanks to Ann Llewellyn, Melanie's mum, for her tireless work in correcting the often ill-punctuated first draft – without her help and friendship I very much doubt this book would ever have seen the light of day. I also owe a great debt of gratitude to Andy Hobsbawm for all the help and advice he has provided.

My thanks are also due to Robert Sutton, Lindsay Treanor, Emily Loudon, Victoria Hobbs and my agent Toby Eady; Victoria Hipps for her work on the editing and Tom Weldon from William Heinemann for having the confidence in my book's potential.

Lastly I would like to thank Amel for, well, just being Amel.

DAISY WAUGH

A Small Town in Africa

In 1990 Daisy Waugh spent six months in the remote Kenyan town of Isiolo. As a middle-class Western girl, she was horror-struck at the poverty and sheer strangeness of life in this remote corner of Africa.

Despite this she takes up the challenge of the people's natural hostility, learns the rhythm of Isiolo life, and with complete honesty and an appealing mix of zany good humour and peevish irritability, discovers that here, like anywhere else, there are people out to cheat you at every opportunity and people who will leave you speechless by their generosity.

'Charming and brutally honest . . . only the purblind and prejudiced will fail to appreciate it'
Big Issue

'Closely observed, sympathetic yet never sentimental . . . very funny, clever and interesting'
Literary Review

'Miss Waugh commands swift, clean prose, an eye for beauty where others would see none, and an acute sense of the ridiculous, including her own'
Spectator

'An observant study proving that small towns everywhere reek with the same vengeance, bickering, jealousy and gossip . . . constantly amusing'
Daily Mail

**To War with Whitaker
The Wartime Diaries of the
Countess of Ranfurly 1939–45**

When World War II broke out, Dan Ranfurly was dispatched to the Middle East with his faithful valet, Whitaker. These are the diaries of his young wife, Hermione, who, defying the War Office, raced off in hot pursuit of her husband. When Dan was taken prisoner, Hermione vowed never to return home until they were reunited. For six years, travelling alone from Cape Town to Palestine, and meeting such charismatic characters as Churchill, Eisenhower, and a parrot called Coco on the way, she kept her promise.

'If you buy one more book this year, do make it
To War with Whitaker'
Dirk Bogarde, *Daily Telegraph*

'An extraordinary story. No review can do justice to the writing'
Robert Rhodes-James, *Sunday Express*

'These absolutely spiffing diaries offer a madcap, aristocratic window behind the lines of war'
Daily Mail

'Few diaries from any era could be as fascinating . . . This is truly compulsive reading'
Woman & Home

BENSON BOBRICK

East of the Sun

East of the Sun is a hitherto untold story. An epic historical and dramatic narrative, covering four centuries, it combines the heroic settlement and conquest of an intractable virgin land, the unremitting extremes, ghastly danger and high drama of Arctic exploration, and the grimmest saga of penal servitude in the chronicles of mankind.

'Benson Bobrick has succeeded in writing a history of Siberia from its conquest in the 16th century right through Stalin's Gulag Archipelago and the break-up of the Soviet empire at the end of the 20th . . . Apart from the fascination of the little-known story he has to tell, Bobrick vividly lights up the importance of the role Siberia may well come to play'
Alan Bullock, author of *Hitler and Stalin*

'An extraordinary story of perseverance . . . powerfully conveyed'
Daniel Farson, *Evening Standard*

TIM PARKS

Italian Neighbours

'This is a clever, entertaining book. And, rare in travel literature, it is charged with a sense of purpose'
Sunday Times

'I recommend his book to all those who are fed up with accounts of roughing it agreeably in Tuscany and similar junk that scarcely scratches the surface of the real Italy'
Paul Bailey, *Daily Telegraph*

'Gradually (he) comes to accept what the locals take for granted: everybody likes the Pope, racism thrives, the barber is a faith healer, the bank manager asks what interest rate you want to pay and the devoted church-going pharmacist upholds Catholicism on a Sunday but shows commercial flair the rest of the week by selling cut-price condoms ... A rich treat from start to finish'
Sunday Express

'Synthesising the experiences of a long-standing resident into a single year ... *Italian Neighbours* is not about the escape of an idyll, but about a different way of living life's idiocies and hardships'
City Limits

'Tough, funny and sceptical'
Tatler

ERROL TRZEBINSKI

The Lives of Beryl Markham
Out of Africa's Hidden Seductress

Hauntingly beautiful, tough as steel, totally amoral and immensely brave, Beryl Markham inspired lust, resentment and admiration, and was chased by scandal wherever she went. Married three times, she counted Edward Prince of Wales, his brother the Duke of Gloucester and Denys Finch Hatton – immortalised by Karen Blixen in *Out of Africa* – among her lovers. Capping notoriety with fame, in 1936 Beryl Markham became the first woman to fly solo west across the Atlantic, the feat described in her bestselling memoir *West with the Night*.

'Beryl's behaviour certainly makes for a wonderful read and I cannot recommend this book too highly'
Lady Antonia Fraser, *Mail on Sunday*

'Trzebinski has provided a richly detailed and memorable account of a woman who achieved much and fascinated and outraged in equal measure across three continents'
Literary Review

'Errol Trzebinski has researched her biography with meticulous care and spun it together with impressive skill'
Elspeth Huxley, *Daily Telegraph*

'Trzebinski combines sympathetic understanding with an evocative style'
Independent

HELEN SUZMAN

In No Uncertain Terms
Memoirs

With new information taking it up to the momentous elections in April 1994, this is the story of Helen Suzman, tireless fighter against apartheid and for the rights of the marginalised and dispossessed of South Africa.

'When the history of South Africa is written, she and her colleagues will be found to have played a very large part in the struggle for human rights – and she is very entertaining as well'
Sir David Steel

'Combative and courageous, Helen Suzman's political life is on an heroic scale'
Observer

'A wonderful woman, brave, formidable, indefatigable, witty, thinking'
Financial Times

'In all the annals of parliamentarism in the English-speaking world, Helen Suzman may have been the best there has ever been'
The Times

'I believe this book should be read by all interested in South Africa'
Nelson Mandela